WE WON'T SEE AUSCHWITZ

WE WON'T SEE AUSCHWITZ

WRITTEN AND ILLUSTRATED BY
JÉRÉMIE DRES

TRANSLATED BY
EDWARD GAUVIN

SELF
MADE
HERO

Published in English in 2012
by SelfMadeHero
5 Upper Wimpole Street
London WIG 6BP
www.selfmadehero.com

Written and illustrated by: Jérémie Dres
Translated from the French edition by: Edward Gauvin

Editorial Assistant and Lettering: Lizzie Kaye
Marketing Director: Doug Wallace
Publishing Director: Emma Hayley
With thanks to: Nick de Somogyi and Jane Laporte

First published in 2011 by Éditions Cambourakis as
Nous N'Irons Pas Voir Auschwitz
Rights arranged through Nicolas Grivel Agency
Copyright © Éditions Cambourakis, 2011.

A CIP record for this book is available from the British Library

ISBN: 978-1-906838-63-8

10 9 8 7 6 5 4 3 2 1

Printed and bound in Slovenia

Preface

There is a paradox in this book. These days, when we are all called on to remember, to honour our dead, to share the burden of memory for last century's great crimes, and to visit Auschwitz – for example – here are two young men who won't be going there. Two young Parisians, Jewish to boot – which is to say, grandchildren of a generation decimated by the Shoah. Worse yet, if they don't go to the camp, they're transgressing a family taboo. They leave for a hostile, even forbidden land, one reduced to a graveyard, an ancestral land others have occupied. Watch out for Polacks, they're told.

The paradox is plain to see. This third generation has put some distance behind them, which isn't the same as forgetting. Today, they can revisit the past, restore life and meaning to it, all while avoiding the commemorative murmurs and paralyzing stereotypes. They can shoulder it differently. These young men and women are no longer obliged to perpetuate family sorrow – on the contrary, they want to know. To understand. To observe. To listen. They grow close to their grandparents, speaking with them directly. Some of them, such as those in this book, are lucky enough to have known and loved a grandmother. Others must make do with stories, archives, or secondhand memories. In either case, their quest breaks free of death to remember life.

We no longer concentrate exclusively on anti-Semitism, the crime suffered, the details of its implementation, its accomplices, the agony of grandparents who must be glorified, avenged, or merely mourned (depending); we would rather reconstruct the life from before, share the little everyday joys and sorrows from a time gone by, a vanished world, a distant culture. We accept the conflicts of the past, an earlier youth in revolt, their illusions, their search for happiness. We wonder what that was like, the better to appreciate what our grandmothers or grandfathers have passed down. We go to the old country to find them again.

This step, common to members of the third generation, has more to do with them building their own identities than meditating on the deeper meaning of the Jewish genocide. In this it is the 21st-century sign of a way to situate oneself amidst continuities, to plant one's roots in a tradition that is, above all, one of family. Witness, in our day and age, the craze for genealogy or all manner of cults of memory...

By not going to Auschwitz, the characters encounter another past, one from before the Catastrophe, and in an unpredictable way, they end up in the present. Therein lies the second surprise. They had not imagined life might go on. They simply set out to gather a few traces, convinced everything had vanished, and at the end of their journey they wind up at the biggest festival of Jewish culture in Europe, in Kraków! They were wary, afraid of revealing their quest, ready to pass themselves off as others, and yet in several cities they were able to speak with Jews of all ages, rabbis, even goys fascinated by that era. They found themselves face to face with living Polish people: warm, open, ready to share their concerns.

They came across an awakening similar to their own, just as enthusiastic and confused, borne on strong feelings, curious, and increasingly effective. A Polish society of multiple reactions that, like them, sought above all to question and understand itself, fascinated by a long-ignored past.

For strange as it may seem, communist Poland has long effaced this history, repressed this memory, affirming an official, purely Polish version in the worst nationalist tradition. The Jews had disappeared. Slaughtered by the Germans (not without a certain Polish complicity), and rejected by History, they were, as victims, reduced to statistics and assimilated into the anonymous mass of "anti-fascists". And yet, with the victory of democracy in 1989, Polish society has, bit by bit, reappropriated this past, free now to interrogate it. But not without media uproar and painful upheavals.

The Jews have returned in the form of questions. How to live with this absence? In territory that was the very seat of the Great Catastrophe, the site where the Nazis exterminated millions of European Jews. How to grow up there without knowing who these victims were, what they lived through and created for centuries – above all, without knowing how one's own parents or grandparents faced the crime? How, indeed, to keep a clear conscience? Why was a world so important to us forgotten, erased, silenced? So many questions, so many good and bad answers, are often expressed in Poland. Their sometimes contradictory variety is made obvious in our two travellers' every encounter. For a good 15 years now, the young, and the less than young, have sought to safeguard this past, to reconstruct it via a network of societies, schools, and institutions. A small Jewish community has finally been able to reorganize itself beyond the supervision of the State and the Communist Party. A rabbinate was rebuilt... along with the quarrels of its rabbis.

This is what our two incredulous travellers found in a few days, and they realized they weren't alone. They'd gone to learn about their grandmother's past, only to be caught up in a flood of questions akin to their own. Just as well they had a sense of humour.

And so this beautiful journey to an ancestral land became an exchange, a veritable conversation among descendants of a world that death had left littered with hate and rancour. By sweeping stereotypes aside, these conversations have made a clean breast of things.

Time now for the pictures to tell their story.

Jean-Yves Potel
Guardian of the Shoah Memorial for Poland

To Grandma Thérèse,
Tema Dres, *née* Barab

Warsaw: First Steps

Sunday, 27 June. 2 p.m. My first instinct on reaching Warsaw was to find where she'd lived. I've been wandering the streets of the capital for two hours now.

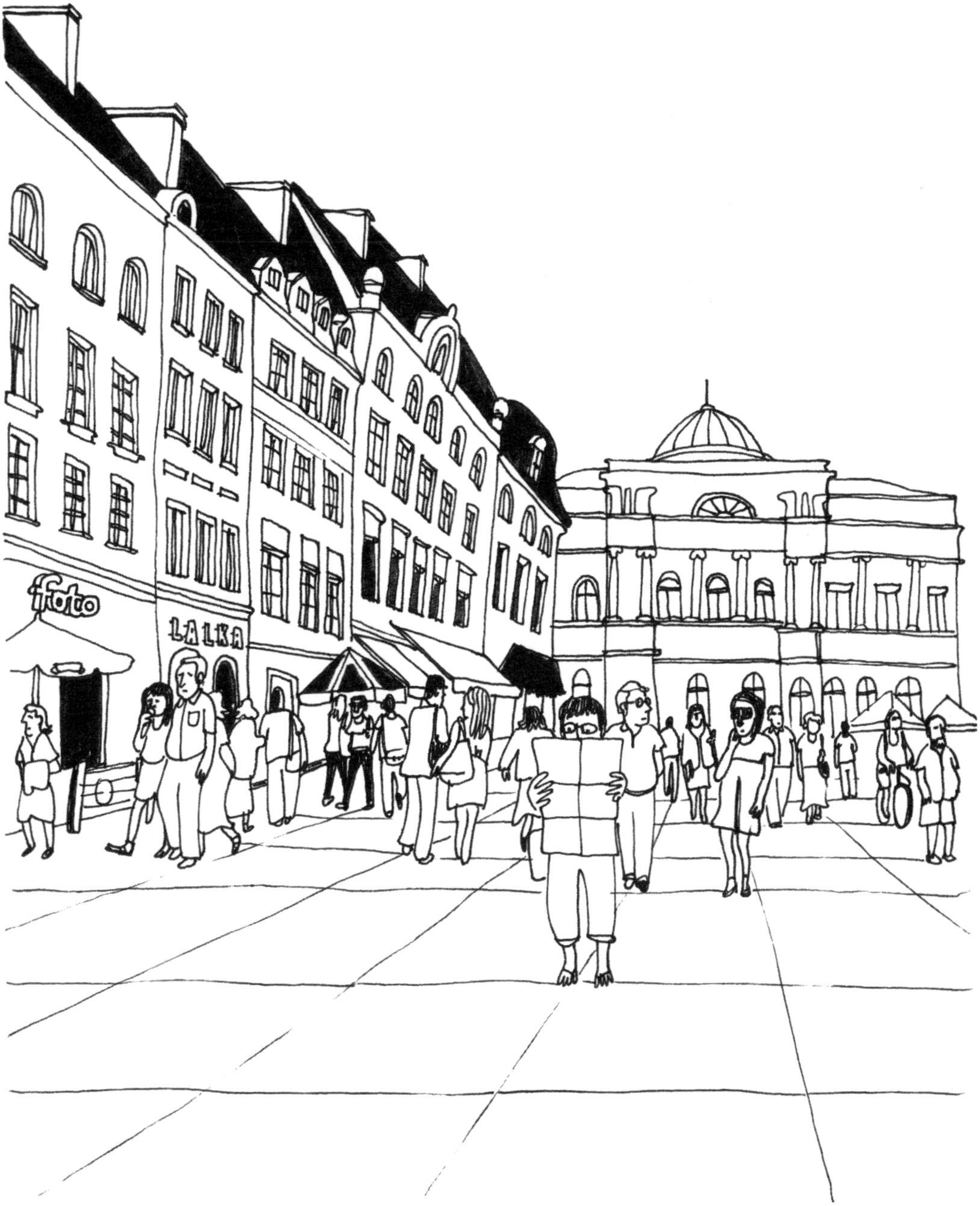
foto
LALKA

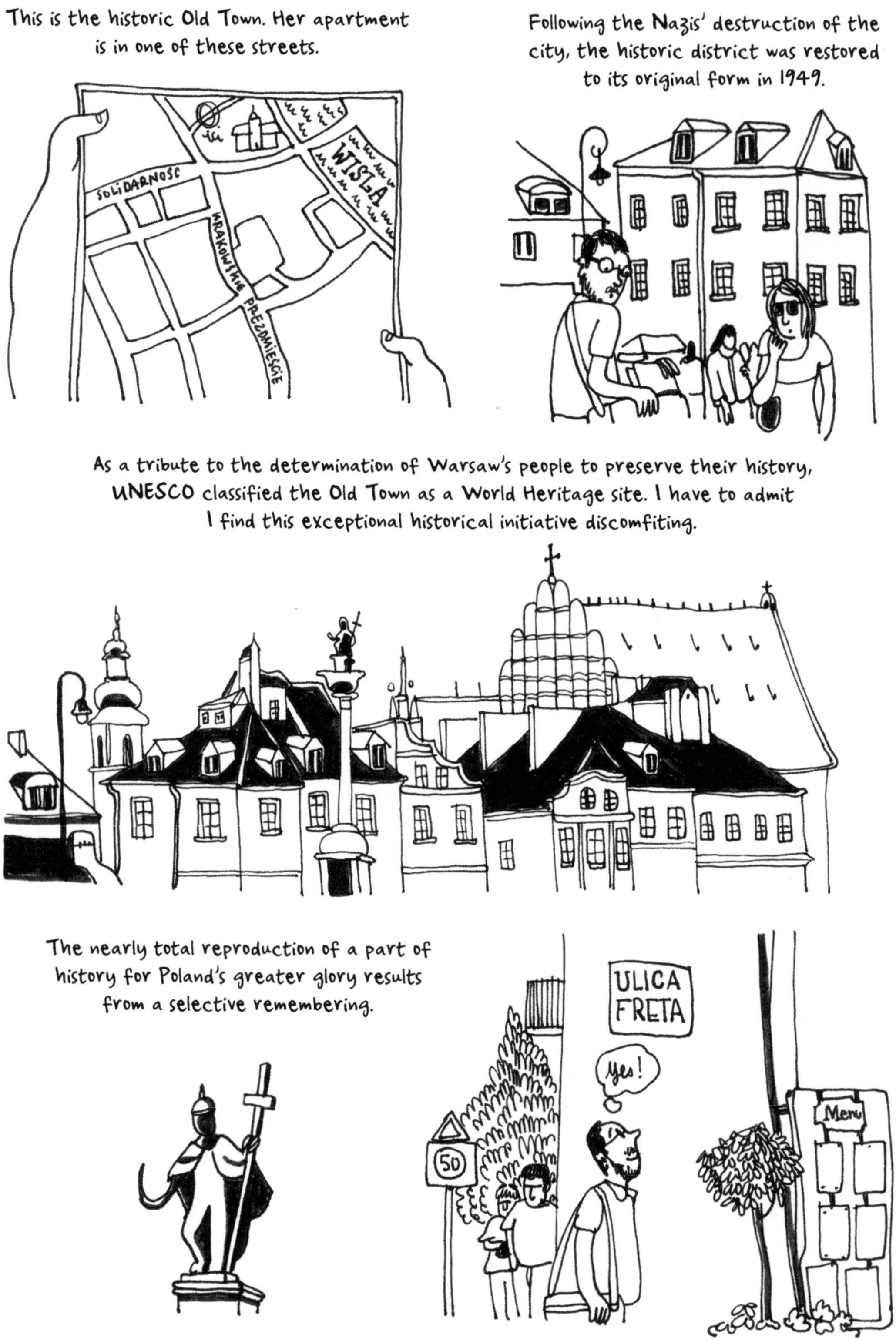
This is the historic Old Town. Her apartment is in one of these streets.
SOLIDARNOSC
KRAKOWSKIE PRZEDMIESCIE
WISLA
Following the Nazis' destruction of the city, the historic district was restored to its original form in 1949.
As a tribute to the determination of Warsaw's people to preserve their history, UNESCO classified the Old Town as a World Heritage site. I have to admit I find this exceptional historical initiative discomfiting.
The nearly total reproduction of a part of history for Poland's greater glory results from a selective remembering.
ULICA FRETA
Yes!
50
Menu

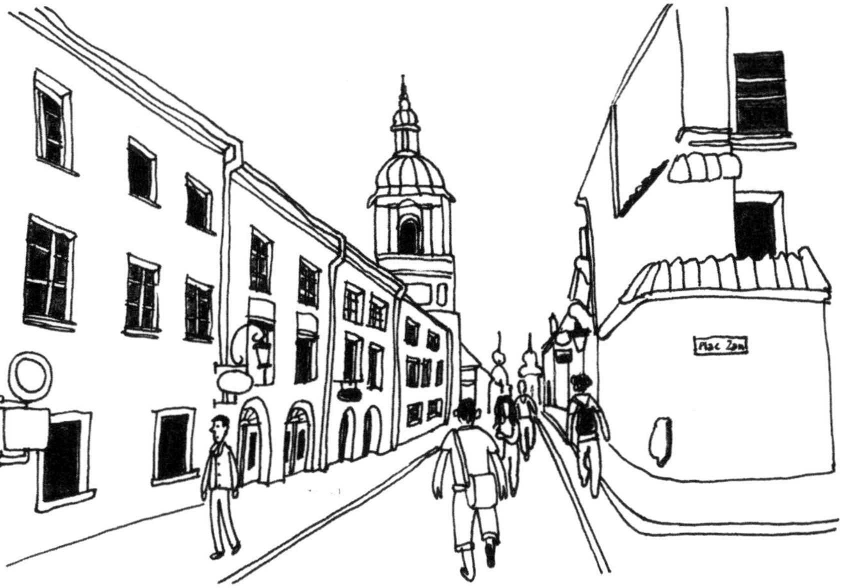

These forgotten things, Warsaw's once-thriving Jewish community...
I've not seen the slightest trace of them since setting foot on the ground.

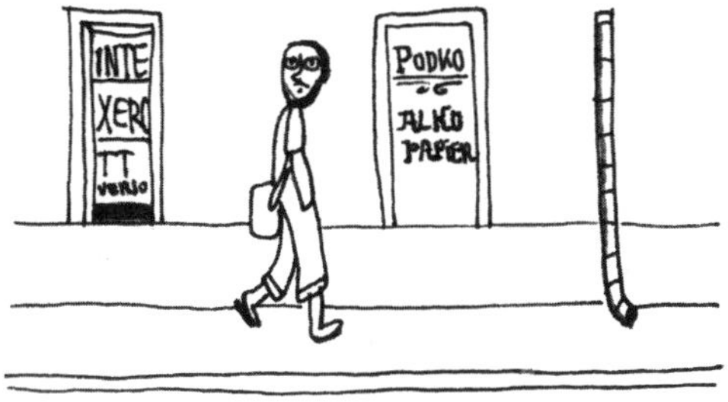
PODKO
ALKO
PAPIER

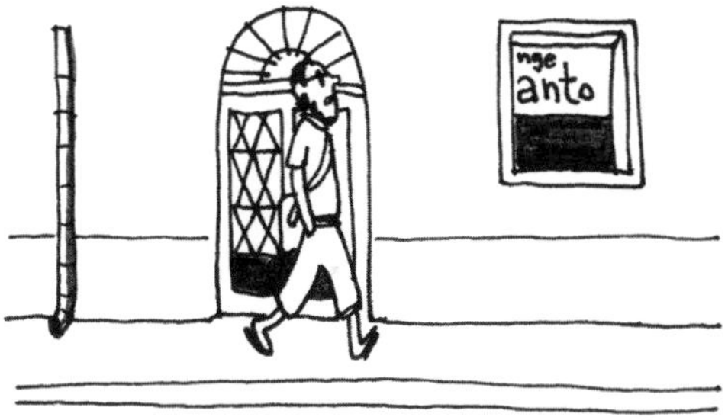
anto

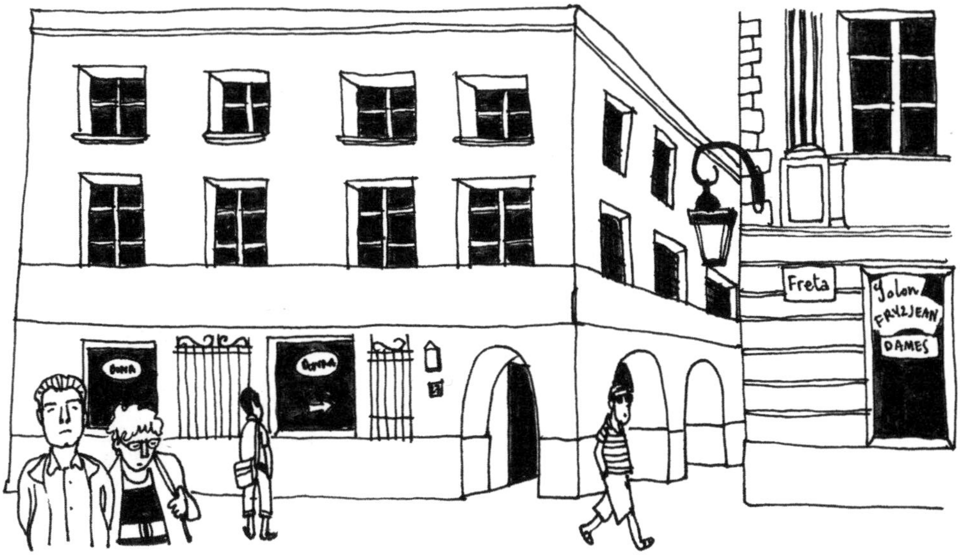
Freta
DAMES

27 Ulica Freta. This is where she lived.

By "she", I mean my grandmother. To get the whole picture, you have to take a step backwards in time: a spring afternoon in Paris, 2008.

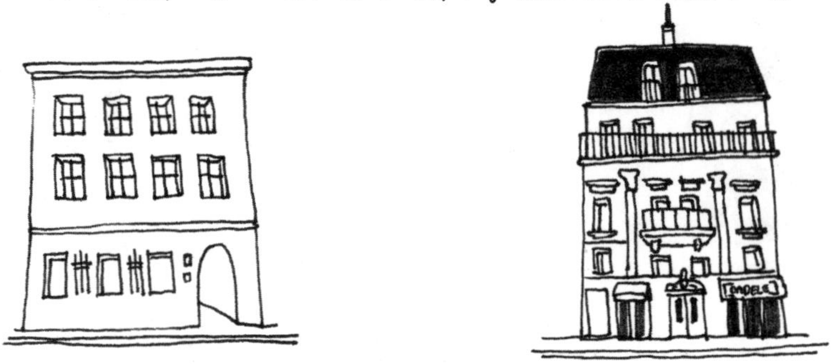

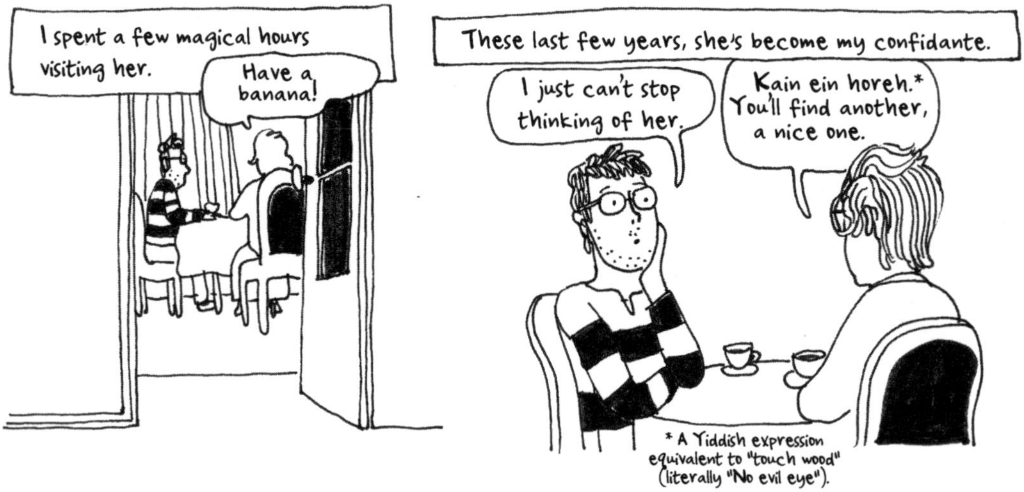
I spent a few magical hours visiting her.
Have a banana!
These last few years, she's become my confidante.
I just can't stop thinking of her.
Kain ein horeh.* You'll find another, a nice one.
* A Yiddish expression equivalent to "touch wood" (literally "No evil eye").

My grandma is a droplet of pure water from a spring over there that has since vanished. Seventy years of French life have done nothing to change her Yiddish accent.

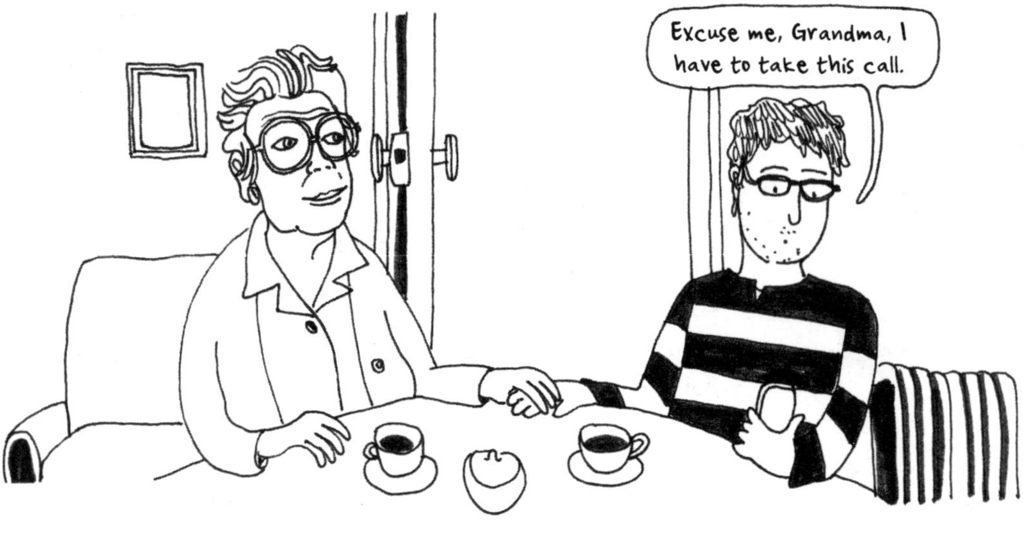
Excuse me, Grandma, I have to take this call.

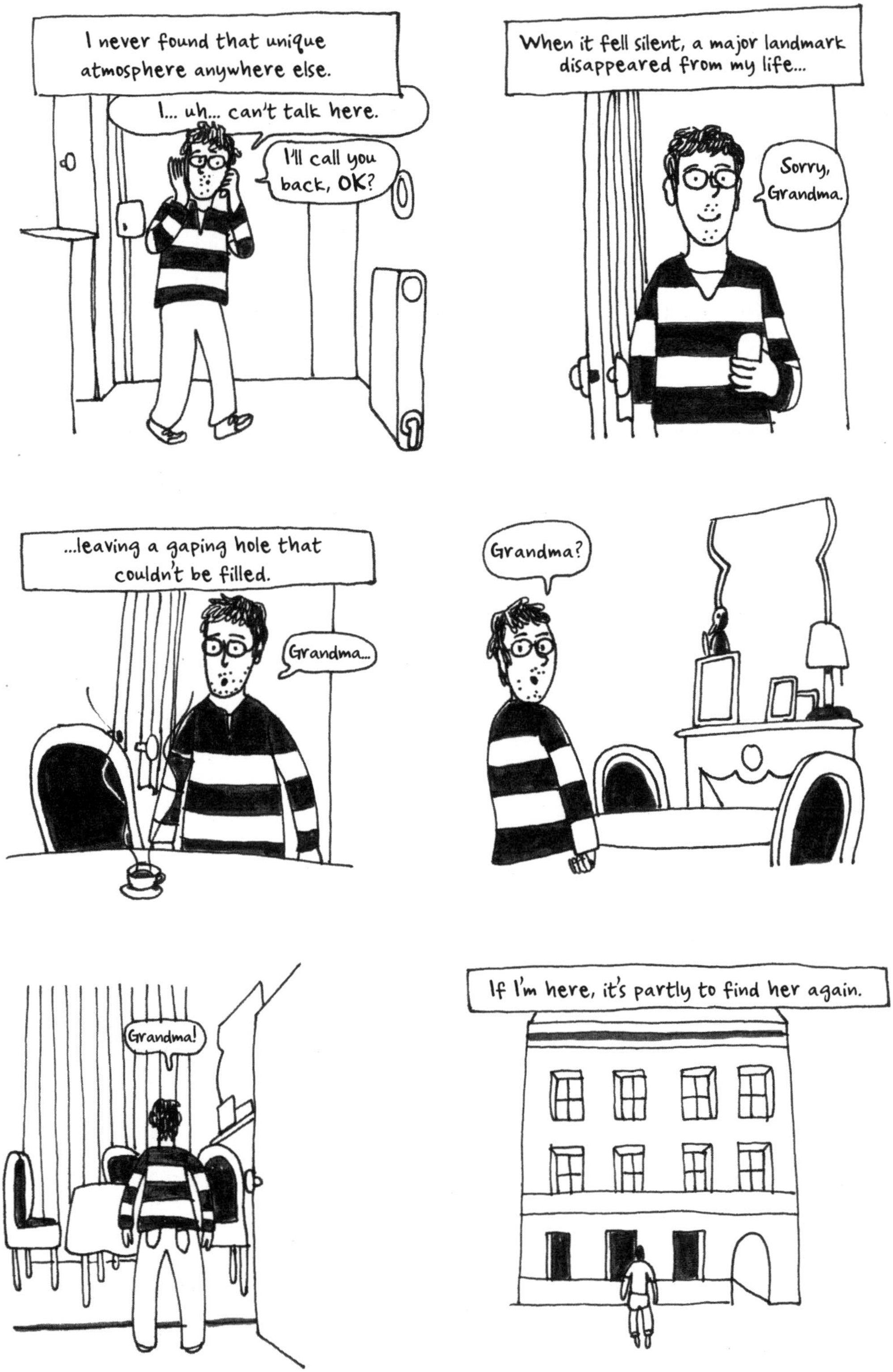
I never found that unique atmosphere anywhere else.
I... uh... can't talk here.
I'll call you back, OK?
When it fell silent, a major landmark disappeared from my life...
Sorry, Grandma.
...leaving a gaping hole that couldn't be filled.
Grandma...
Grandma?
Grandma!
If I'm here, it's partly to find her again.

Watch Out for Polacks

I'd envisioned all sorts of possible scenarios.

 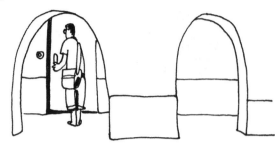

Excuse me, there was a lady who used to live here a long time ago... Tema Barab?

Tema! Yes, I remember! We used to play together when we were kids!

Come in! Tema! How is she? Oooh, you must be hungry!

Come in!

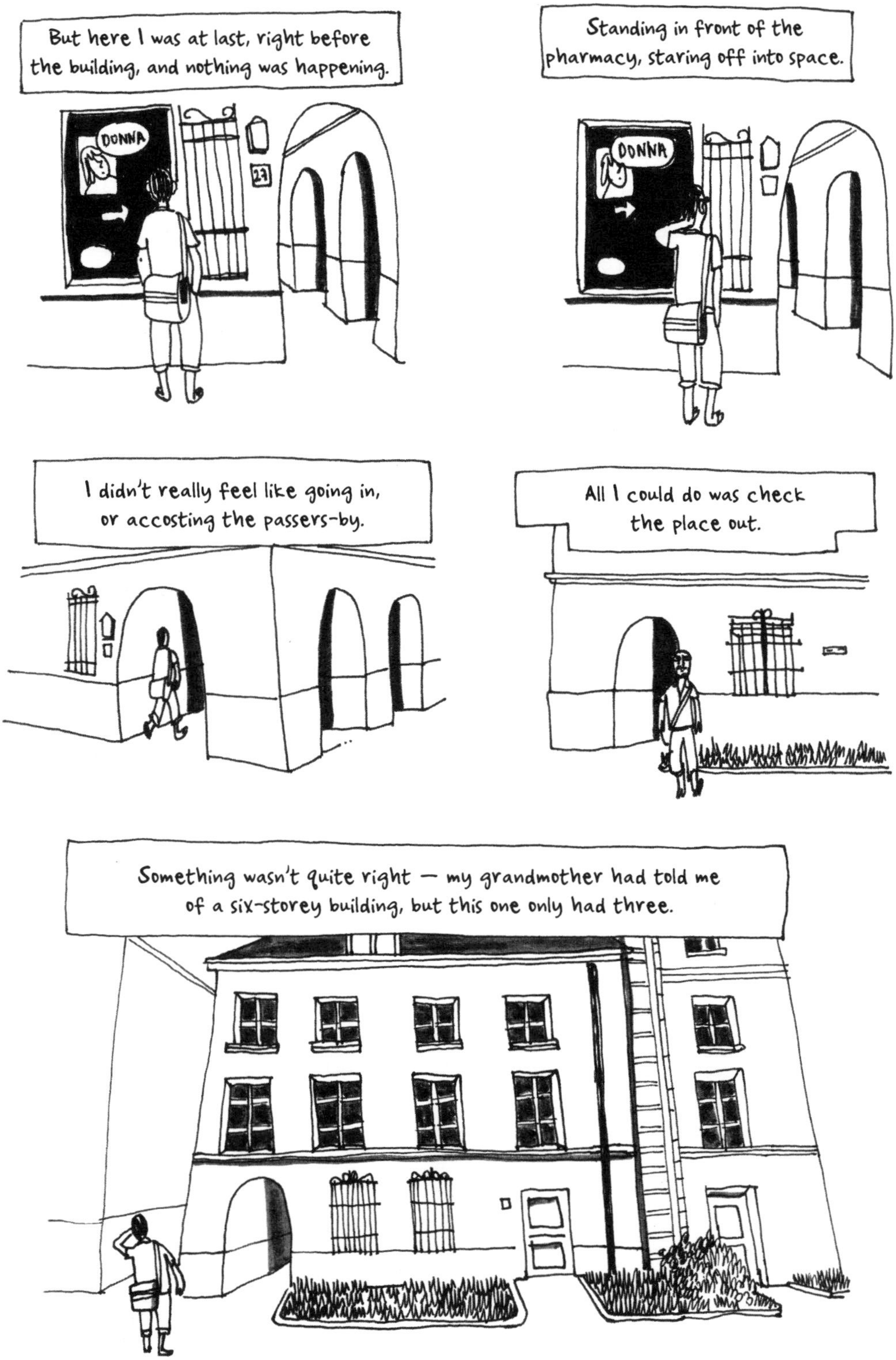

But here I was at last, right before the building, and nothing was happening.
DONNA
Standing in front of the pharmacy, staring off into space.
DONNA
I didn't really feel like going in, or accosting the passers-by.
All I could do was check the place out.
Something wasn't quite right — my grandmother had told me of a six-storey building, but this one only had three.

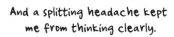

And a splitting headache kept me from thinking clearly.

Let me just sit down and get my thoughts in order...

Paris, France, 19th arrondissement. Jaurès. My room. My bed. A week ago.

Prepping this trip was no mean affair.

Spreading the word, dreading everyone's reactions.

other actions ▼

Poland   [Inbox | x]   More

☆ Jérémie Dres   Hi, Dad! I should be   30/05/10
☆ Dad to me   show details 31/05/10

Hello Jérémie,
If you're going to Poland, above all,
watch out for Polacks.
Hugs,
Dad

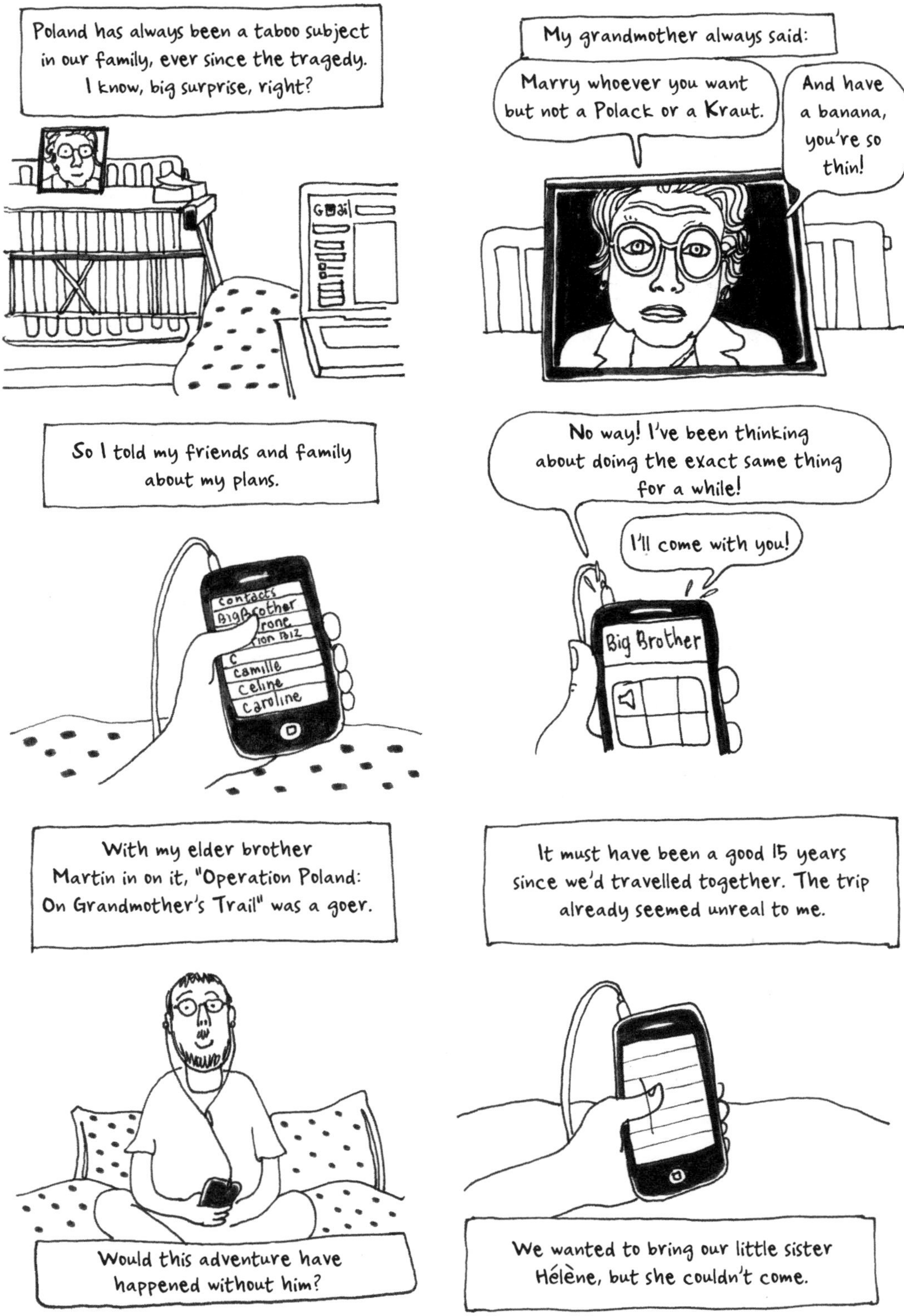
Poland has always been a taboo subject in our family, ever since the tragedy. I know, big surprise, right?
My grandmother always said:
Marry whoever you want but not a Polack or a Kraut.
And have a banana, you're so thin!
So I told my friends and family about my plans.
Contacts
camille
celine
caroline
No way! I've been thinking about doing the exact same thing for a while!
I'll come with you!
Big Brother
With my elder brother Martin in on it, "Operation Poland: On Grandmother's Trail" was a goer.
It must have been a good 15 years since we'd travelled together. The trip already seemed unreal to me.
Would this adventure have happened without him?
We wanted to bring our little sister Hélène, but she couldn't come.

Next on the list: my cousin.

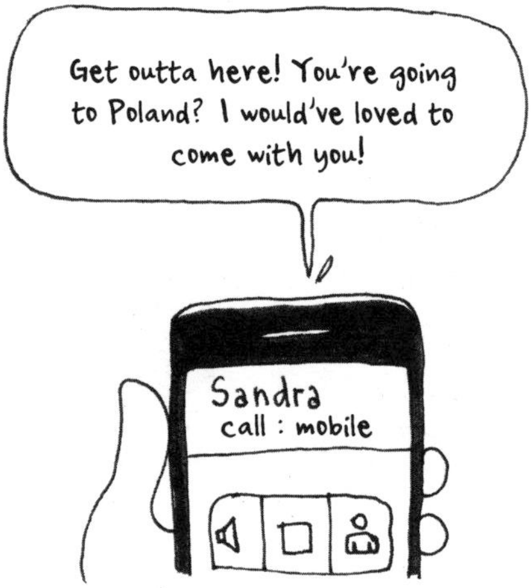
Get outta here! You're going to Poland? I would've loved to come with you!
Sandra
call : mobile

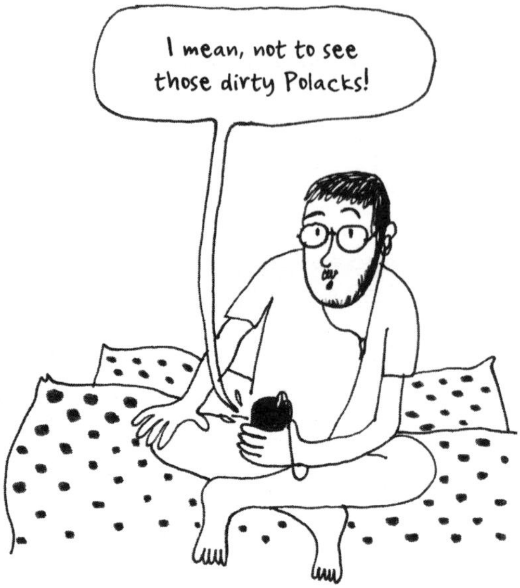
I mean, not to see those dirty Polacks!

And last of all my aunt, whom I hardly dared speak to.

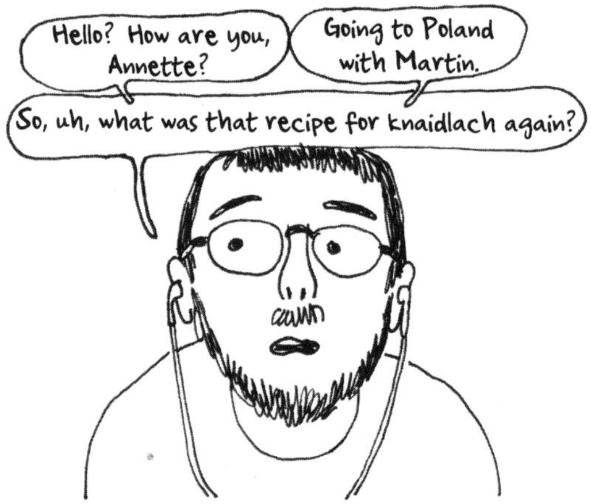
Hello? How are you, Annette?
Going to Poland with Martin.
So, uh, what was that recipe for knaidlach again?

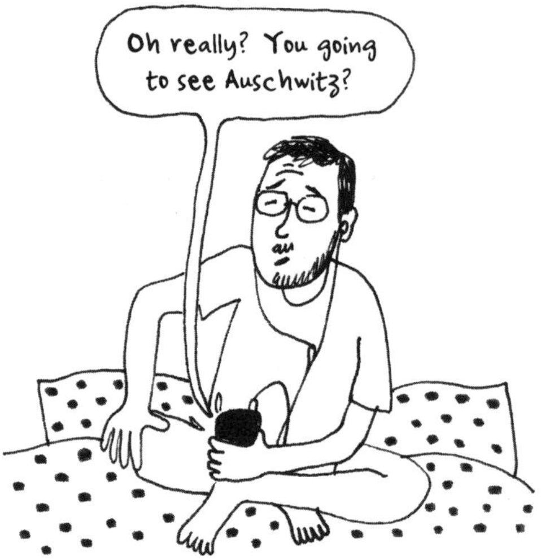
Oh really? You going to see Auschwitz?

Auschwitz: five years of devastation for more than a thousand years of Jewish life and history.

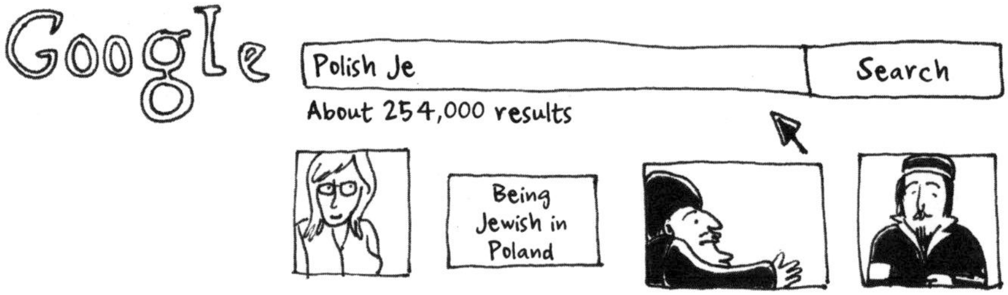
Google
Polish Je
Search
About 254,000 results
Being Jewish in Poland

Before the Holocaust, Poland ranked second among countries in terms of a Jewish population (three and a half million). It was the cradle of Yiddish culture, which spread throughout Europe.

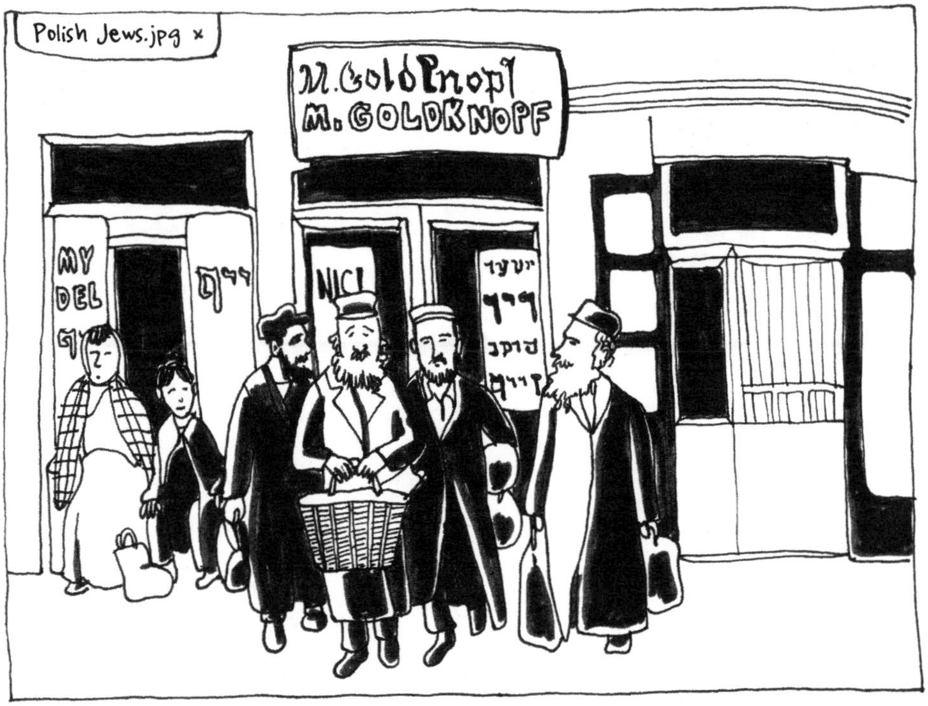
Polish Jews.jpg ×
M. GOLDKNOPF

Auschwitz, a trauma still so present as to overshadow all the rest. But the rest was what I'd gone looking for in Poland.

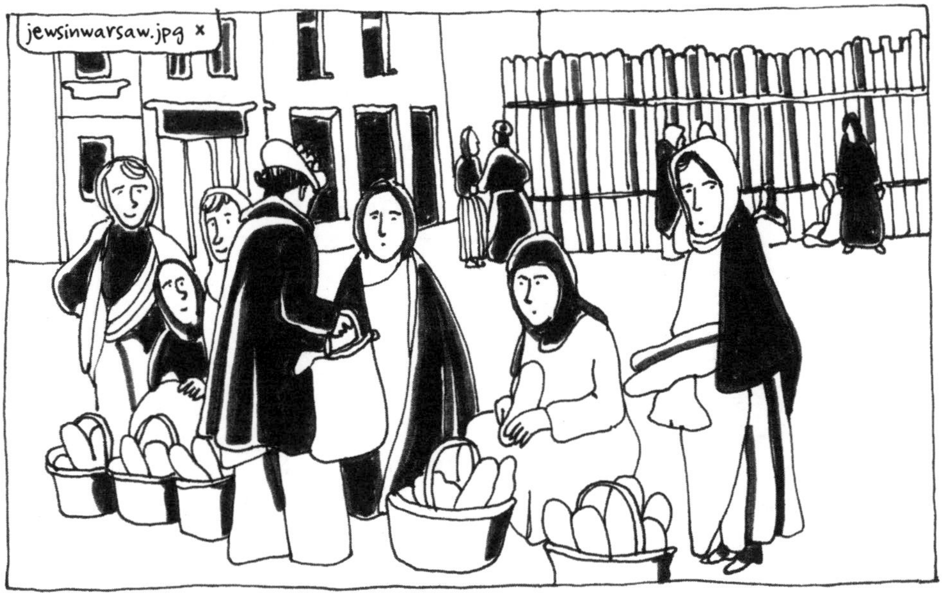
jewsinwarsaw.jpg ×

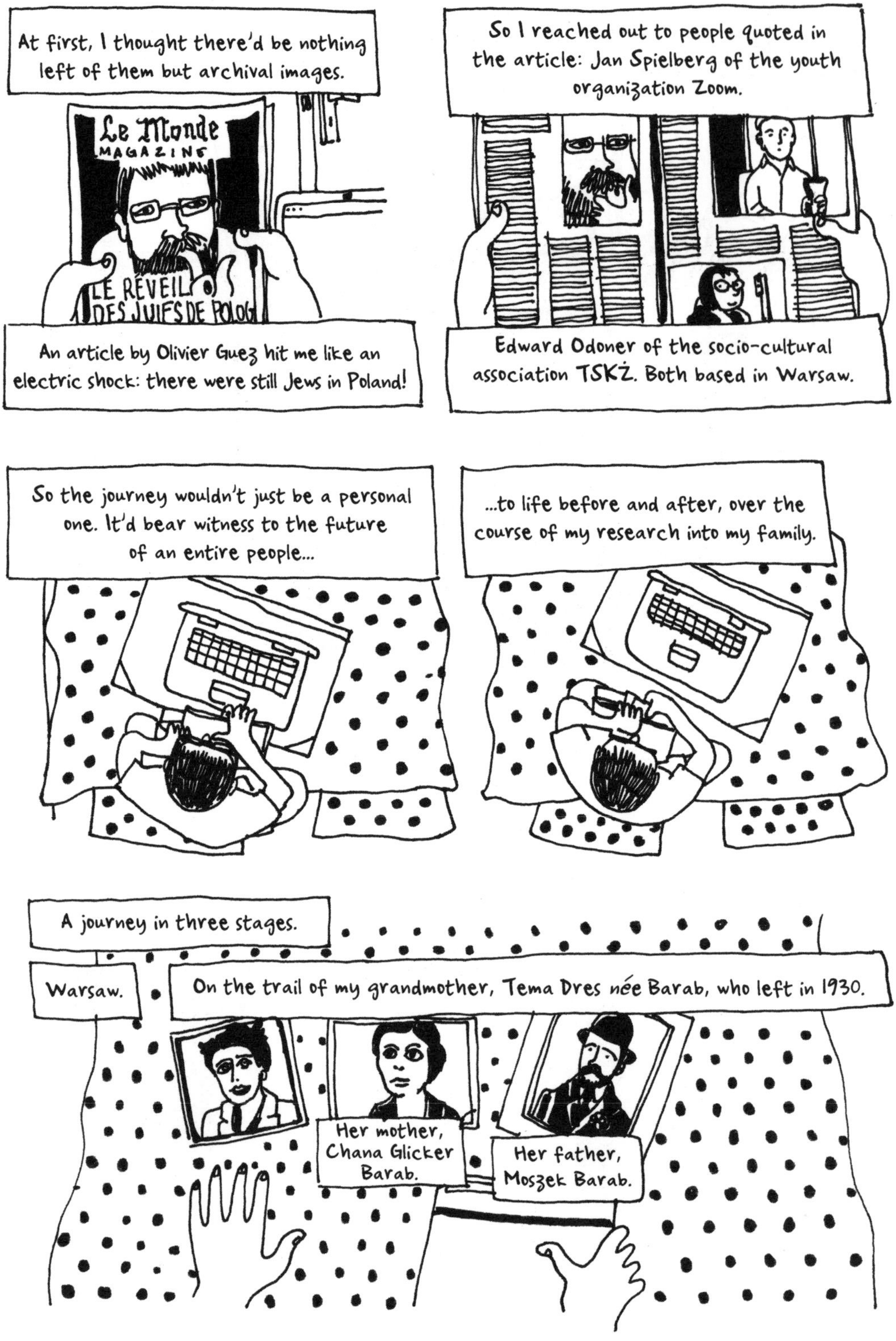

At first, I thought there'd be nothing left of them but archival images.
Le Monde MAGAZINE
LE RÉVEIL DES JUIFS DE POLOG
An article by Olivier Guez hit me like an electric shock: there were still Jews in Poland!
So I reached out to people quoted in the article: Jan Spielberg of the youth organization Zoom.
Edward Odoner of the socio-cultural association TSKŻ. Both based in Warsaw.
So the journey wouldn't just be a personal one. It'd bear witness to the future of an entire people...
...to life before and after, over the course of my research into my family.
A journey in three stages.
Warsaw.
On the trail of my grandmother, Tema Dres née Barab, who left in 1930.
Her mother, Chana Glicker Barab.
Her father, Moszek Barab.

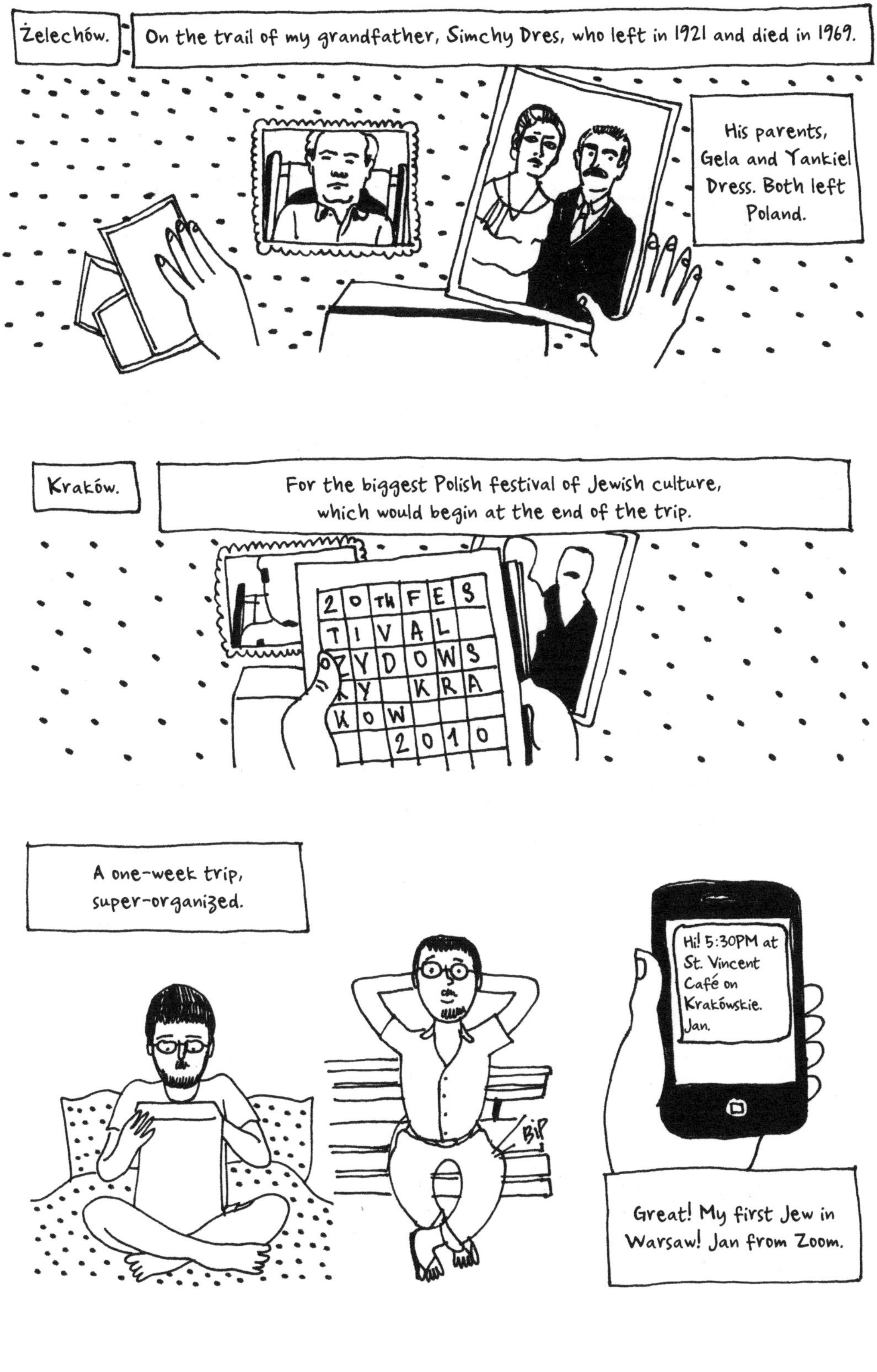

Żelechów.
On the trail of my grandfather, Simchy Dres, who left in 1921 and died in 1969.
His parents, Gela and Yankiel Dress. Both left Poland.
Kraków.
For the biggest Polish festival of Jewish culture, which would begin at the end of the trip.
20TH FES
TIVAL
ZYDOWS
Y KRA
KOW
2010
A one-week trip, super-organized.
BiP
Hi! 5:30PM at St. Vincent Café on Krakówskie. Jan.
Great! My first Jew in Warsaw! Jan from Zoom.

Young, Jewish, and Polish

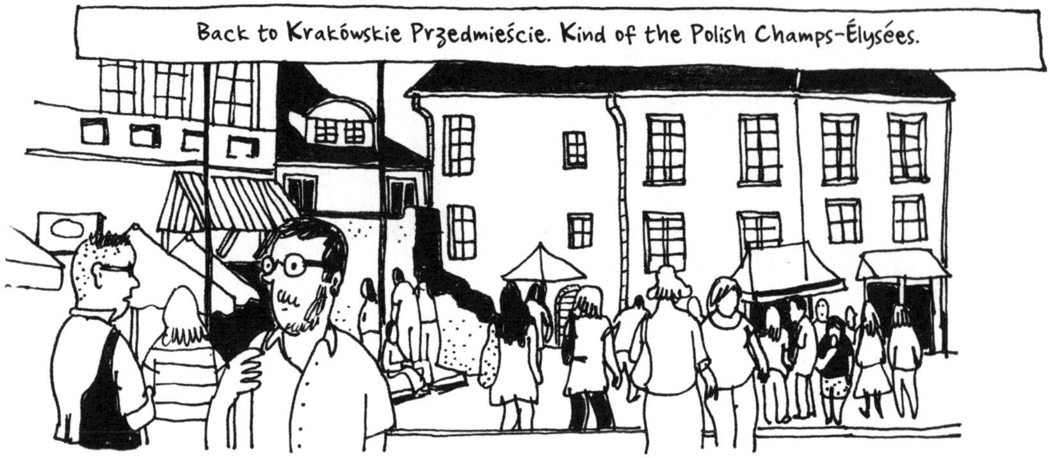
Back to Krakówskie Przedmieście. Kind of the Polish Champs-Élysées.

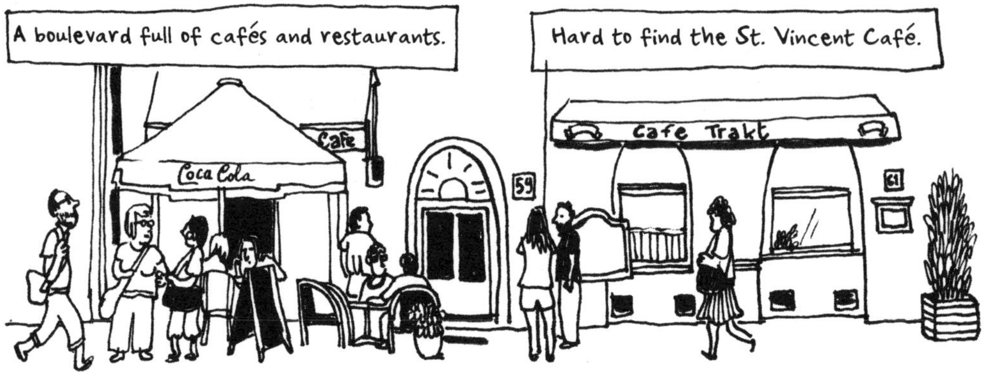
A boulevard full of cafés and restaurants.
Cafe
Coca Cola
59
Hard to find the St. Vincent Café.
Cafe Trakt
61

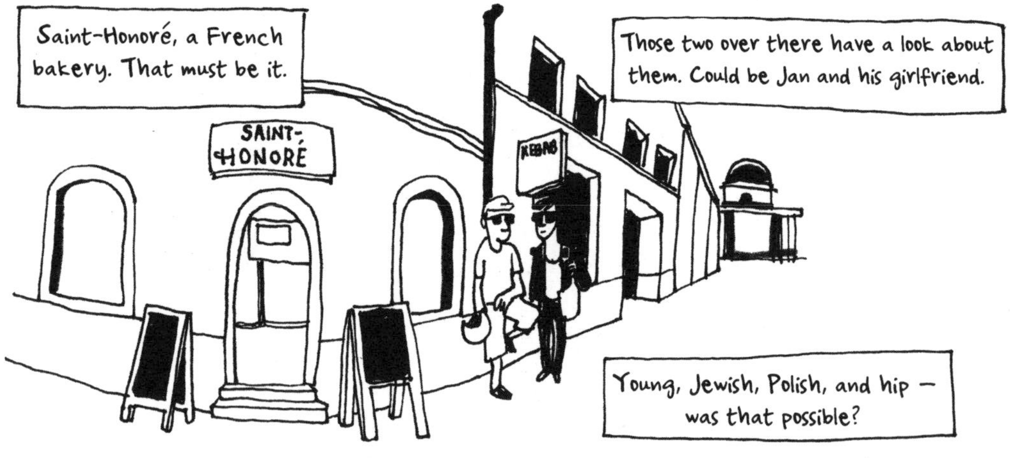
Saint-Honoré, a French bakery. That must be it.
SAINT-HONORÉ
Those two over there have a look about them. Could be Jan and his girlfriend.
Young, Jewish, Polish, and hip — was that possible?

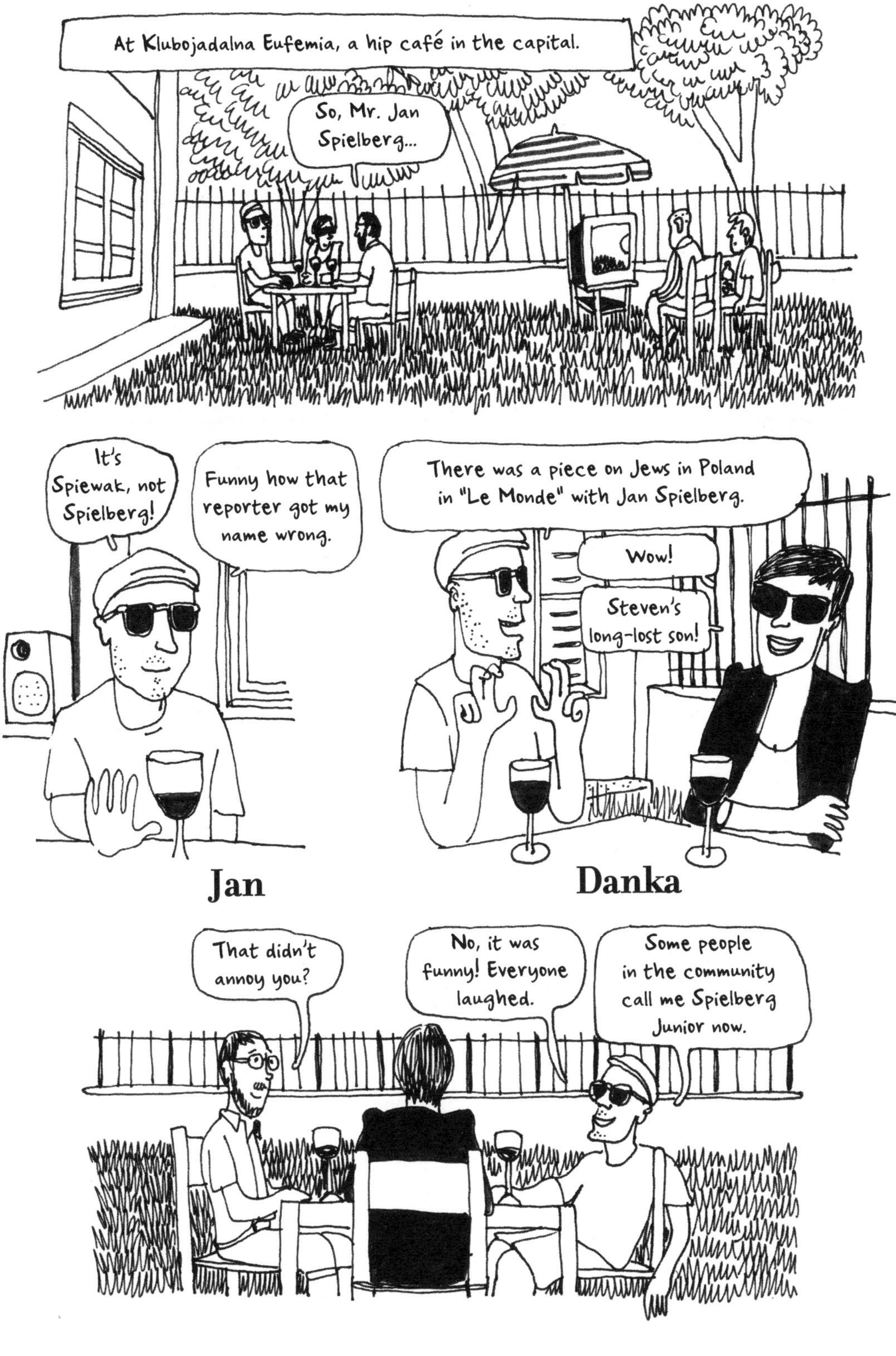
At Klubojadalna Eufemia, a hip café in the capital.
So, Mr. Jan Spielberg...
It's Spiewak, not Spielberg!
Funny how that reporter got my name wrong.
There was a piece on Jews in Poland in "Le Monde" with Jan Spielberg.
Wow!
Steven's long-lost son!
Jan
Danka
That didn't annoy you?
No, it was funny! Everyone laughed.
Some people in the community call me Spielberg Junior now.

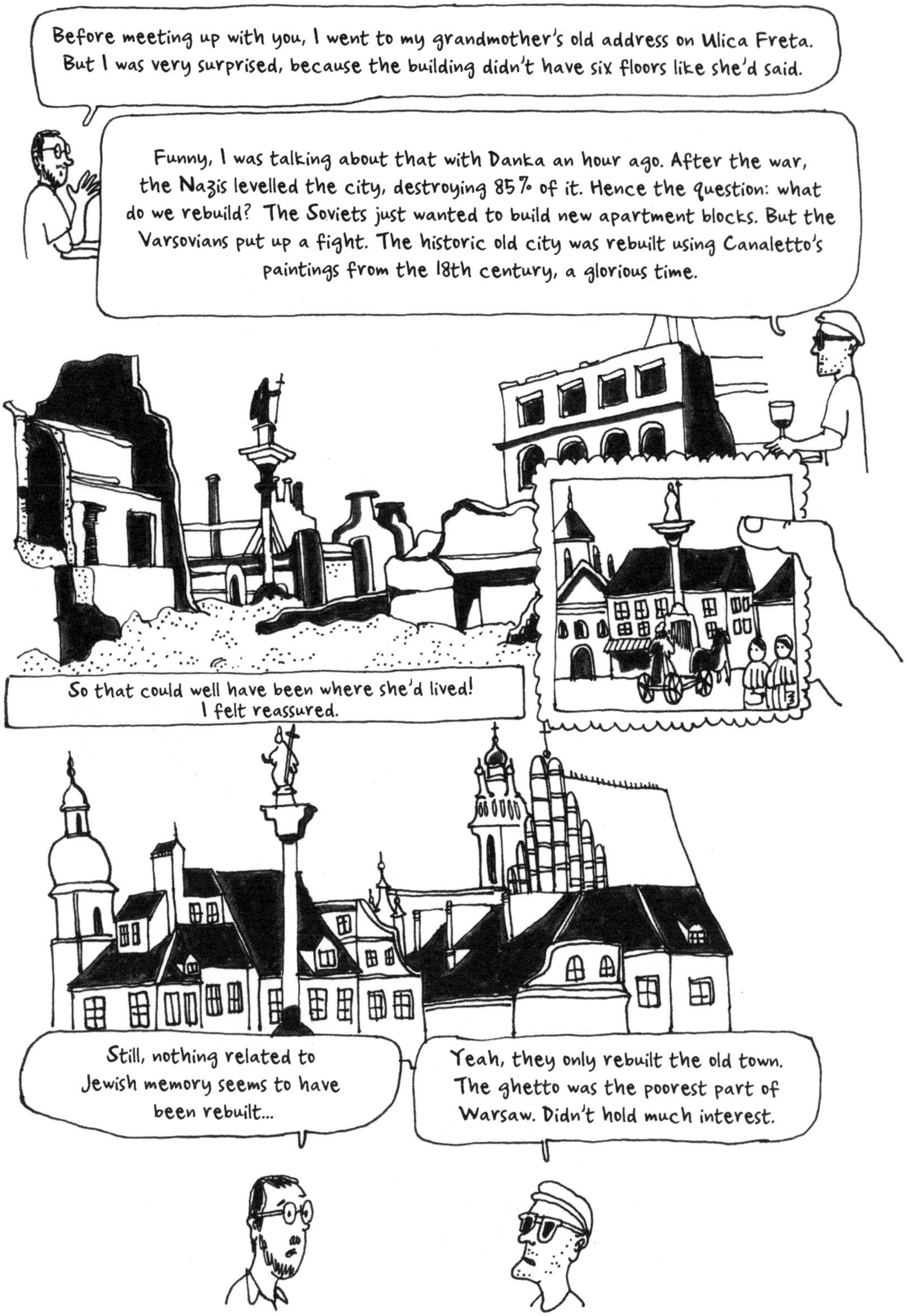
Before meeting up with you, I went to my grandmother's old address on Ulica Freta. But I was very surprised, because the building didn't have six floors like she'd said.
Funny, I was talking about that with Danka an hour ago. After the war, the Nazis levelled the city, destroying 85% of it. Hence the question: what do we rebuild? The Soviets just wanted to build new apartment blocks. But the Varsovians put up a fight. The historic old city was rebuilt using Canaletto's paintings from the 18th century, a glorious time.
So that could well have been where she'd lived! I felt reassured.
Still, nothing related to Jewish memory seems to have been rebuilt...
Yeah, they only rebuilt the old town. The ghetto was the poorest part of Warsaw. Didn't hold much interest.

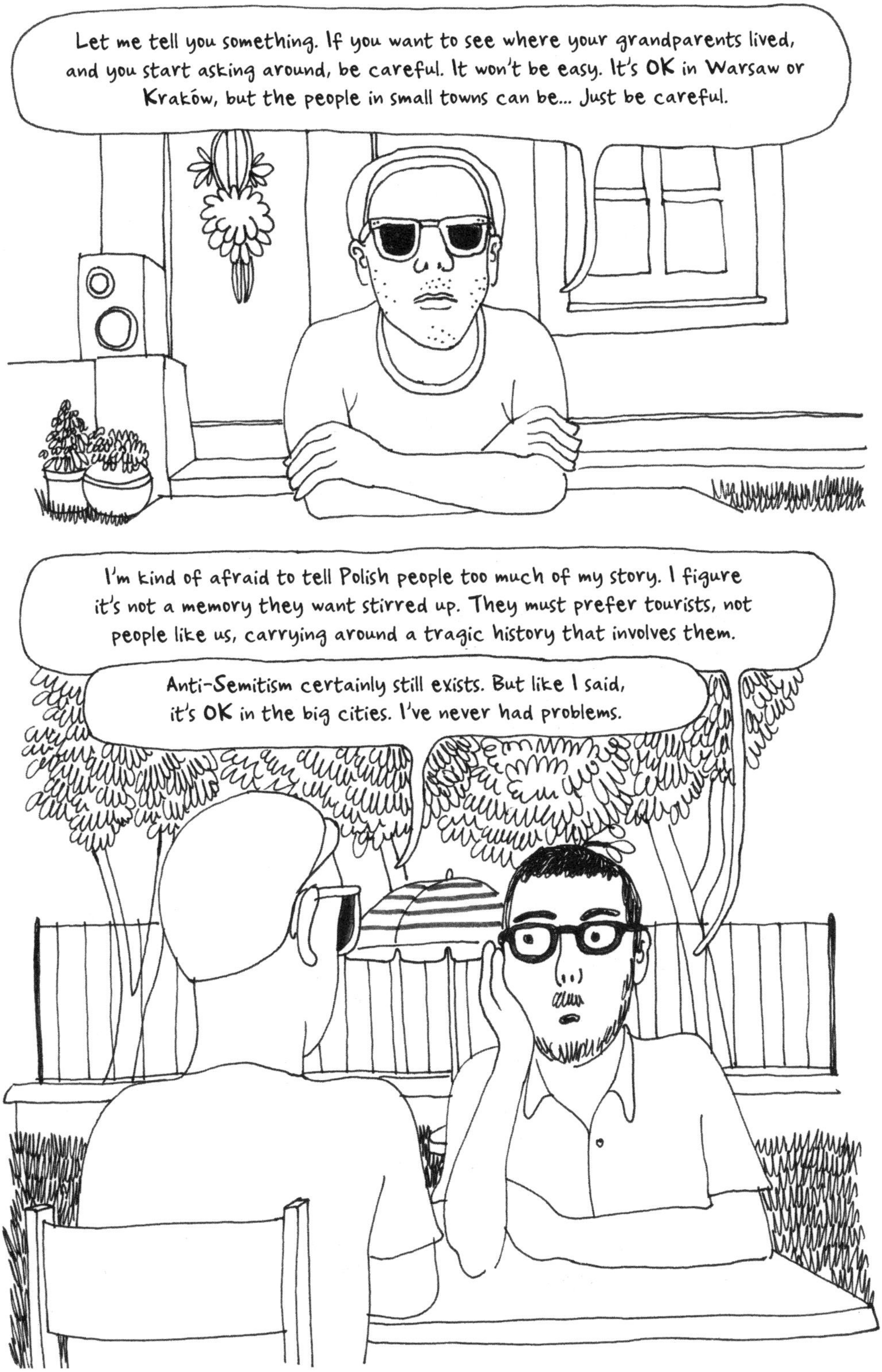
Let me tell you something. If you want to see where your grandparents lived, and you start asking around, be careful. It won't be easy. It's OK in Warsaw or Kraków, but the people in small towns can be... Just be careful.
I'm kind of afraid to tell Polish people too much of my story. I figure it's not a memory they want stirred up. They must prefer tourists, not people like us, carrying around a tragic history that involves them.
Anti-Semitism certainly still exists. But like I said, it's OK in the big cities. I've never had problems.

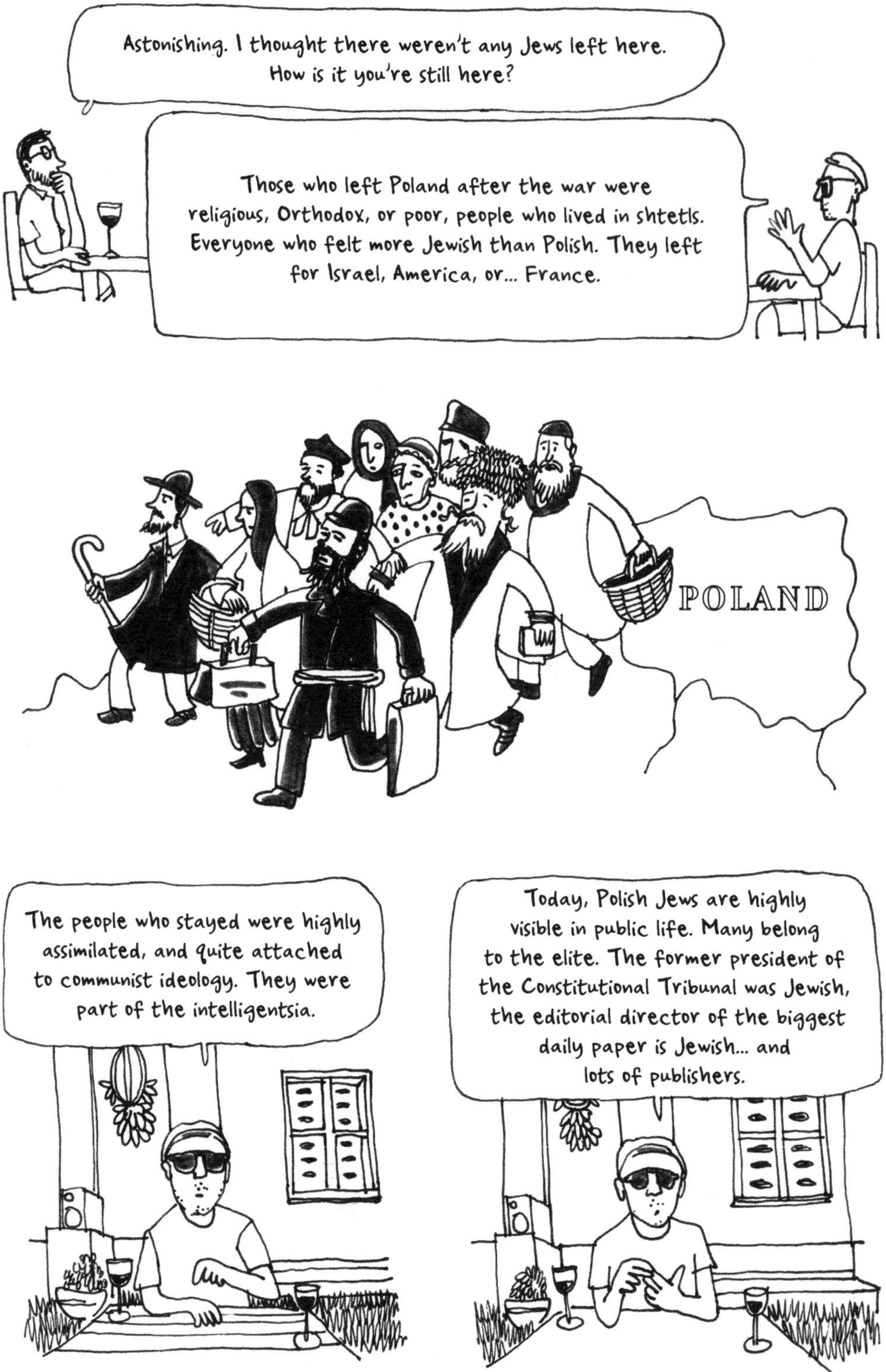
Astonishing. I thought there weren't any Jews left here. How is it you're still here?
Those who left Poland after the war were religious, Orthodox, or poor, people who lived in shtetls. Everyone who felt more Jewish than Polish. They left for Israel, America, or... France.
POLAND
The people who stayed were highly assimilated, and quite attached to communist ideology. They were part of the intelligentsia.
Today, Polish Jews are highly visible in public life. Many belong to the elite. The former president of the Constitutional Tribunal was Jewish, the editorial director of the biggest daily paper is Jewish... and lots of publishers.

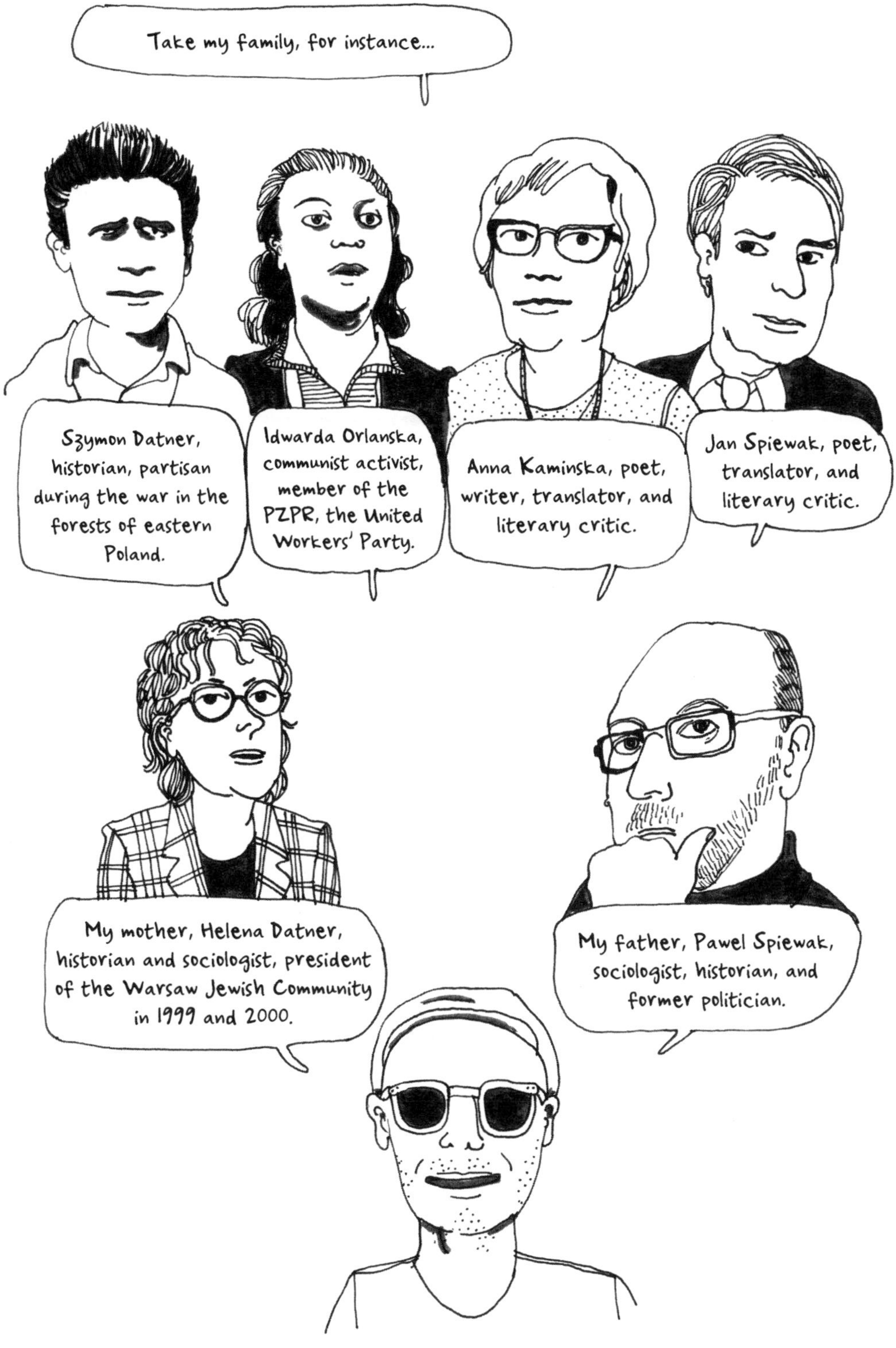
Take my family, for instance...
Szymon Datner, historian, partisan during the war in the forests of eastern Poland.
Idwarda Orlanska, communist activist, member of the PZPR, the United Workers' Party.
Anna Kaminska, poet, writer, translator, and literary critic.
Jan Spiewak, poet, translator, and literary critic.
My mother, Helena Datner, historian and sociologist, president of the Warsaw Jewish Community in 1999 and 2000.
My father, Pawel Spiewak, sociologist, historian, and former politician.

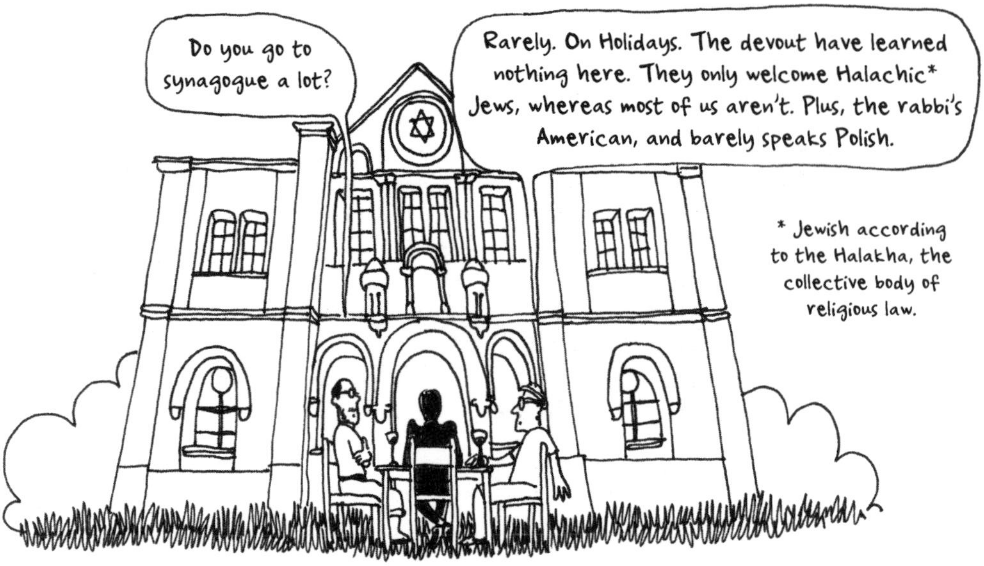
Do you go to synagogue a lot?
Rarely. On Holidays. The devout have learned nothing here. They only welcome Halachic* Jews, whereas most of us aren't. Plus, the rabbi's American, and barely speaks Polish.
* Jewish according to the Halakha, the collective body of religious law.

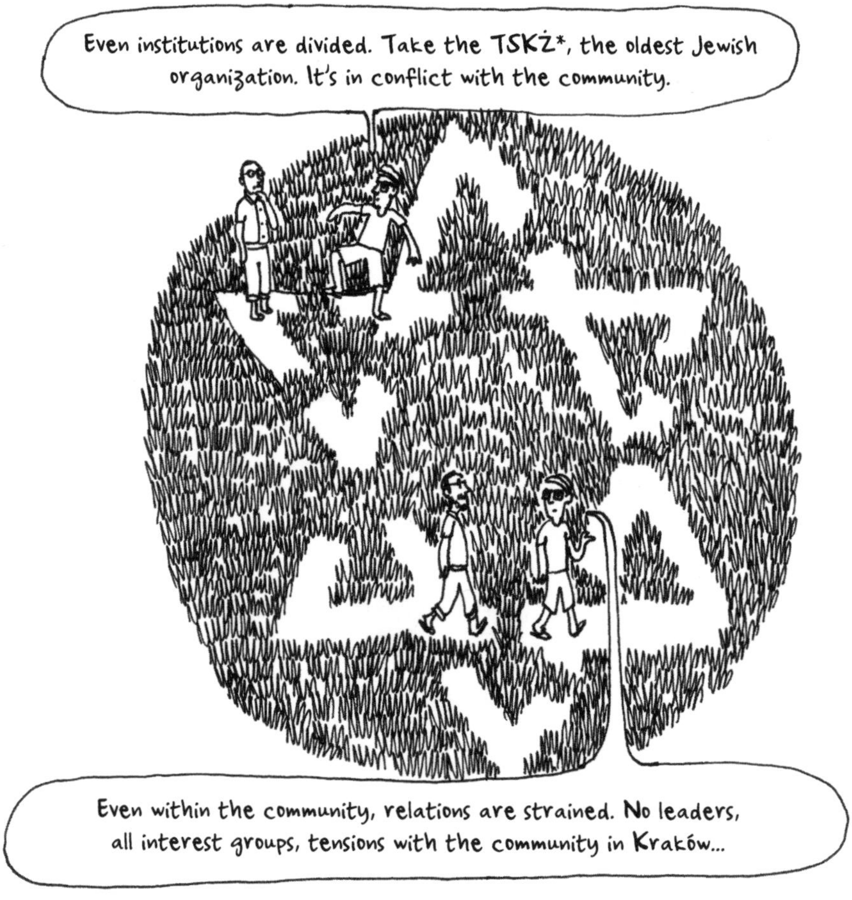
Even institutions are divided. Take the TSKŻ*, the oldest Jewish organization. It's in conflict with the community.
Even within the community, relations are strained. No leaders, all interest groups, tensions with the community in Kraków...

* Towarzystwo Społeczno-Kulturalne Żwydów w Polsce, formerly the Central Committee of Polish Jews (CKŻP).

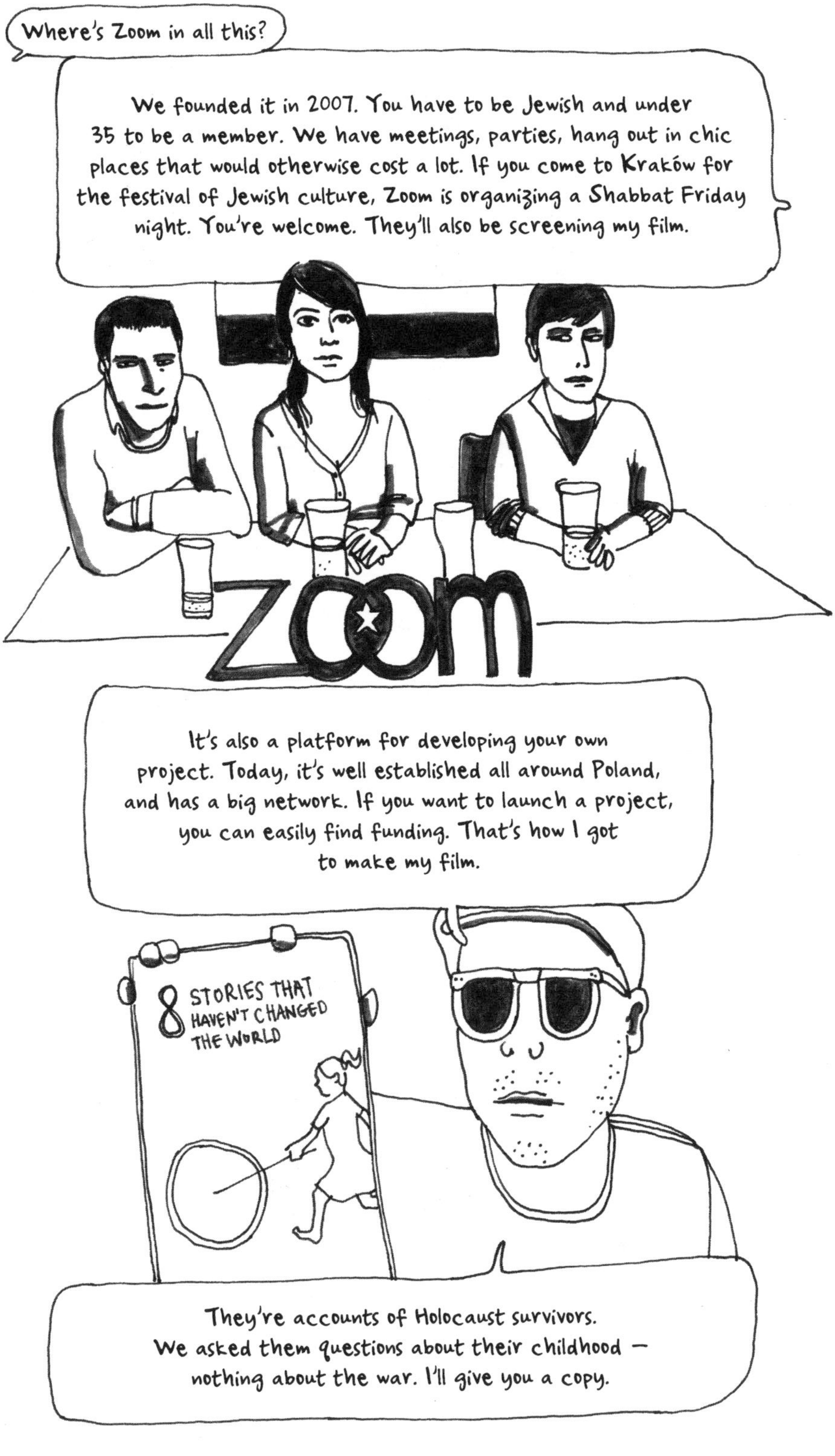
Where's Zoom in all this?
We founded it in 2007. You have to be Jewish and under 35 to be a member. We have meetings, parties, hang out in chic places that would otherwise cost a lot. If you come to Kraków for the festival of Jewish culture, Zoom is organizing a Shabbat Friday night. You're welcome. They'll also be screening my film.
ZOOM
It's also a platform for developing your own project. Today, it's well established all around Poland, and has a big network. If you want to launch a project, you can easily find funding. That's how I got to make my film.
8 STORIES THAT HAVEN'T CHANGED THE WORLD
They're accounts of Holocaust survivors. We asked them questions about their childhood — nothing about the war. I'll give you a copy.

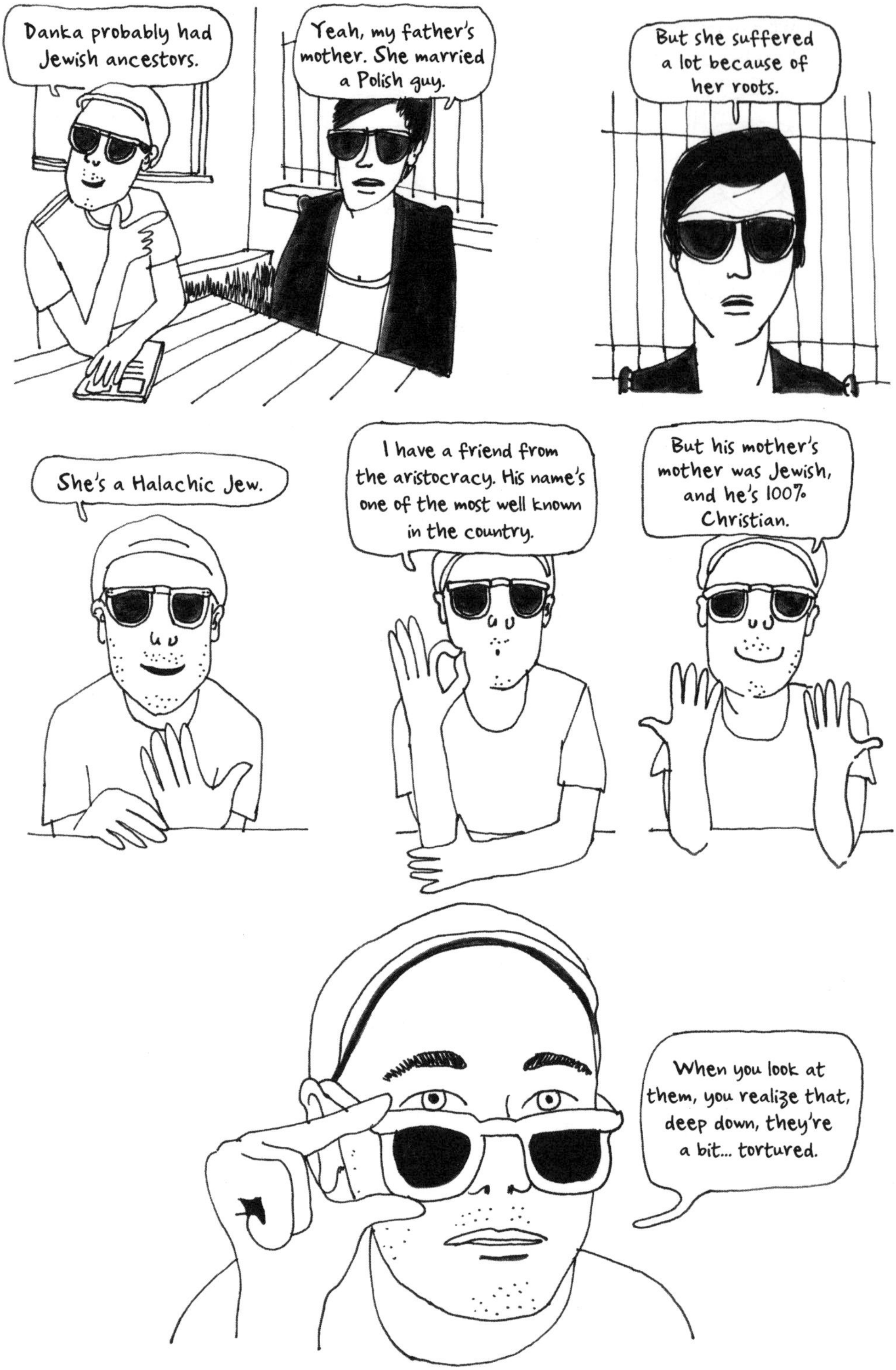
Danka probably had Jewish ancestors.
Yeah, my father's mother. She married a Polish guy.
But she suffered a lot because of her roots.
She's a Halachic Jew.
I have a friend from the aristocracy. His name's one of the most well known in the country.
But his mother's mother was Jewish, and he's 100% Christian.
When you look at them, you realize that, deep down, they're a bit... tortured.

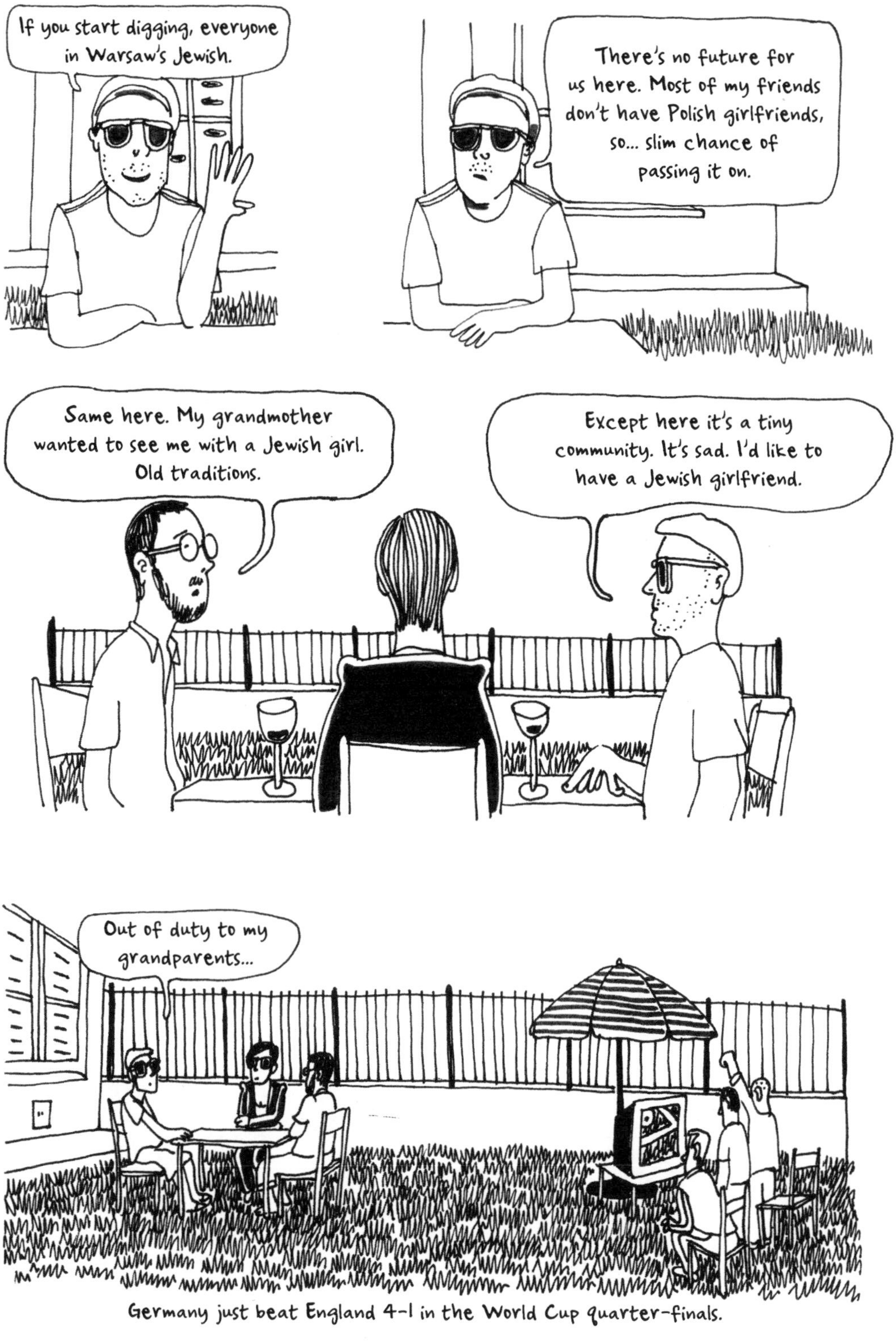
If you start digging, everyone in Warsaw's Jewish.
There's no future for us here. Most of my friends don't have Polish girlfriends, so... slim chance of passing it on.
Same here. My grandmother wanted to see me with a Jewish girl. Old traditions.
Except here it's a tiny community. It's sad. I'd like to have a Jewish girlfriend.
Out of duty to my grandparents...

Germany just beat England 4-1 in the World Cup quarter-finals.

Any Kippahs in Town?

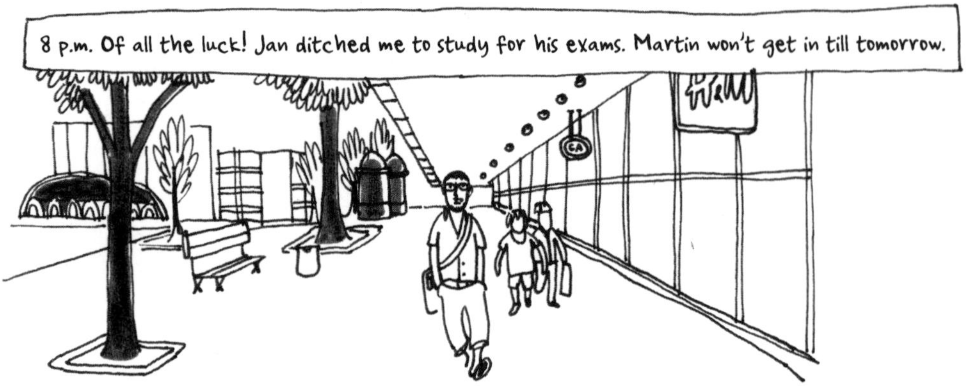
8 p.m. Of all the luck! Jan ditched me to study for his exams. Martin won't get in till tomorrow.
H&M
C&A

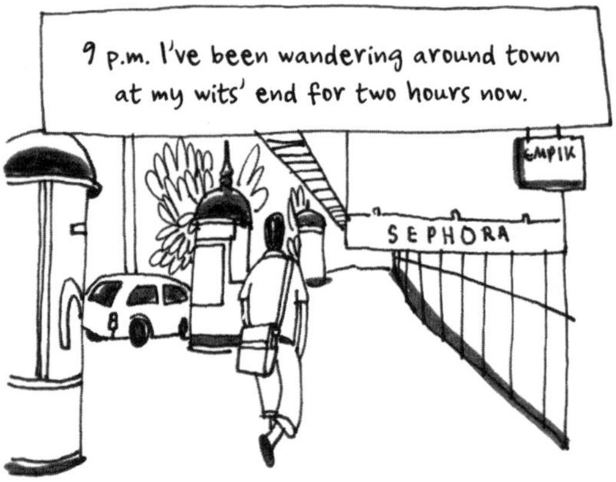
9 p.m. I've been wandering around town at my wits' end for two hours now.
EMPIK
SEPHORA

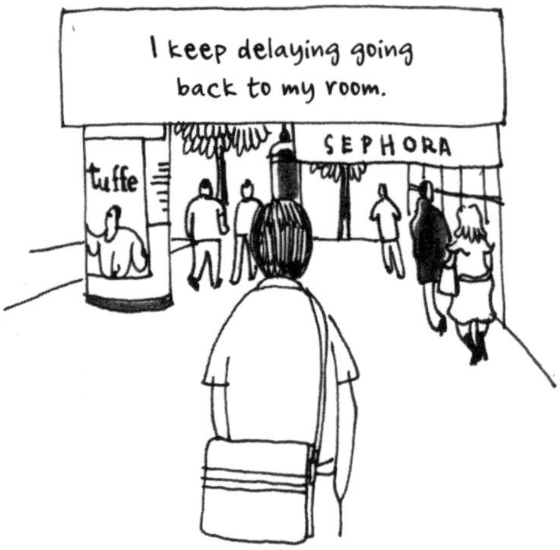
I keep delaying going back to my room.
tuffe
SEPHORA

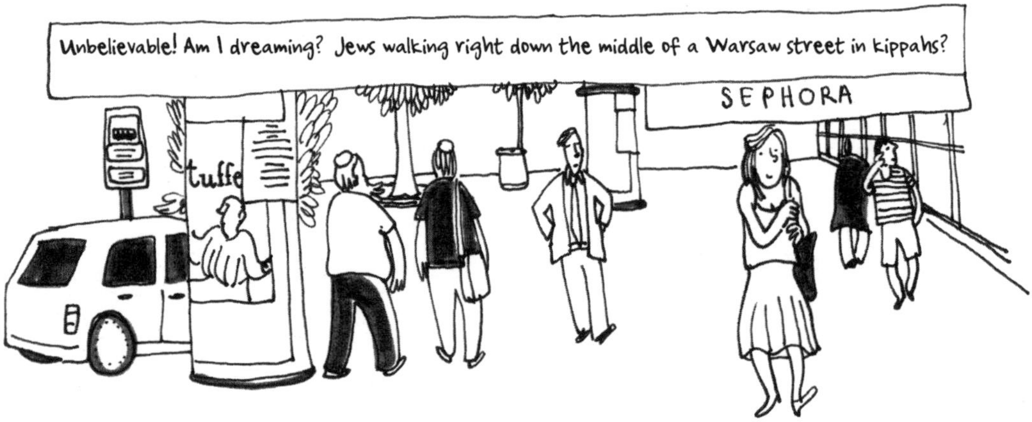
Unbelievable! Am I dreaming? Jews walking right down the middle of a Warsaw street in kippahs?
tuffe
SEPHORA

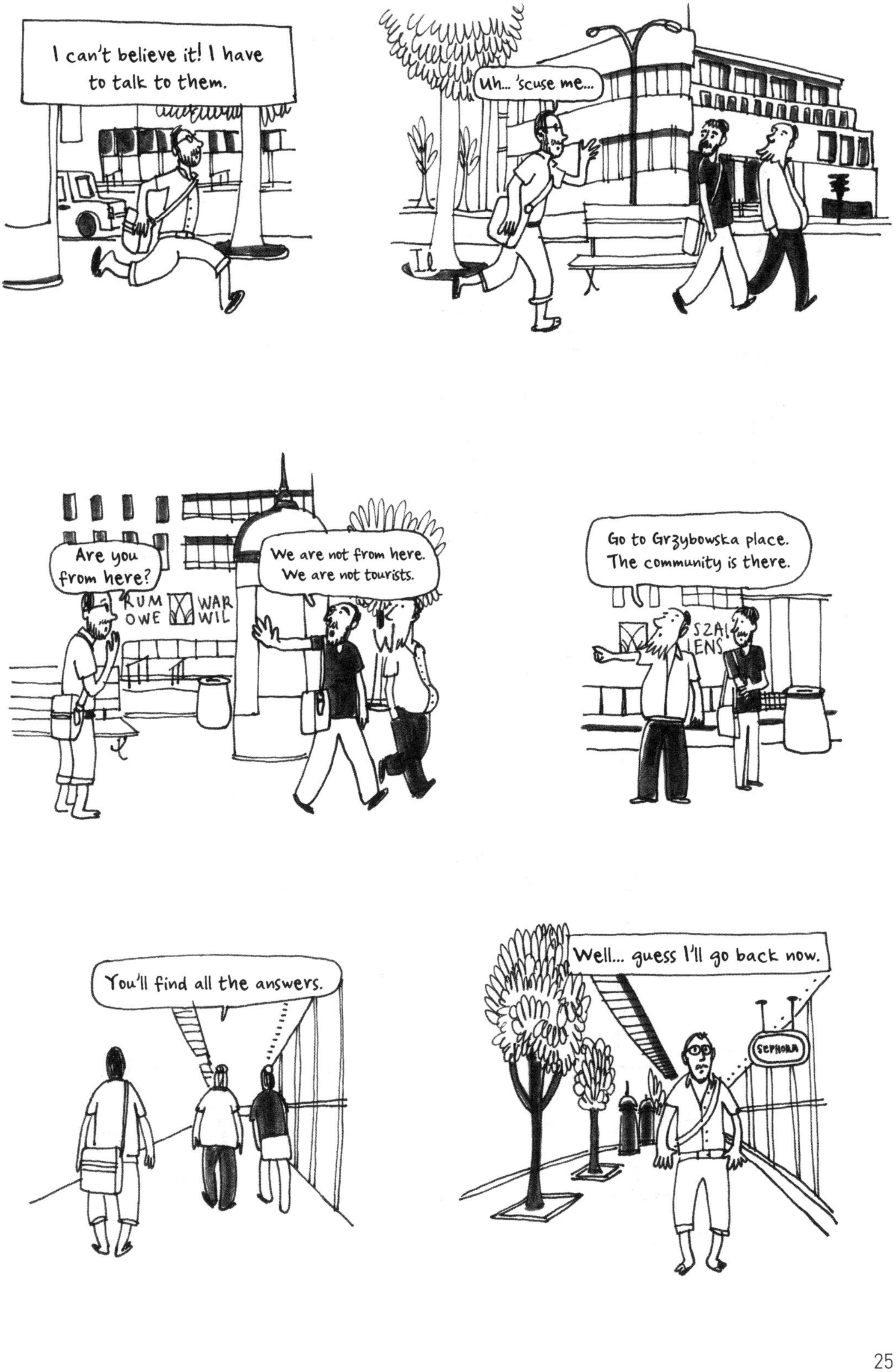
I can't believe it! I have to talk to them.
Uh... 'scuse me...
Are you from here?
RUM OWE
WAR WIL
We are not from here. We are not tourists.
Go to Grzybowska place. The community is there.
SZA LENS
You'll find all the answers.
Well... guess I'll go back now.
SEPHORA

S.O.S. Distress?

9:30 p.m. The Oki Doki youth hostel. The bar's an ideal place to meet people.

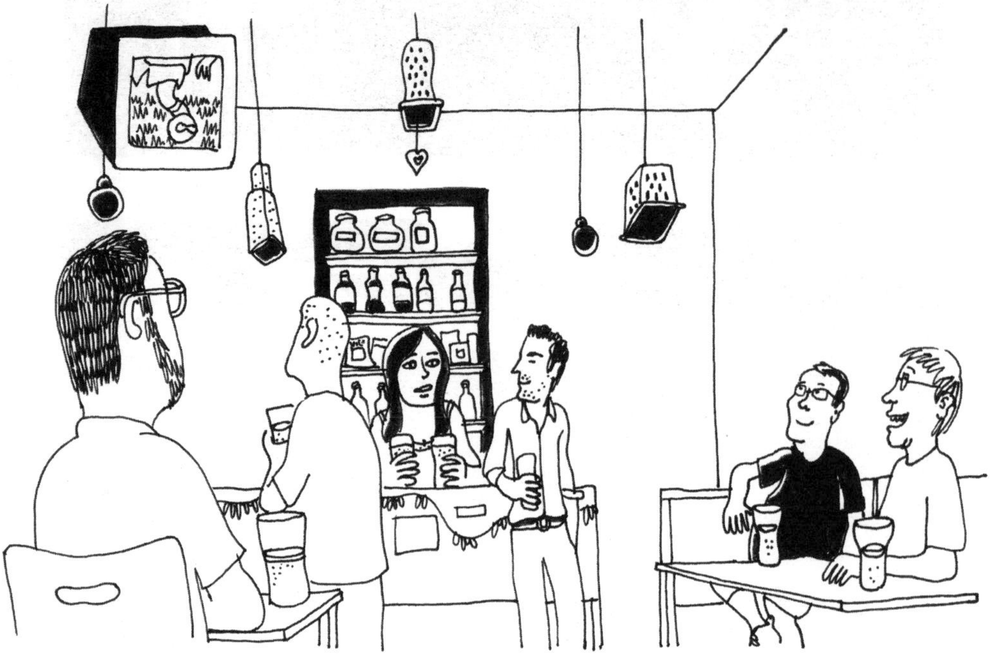

At least if I go to bed now, I'll be in top shape tomorrow.

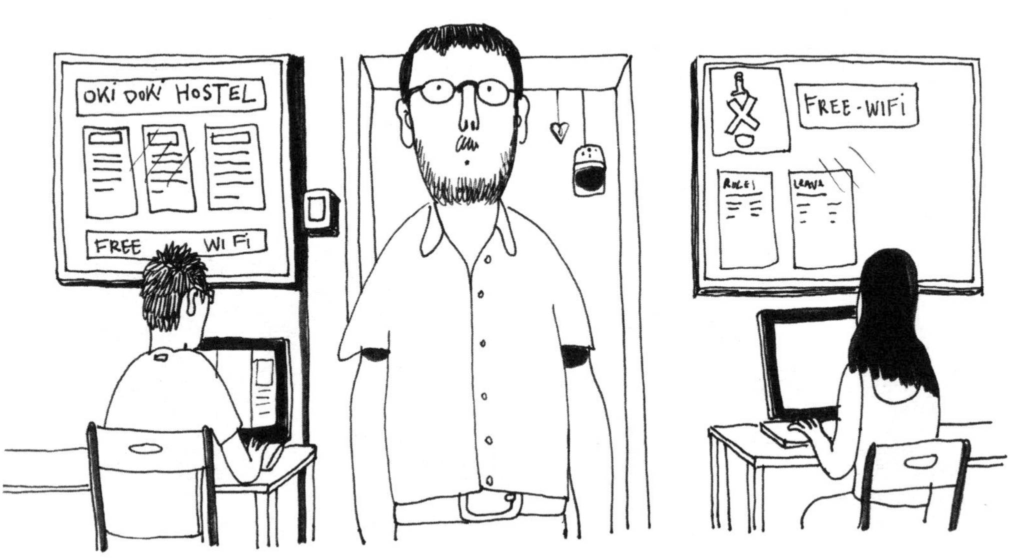
OKi DOKi HOSTEL
FREE WI Fi
FREE-WIFi

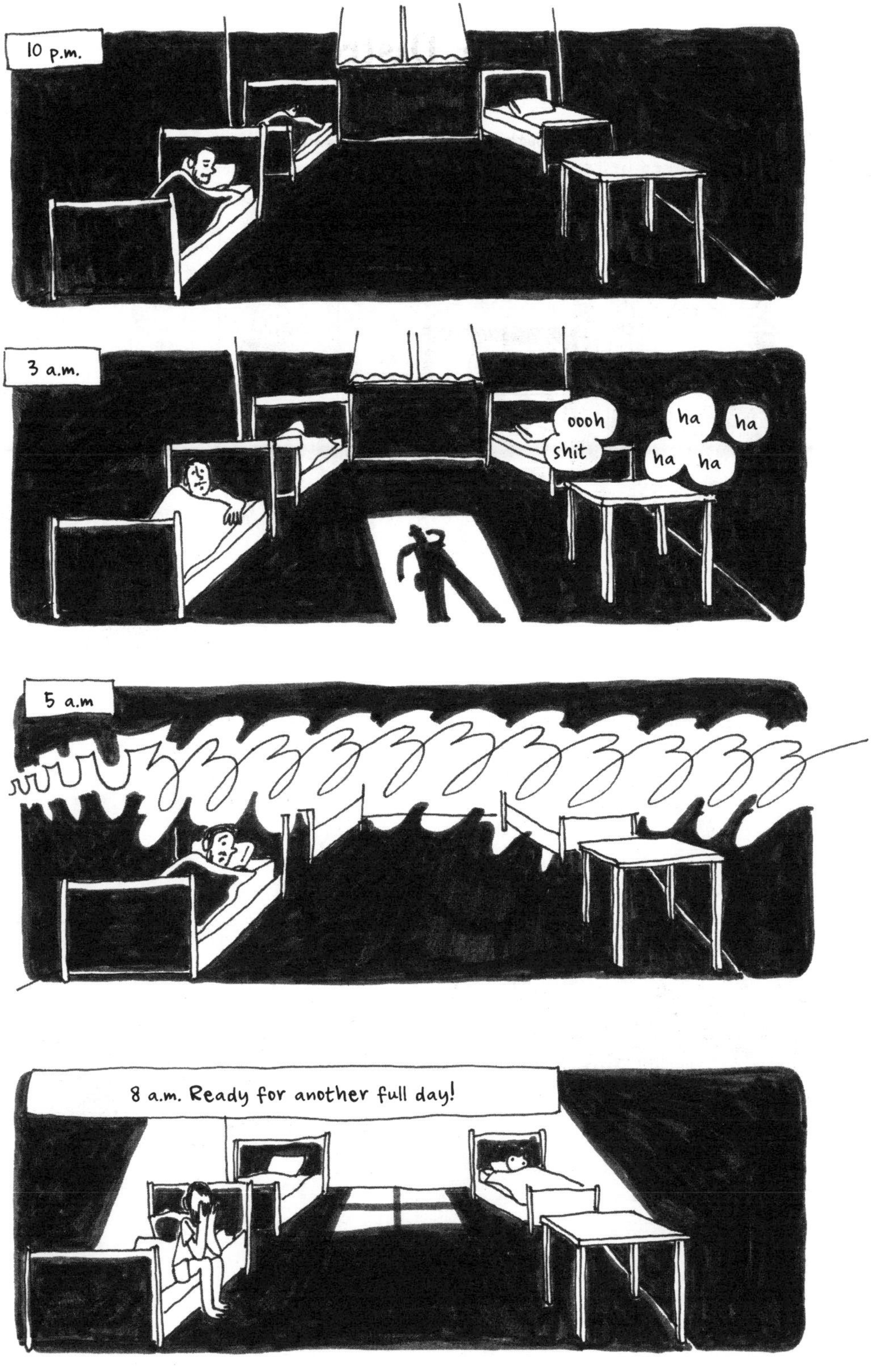
10 p.m.
3 a.m.
oooh shit
ha
ha
ha
ha
5 a.m
8 a.m. Ready for another full day!

The Words of Elders

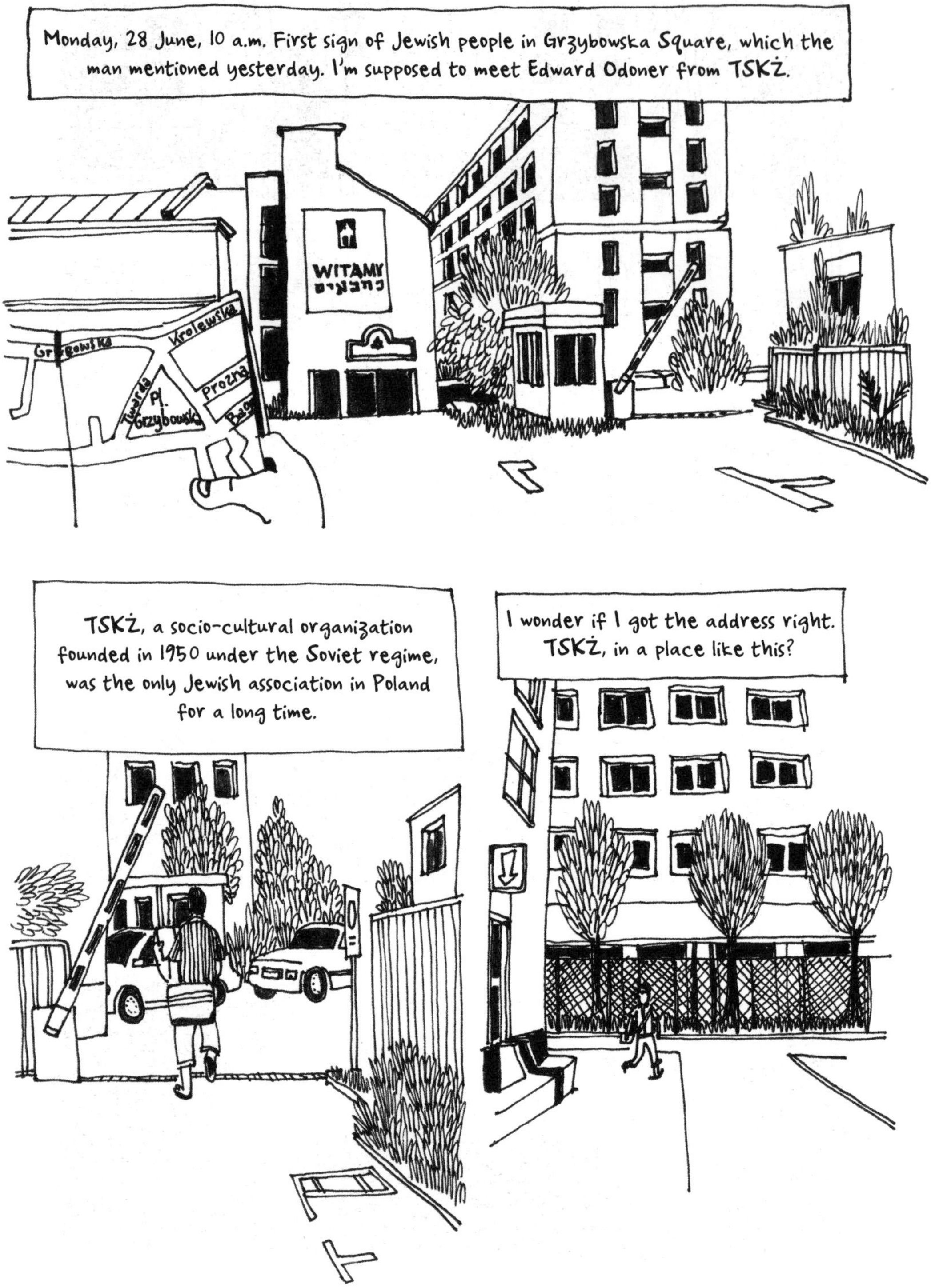
Monday, 28 June, 10 a.m. First sign of Jewish people in Grzybowska Square, which the man mentioned yesterday. I'm supposed to meet Edward Odoner from TSKŻ.
WITAMY
Krolewska
Prozna
Pl. Grzybowski
Twarda
TSKŻ, a socio-cultural organization founded in 1950 under the Soviet regime, was the only Jewish association in Poland for a long time.
I wonder if I got the address right. TSKŻ, in a place like this?

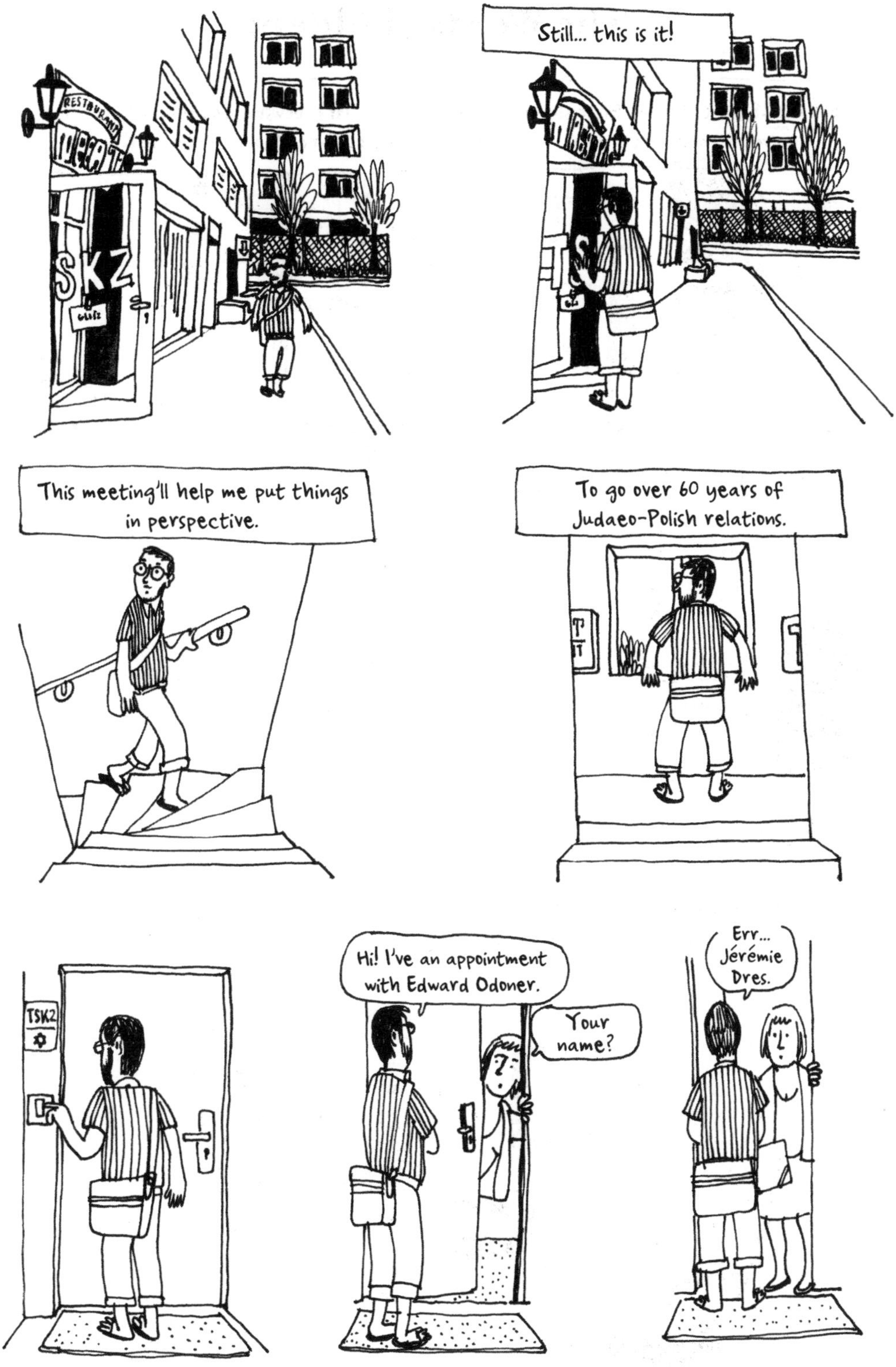
SKZ
Still... this is it!
This meeting'll help me put things in perspective.
To go over 60 years of Judaeo-Polish relations.
TSKZ
Hi! I've an appointment with Edward Odoner.
Your name?
Err... Jérémie Dres.

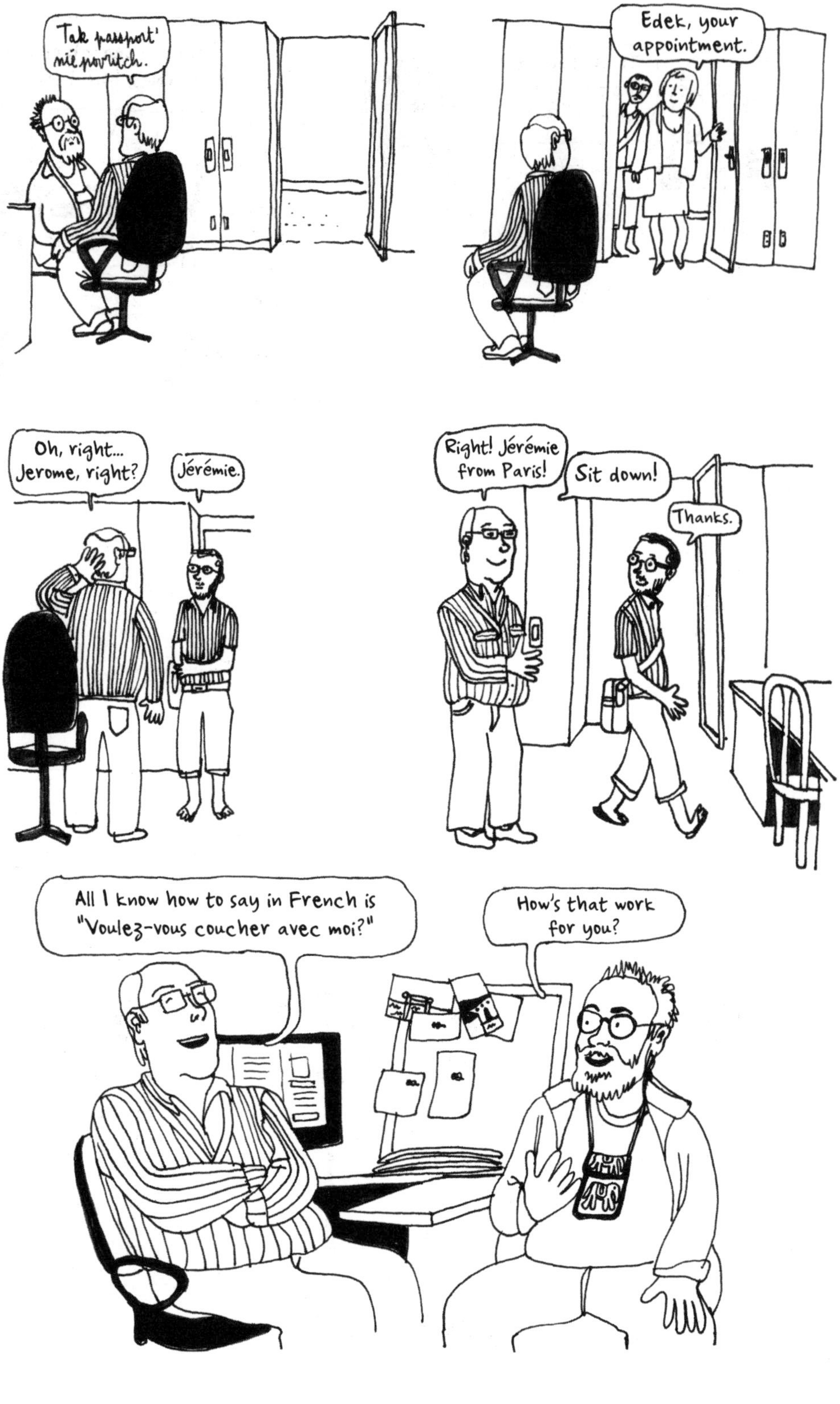
Tak passport' nié povritch.
Edek, your appointment.
Oh, right... Jerome, right?
Jérémie.
Right! Jérémie from Paris!
Sit down!
Thanks.
All I know how to say in French is "Voulez-vous coucher avec moi?"
How's that work for you?

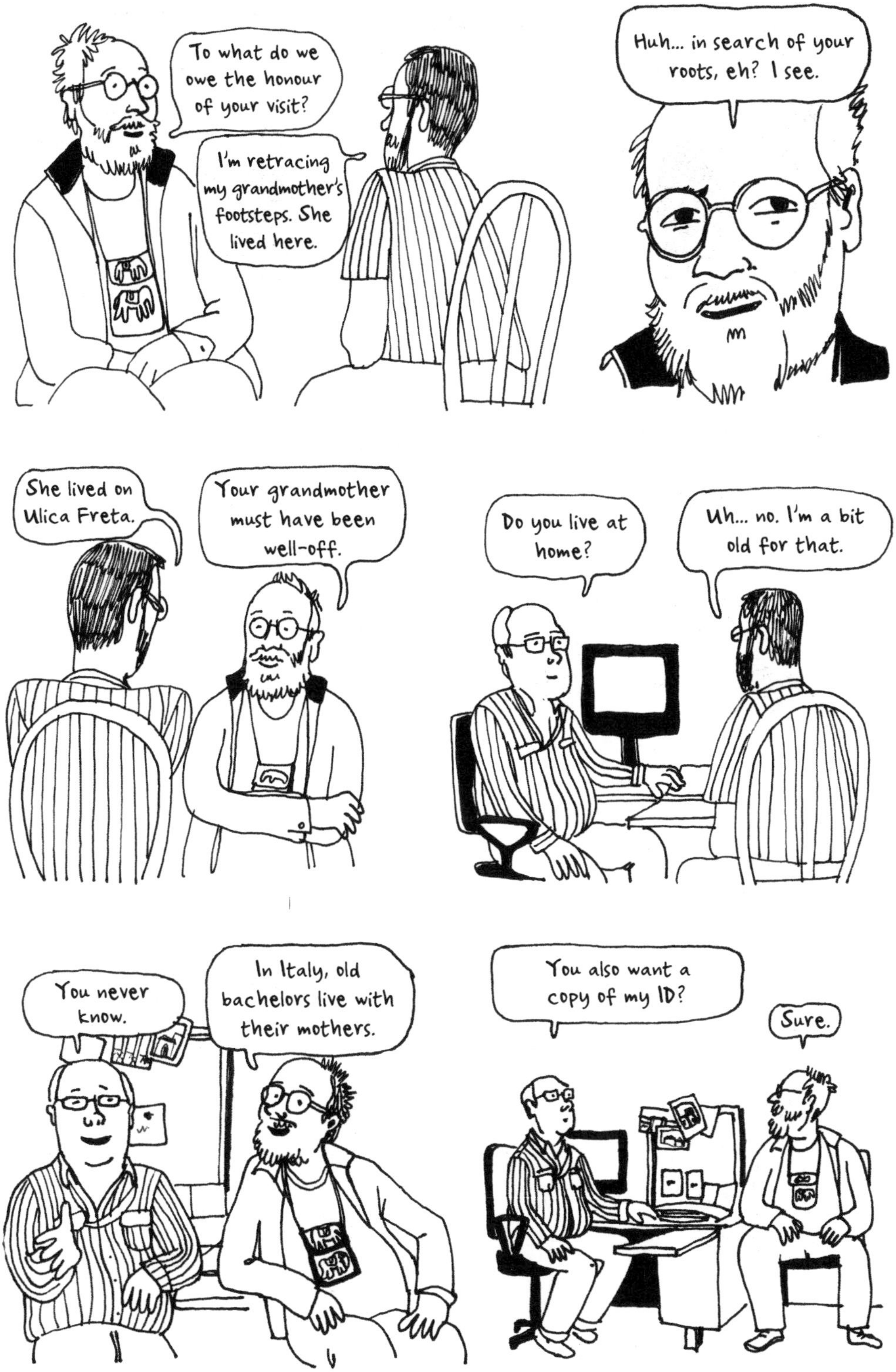
To what do we owe the honour of your visit?
I'm retracing my grandmother's footsteps. She lived here.
Huh... in search of your roots, eh? I see.
She lived on Ulica Freta.
Your grandmother must have been well-off.
Do you live at home?
Uh... no. I'm a bit old for that.
You never know.
In Italy, old bachelors live with their mothers.
You also want a copy of my ID?
Sure.

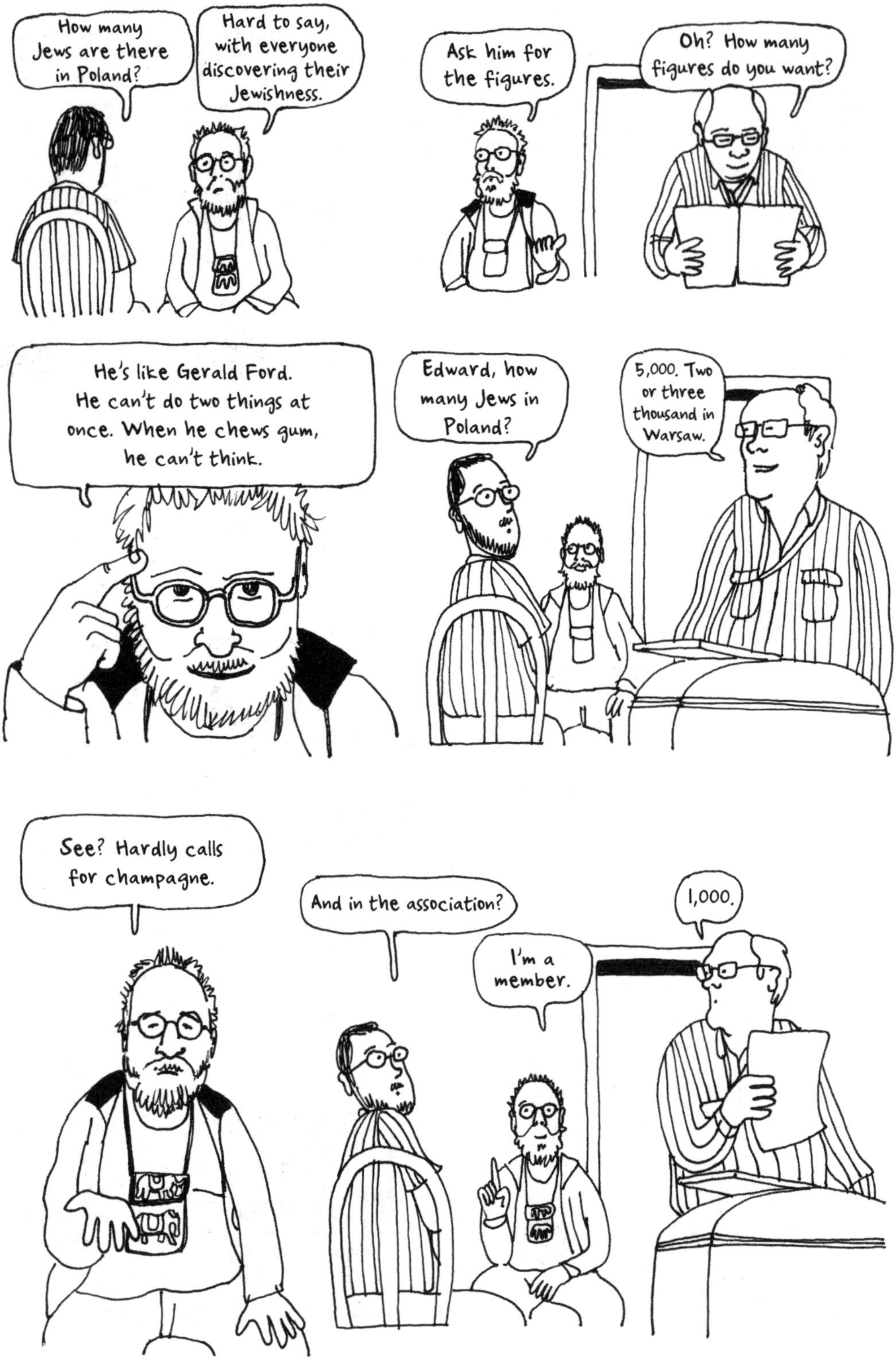
How many Jews are there in Poland?
Hard to say, with everyone discovering their Jewishness.
Ask him for the figures.
Oh? How many figures do you want?
He's like Gerald Ford. He can't do two things at once. When he chews gum, he can't think.
Edward, how many Jews in Poland?
5,000. Two or three thousand in Warsaw.
See? Hardly calls for champagne.
And in the association?
I'm a member.
1,000.

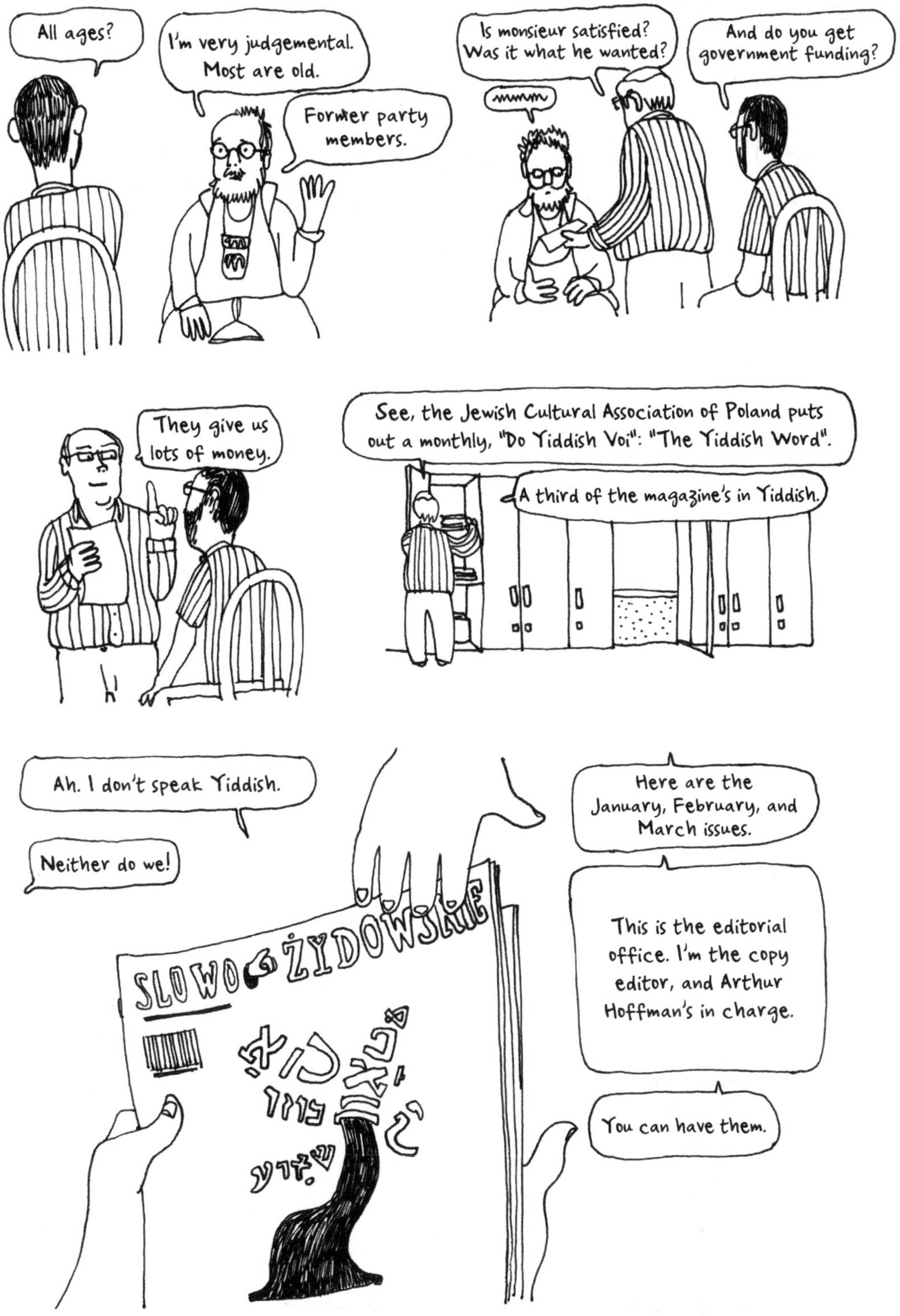
All ages?
I'm very judgemental. Most are old.
Former party members.
Is monsieur satisfied? Was it what he wanted?
mmmm
And do you get government funding?
They give us lots of money.
See, the Jewish Cultural Association of Poland puts out a monthly, "Do Yiddish Voi": "The Yiddish Word".
A third of the magazine's in Yiddish.
Ah. I don't speak Yiddish.
Neither do we!
SLOWO ŻYDOWSKIE
Here are the January, February, and March issues.
This is the editorial office. I'm the copy editor, and Arthur Hoffman's in charge.
You can have them.

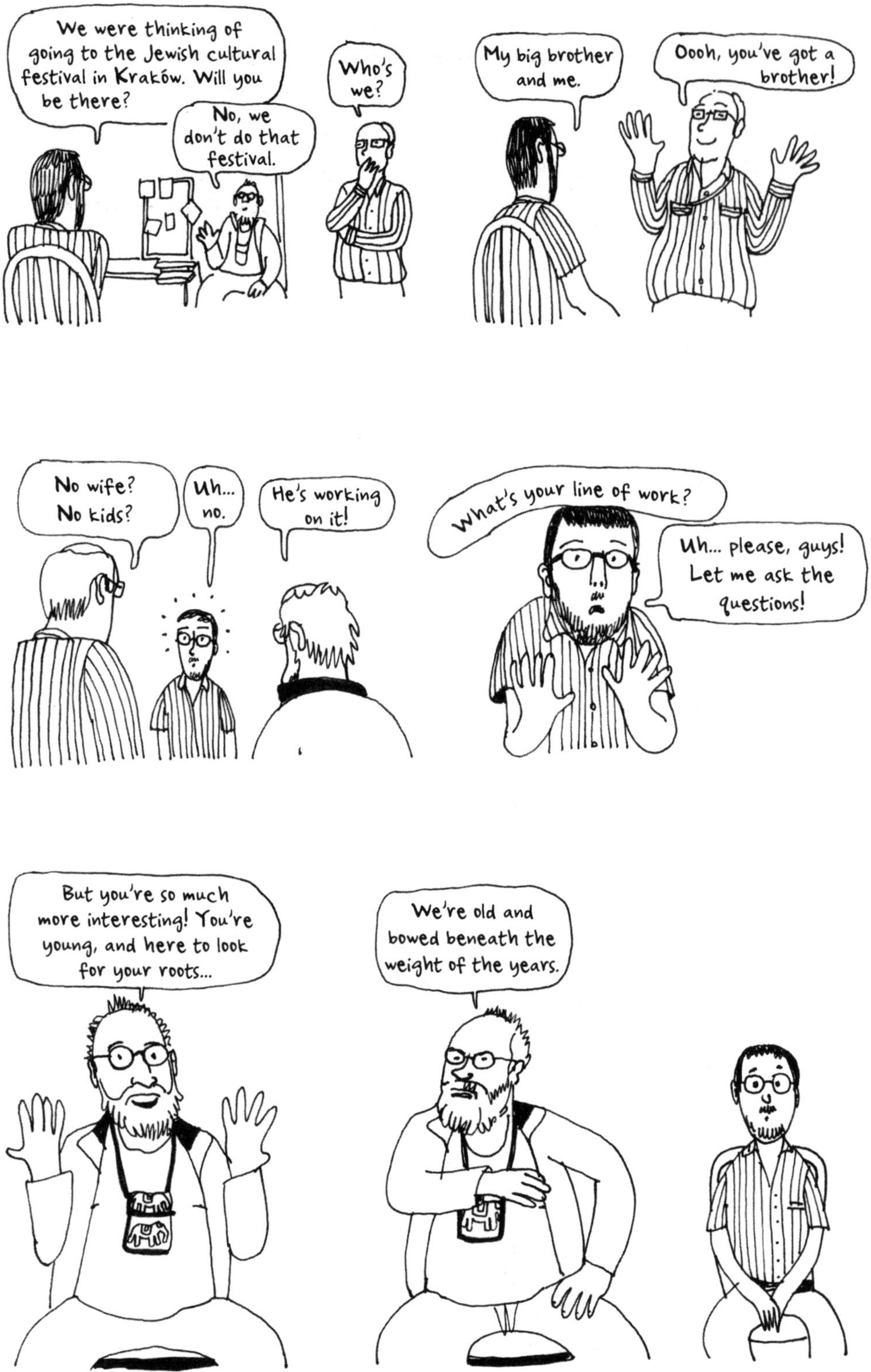
We were thinking of going to the Jewish cultural festival in Kraków. Will you be there?
No, we don't do that festival.
Who's we?
My big brother and me.
Oooh, you've got a brother!
No wife? No kids?
Uh... no.
He's working on it!
What's your line of work?
Uh... please, guys! Let me ask the questions!
But you're so much more interesting! You're young, and here to look for your roots...
We're old and bowed beneath the weight of the years.

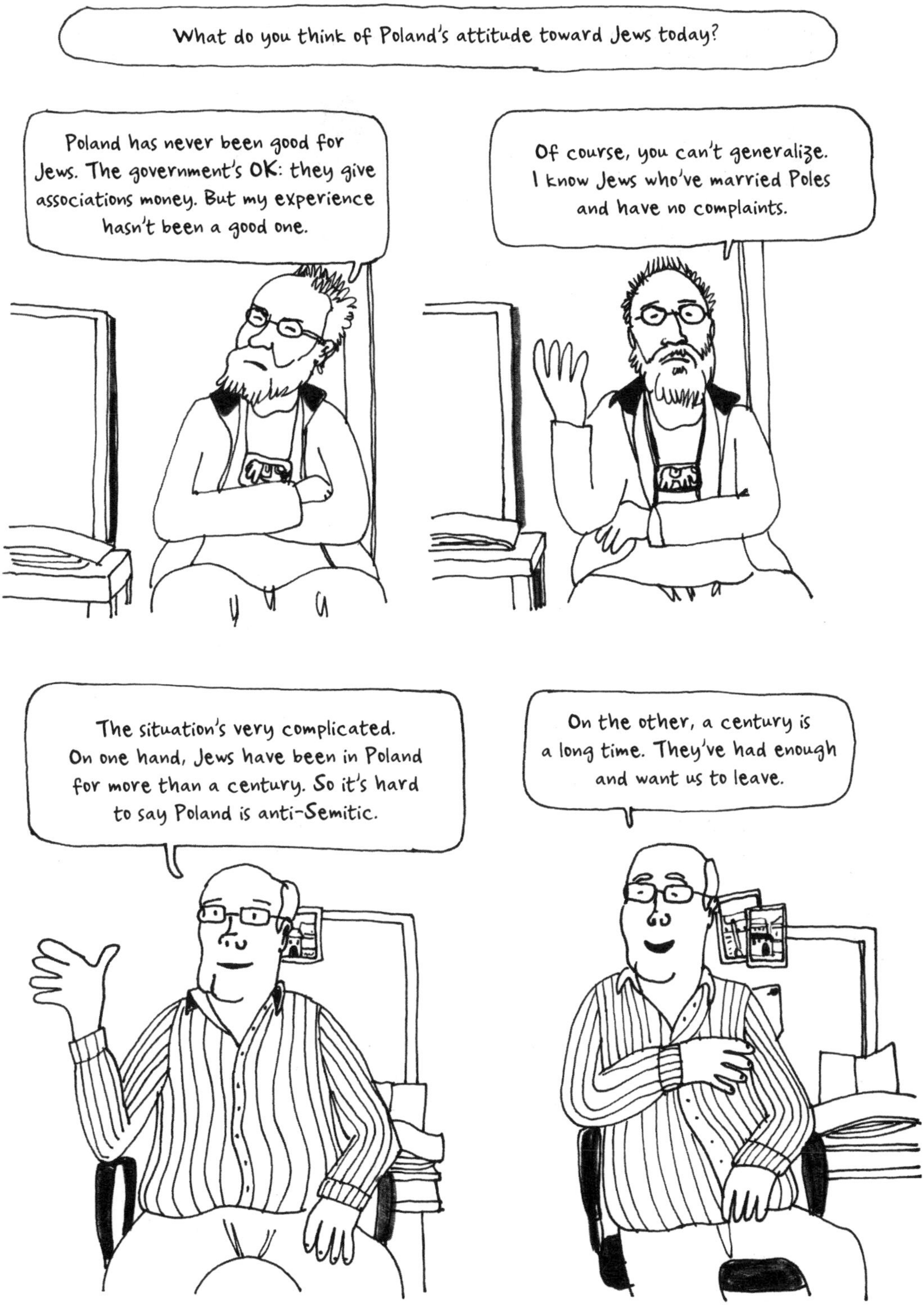
What do you think of Poland's attitude toward Jews today?
Poland has never been good for Jews. The government's OK: they give associations money. But my experience hasn't been a good one.
Of course, you can't generalize. I know Jews who've married Poles and have no complaints.
The situation's very complicated. On one hand, Jews have been in Poland for more than a century. So it's hard to say Poland is anti-Semitic.
On the other, a century is a long time. They've had enough and want us to leave.

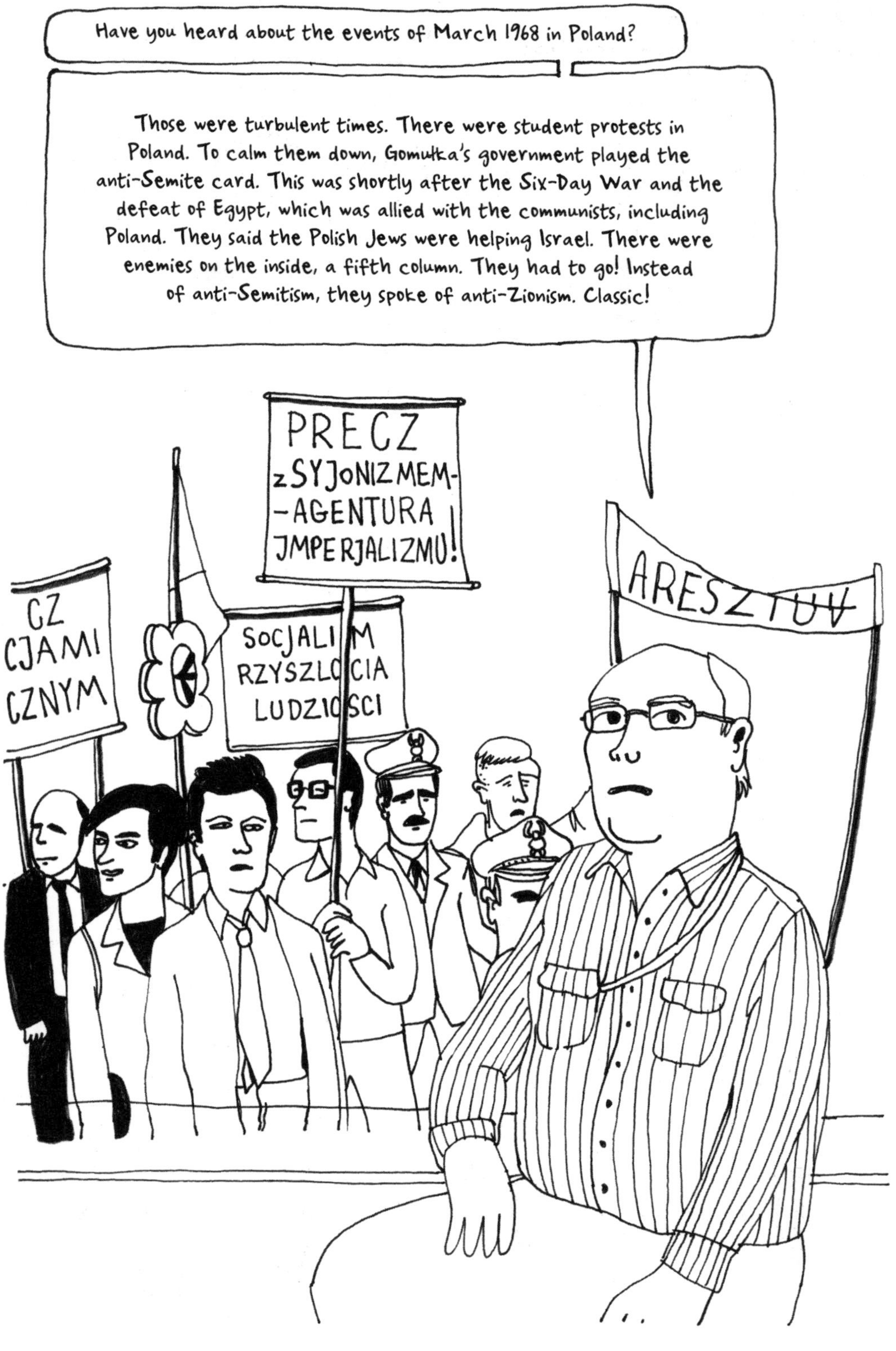
Have you heard about the events of March 1968 in Poland?
Those were turbulent times. There were student protests in Poland. To calm them down, Gomułka's government played the anti-Semite card. This was shortly after the Six-Day War and the defeat of Egypt, which was allied with the communists, including Poland. They said the Polish Jews were helping Israel. There were enemies on the inside, a fifth column. They had to go! Instead of anti-Semitism, they spoke of anti-Zionism. Classic!
PRECZ zSYJONIZMEM- -AGENTURA JMPERJALIZMU!
CZ CJAMI CZNYM
SOCJALI M RZYSZLO CIA LUDZIO SCI
ARESZT

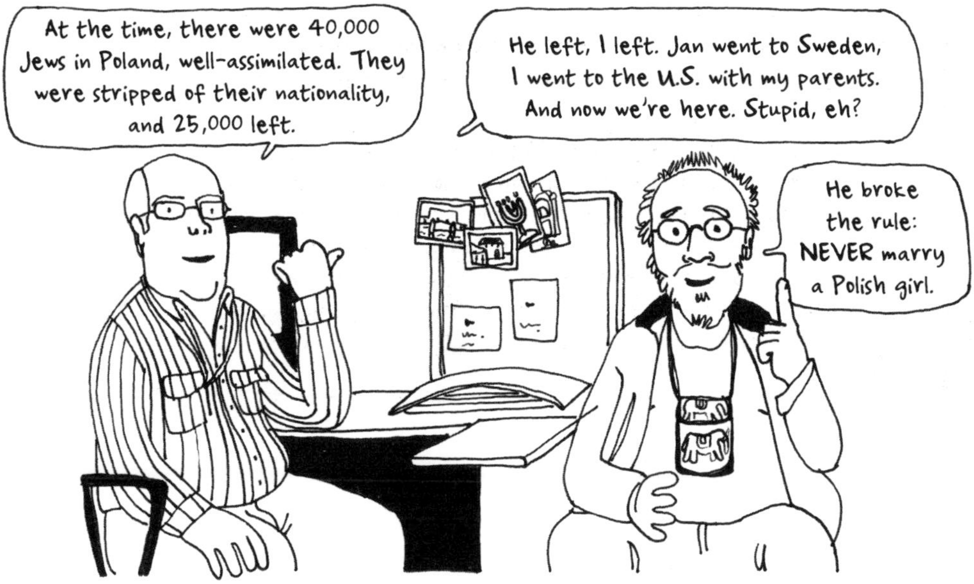
At the time, there were 40,000 Jews in Poland, well-assimilated. They were stripped of their nationality, and 25,000 left.
He left, I left. Jan went to Sweden, I went to the U.S. with my parents. And now we're here. Stupid, eh?
He broke the rule: NEVER marry a Polish girl.

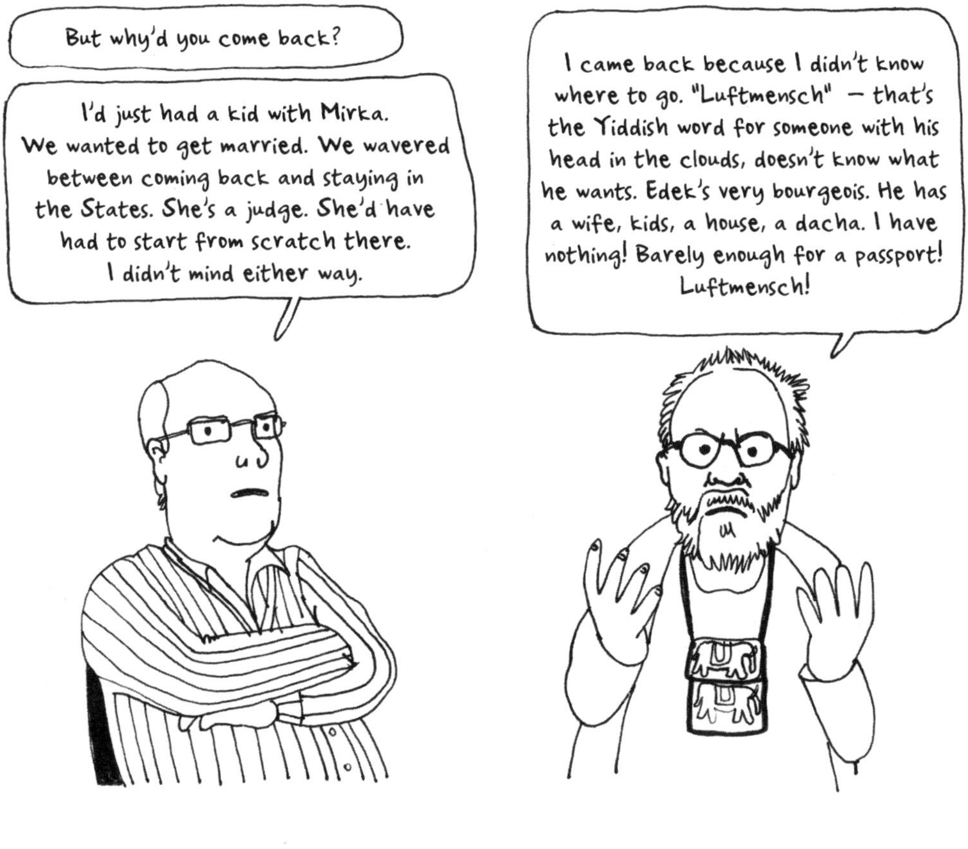
But why'd you come back?
I'd just had a kid with Mirka. We wanted to get married. We wavered between coming back and staying in the States. She's a judge. She'd have had to start from scratch there. I didn't mind either way.
I came back because I didn't know where to go. "Luftmensch" – that's the Yiddish word for someone with his head in the clouds, doesn't know what he wants. Edek's very bourgeois. He has a wife, kids, a house, a dacha. I have nothing! Barely enough for a passport! Luftmensch!

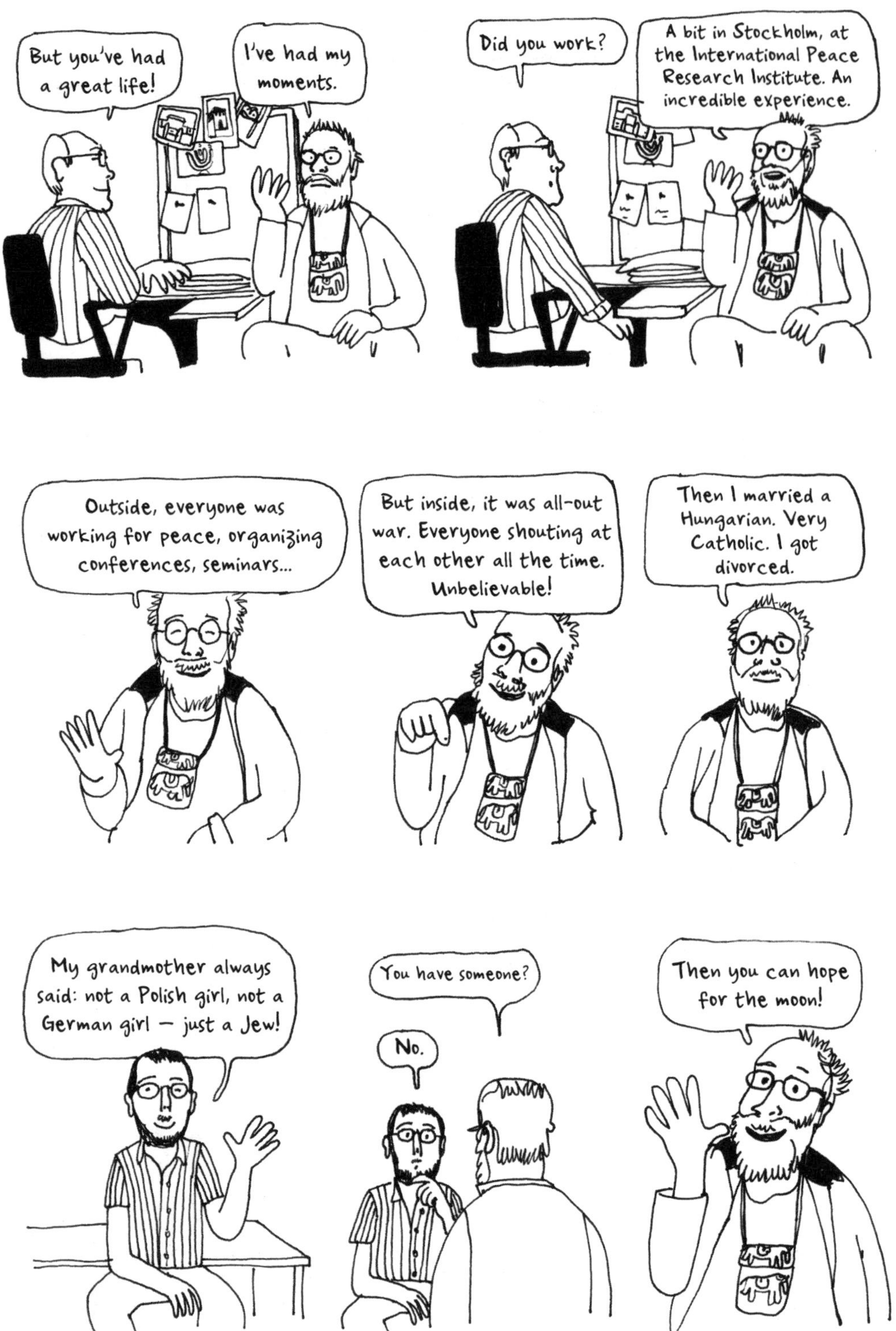
But you've had a great life!
I've had my moments.
Did you work?
A bit in Stockholm, at the International Peace Research Institute. An incredible experience.
Outside, everyone was working for peace, organizing conferences, seminars...
But inside, it was all-out war. Everyone shouting at each other all the time. Unbelievable!
Then I married a Hungarian. Very Catholic. I got divorced.
My grandmother always said: not a Polish girl, not a German girl — just a Jew!
You have someone?
No.
Then you can hope for the moon!

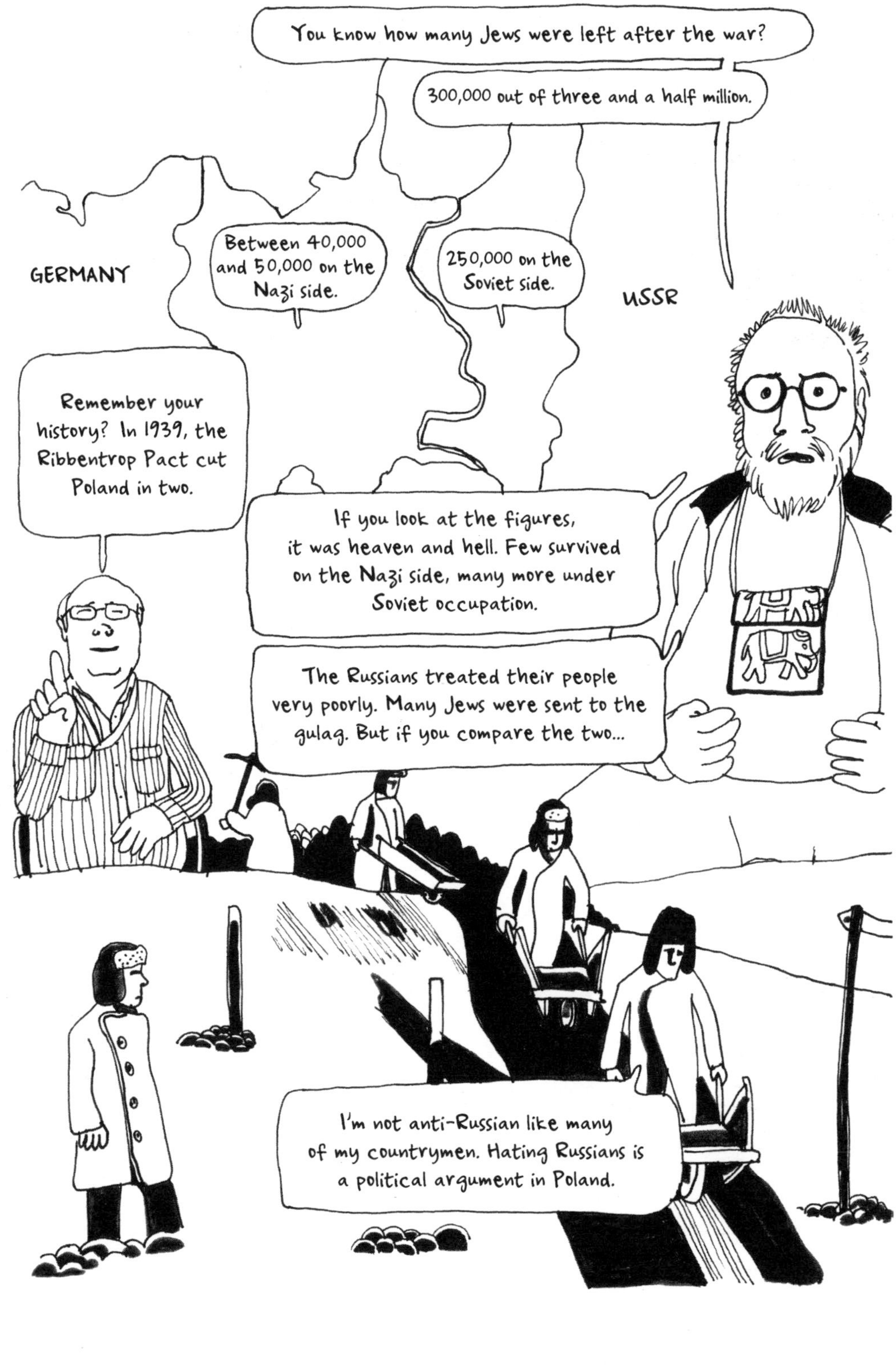
You know how many Jews were left after the war?
300,000 out of three and a half million.
GERMANY
Between 40,000 and 50,000 on the Nazi side.
250,000 on the Soviet side.
USSR
Remember your history? In 1939, the Ribbentrop Pact cut Poland in two.
If you look at the figures, it was heaven and hell. Few survived on the Nazi side, many more under Soviet occupation.
The Russians treated their people very poorly. Many Jews were sent to the gulag. But if you compare the two...
I'm not anti-Russian like many of my countrymen. Hating Russians is a political argument in Poland.

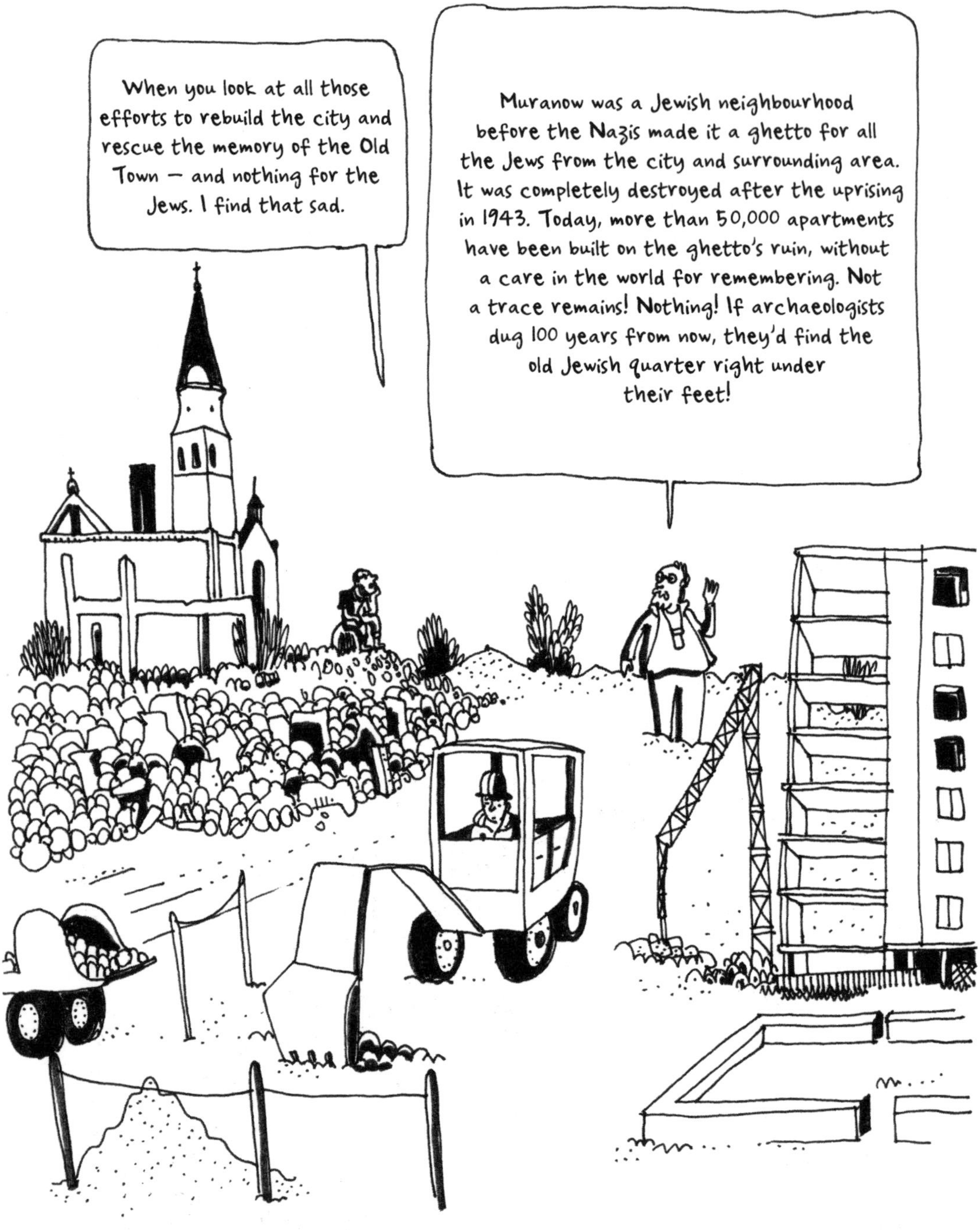
When you look at all those efforts to rebuild the city and rescue the memory of the Old Town — and nothing for the Jews. I find that sad.
Muranow was a Jewish neighbourhood before the Nazis made it a ghetto for all the Jews from the city and surrounding area. It was completely destroyed after the uprising in 1943. Today, more than 50,000 apartments have been built on the ghetto's ruin, without a care in the world for remembering. Not a trace remains! Nothing! If archaeologists dug 100 years from now, they'd find the old Jewish quarter right under their feet!

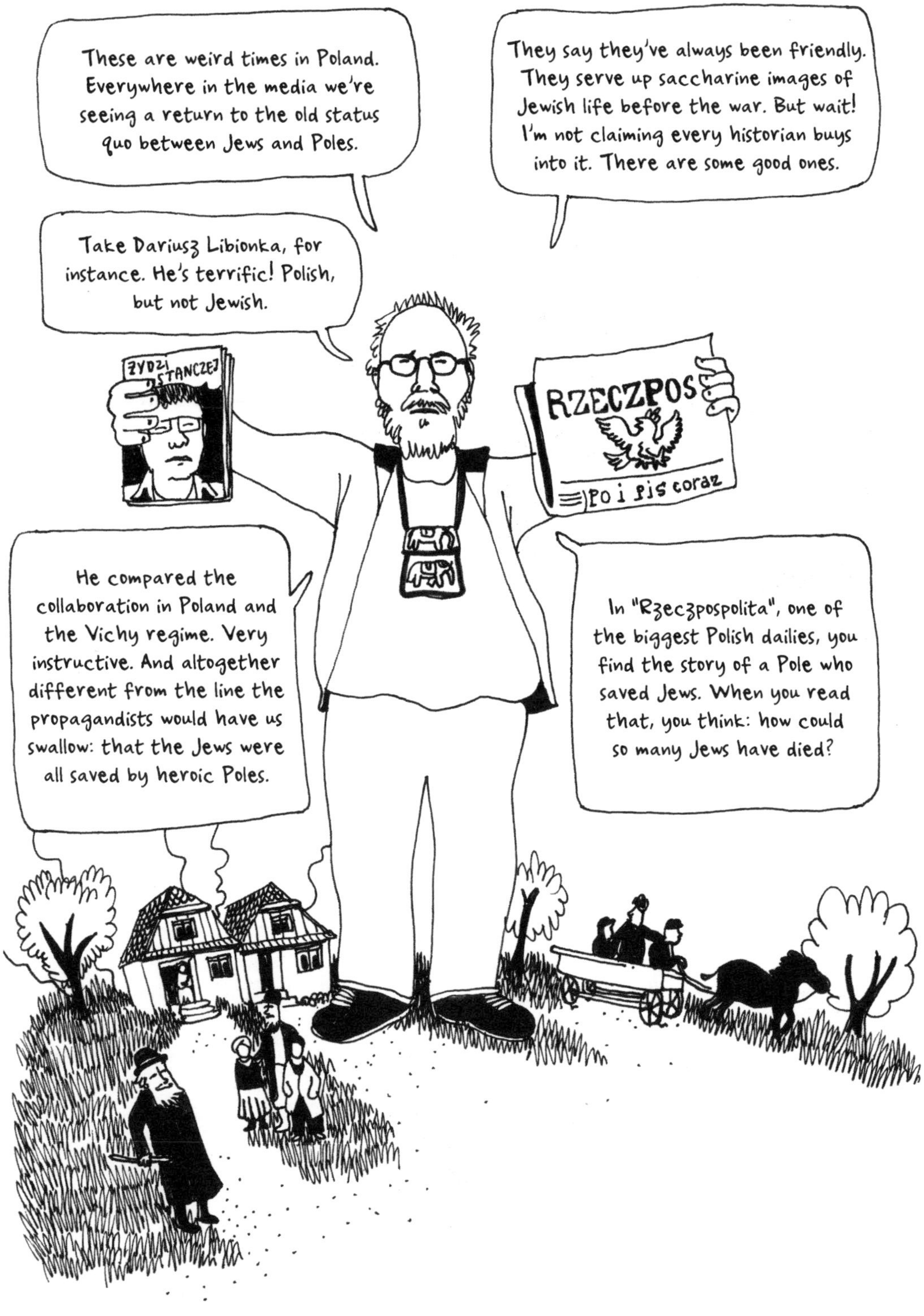
These are weird times in Poland. Everywhere in the media we're seeing a return to the old status quo between Jews and Poles.
They say they've always been friendly. They serve up saccharine images of Jewish life before the war. But wait! I'm not claiming every historian buys into it. There are some good ones.
Take Dariusz Libionka, for instance. He's terrific! Polish, but not Jewish.
ŻYDZI STAŃCZEJ
RZECZPOS
PO i PiS coraz
He compared the collaboration in Poland and the Vichy regime. Very instructive. And altogether different from the line the propagandists would have us swallow: that the Jews were all saved by heroic Poles.
In "Rzeczpospolita", one of the biggest Polish dailies, you find the story of a Pole who saved Jews. When you read that, you think: how could so many Jews have died?

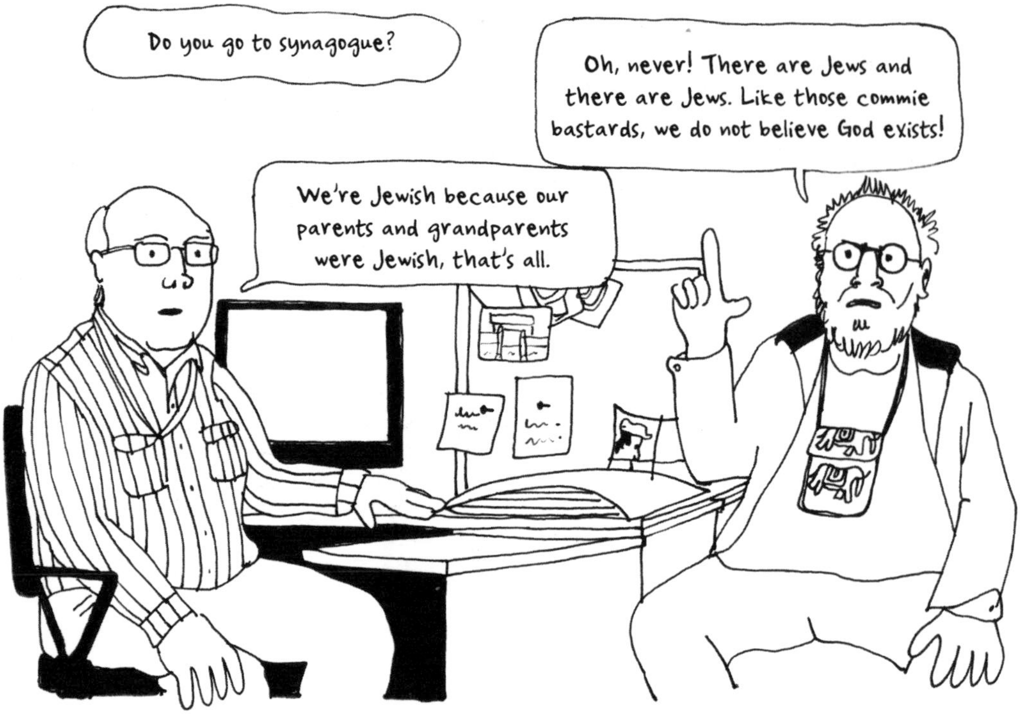
Do you go to synagogue?
Oh, never! There are Jews and there are Jews. Like those commie bastards, we do not believe God exists!
We're Jewish because our parents and grandparents were Jewish, that's all.

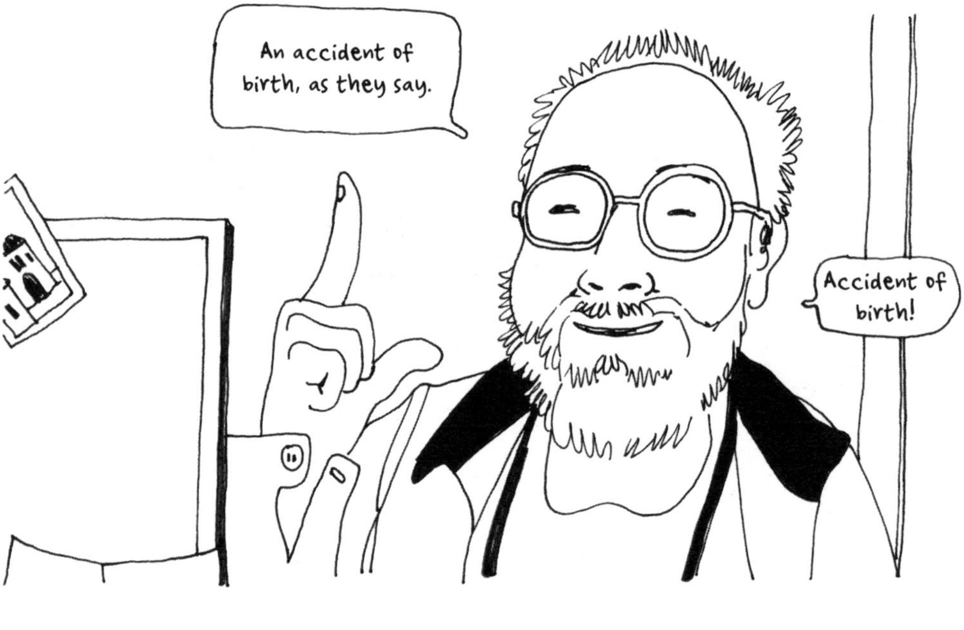
An accident of birth, as they say.
Accident of birth!

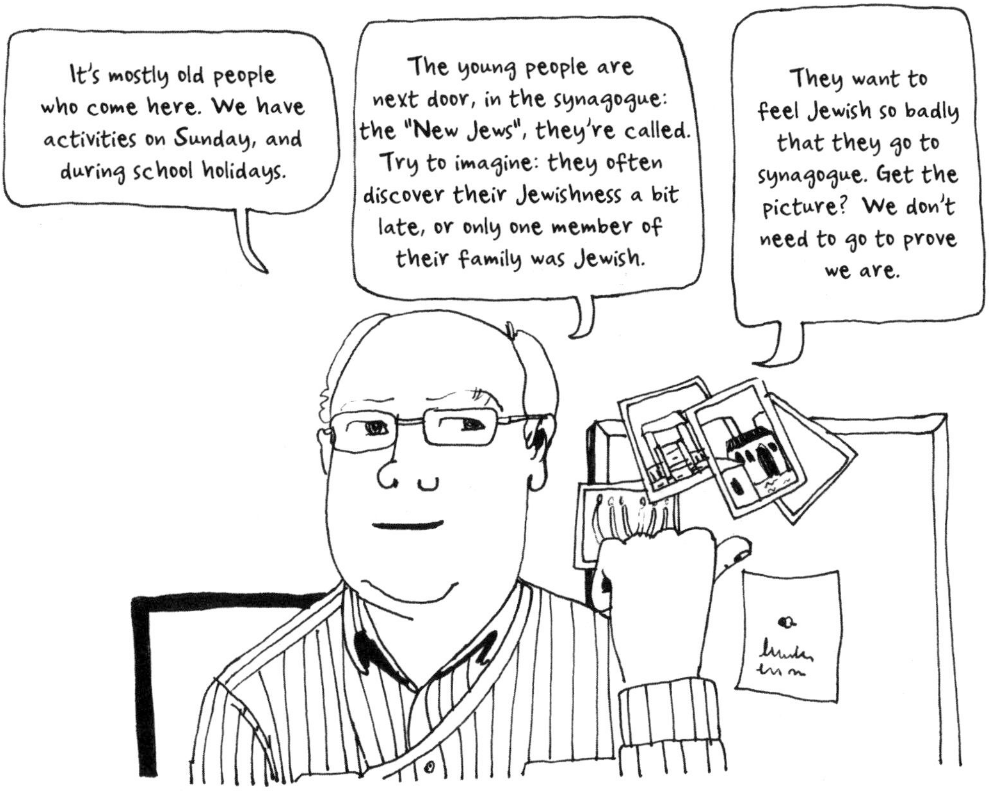
It's mostly old people who come here. We have activities on Sunday, and during school holidays.
The young people are next door, in the synagogue: the "New Jews", they're called. Try to imagine: they often discover their Jewishness a bit late, or only one member of their family was Jewish.
They want to feel Jewish so badly that they go to synagogue. Get the picture? We don't need to go to prove we are.

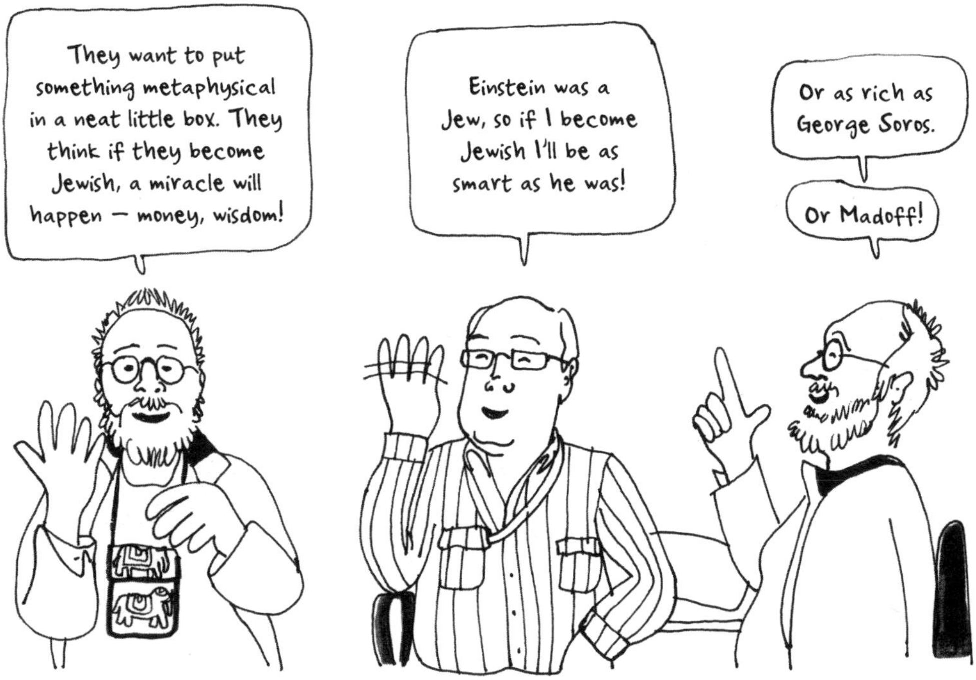
They want to put something metaphysical in a neat little box. They think if they become Jewish, a miracle will happen – money, wisdom!
Einstein was a Jew, so if I become Jewish I'll be as smart as he was!
Or as rich as George Soros.
Or Madoff!

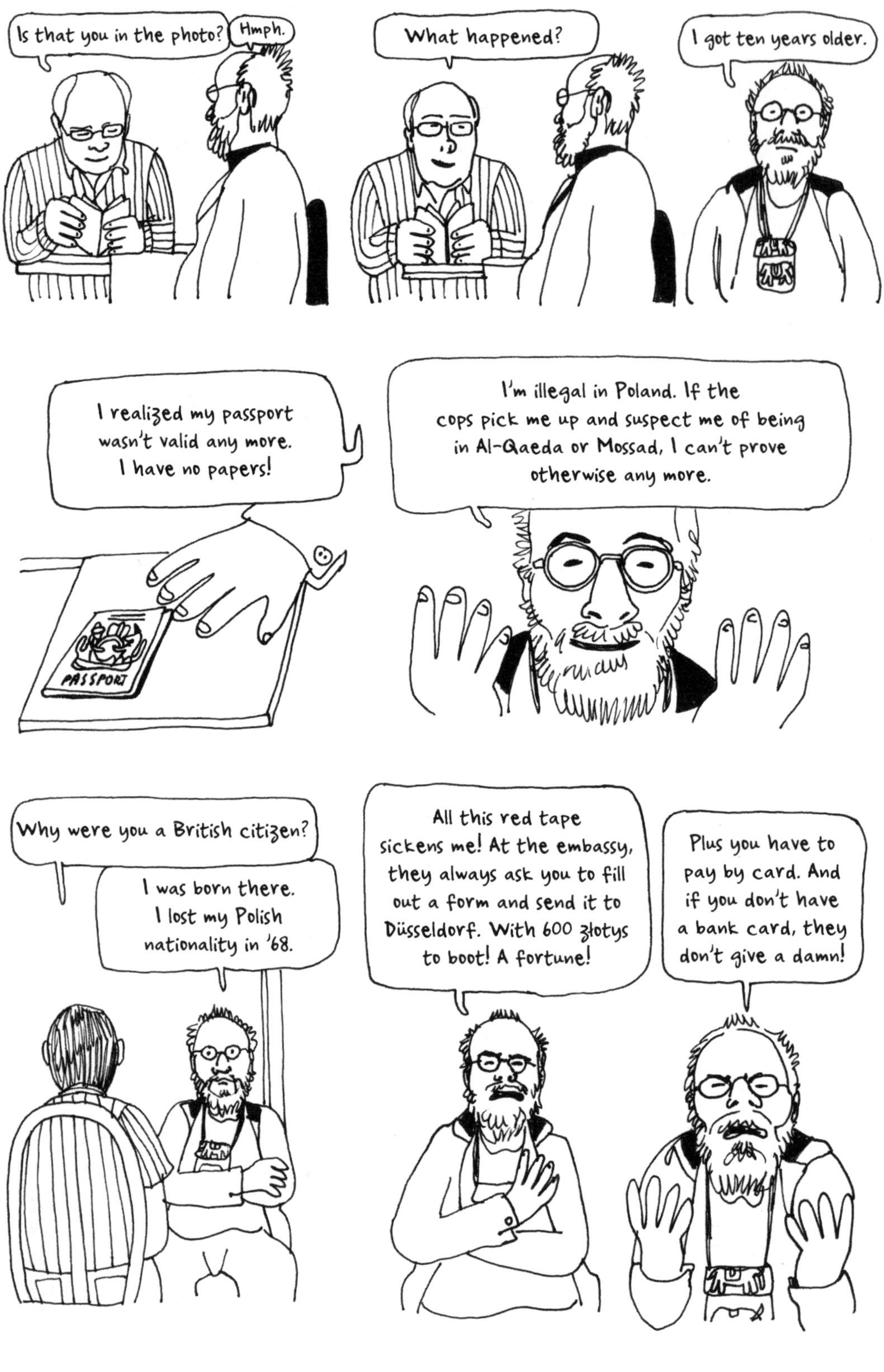
Is that you in the photo?
Hmph.
What happened?
I got ten years older.
I realized my passport wasn't valid any more. I have no papers!
I'm illegal in Poland. If the cops pick me up and suspect me of being in Al-Qaeda or Mossad, I can't prove otherwise any more.
PASSPORT
Why were you a British citizen?
I was born there. I lost my Polish nationality in '68.
All this red tape sickens me! At the embassy, they always ask you to fill out a form and send it to Düsseldorf. With 600 złotys to boot! A fortune!
Plus you have to pay by card. And if you don't have a bank card, they don't give a damn!

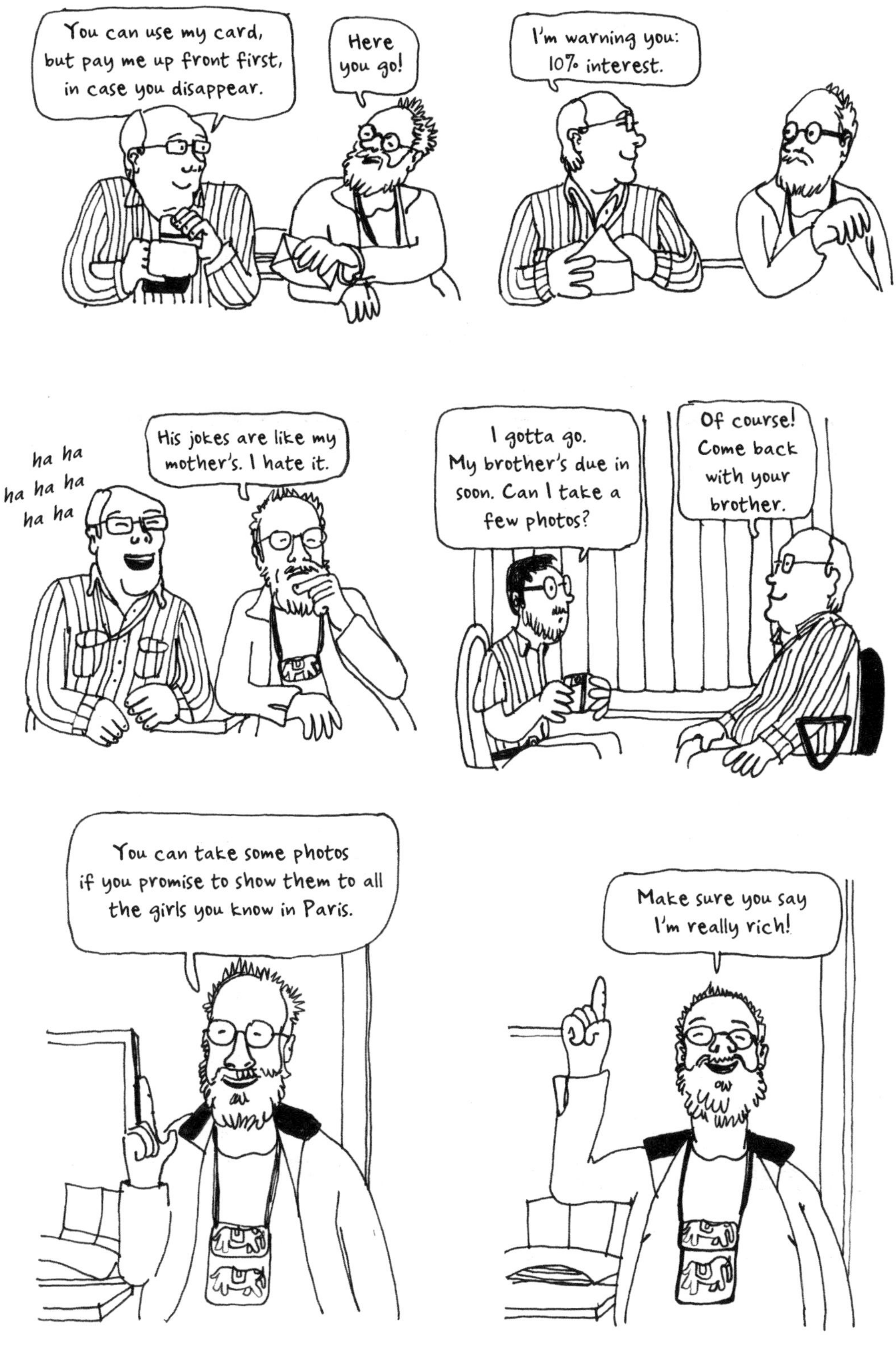
You can use my card, but pay me up front first, in case you disappear.
Here you go!
I'm warning you: 10% interest.
ha ha ha ha ha ha ha
His jokes are like my mother's. I hate it.
I gotta go. My brother's due in soon. Can I take a few photos?
Of course! Come back with your brother.
You can take some photos if you promise to show them to all the girls you know in Paris.
Make sure you say I'm really rich!

Together!

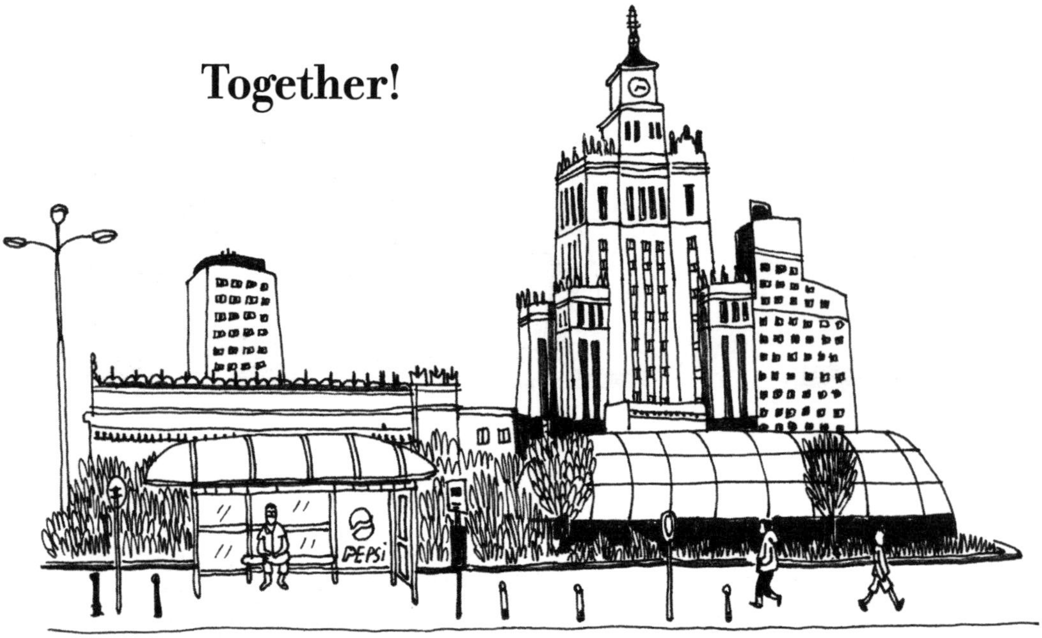
PEPSi

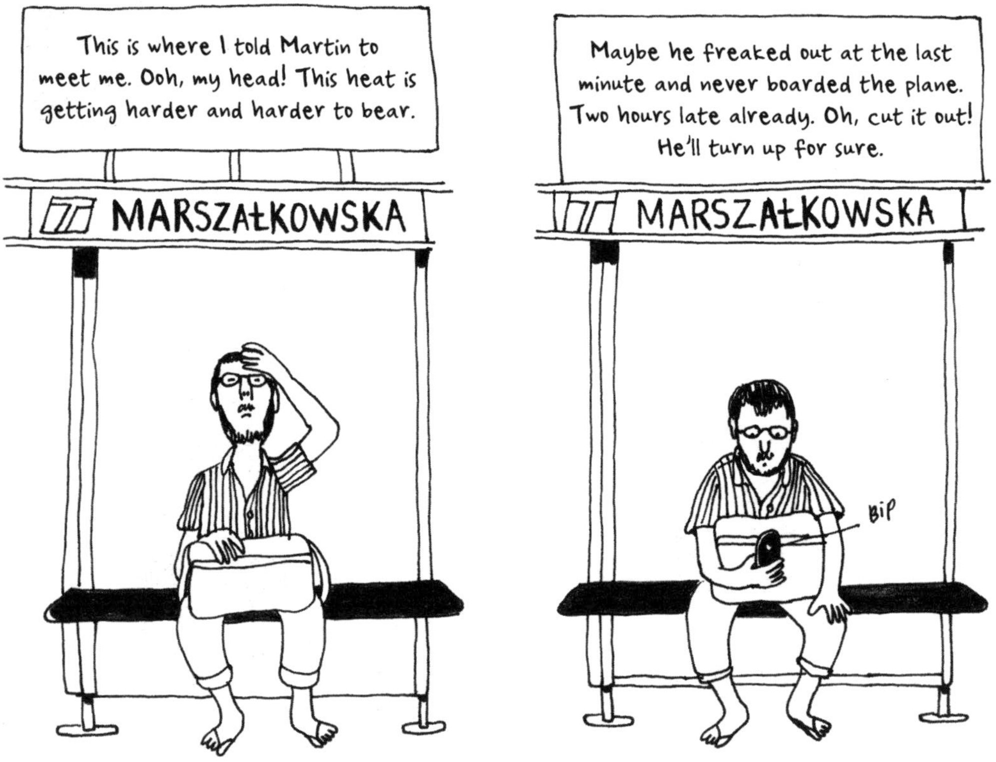
This is where I told Martin to meet me. Ooh, my head! This heat is getting harder and harder to bear.
MARSZAŁKOWSKA
Maybe he freaked out at the last minute and never boarded the plane. Two hours late already. Oh, cut it out! He'll turn up for sure.
MARSZAŁKOWSKA
BiP

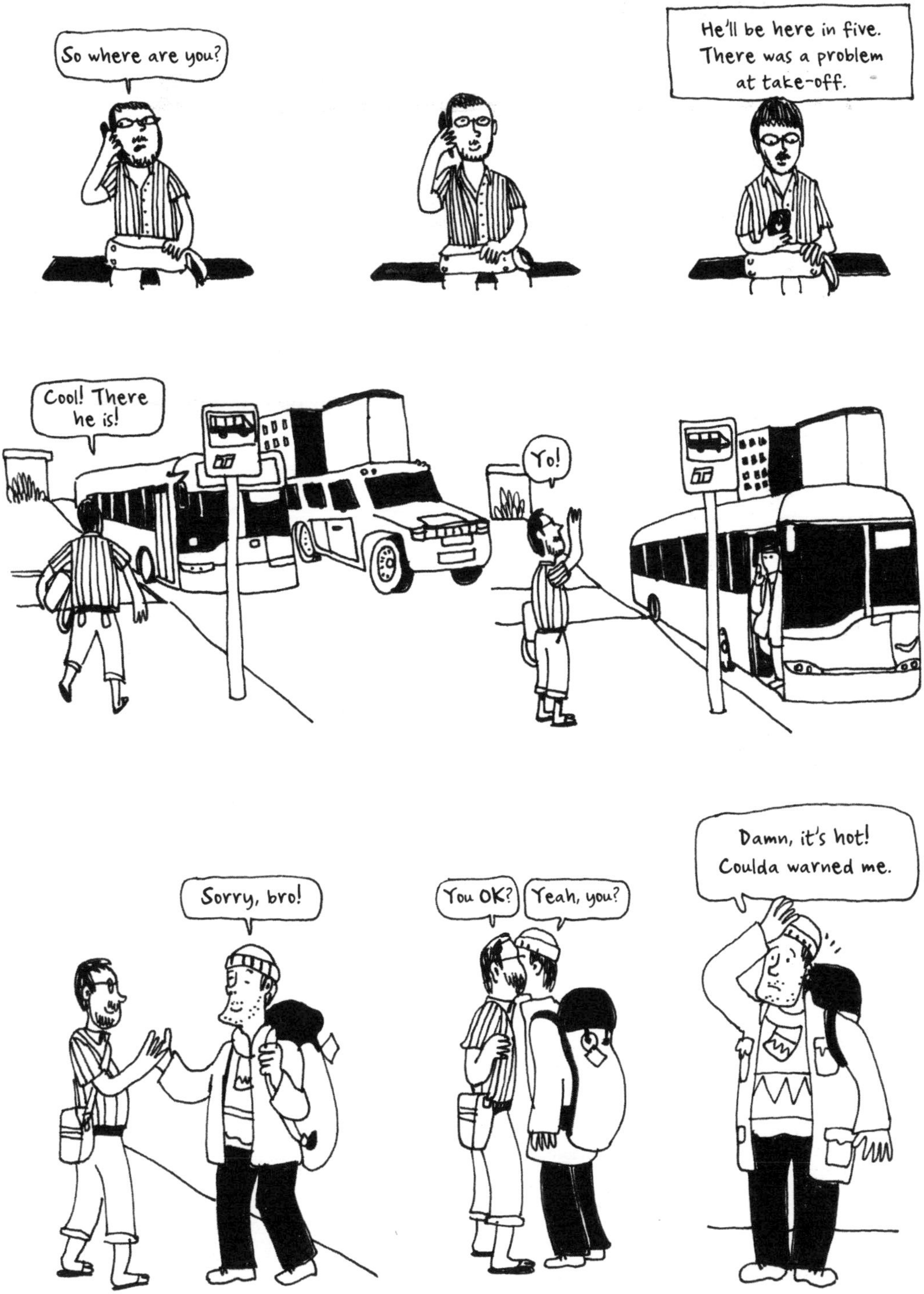
So where are you?
He'll be here in five. There was a problem at take-off.
Cool! There he is!
Yo!
Sorry, bro!
You OK?
Yeah, you?
Damn, it's hot! Coulda warned me.

On the Trail of the Jewish Atlantis

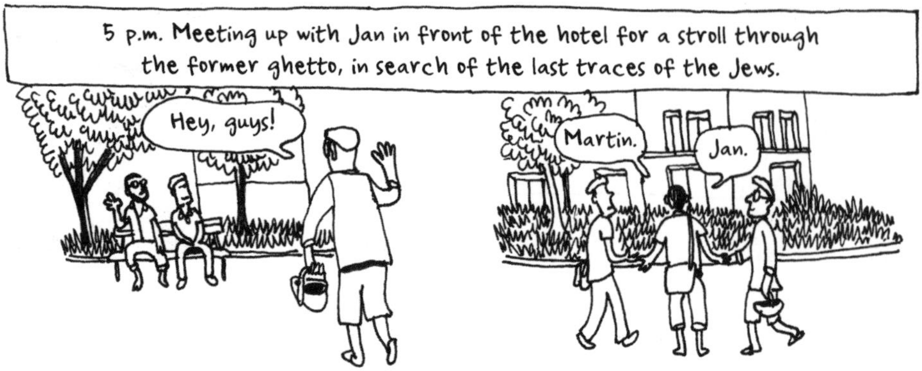
5 p.m. Meeting up with Jan in front of the hotel for a stroll through the former ghetto, in search of the last traces of the Jews.
Hey, guys!
Martin.
Jan.

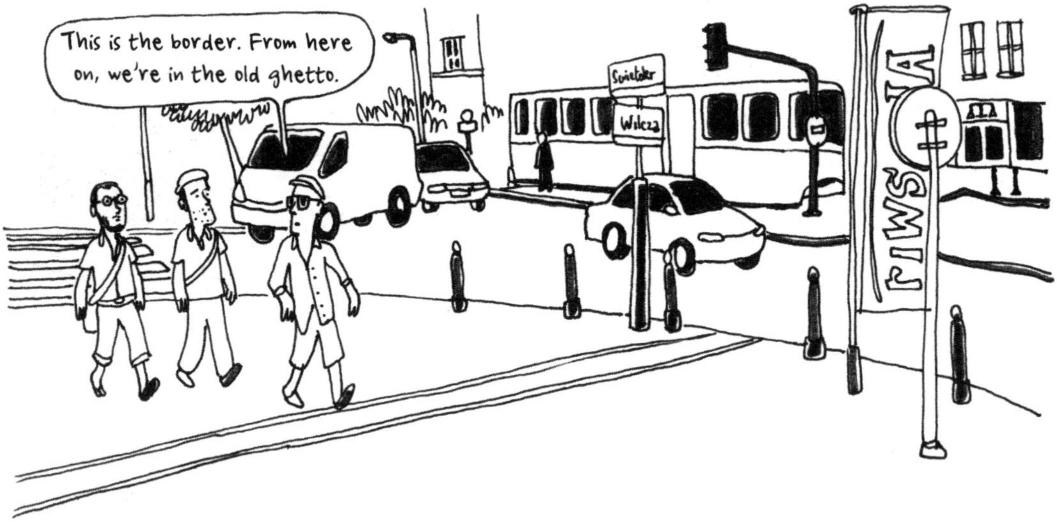
This is the border. From here on, we're in the old ghetto.
Wilcza

The wall was created in 1940 from the old Jewish quarter. It stretched around several hundred hectares and was surrounded in turn by ten-foot walls. These are the remnants.

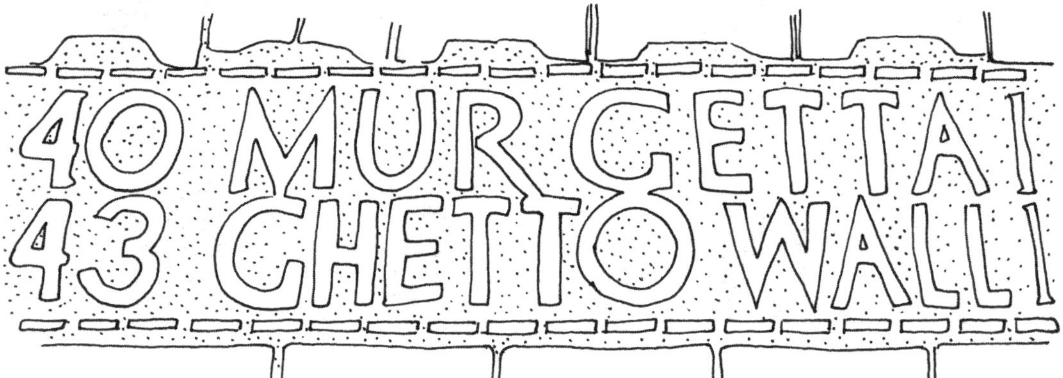
40 MUR GETTA
43 GHETTO WALL

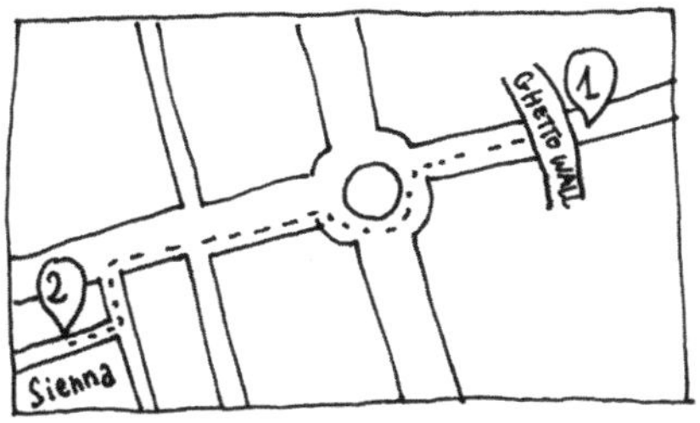
1
GHETTO WALL
2
Sienna

A few streets on, in the courtyard of an apartment building, one of the last pieces of the wall.

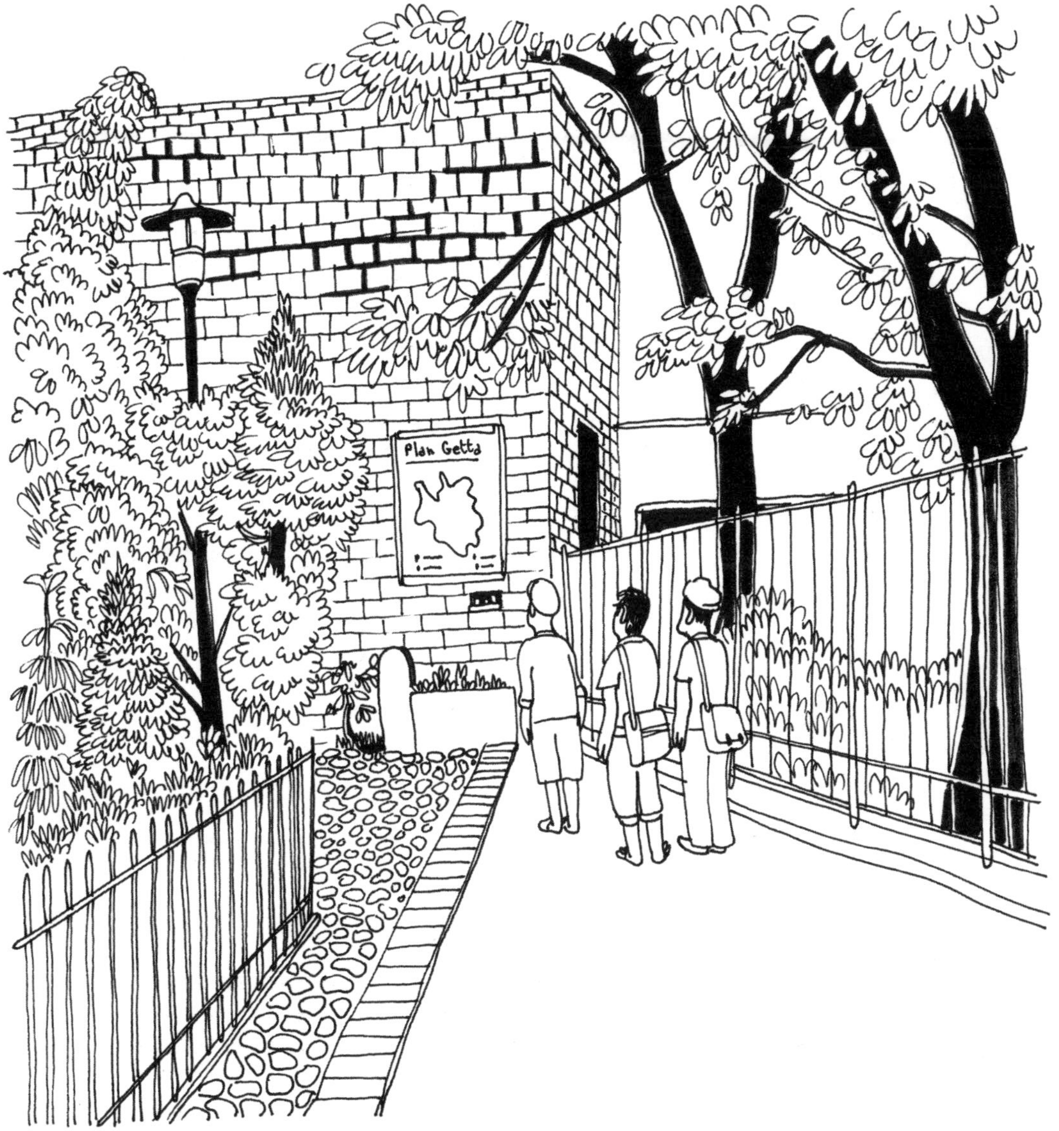
Plan Getta

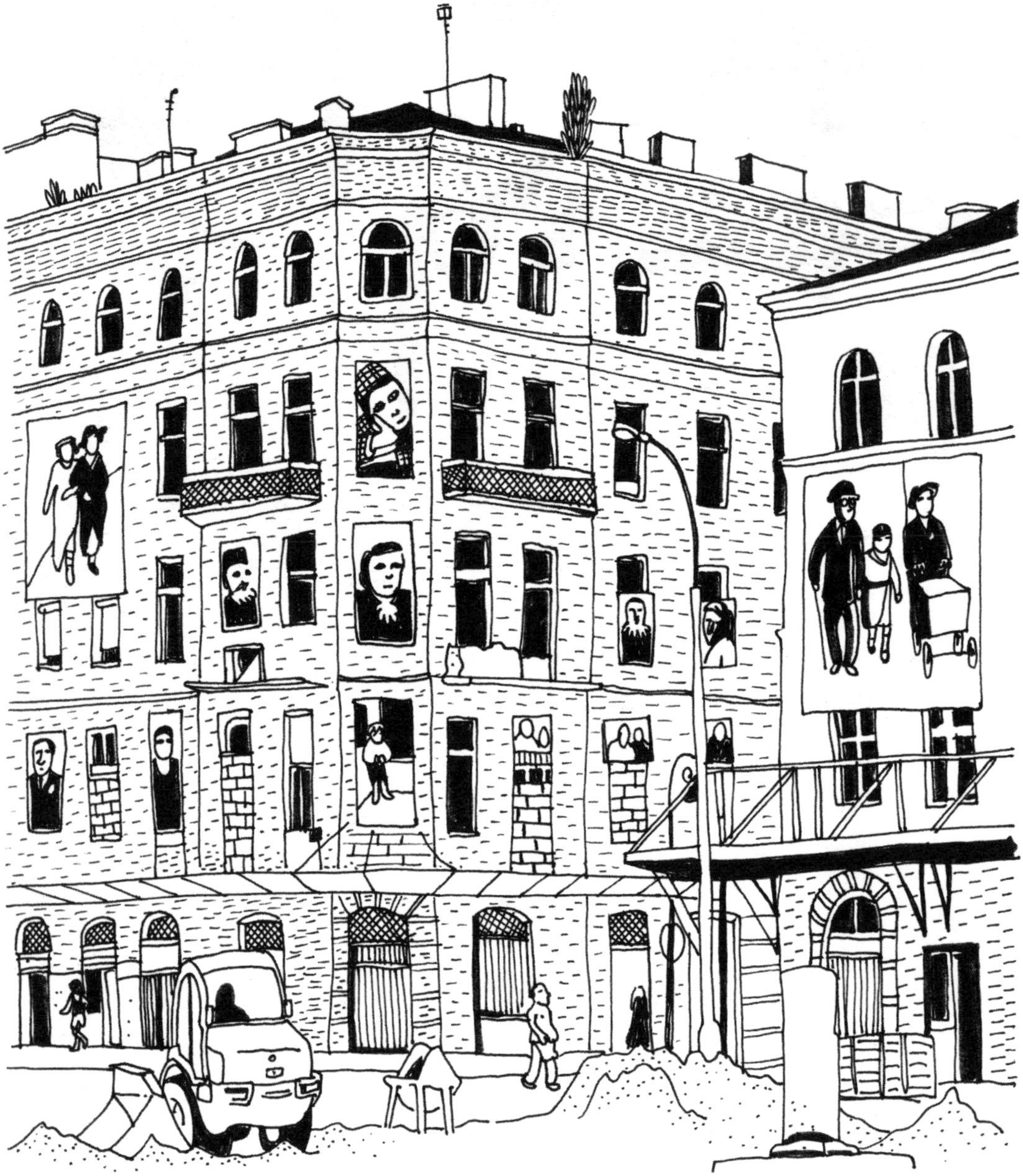

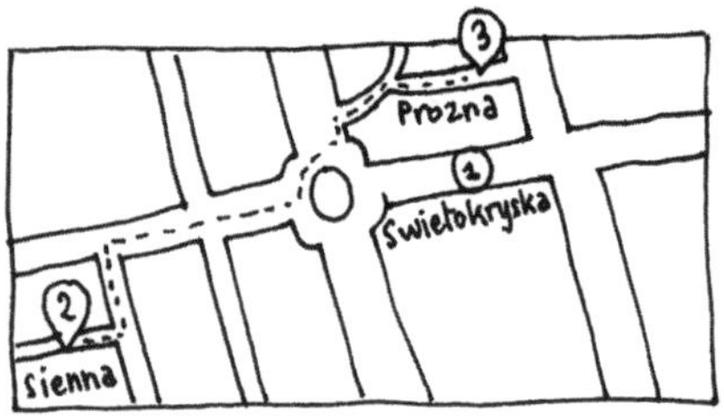
Prozna
Swietokryska
Sienna

The famous Ulica Prozna, the last actual trace of former Jewish life. But the facades have never been cleaned, and the buildings are in terrible condition.

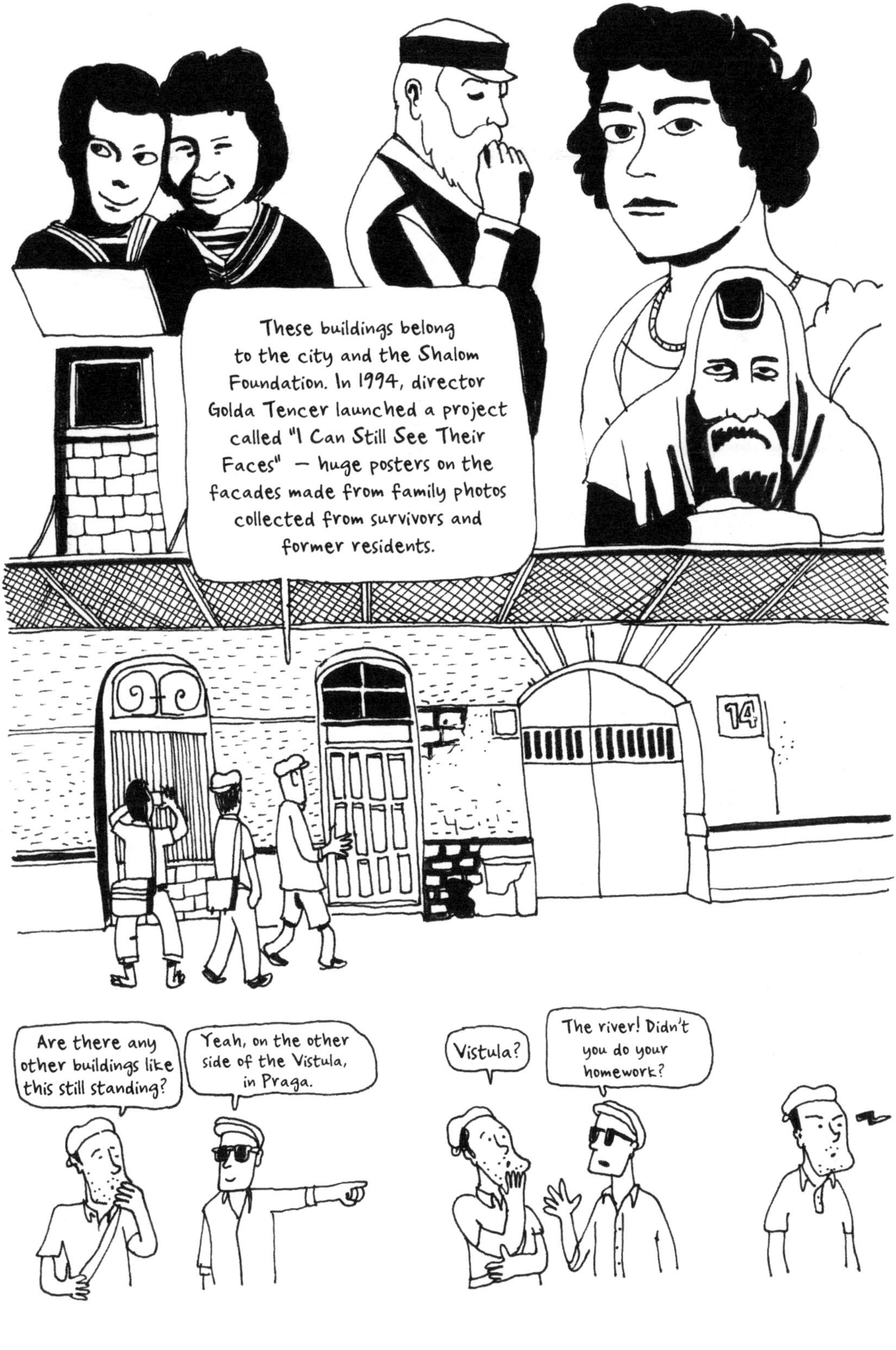

These buildings belong to the city and the Shalom Foundation. In 1994, director Golda Tencer launched a project called "I Can Still See Their Faces" – huge posters on the facades made from family photos collected from survivors and former residents.
14
Are there any other buildings like this still standing?
Yeah, on the other side of the Vistula, in Praga.
Vistula?
The river! Didn't you do your homework?

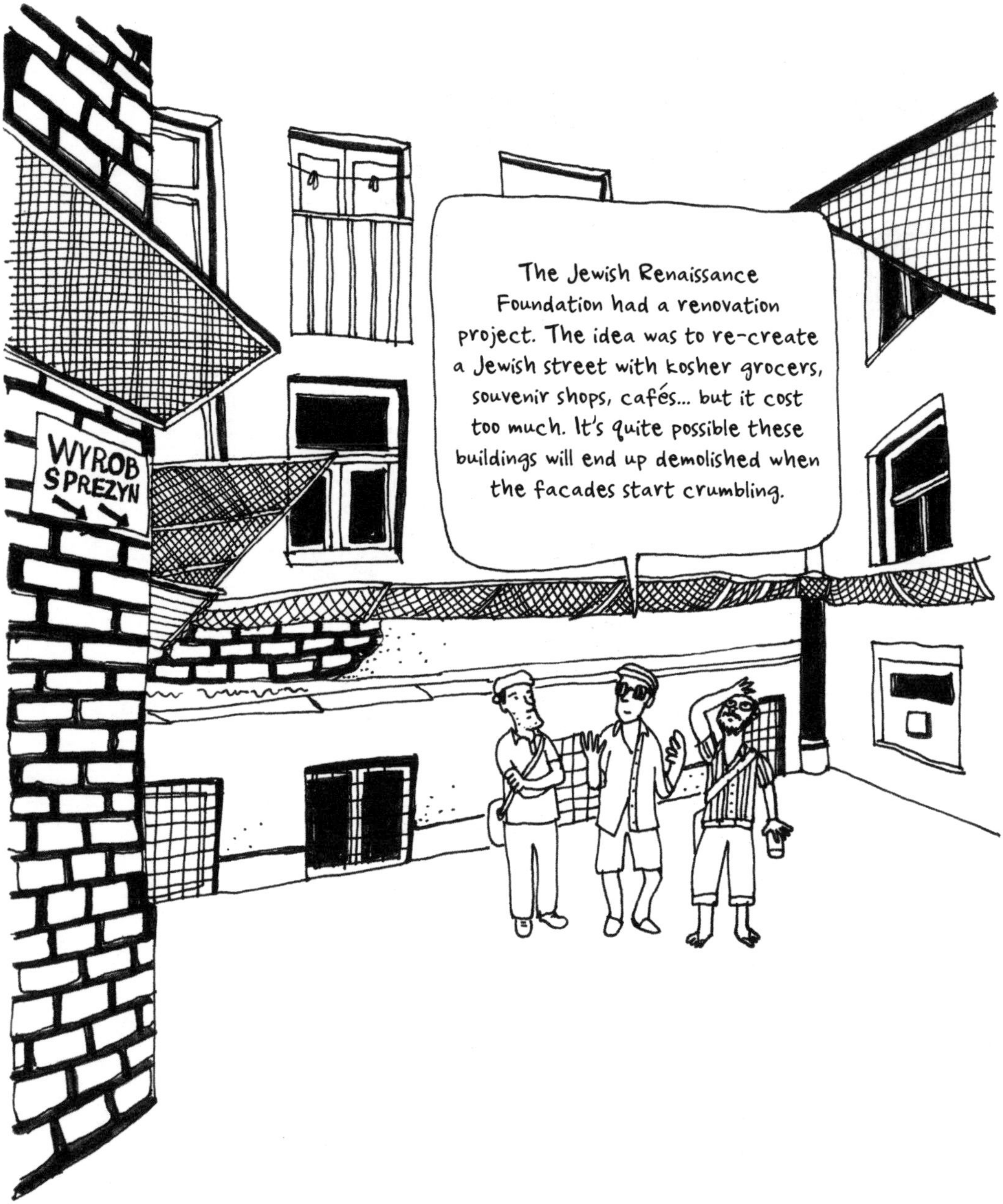
WYROB SPREZYN
The Jewish Renaissance Foundation had a renovation project. The idea was to re-create a Jewish street with kosher grocers, souvenir shops, cafés... but it cost too much. It's quite possible these buildings will end up demolished when the facades start crumbling.

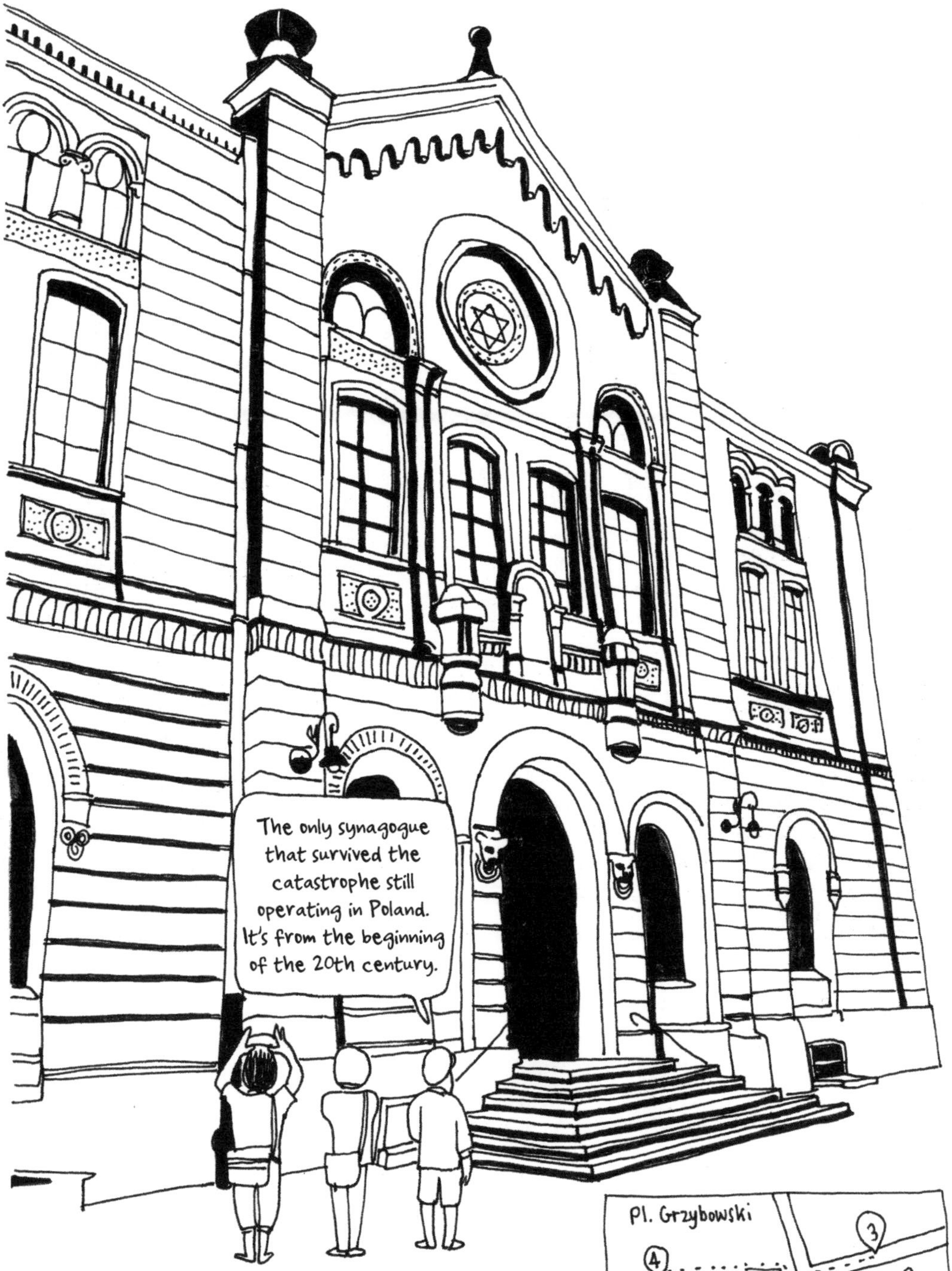
The only synagogue that survived the catastrophe still operating in Poland. It's from the beginning of the 20th century.

Last stop: Nożyk Synagogue.

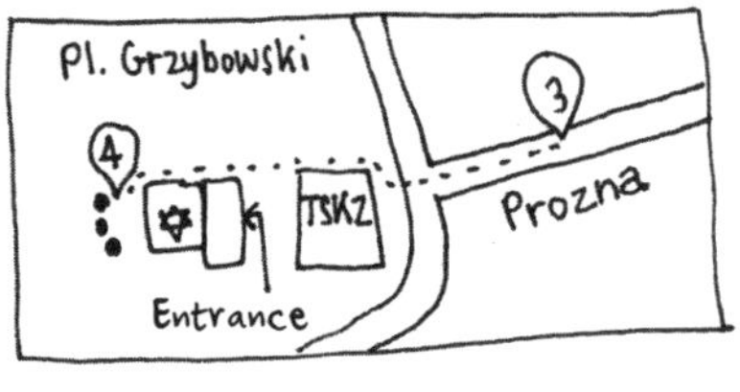
Pl. Grzybowski
3
4
TSKŻ
Prozna
Entrance

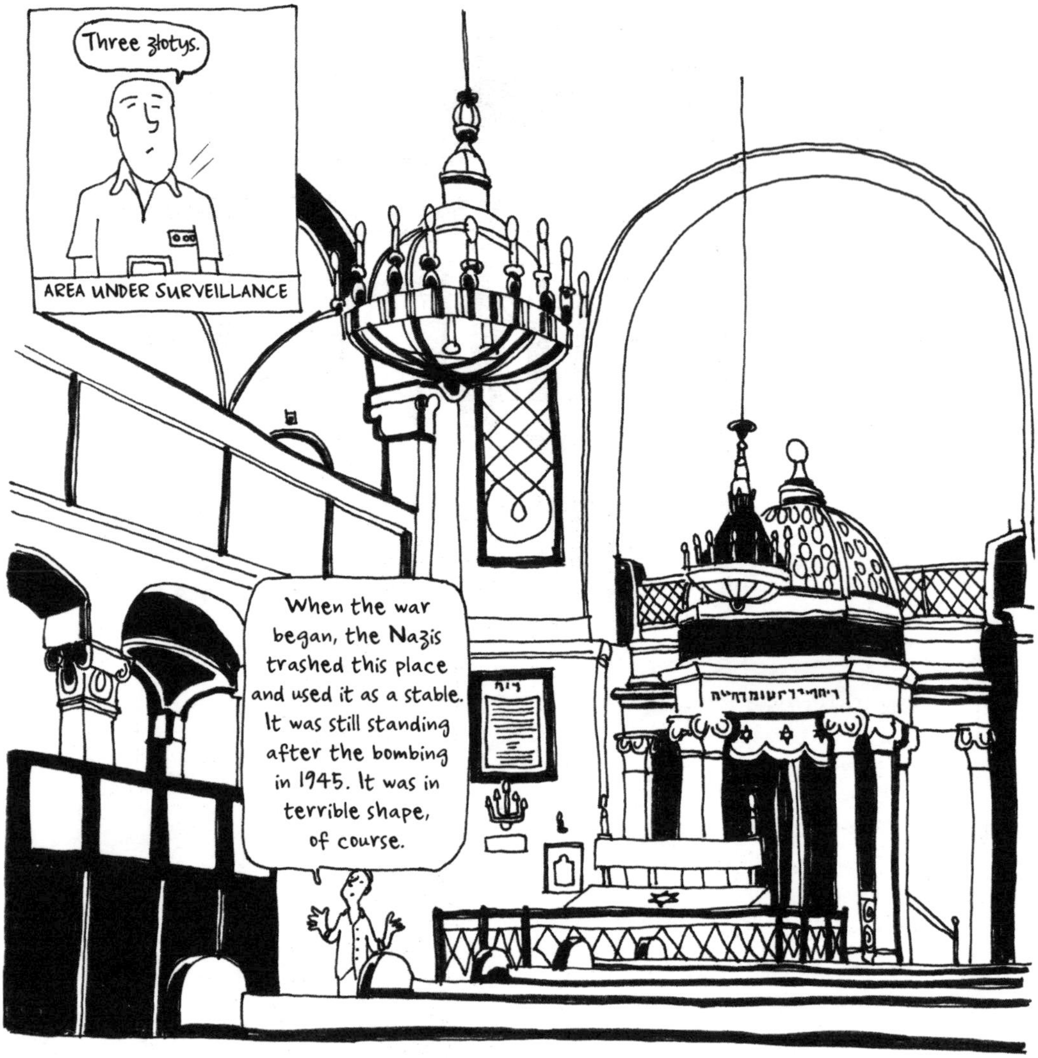
Three złotys.
AREA UNDER SURVEILLANCE
When the war began, the Nazis trashed this place and used it as a stable. It was still standing after the bombing in 1945. It was in terrible shape, of course.

MARTIN STRIKES BACK

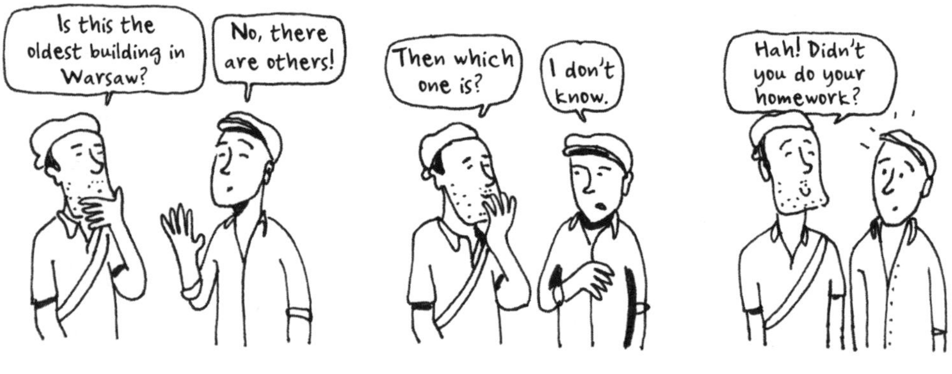
Is this the oldest building in Warsaw?
No, there are others!
Then which one is?
I don't know.
Hah! Didn't you do your homework?

After the war, the city council and the community fought over ownership. In the end, the court delivered its verdict, and today the synagogue belongs to the community. The mayor's office helped a lot with the reconstruction.

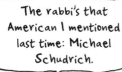

The rabbi's that American I mentioned last time: Michael Schudrich.

BZZZZZZ

Oh... sorry, guys, got a date.

Ciao! Happy touring!

Tomorrow night I'm mixing at Kamieniolomy, if you're into that.

Let's go and see the rabbi!

A Jewish Welcome

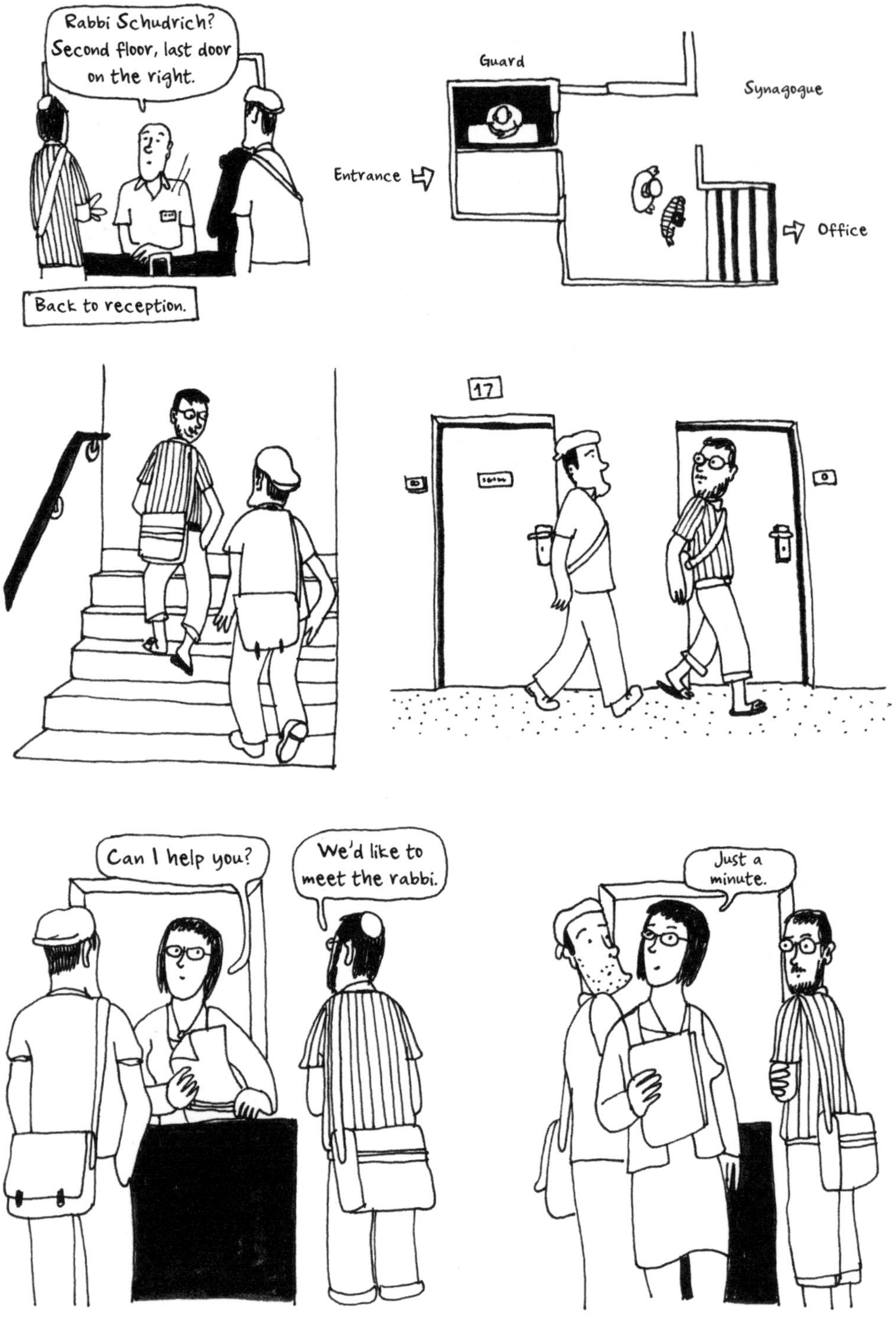
Rabbi Schudrich? Second floor, last door on the right.
Back to reception.
Guard
Synagogue
Entrance
Office
17
Can I help you?
We'd like to meet the rabbi.
Just a minute.

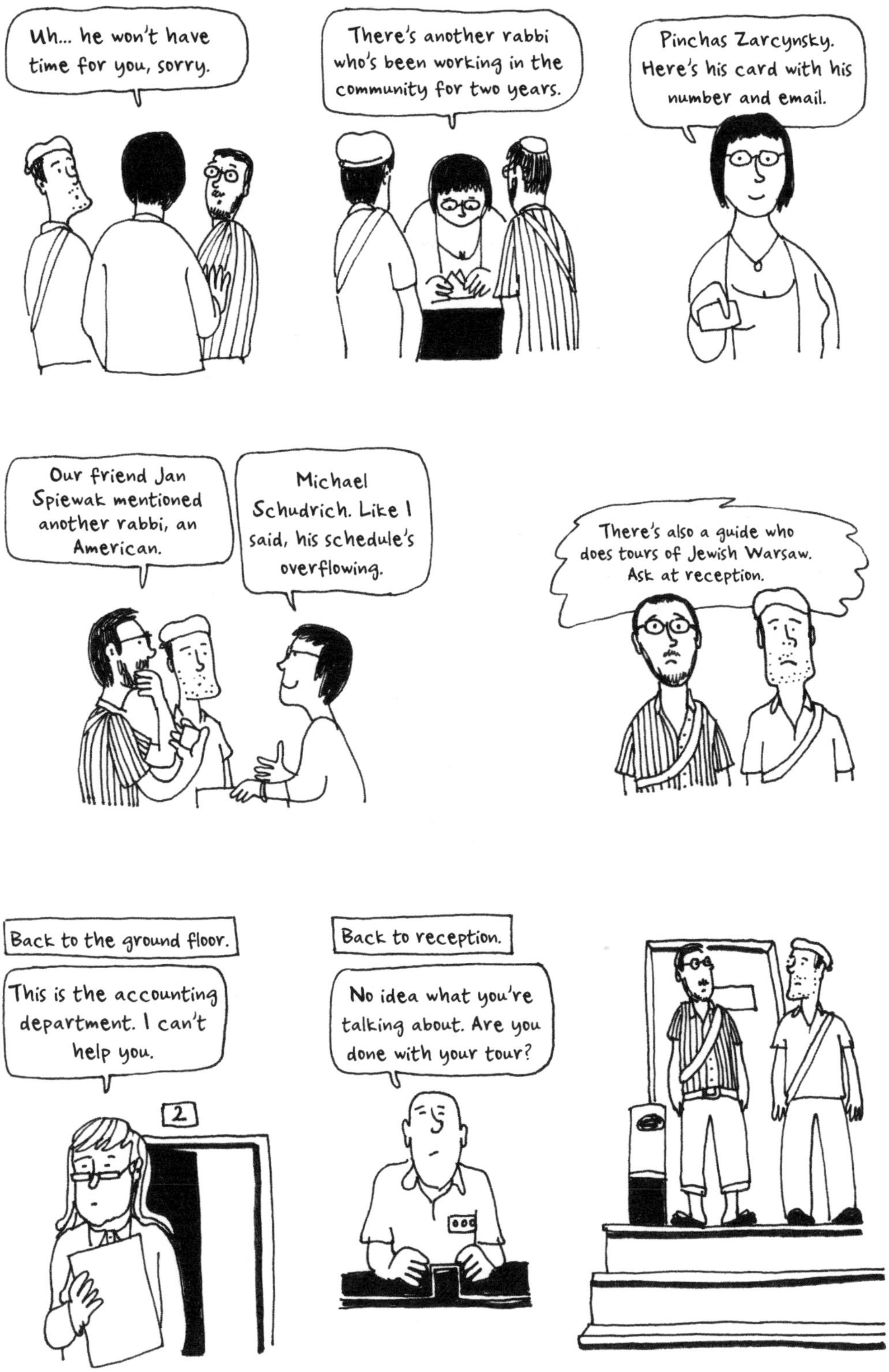
Uh... he won't have time for you, sorry.
There's another rabbi who's been working in the community for two years.
Pinchas Zarcynsky. Here's his card with his number and email.
Our friend Jan Spiewak mentioned another rabbi, an American.
Michael Schudrich. Like I said, his schedule's overflowing.
There's also a guide who does tours of Jewish Warsaw. Ask at reception.
Back to the ground floor.
This is the accounting department. I can't help you.
2
Back to reception.
No idea what you're talking about. Are you done with your tour?

Smacznego (Bon Appétit)

8 p.m. Pdowale Piwna Kompania. Polish cuisine, recommended by the Routard guidebook.

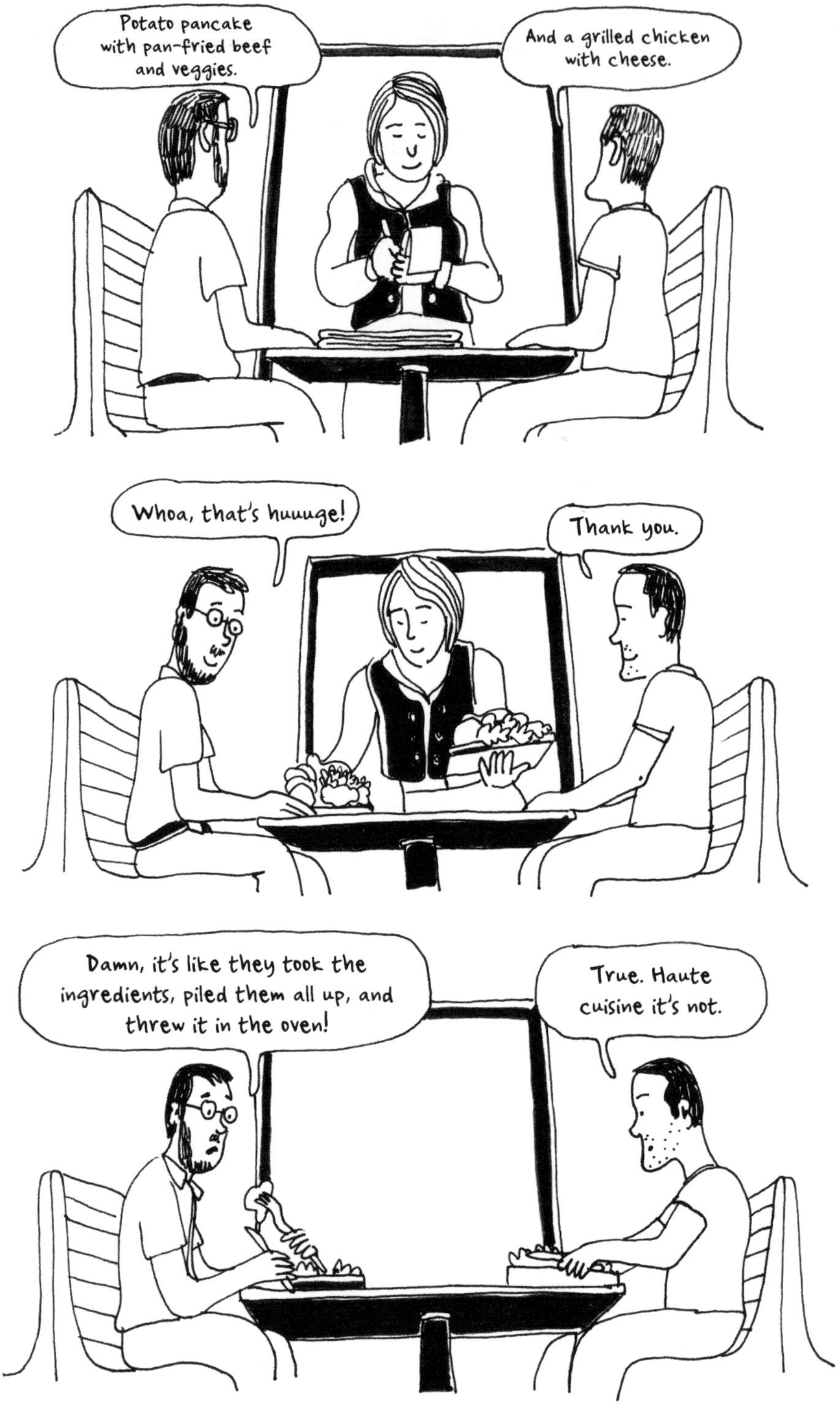

Potato pancake with pan-fried beef and veggies.
And a grilled chicken with cheese.
Whoa, that's huuuge!
Thank you.
Damn, it's like they took the ingredients, piled them all up, and threw it in the oven!
True. Haute cuisine it's not.

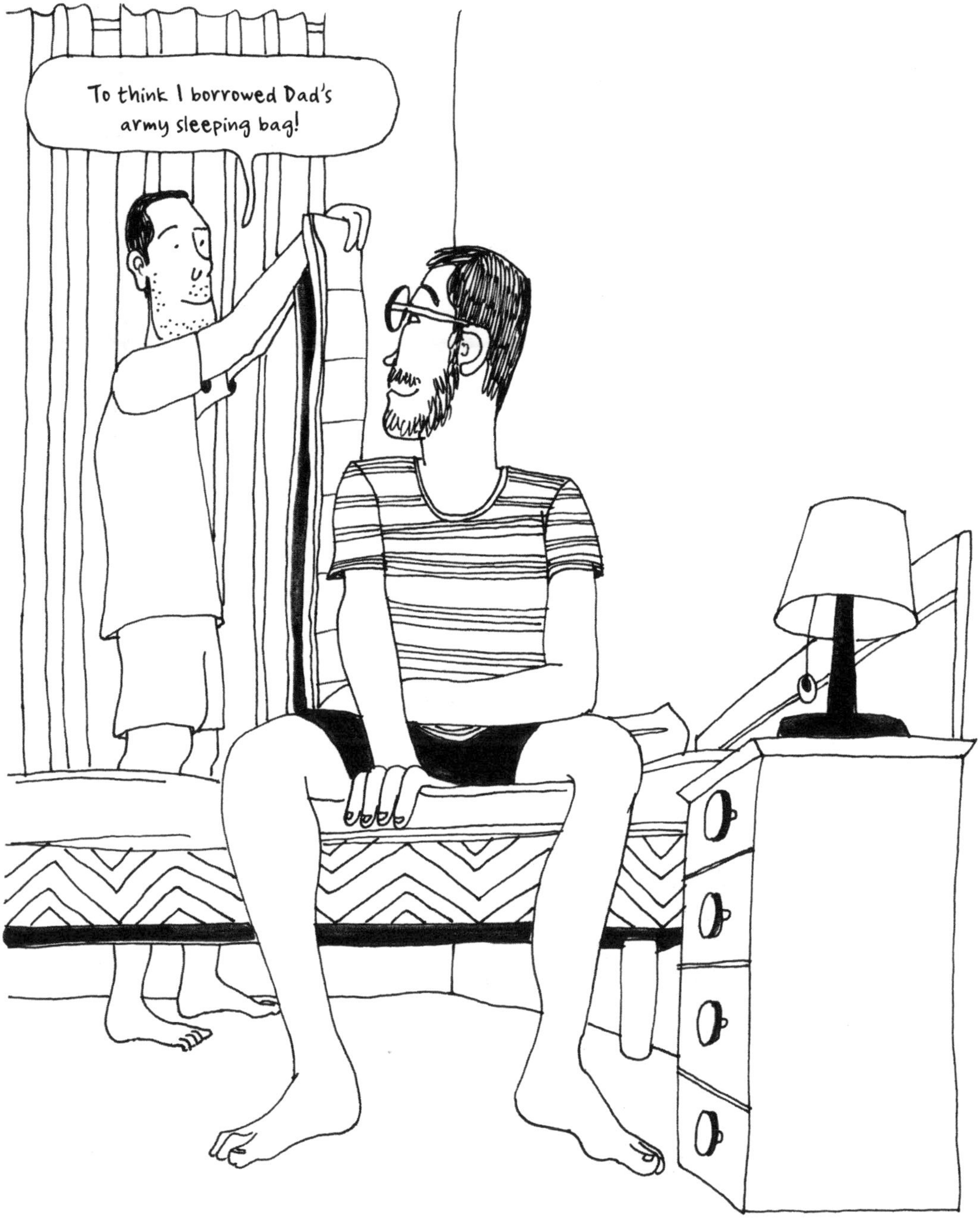
To think I borrowed Dad's army sleeping bag!

Looking for a Rabbi

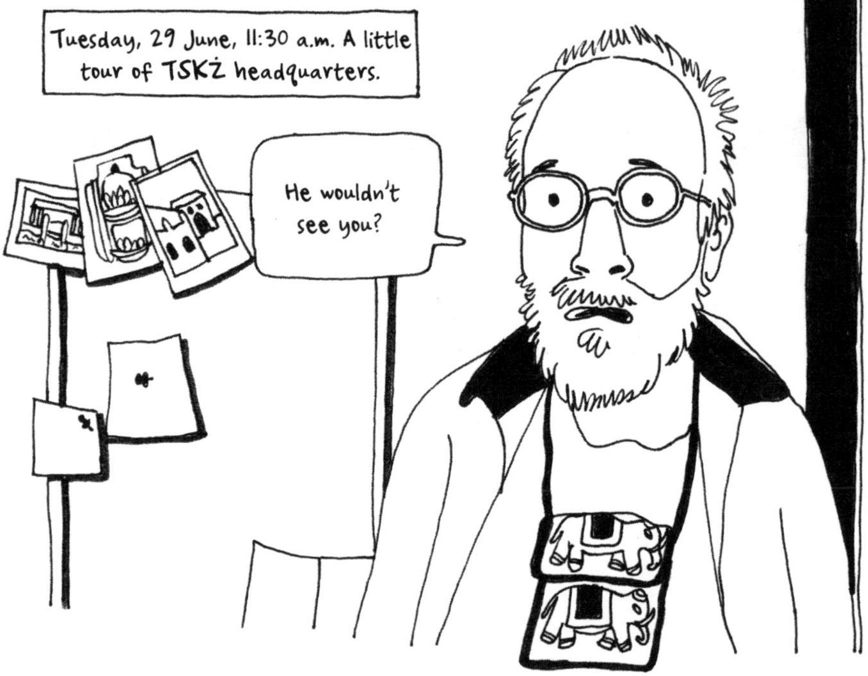
Tuesday, 29 June, 11:30 a.m. A little tour of TSKŻ headquarters.
He wouldn't see you?

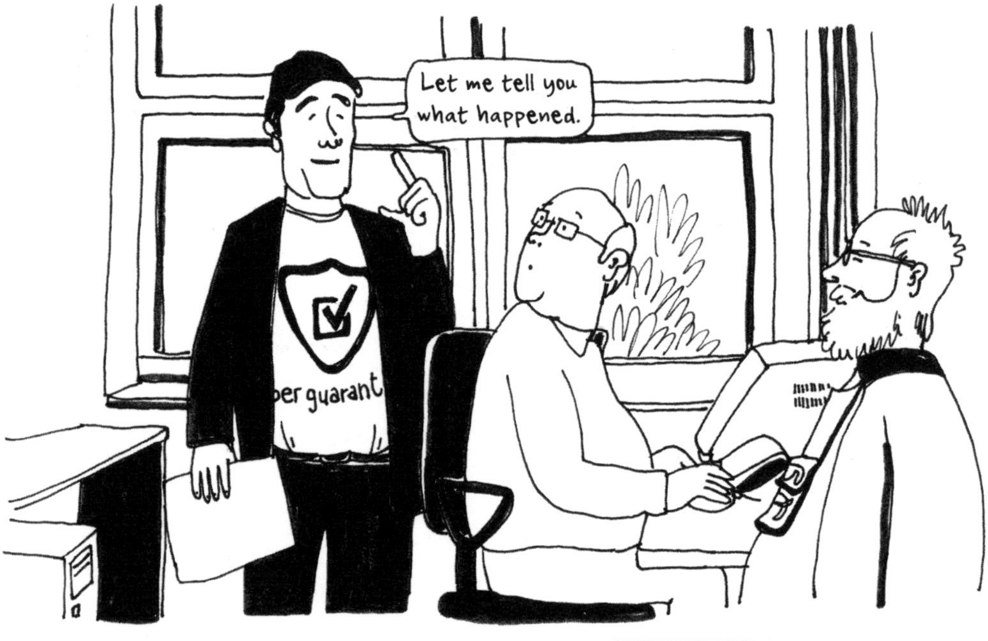
Let me tell you what happened.
per guarant

Jacob "Kobi"

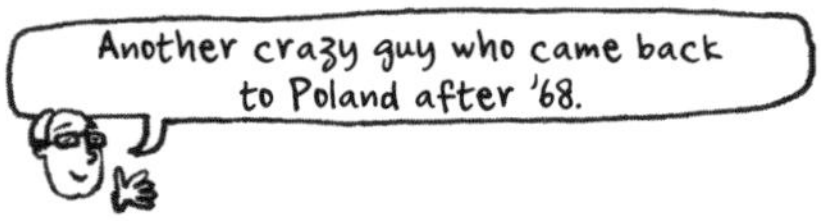
Another crazy guy who came back to Poland after '68.

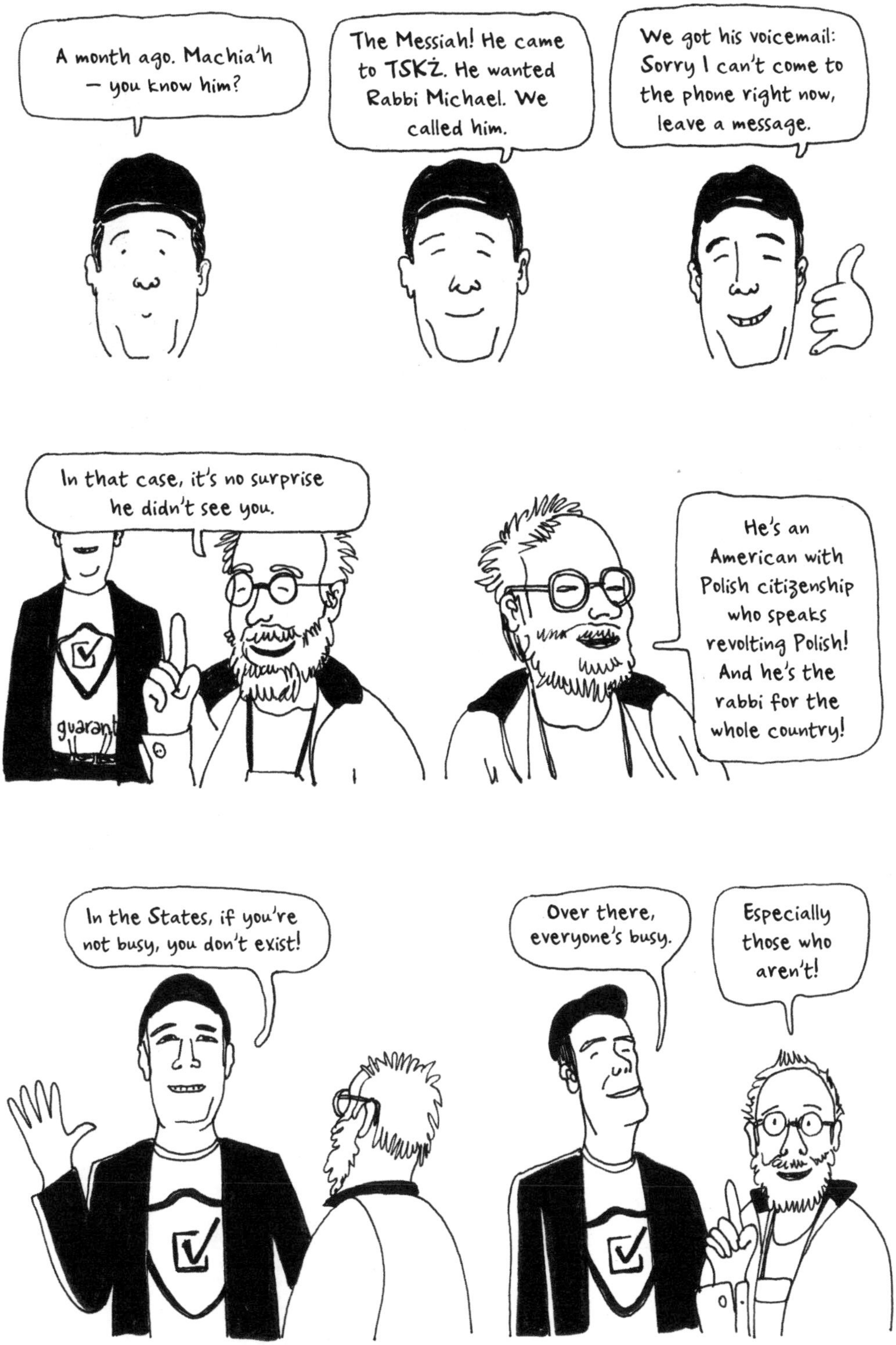
A month ago. Machia'h — you know him?
The Messiah! He came to TSKŻ. He wanted Rabbi Michael. We called him.
We got his voicemail: Sorry I can't come to the phone right now, leave a message.
In that case, it's no surprise he didn't see you.
guarant
He's an American with Polish citizenship who speaks revolting Polish! And he's the rabbi for the whole country!
In the States, if you're not busy, you don't exist!
Over there, everyone's busy.
Especially those who aren't!

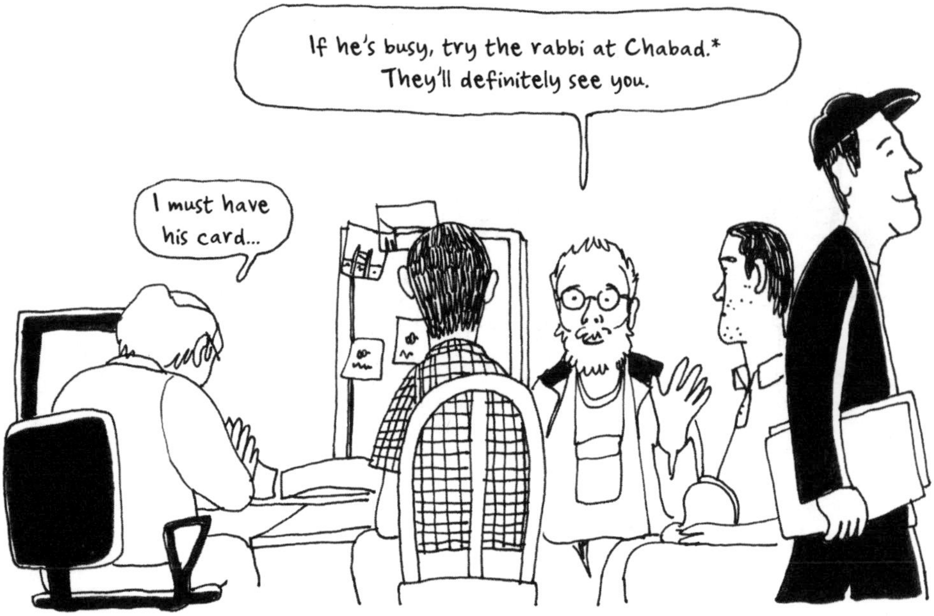
I must have his card...
If he's busy, try the rabbi at Chabad.* They'll definitely see you.

* An Orthodox movement.

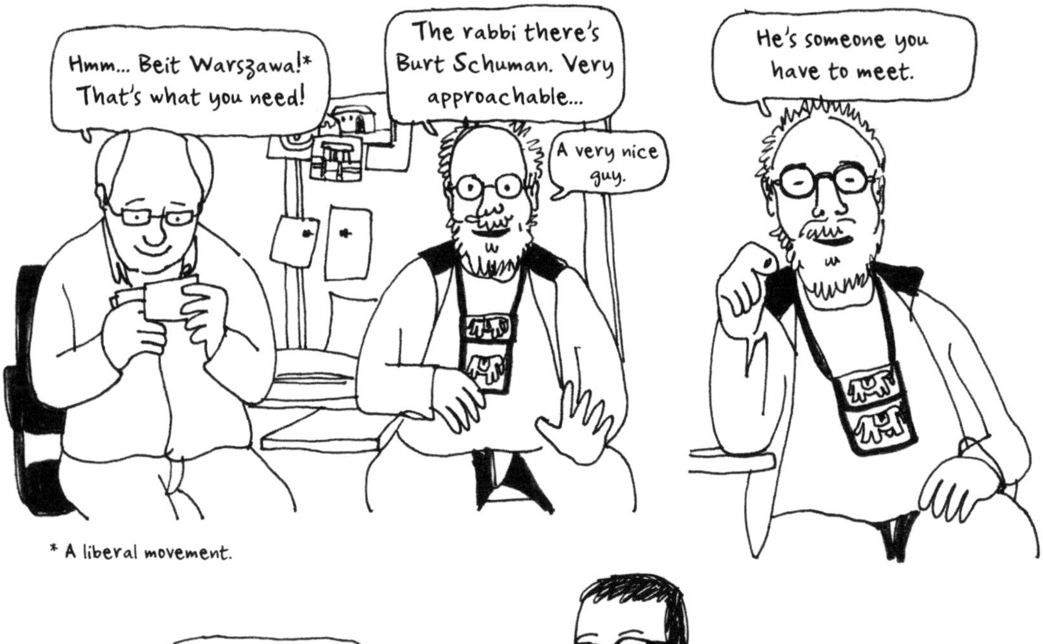
Hmm... Beit Warszawa!* That's what you need!
The rabbi there's Burt Schuman. Very approachable...
A very nice guy.
He's someone you have to meet.

* A liberal movement.

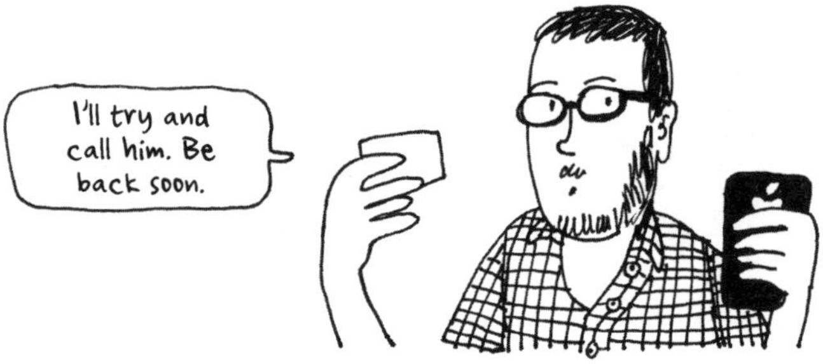
I'll try and call him. Be back soon.

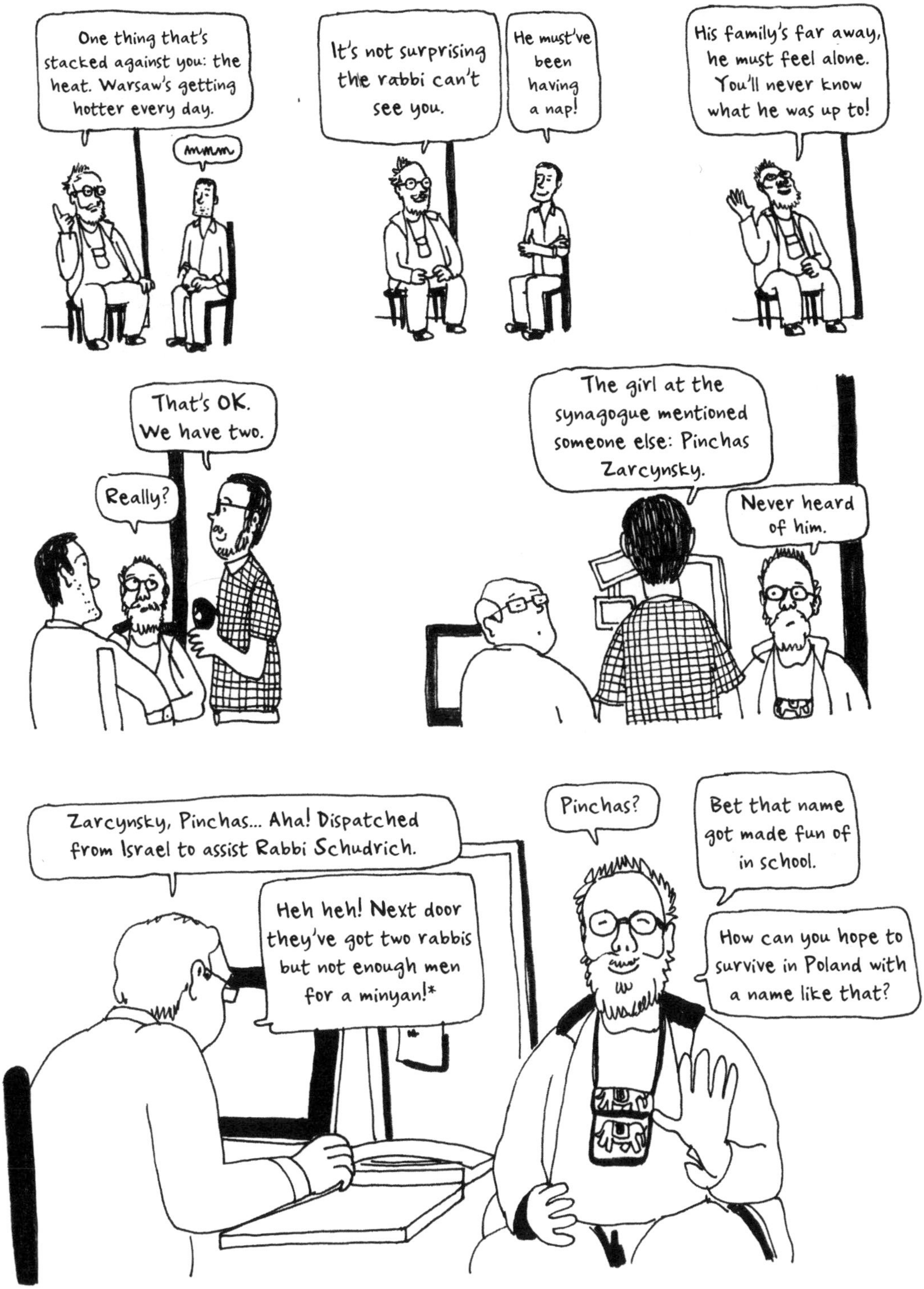
One thing that's stacked against you: the heat. Warsaw's getting hotter every day.
mmm
It's not surprising the rabbi can't see you.
He must've been having a nap!
His family's far away, he must feel alone. You'll never know what he was up to!
That's OK. We have two.
Really?
The girl at the synagogue mentioned someone else: Pinchas Zarcynsky.
Never heard of him.
Zarcynsky, Pinchas... Aha! Dispatched from Israel to assist Rabbi Schudrich.
Heh heh! Next door they've got two rabbis but not enough men for a minyan!*
Pinchas?
Bet that name got made fun of in school.
How can you hope to survive in Poland with a name like that?

* The quorum of ten adult Jewish men required to recite the most important prayers.

Brudny Zyd

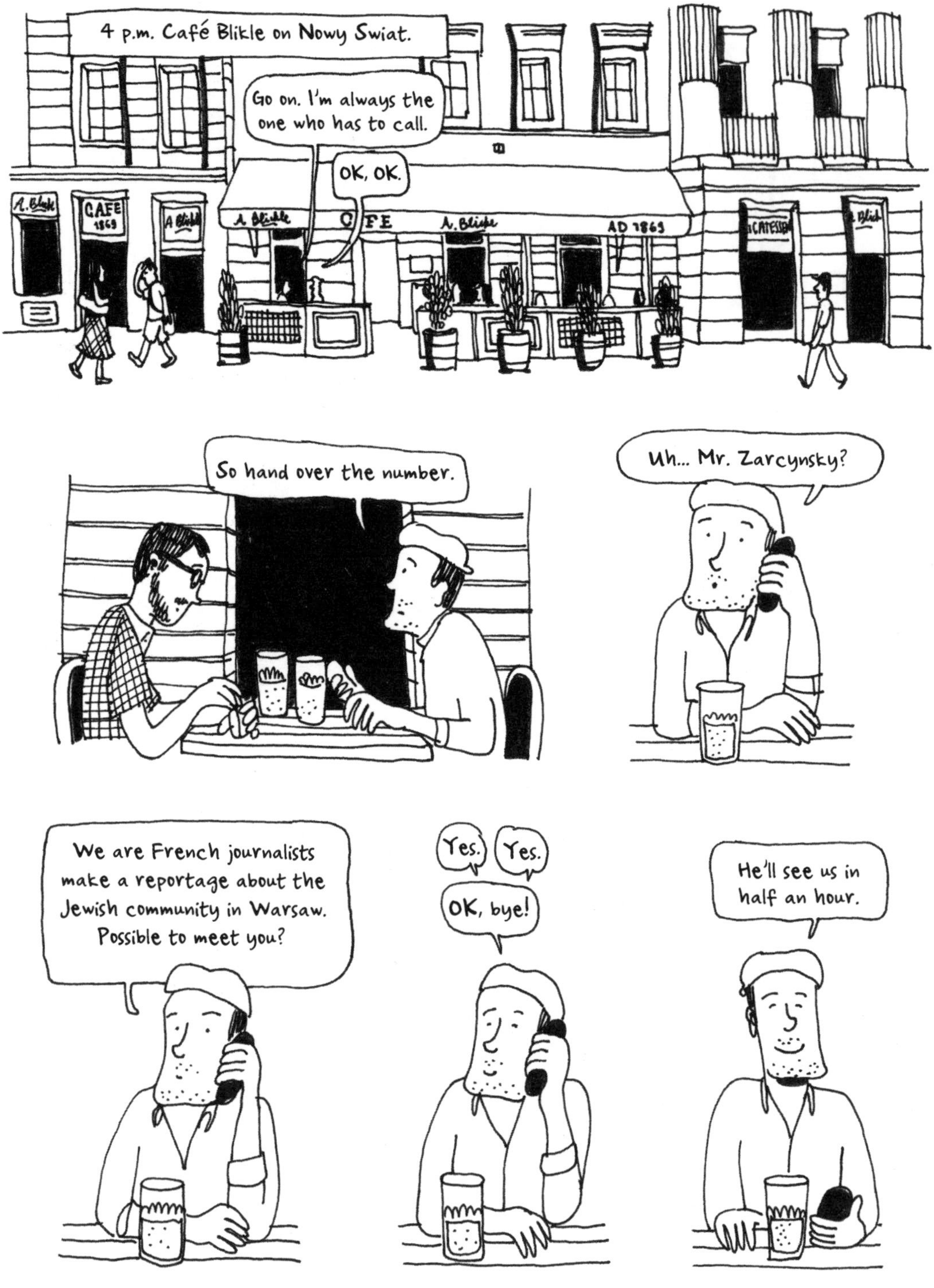
4 p.m. Café Blikle on Nowy Swiat.
Go on. I'm always the one who has to call.
OK, OK.
A. Blikle
CAFE 1869
A. Blikle
A. Blikle
CAFE
A. Blikle
AD 1869
So hand over the number.
Uh... Mr. Zarcynsky?
We are French journalists make a reportage about the Jewish community in Warsaw. Possible to meet you?
Yes.
Yes.
OK, bye!
He'll see us in half an hour.

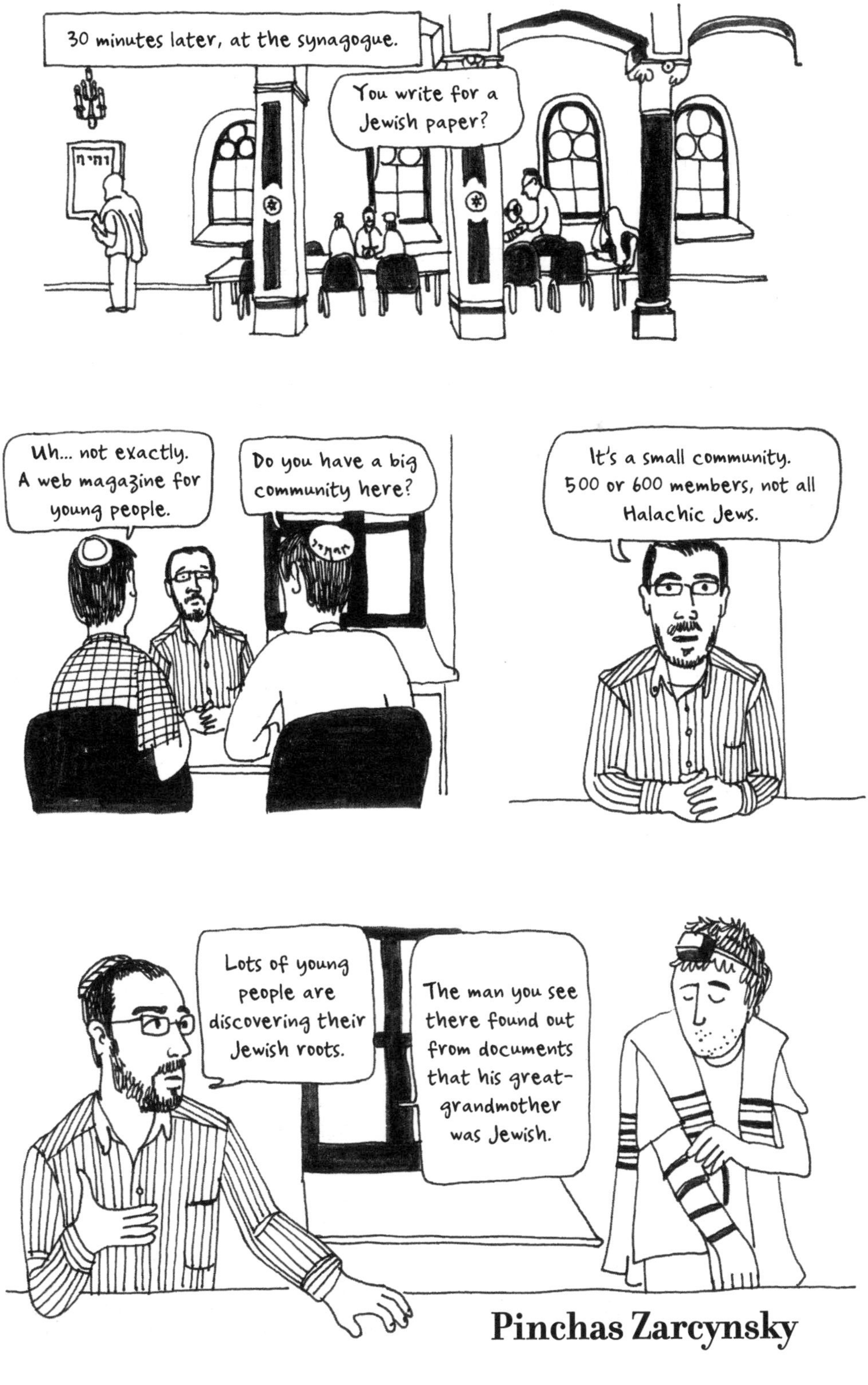
30 minutes later, at the synagogue.
You write for a Jewish paper?
Uh... not exactly. A web magazine for young people.
Do you have a big community here?
It's a small community. 500 or 600 members, not all Halachic Jews.
Lots of young people are discovering their Jewish roots.
The man you see there found out from documents that his great-grandmother was Jewish.
Pinchas Zarcynsky

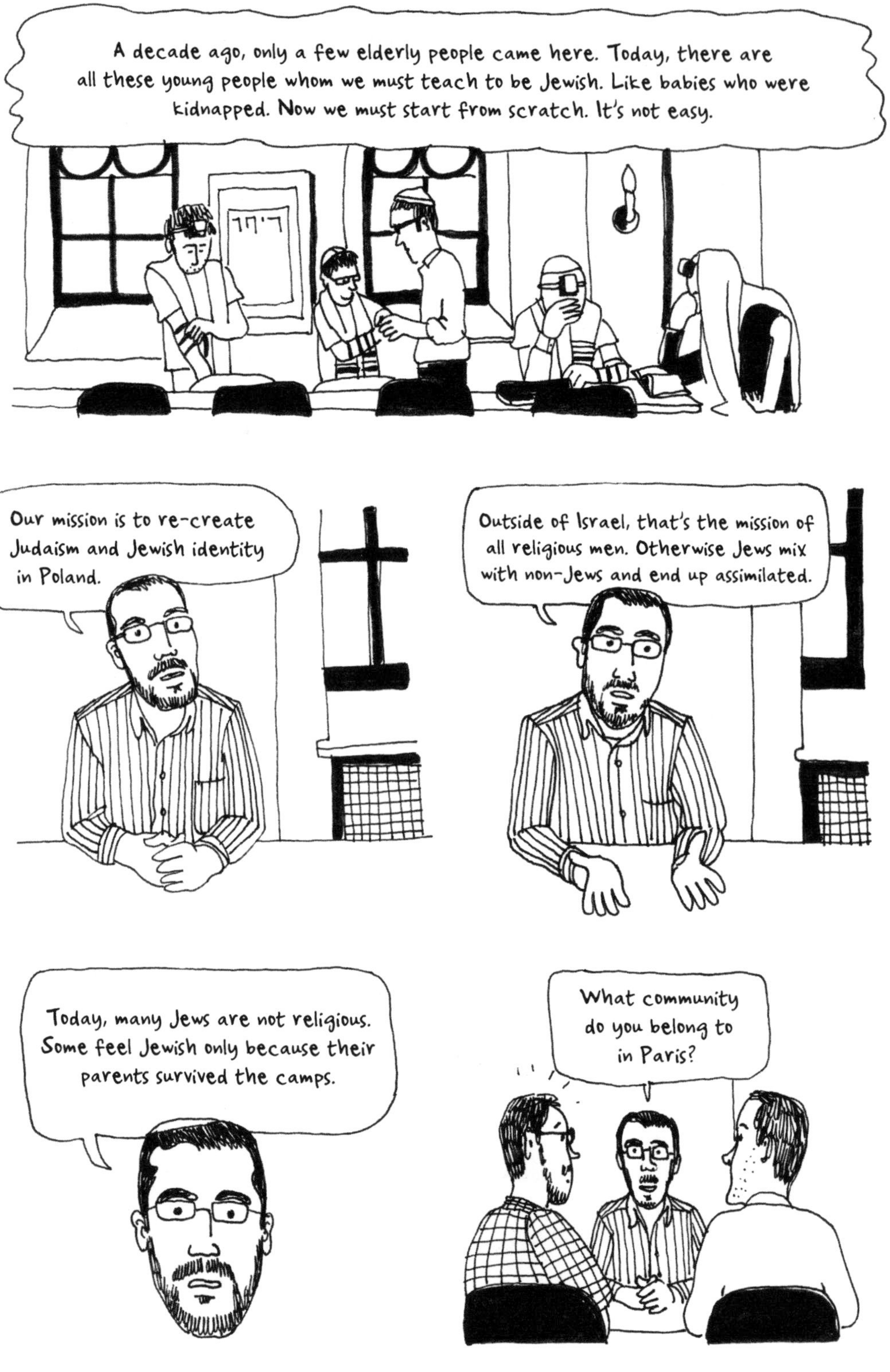
A decade ago, only a few elderly people came here. Today, there are all these young people whom we must teach to be Jewish. Like babies who were kidnapped. Now we must start from scratch. It's not easy.
Our mission is to re-create Judaism and Jewish identity in Poland.
Outside of Israel, that's the mission of all religious men. Otherwise Jews mix with non-Jews and end up assimilated.
Today, many Jews are not religious. Some feel Jewish only because their parents survived the camps.
What community do you belong to in Paris?

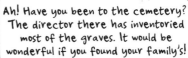

None.

Uh... actually, our grandmother was from Warsaw.

Ah! Have you been to the cemetery? The director there has inventoried most of the graves. It would be wonderful if you found your family's!

You're related?

We're brothers.

For a Jew, a trip to Poland is an incredible thing.

For the non-practising, it's also a way of finding religion.

right, sure

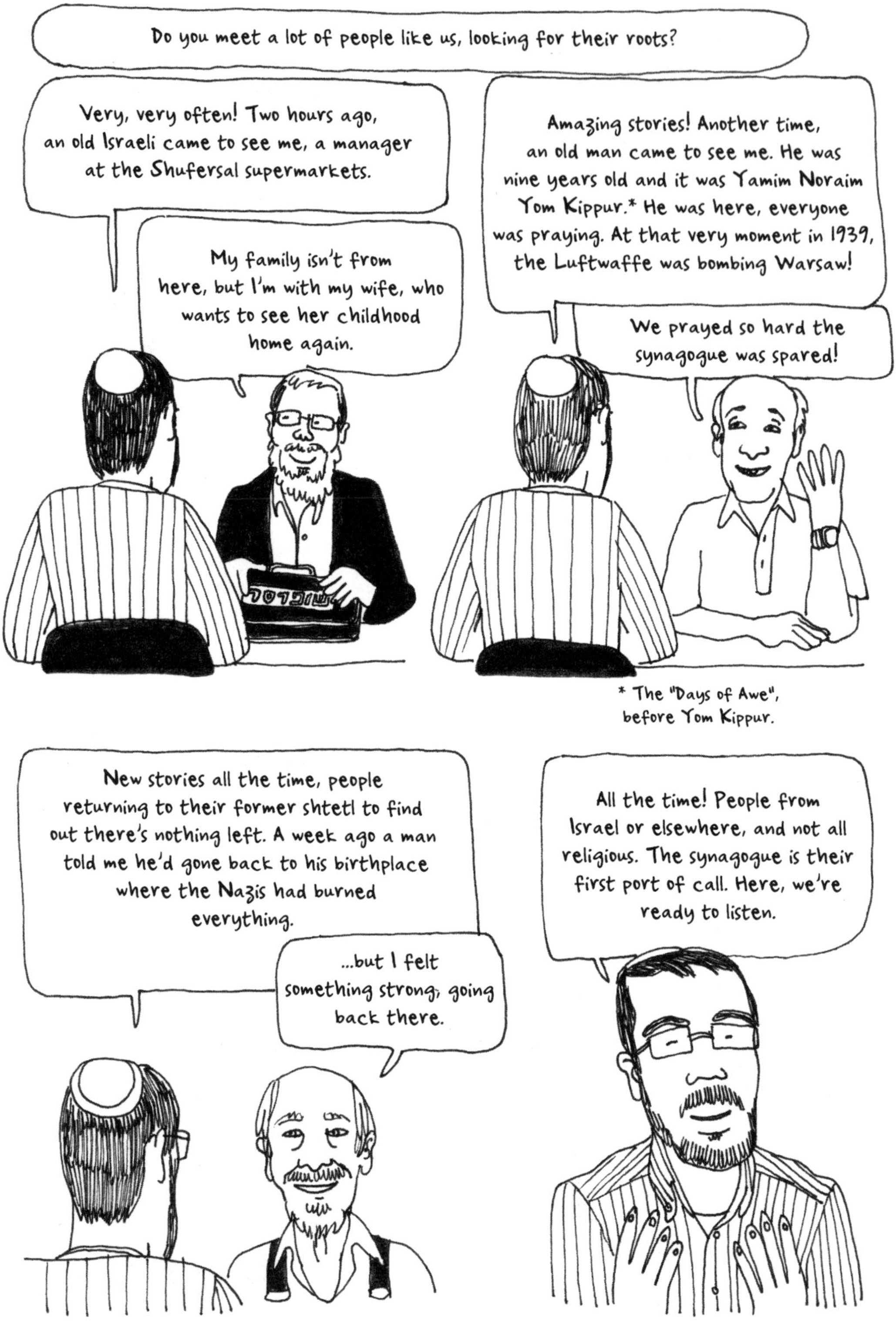

Do you meet a lot of people like us, looking for their roots?
Very, very often! Two hours ago, an old Israeli came to see me, a manager at the Shufersal supermarkets.
My family isn't from here, but I'm with my wife, who wants to see her childhood home again.
Amazing stories! Another time, an old man came to see me. He was nine years old and it was Yamim Noraim Yom Kippur.* He was here, everyone was praying. At that very moment in 1939, the Luftwaffe was bombing Warsaw!
We prayed so hard the synagogue was spared!
* The "Days of Awe", before Yom Kippur.
New stories all the time, people returning to their former shtetl to find out there's nothing left. A week ago a man told me he'd gone back to his birthplace where the Nazis had burned everything.
...but I felt something strong, going back there.
All the time! People from Israel or elsewhere, and not all religious. The synagogue is their first port of call. Here, we're ready to listen.

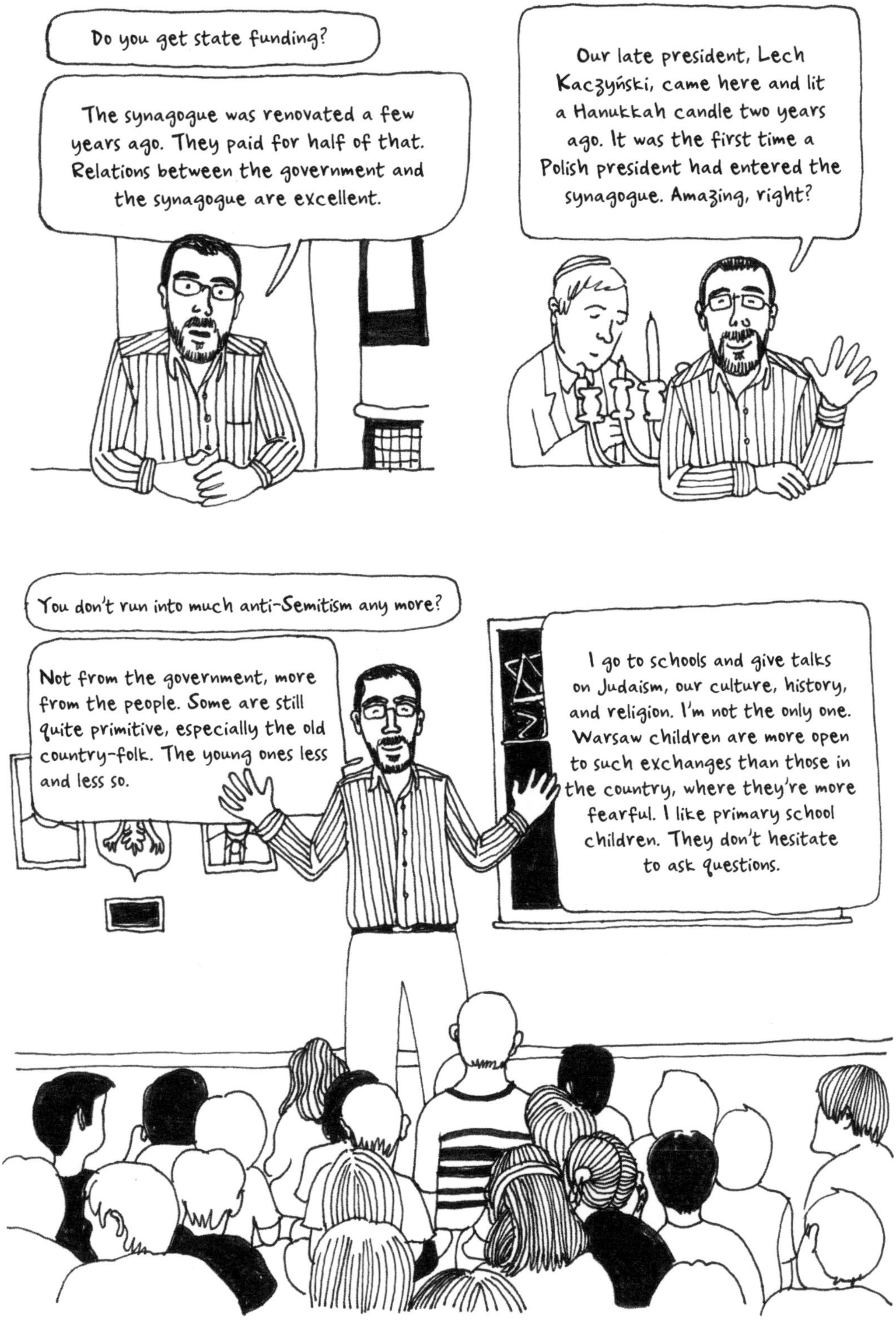

Do you get state funding?
The synagogue was renovated a few years ago. They paid for half of that. Relations between the government and the synagogue are excellent.
Our late president, Lech Kaczyński, came here and lit a Hanukkah candle two years ago. It was the first time a Polish president had entered the synagogue. Amazing, right?
You don't run into much anti-Semitism any more?
Not from the government, more from the people. Some are still quite primitive, especially the old country-folk. The young ones less and less so.
I go to schools and give talks on Judaism, our culture, history, and religion. I'm not the only one. Warsaw children are more open to such exchanges than those in the country, where they're more fearful. I like primary school children. They don't hesitate to ask questions.

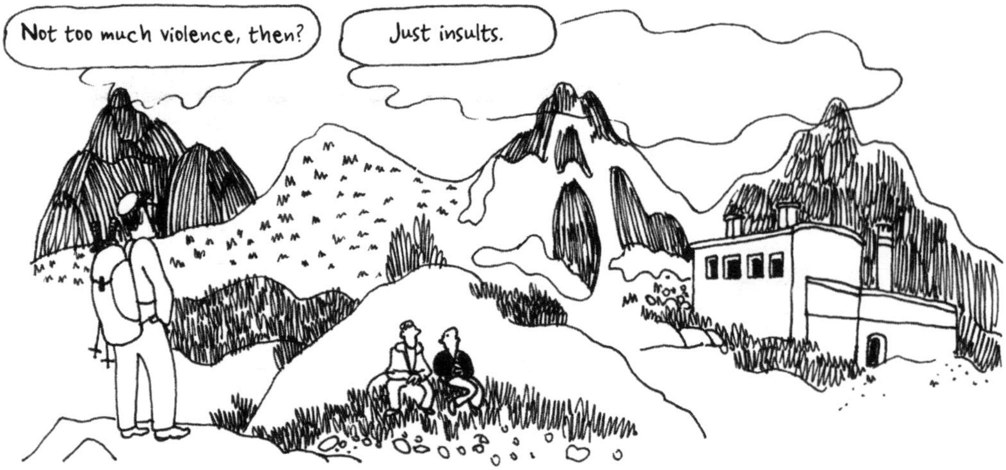
Not too much violence, then?
Just insults.

One day, I was up in the Tatra mountains, alone. Night was falling.

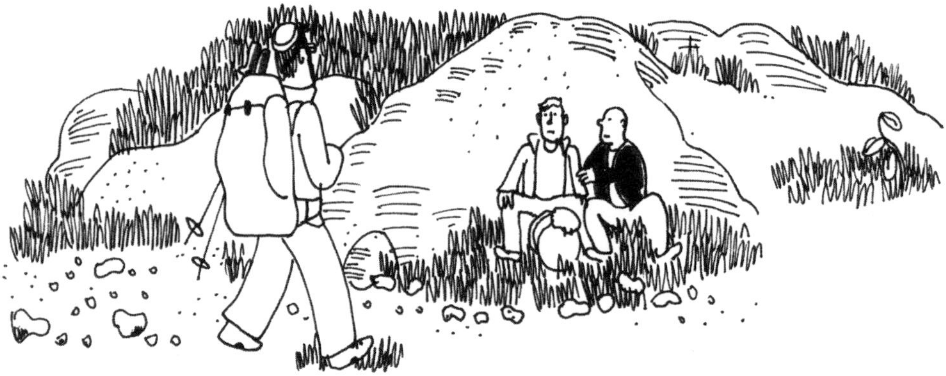

I was walking peacefully along. I passed two young people, and heard:

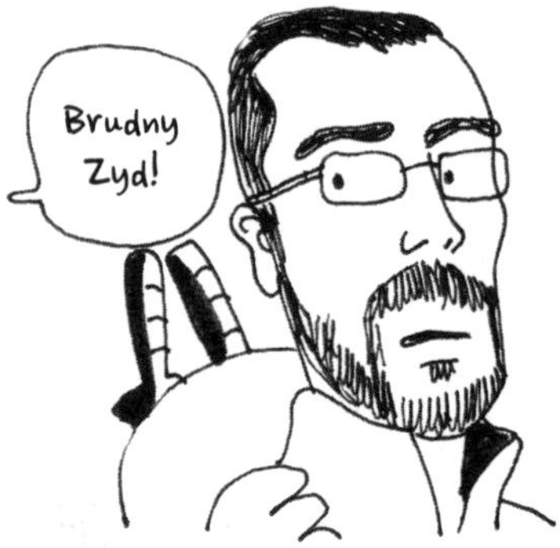
Brudny Zyd!

Brudny Zyd means "dirty Jew".

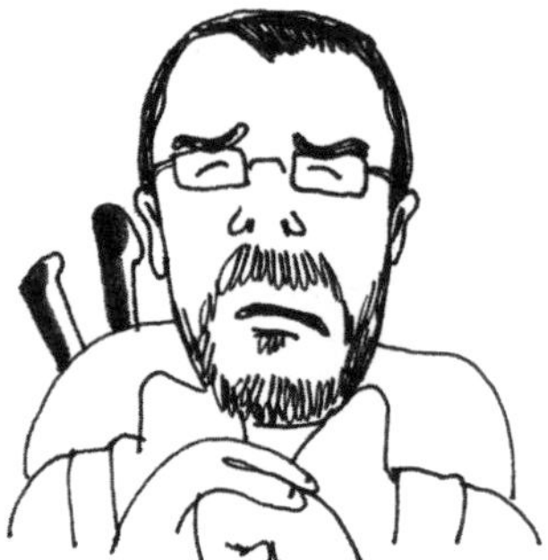

I thought: OK! I've been in the army, I'll fight like Samson.

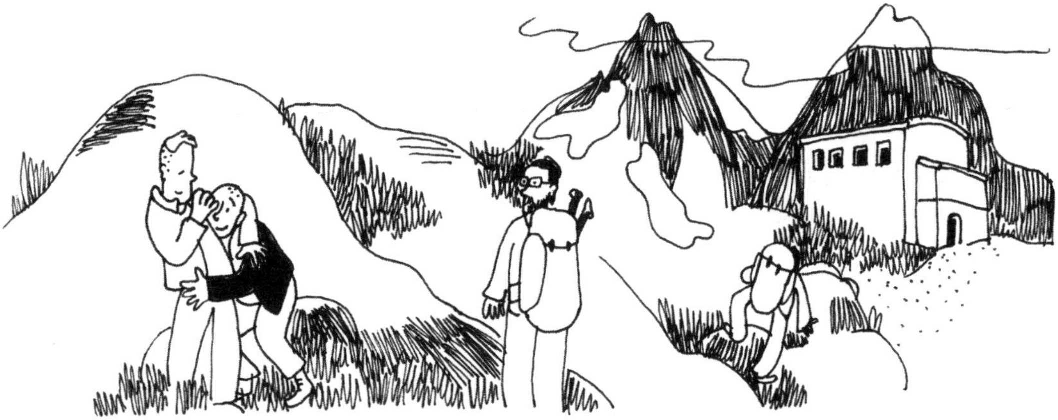

Actually, they were just messing around with each other. They hadn't seen me. I left.

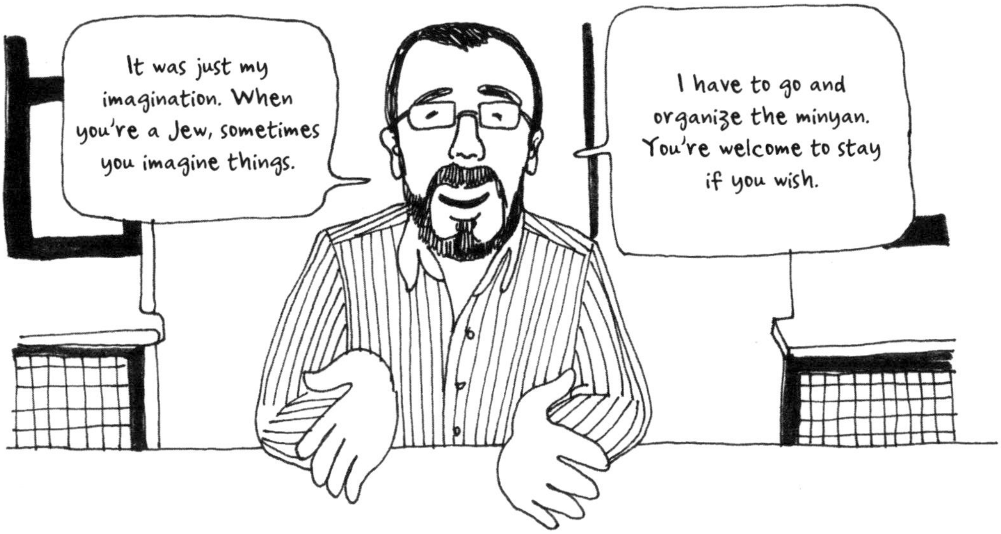
It was just my imagination. When you're a Jew, sometimes you imagine things.
I have to go and organize the minyan. You're welcome to stay if you wish.

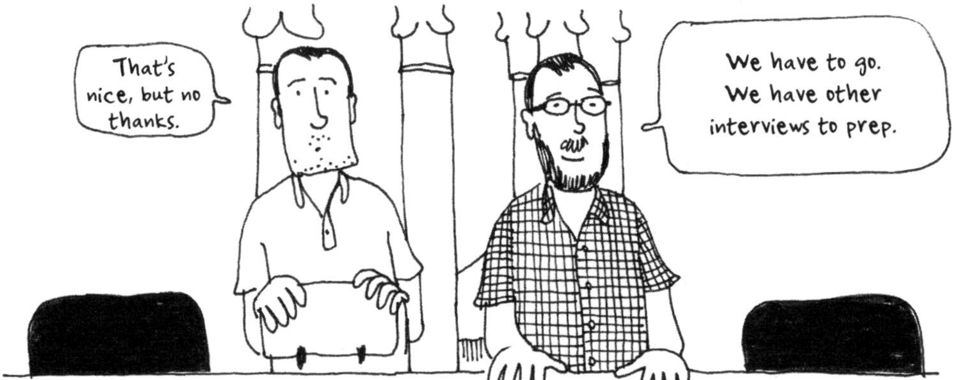
That's nice, but no thanks.
We have to go. We have other interviews to prep.

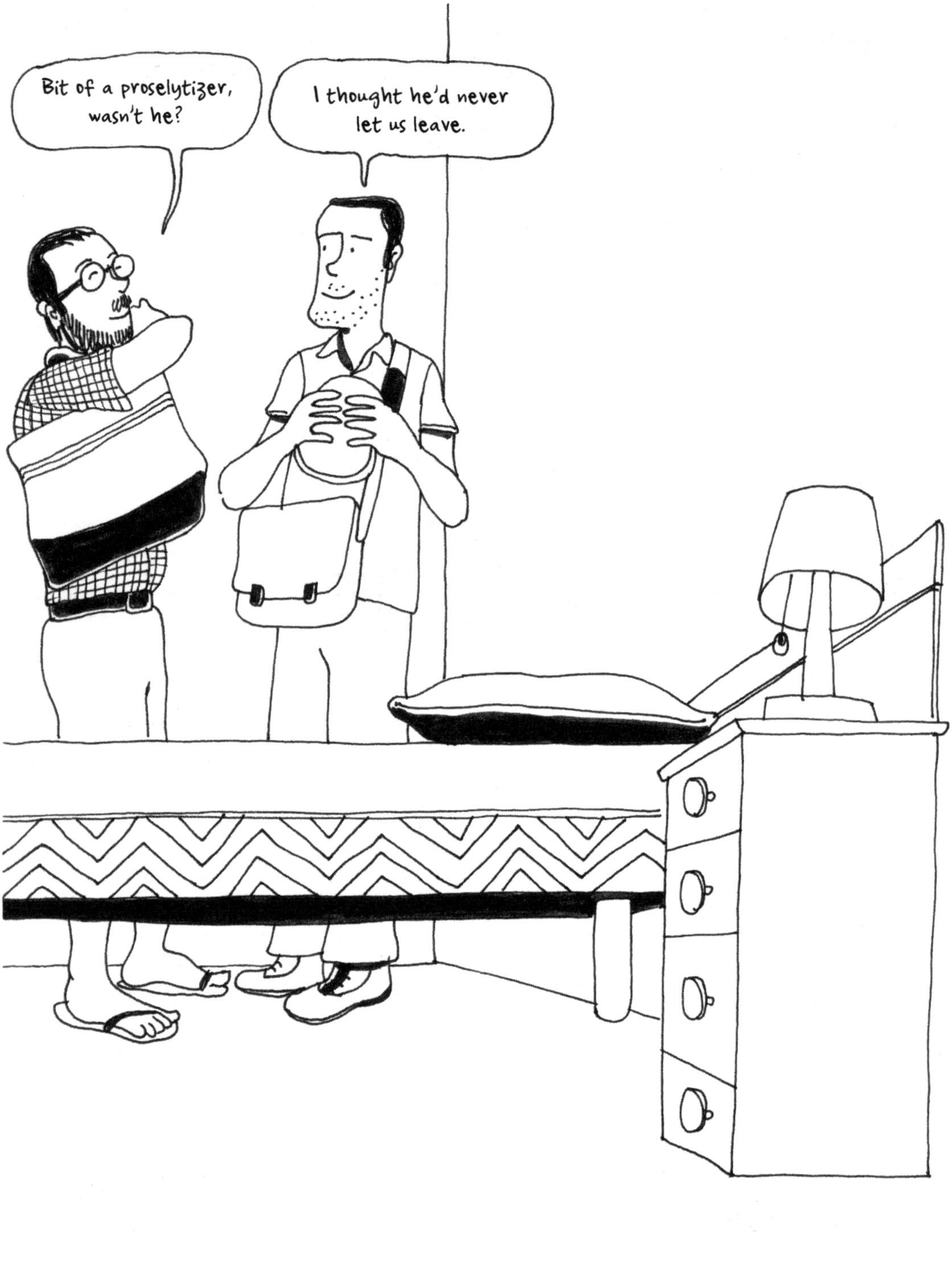
Bit of a proselytizer, wasn't he?
I thought he'd never let us leave.

Hmph! Journalists!

Super-Rabbi

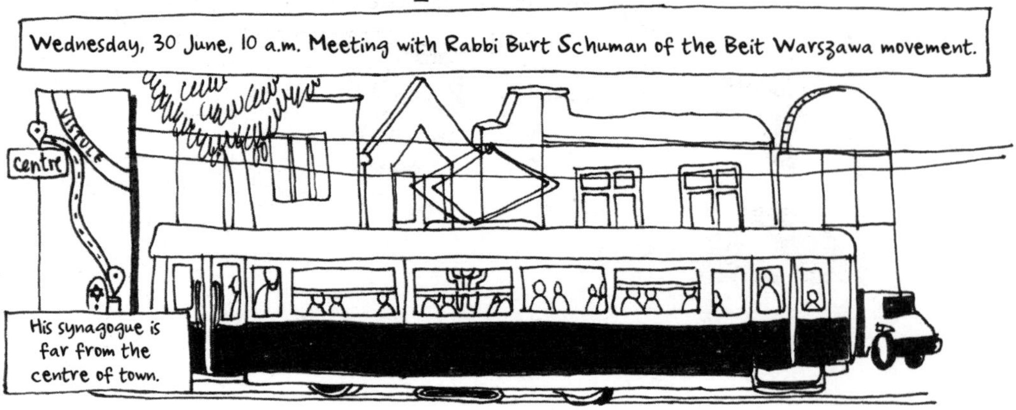
Wednesday, 30 June, 10 a.m. Meeting with Rabbi Burt Schuman of the Beit Warszawa movement.
VISTULE
Centre
His synagogue is far from the centre of town.

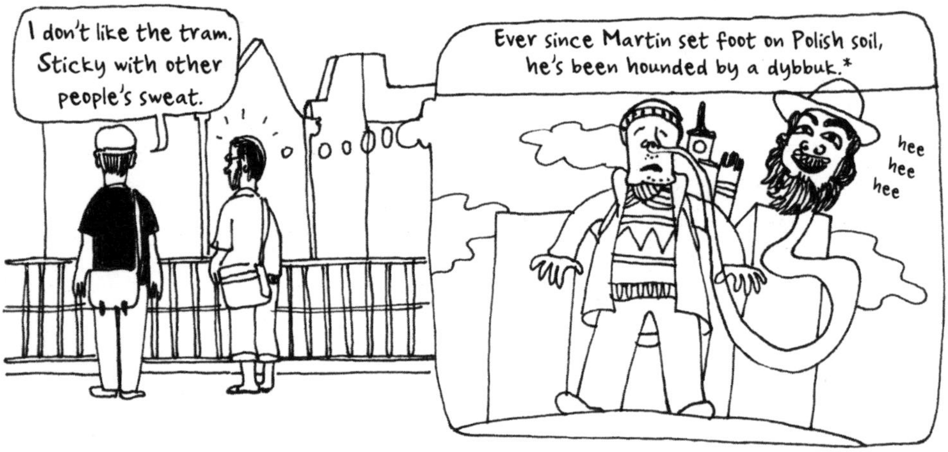
I don't like the tram. Sticky with other people's sweat.
Ever since Martin set foot on Polish soil, he's been hounded by a dybbuk.*
hee hee hee

* Dybbuk: a demon from Yiddish folklore.

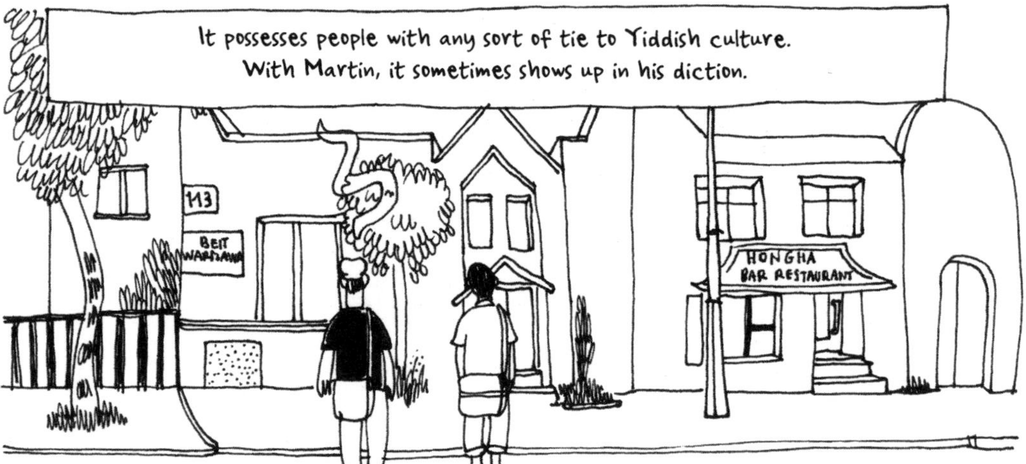
It possesses people with any sort of tie to Yiddish culture. With Martin, it sometimes shows up in his diction.
113
BEIT WARSZAWA
HONGHA
BAR RESTAURANT

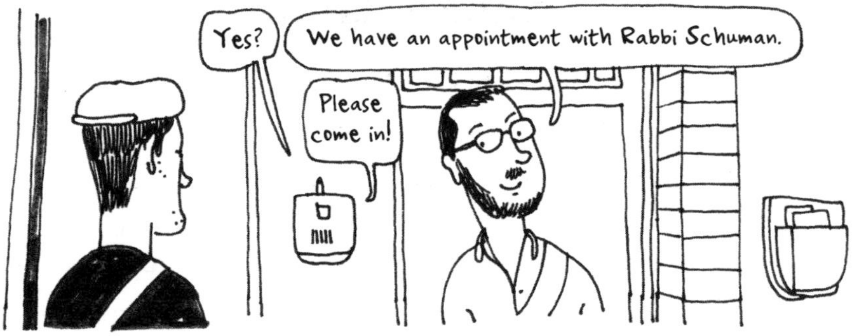
Yes?
We have an appointment with Rabbi Schuman.
Please come in!

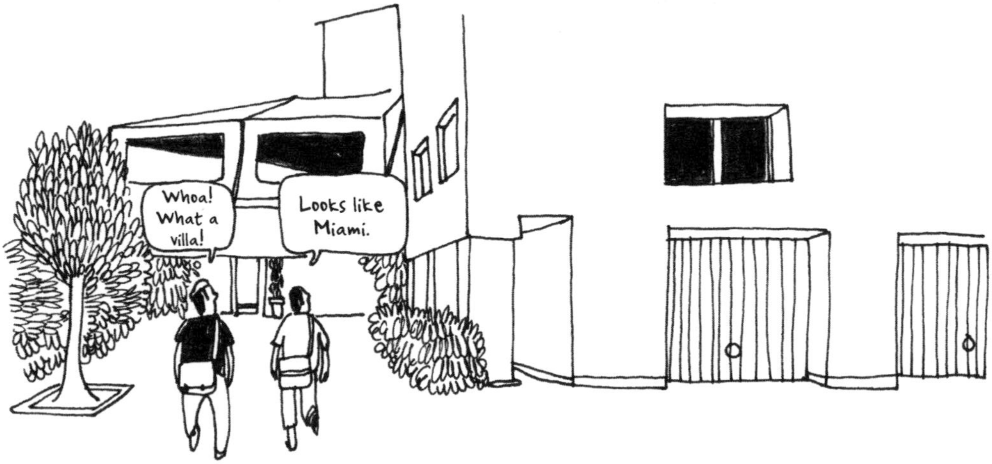
Whoa! What a villa!
Looks like Miami.

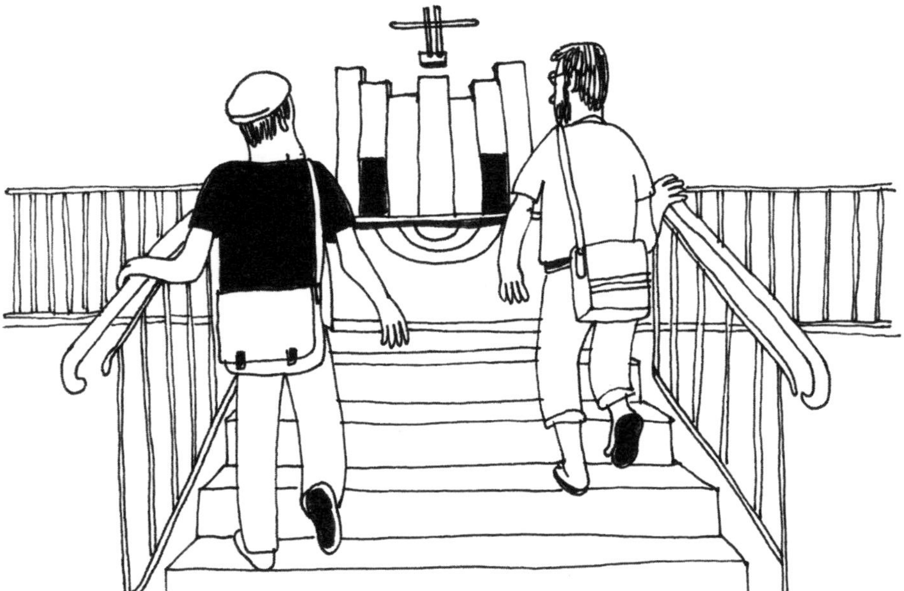

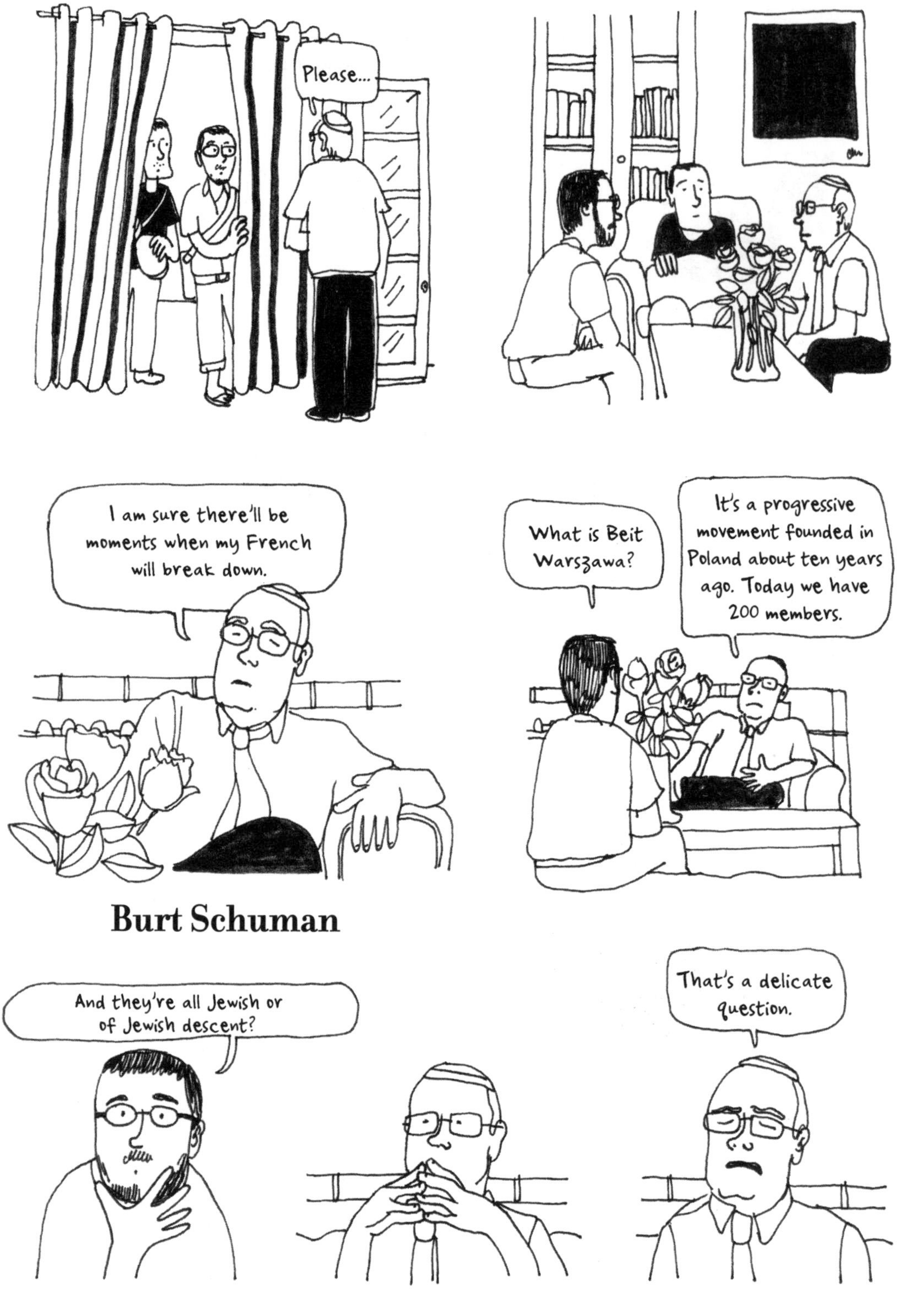
Please...
I am sure there'll be moments when my French will break down.
What is Beit Warszawa?
It's a progressive movement founded in Poland about ten years ago. Today we have 200 members.
And they're all Jewish or of Jewish descent?
That's a delicate question.

Burt Schuman

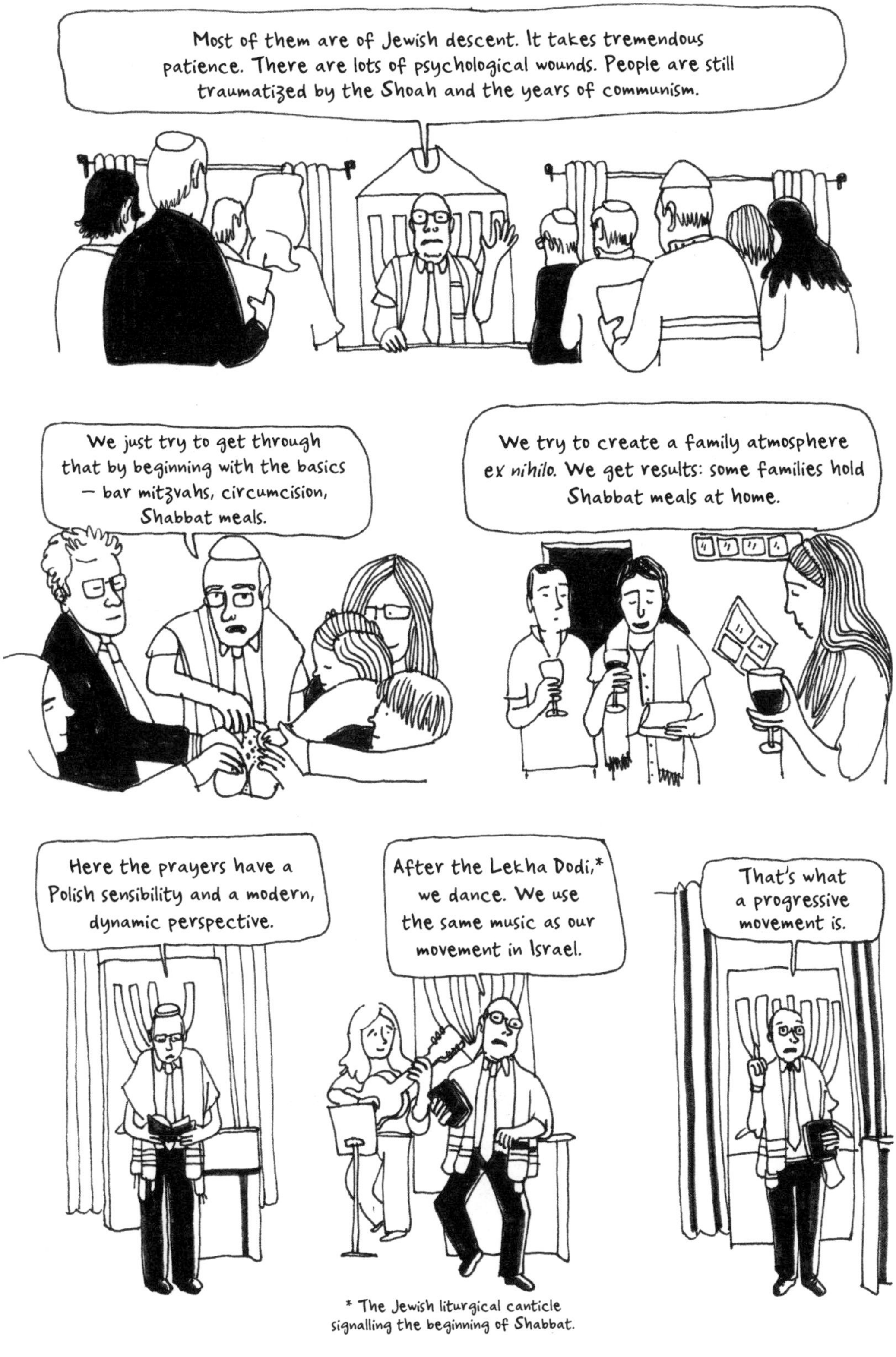
Most of them are of Jewish descent. It takes tremendous patience. There are lots of psychological wounds. People are still traumatized by the Shoah and the years of communism.
We just try to get through that by beginning with the basics — bar mitzvahs, circumcision, Shabbat meals.
We try to create a family atmosphere ex nihilo. We get results: some families hold Shabbat meals at home.
Here the prayers have a Polish sensibility and a modern, dynamic perspective.
After the Lekha Dodi,* we dance. We use the same music as our movement in Israel.
That's what a progressive movement is.

* The Jewish liturgical canticle signalling the beginning of Shabbat.

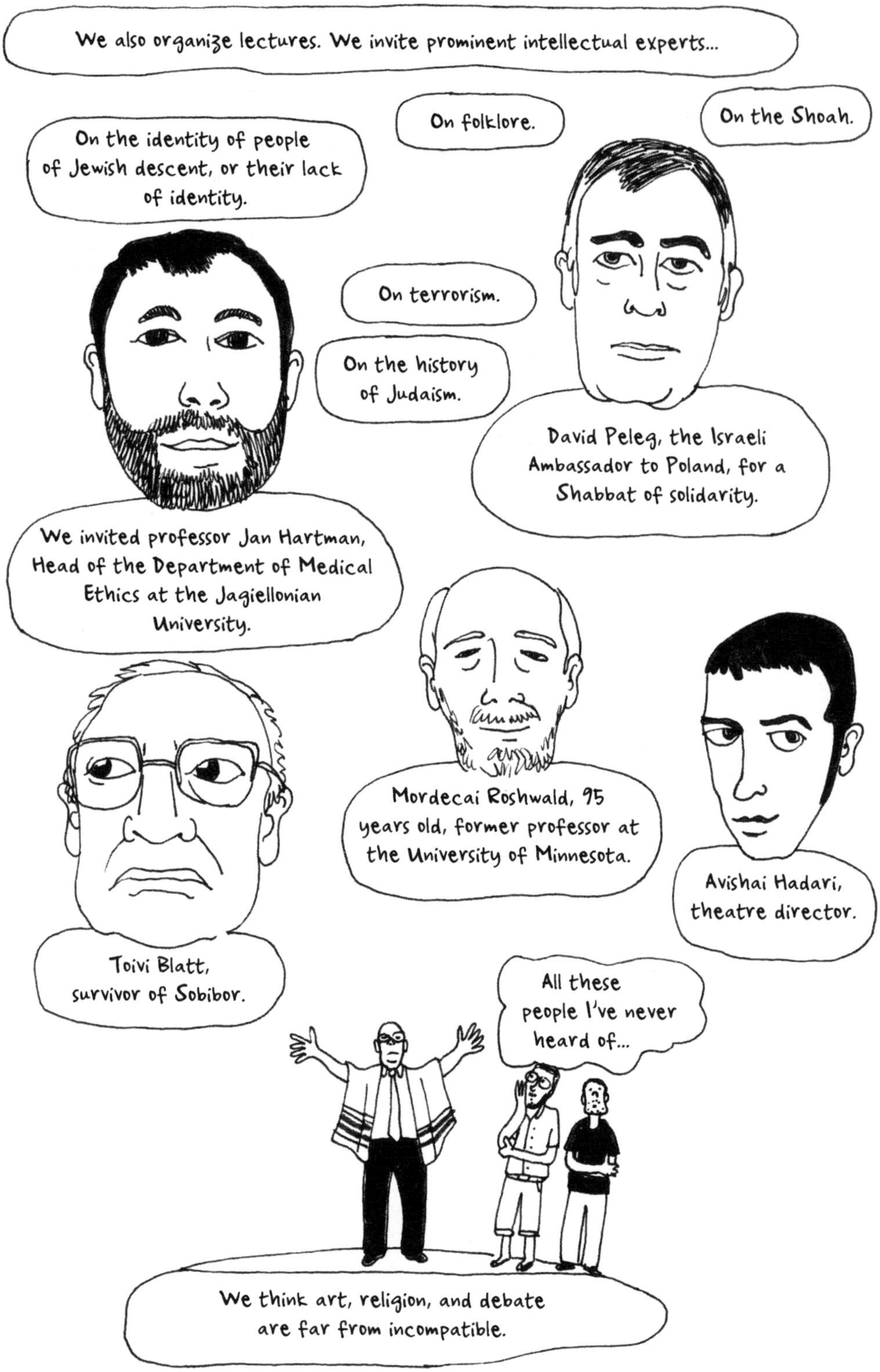
We also organize lectures. We invite prominent intellectual experts...
On the identity of people of Jewish descent, or their lack of identity.
On folklore.
On the Shoah.
On terrorism.
On the history of Judaism.
We invited professor Jan Hartman, Head of the Department of Medical Ethics at the Jagiellonian University.
David Peleg, the Israeli Ambassador to Poland, for a Shabbat of solidarity.
Toivi Blatt, survivor of Sobibor.
Mordecai Roshwald, 95 years old, former professor at the University of Minnesota.
Avishai Hadari, theatre director.
All these people I've never heard of...
We think art, religion, and debate are far from incompatible.

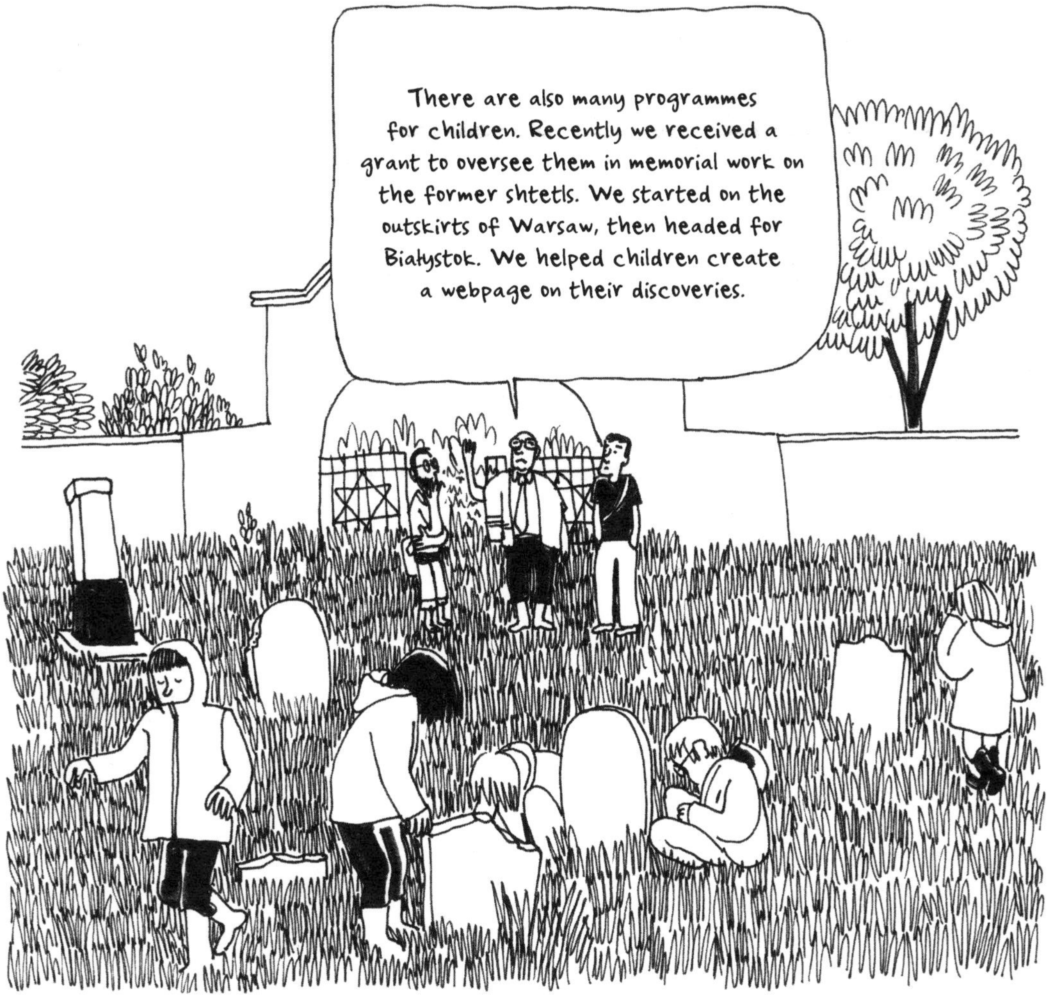
There are also many programmes for children. Recently we received a grant to oversee them in memorial work on the former shtetls. We started on the outskirts of Warsaw, then headed for Białystok. We helped children create a webpage on their discoveries.

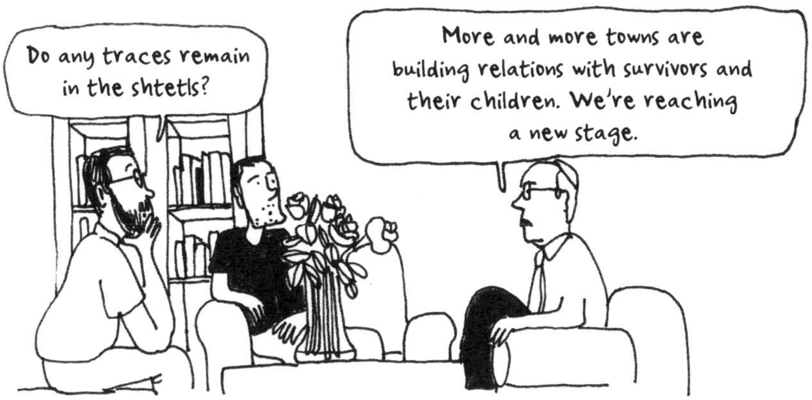
Do any traces remain in the shtetls?
More and more towns are building relations with survivors and their children. We're reaching a new stage.

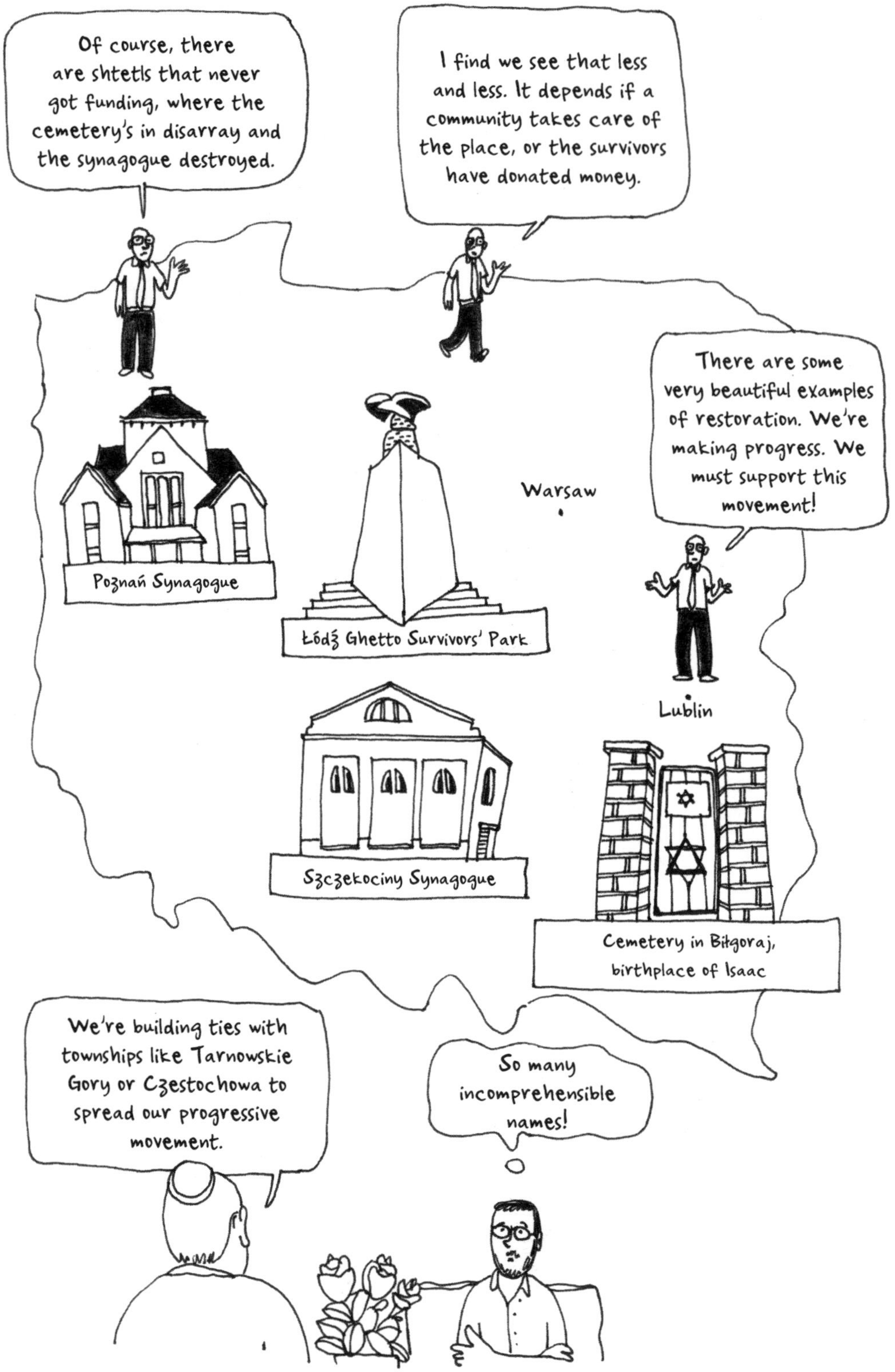
Of course, there are shtetls that never got funding, where the cemetery's in disarray and the synagogue destroyed.
I find we see that less and less. It depends if a community takes care of the place, or the survivors have donated money.
There are some very beautiful examples of restoration. We're making progress. We must support this movement!
Warsaw
Poznań Synagogue
Łódź Ghetto Survivors' Park
Lublin
Szczekociny Synagogue
Cemetery in Biłgoraj, birthplace of Isaac
We're building ties with townships like Tarnowskie Gory or Czestochowa to spread our progressive movement.
So many incomprehensible names!

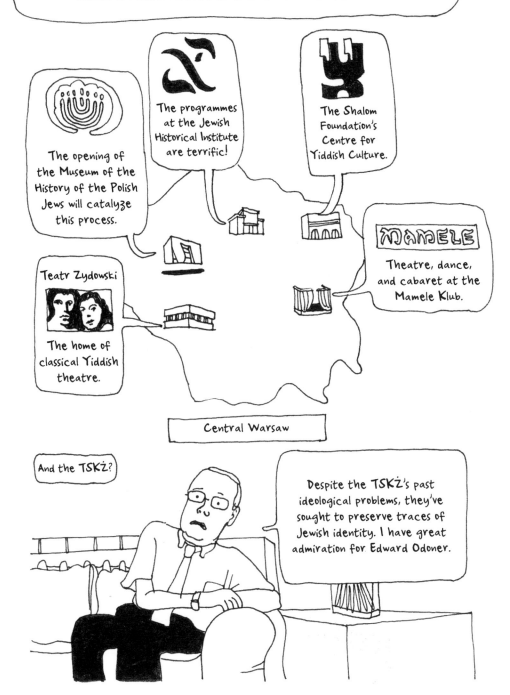

More and more people — Jews, those of Jewish descent, non-Jews — are working to maintain their heritage and this revival of Jewish life. There's a whole bunch of initiatives. Take Warsaw, for instance.

The programmes at the Jewish Historical Institute are terrific!

The Shalom Foundation's Centre for Yiddish Culture.

The opening of the Museum of the History of the Polish Jews will catalyze this process.

Teatr Żydowski

The home of classical Yiddish theatre.

MAMELE

Theatre, dance, and cabaret at the Mamele Klub.

Central Warsaw

And the TSKŻ?

Despite the TSKŻ's past ideological problems, they've sought to preserve traces of Jewish identity. I have great admiration for Edward Odoner.

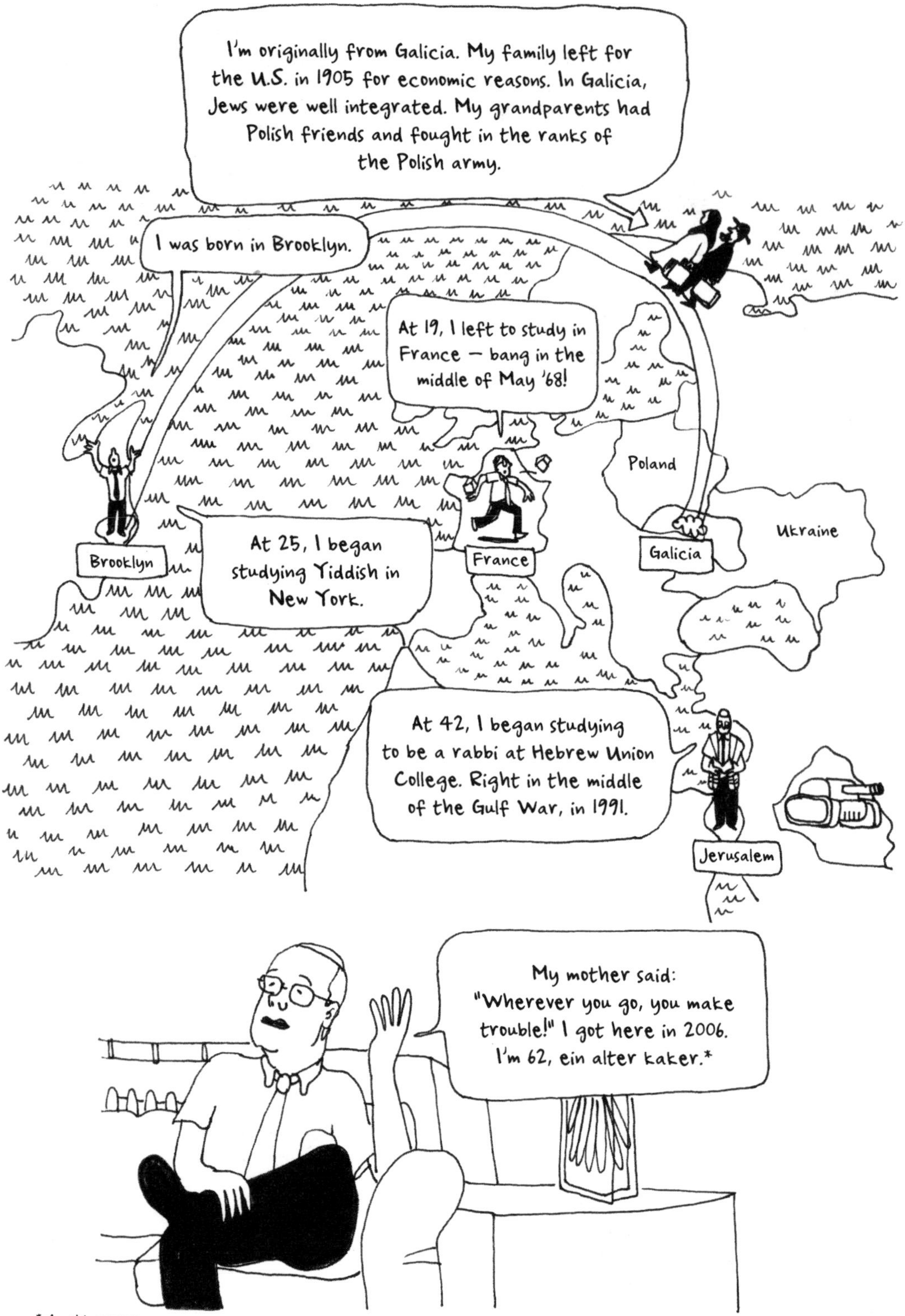
I'm originally from Galicia. My family left for the U.S. in 1905 for economic reasons. In Galicia, Jews were well integrated. My grandparents had Polish friends and fought in the ranks of the Polish army.
I was born in Brooklyn.
At 19, I left to study in France — bang in the middle of May '68!
Poland
Ukraine
Brooklyn
France
Galicia
At 25, I began studying Yiddish in New York.
At 42, I began studying to be a rabbi at Hebrew Union College. Right in the middle of the Gulf War, in 1991.
Jerusalem
My mother said: "Wherever you go, you make trouble!" I got here in 2006. I'm 62, ein alter kaker.*

* An old geezer.

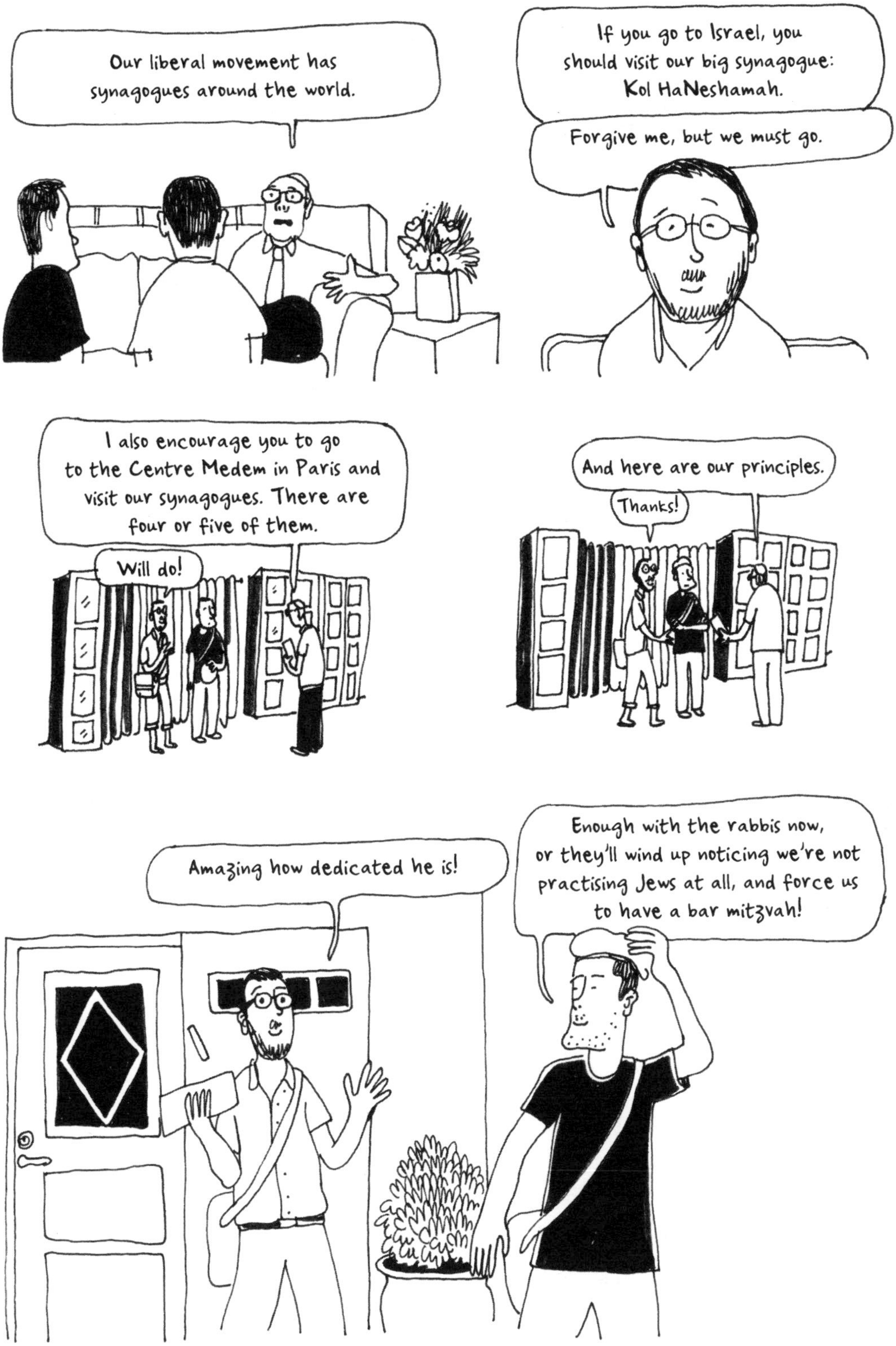
Our liberal movement has synagogues around the world.
If you go to Israel, you should visit our big synagogue: Kol HaNeshamah.
Forgive me, but we must go.
I also encourage you to go to the Centre Medem in Paris and visit our synagogues. There are four or five of them.
Will do!
And here are our principles.
Thanks!
Amazing how dedicated he is!
Enough with the rabbis now, or they'll wind up noticing we're not practising Jews at all, and force us to have a bar mitzvah!

Culinary Interlude

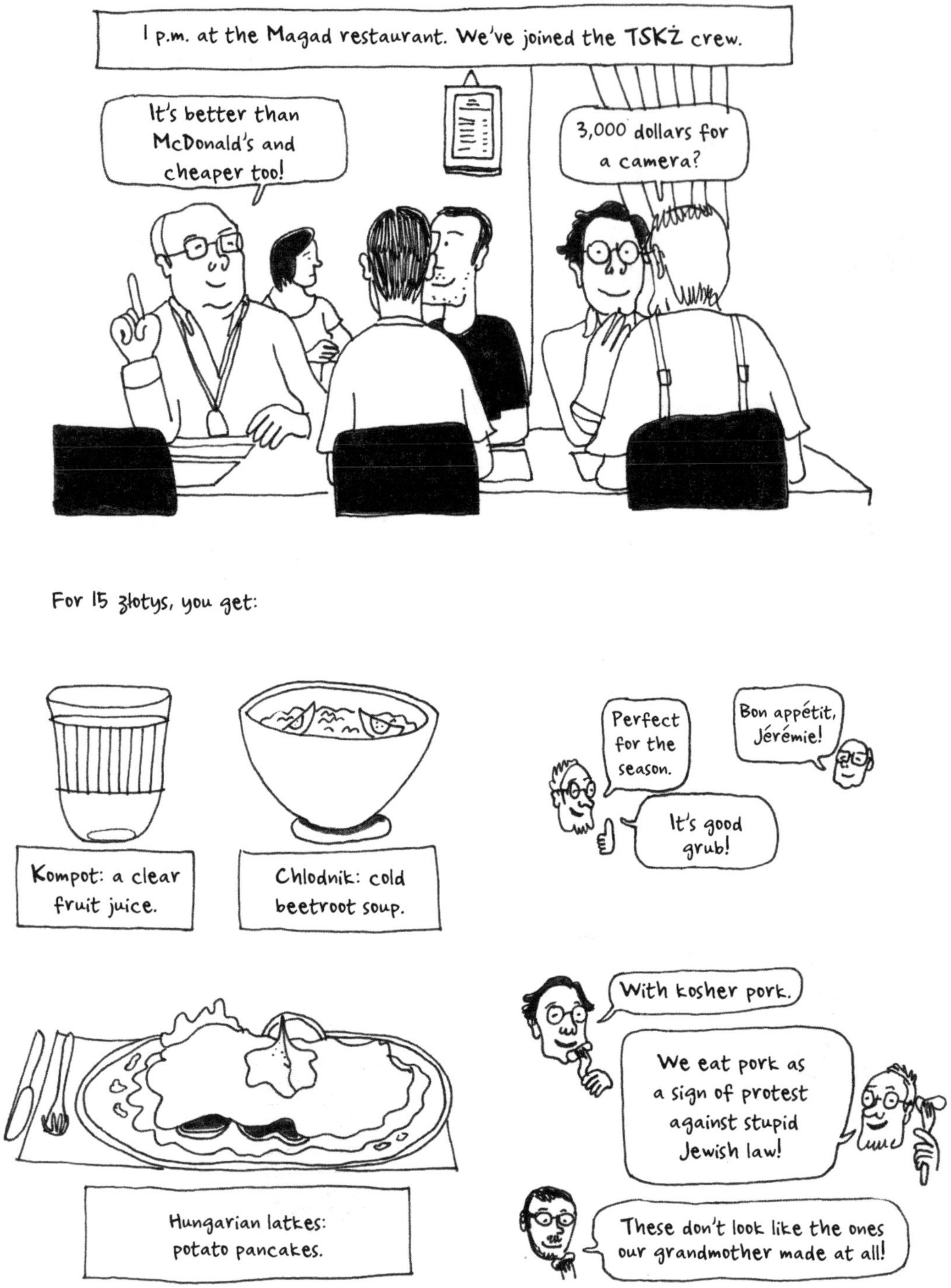
1 p.m. at the Magad restaurant. We've joined the TSKŻ crew.
It's better than McDonald's and cheaper too!
3,000 dollars for a camera?
For 15 złotys, you get:
Kompot: a clear fruit juice.
Chlodnik: cold beetroot soup.
Perfect for the season.
Bon appétit, Jérémie!
It's good grub!
Hungarian latkes: potato pancakes.
With kosher pork.
We eat pork as a sign of protest against stupid Jewish law!
These don't look like the ones our grandmother made at all!

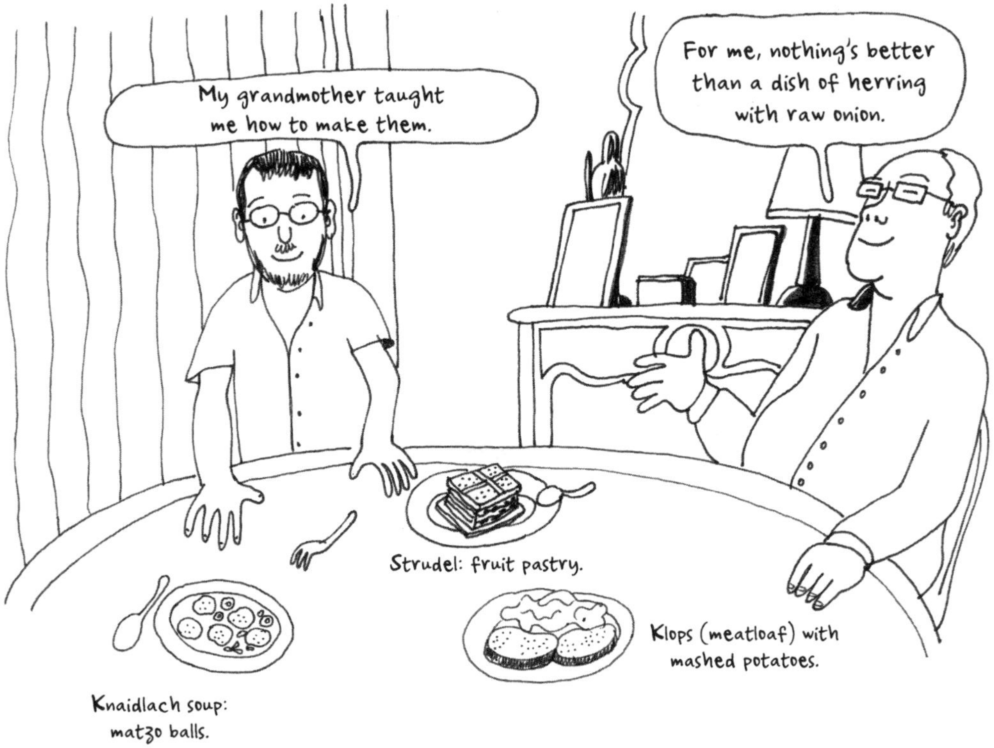
My grandmother taught me how to make them.
For me, nothing's better than a dish of herring with raw onion.
Strudel: fruit pastry.
Klops (meatloaf) with mashed potatoes.
Knaidlach soup: matzo balls.

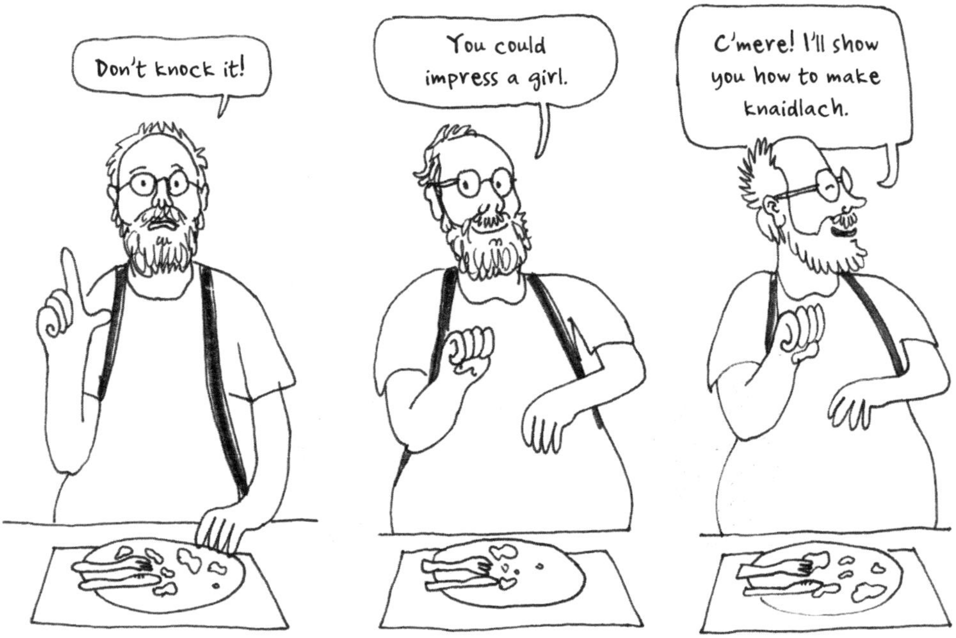
Don't knock it!
You could impress a girl.
C'mere! I'll show you how to make knaidlach.

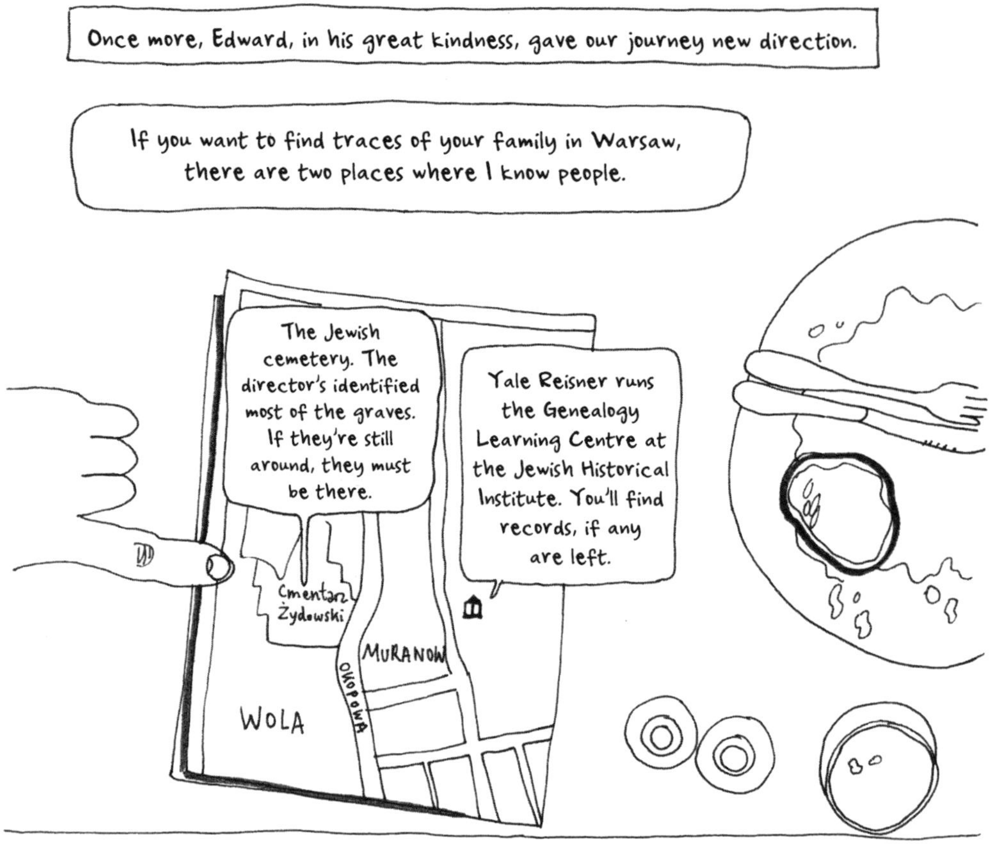
Once more, Edward, in his great kindness, gave our journey new direction.
If you want to find traces of your family in Warsaw, there are two places where I know people.
The Jewish cemetery. The director's identified most of the graves. If they're still around, they must be there.
Yale Reisner runs the Genealogy Learning Centre at the Jewish Historical Institute. You'll find records, if any are left.
Cmentarz Żydowski
MURANOW
OKOPOWA
WOLA

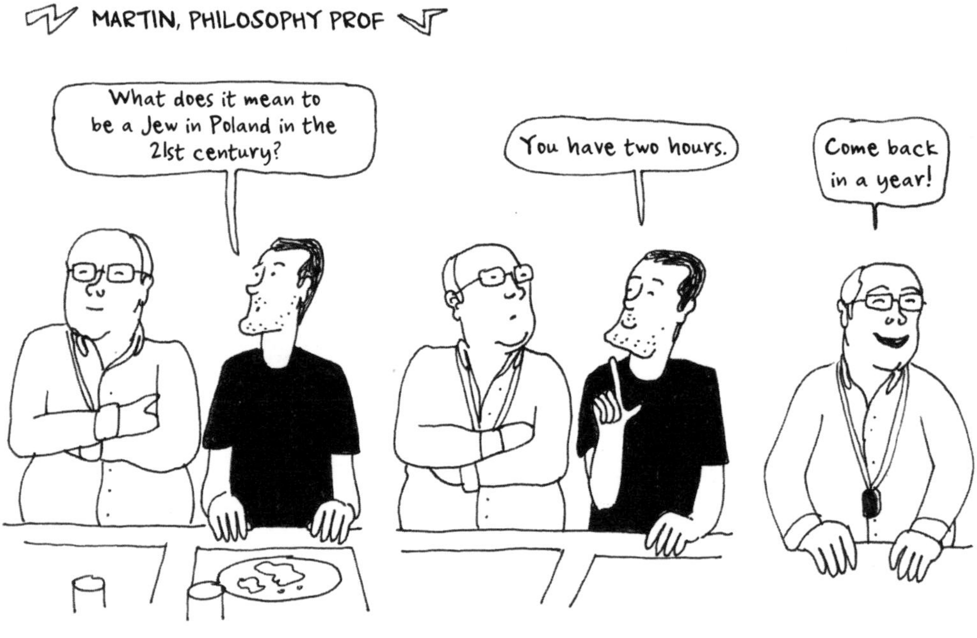
MARTIN, PHILOSOPHY PROF
What does it mean to be a Jew in Poland in the 21st century?
You have two hours.
Come back in a year!

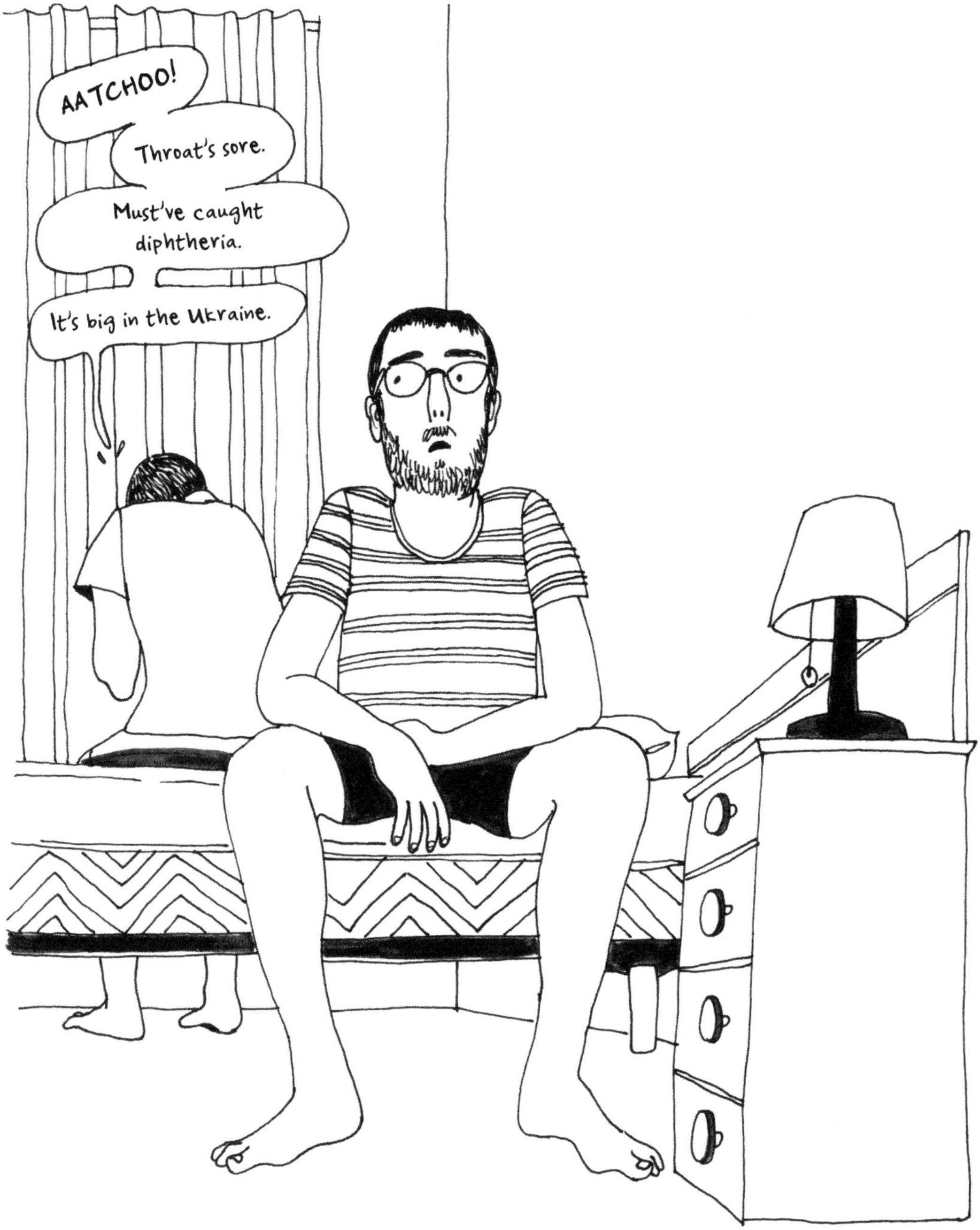
AATCHOO!
Throat's sore.
Must've caught diphtheria.
It's big in the Ukraine.

The Jungle of the Forgotten

Thursday, 1 July, 10 a.m. We reach the cemetery. If traces of our family still remain in Poland, this is where we'll find them. We're looking for the graves of Moszek and Chana, my grandmother's parents.

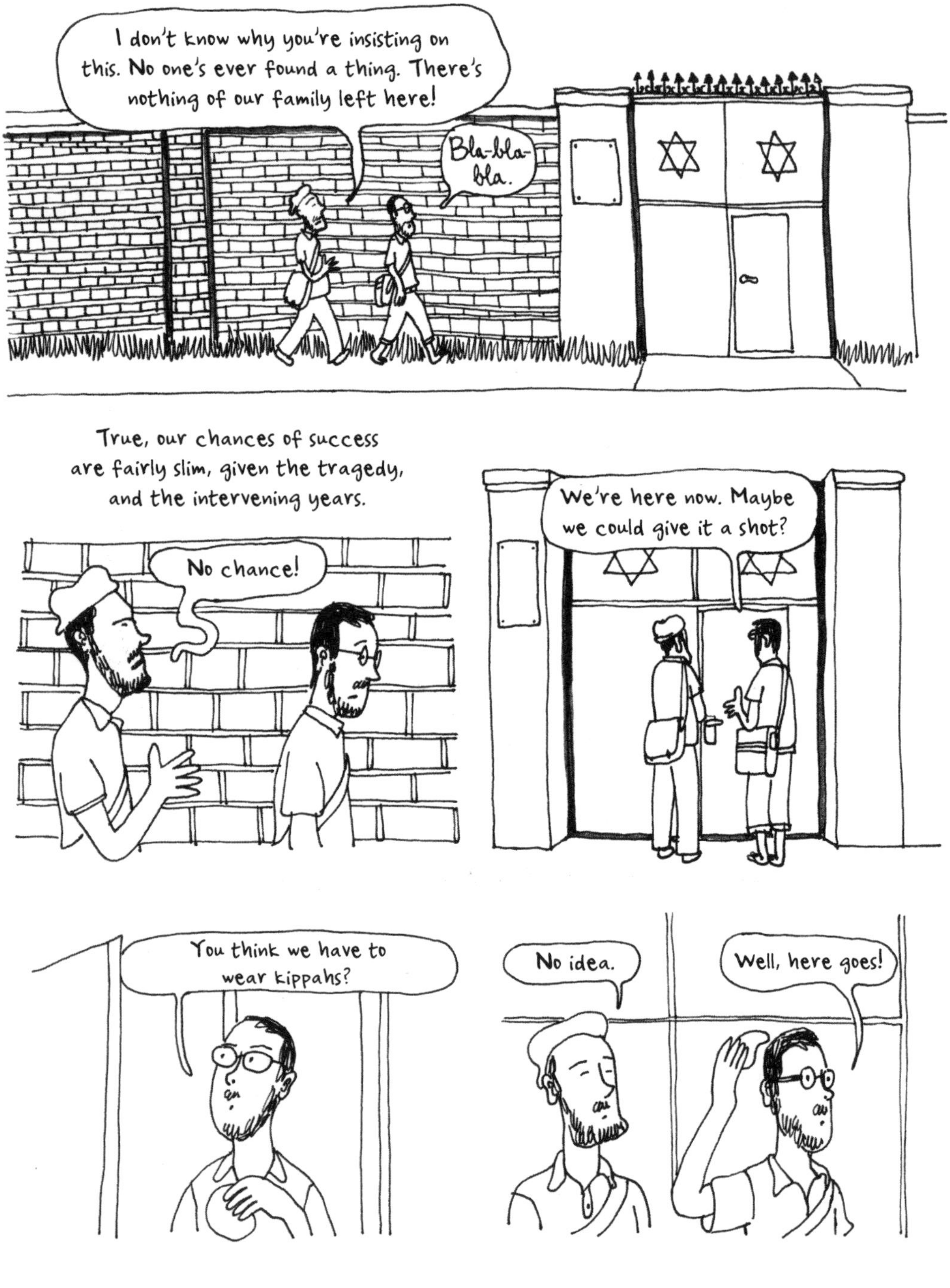
I don't know why you're insisting on this. No one's ever found a thing. There's nothing of our family left here!
Bla-bla-bla.
True, our chances of success are fairly slim, given the tragedy, and the intervening years.
No chance!
We're here now. Maybe we could give it a shot?
You think we have to wear kippahs?
No idea.
Well, here goes!

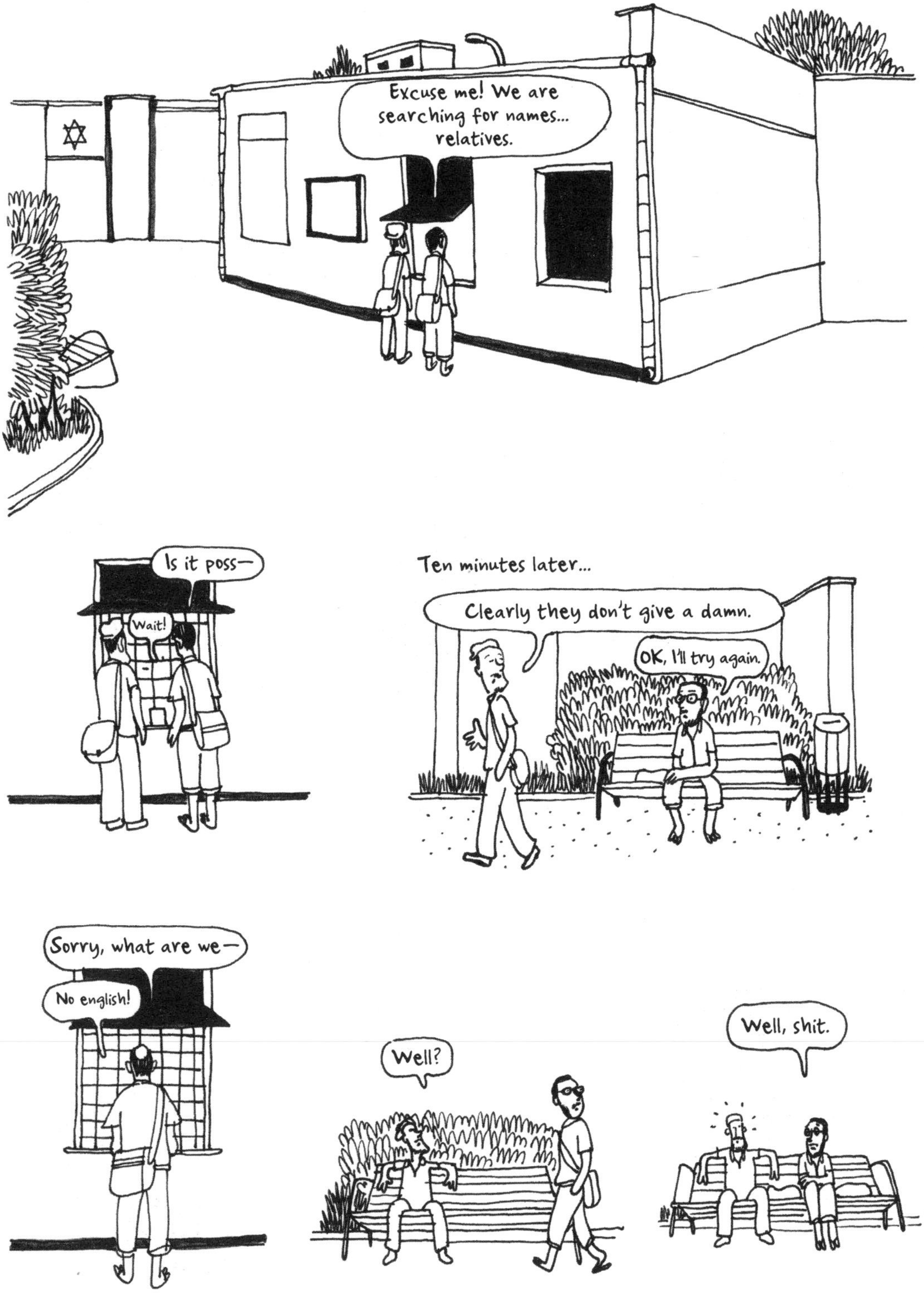
Excuse me! We are searching for names... relatives.
Is it poss—
Wait!
Ten minutes later...
Clearly they don't give a damn.
OK, I'll try again.
Sorry, what are we—
No english!
Well?
Well, shit.

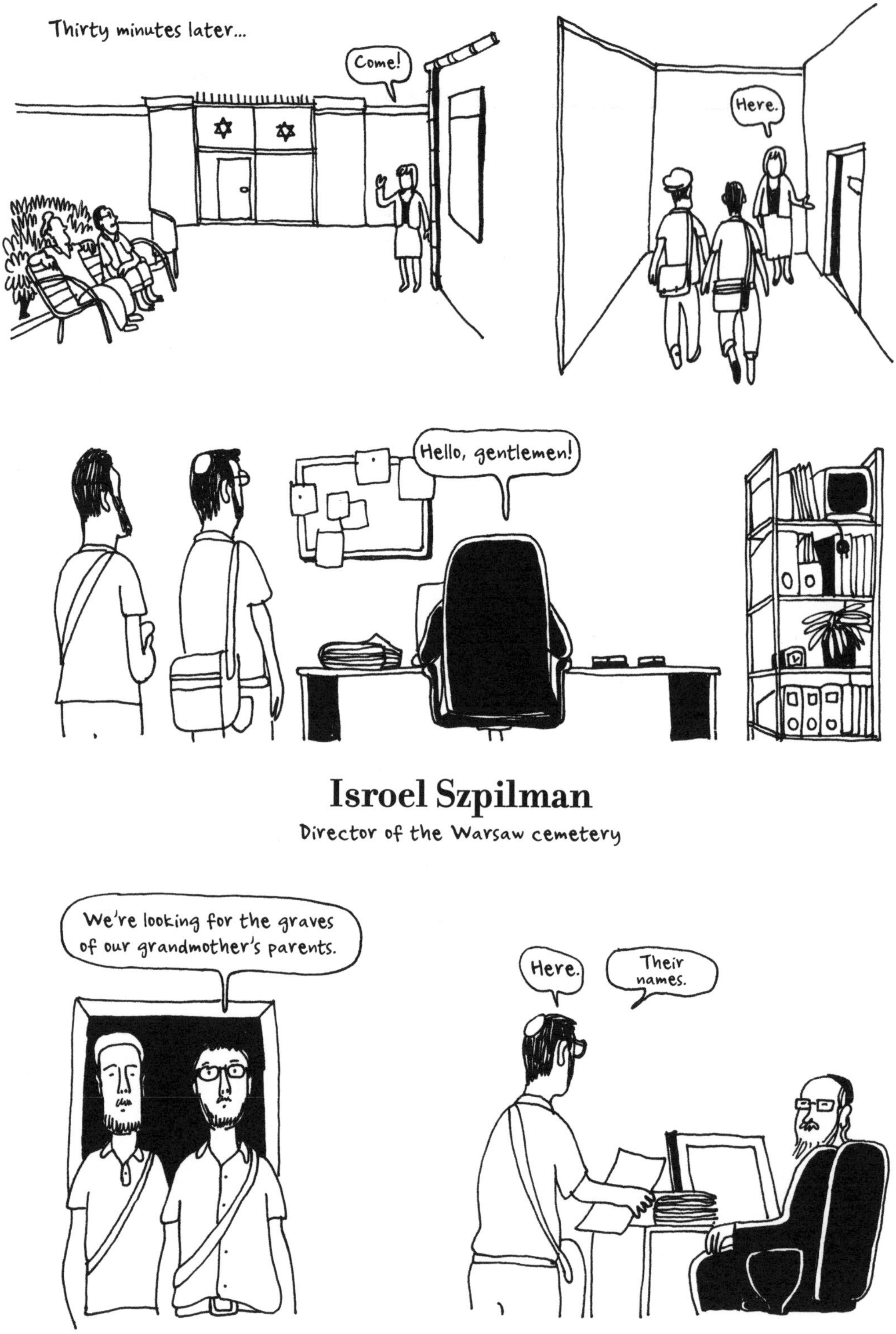
Thirty minutes later...
Come!
Here.
Hello, gentlemen!
Isroel Szpilman
Director of the Warsaw cemetery
We're looking for the graves of our grandmother's parents.
Here.
Their names.

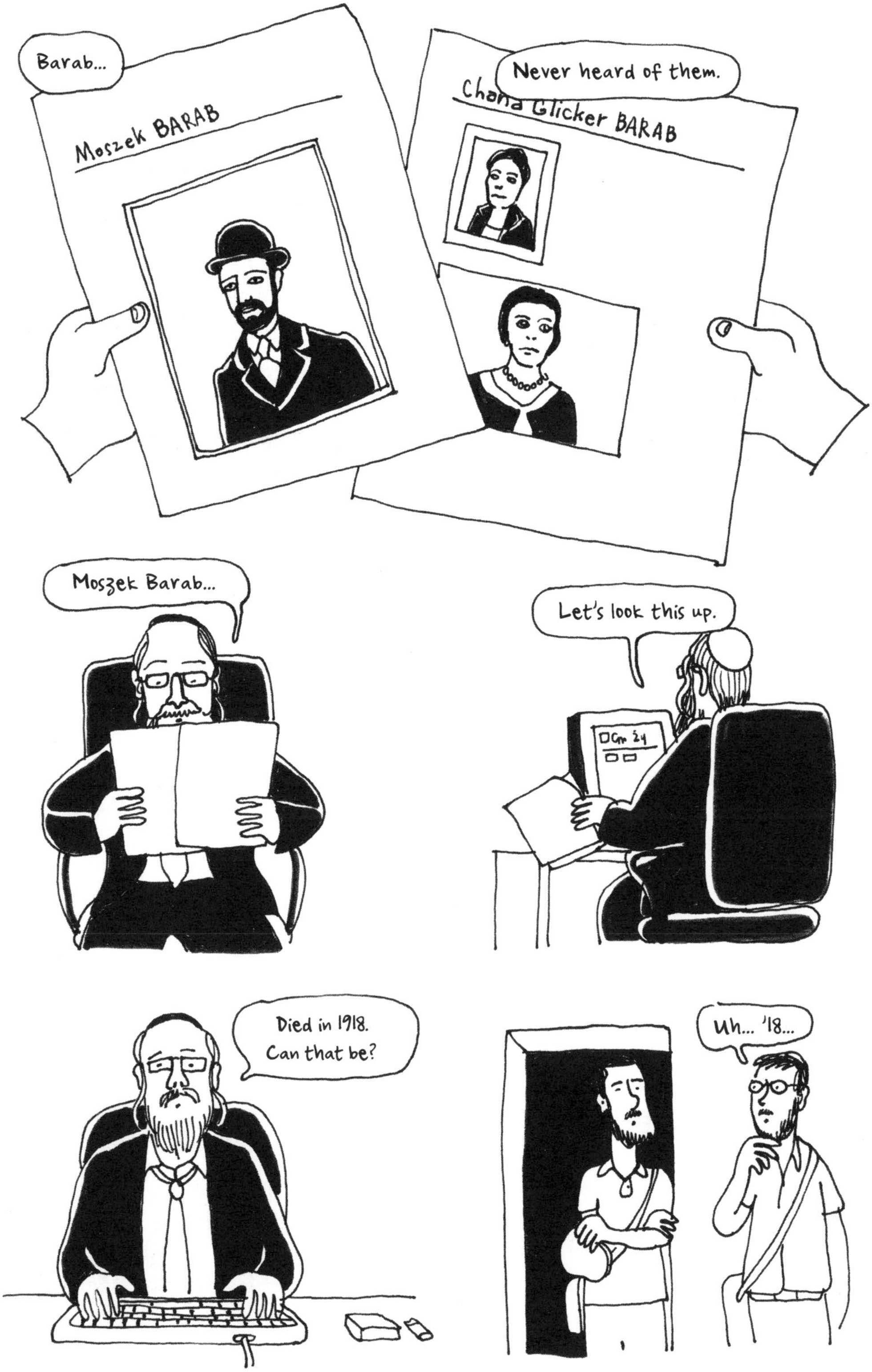
Barab...
Moszek BARAB
Never heard of them.
Chana Glicker BARAB
Moszek Barab...
Let's look this up.
Died in 1918.
Can that be?
Uh... '18...

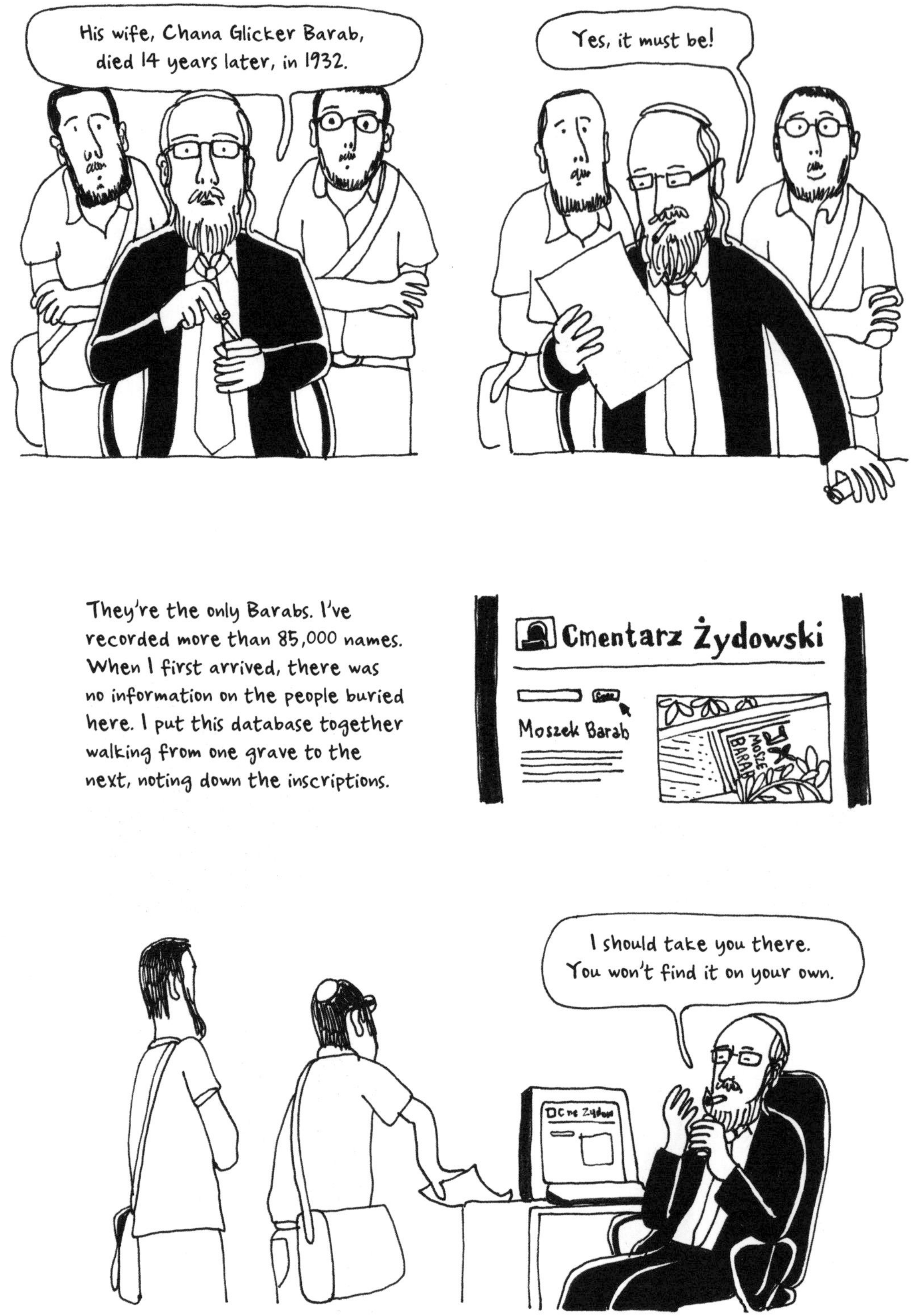
His wife, Chana Glicker Barab, died 14 years later, in 1932.
Yes, it must be!
They're the only Barabs. I've recorded more than 85,000 names. When I first arrived, there was no information on the people buried here. I put this database together walking from one grave to the next, noting down the inscriptions.
Cmentarz Żydowski
Moszek Barab
MOSZE BARAB
I should take you there. You won't find it on your own.

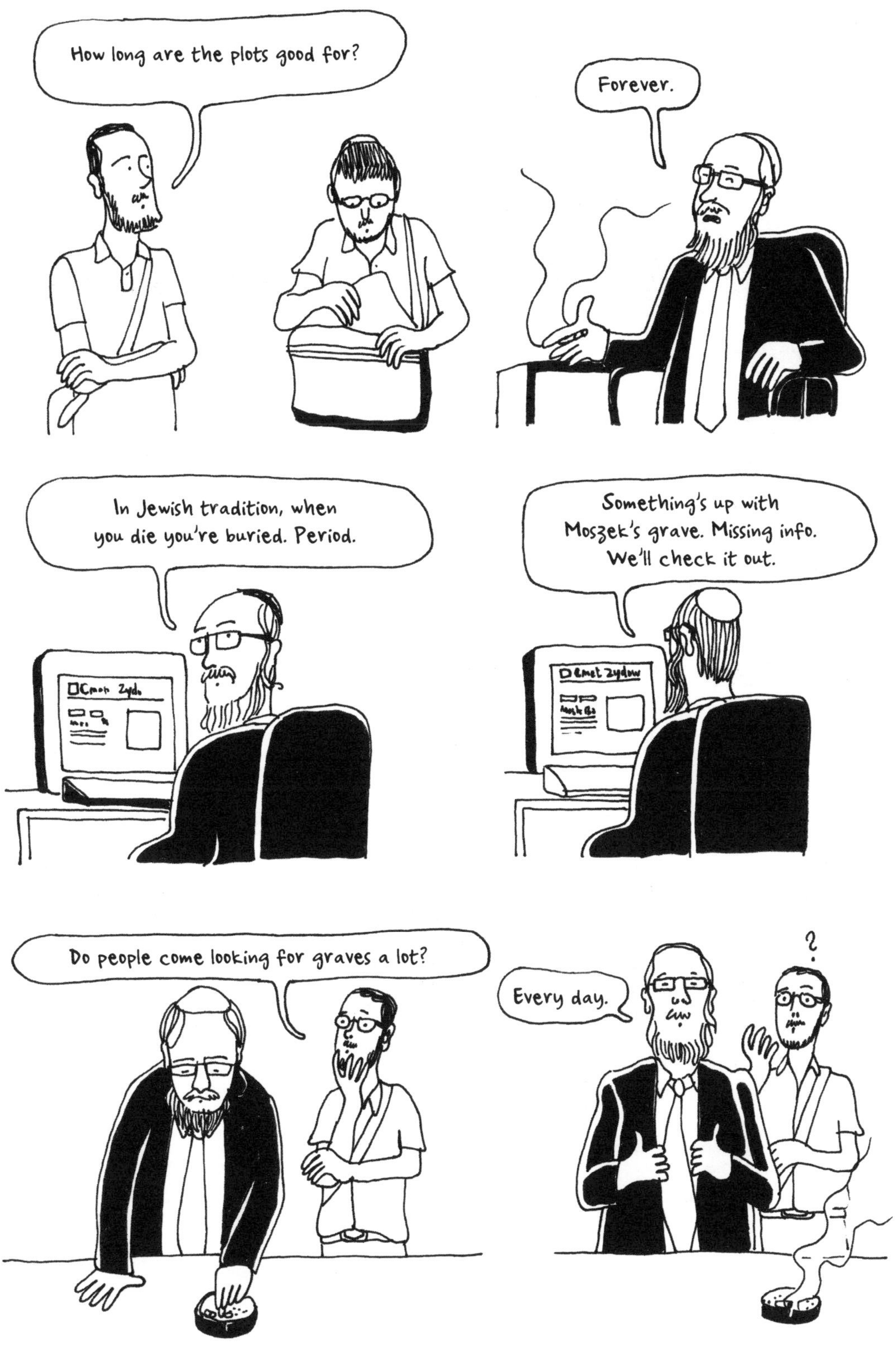
How long are the plots good for?
Forever.
In Jewish tradition, when you die you're buried. Period.
Something's up with Moszek's grave. Missing info. We'll check it out.
Do people come looking for graves a lot?
Every day.
?

Mr. Szpilman asked us to wait outside.

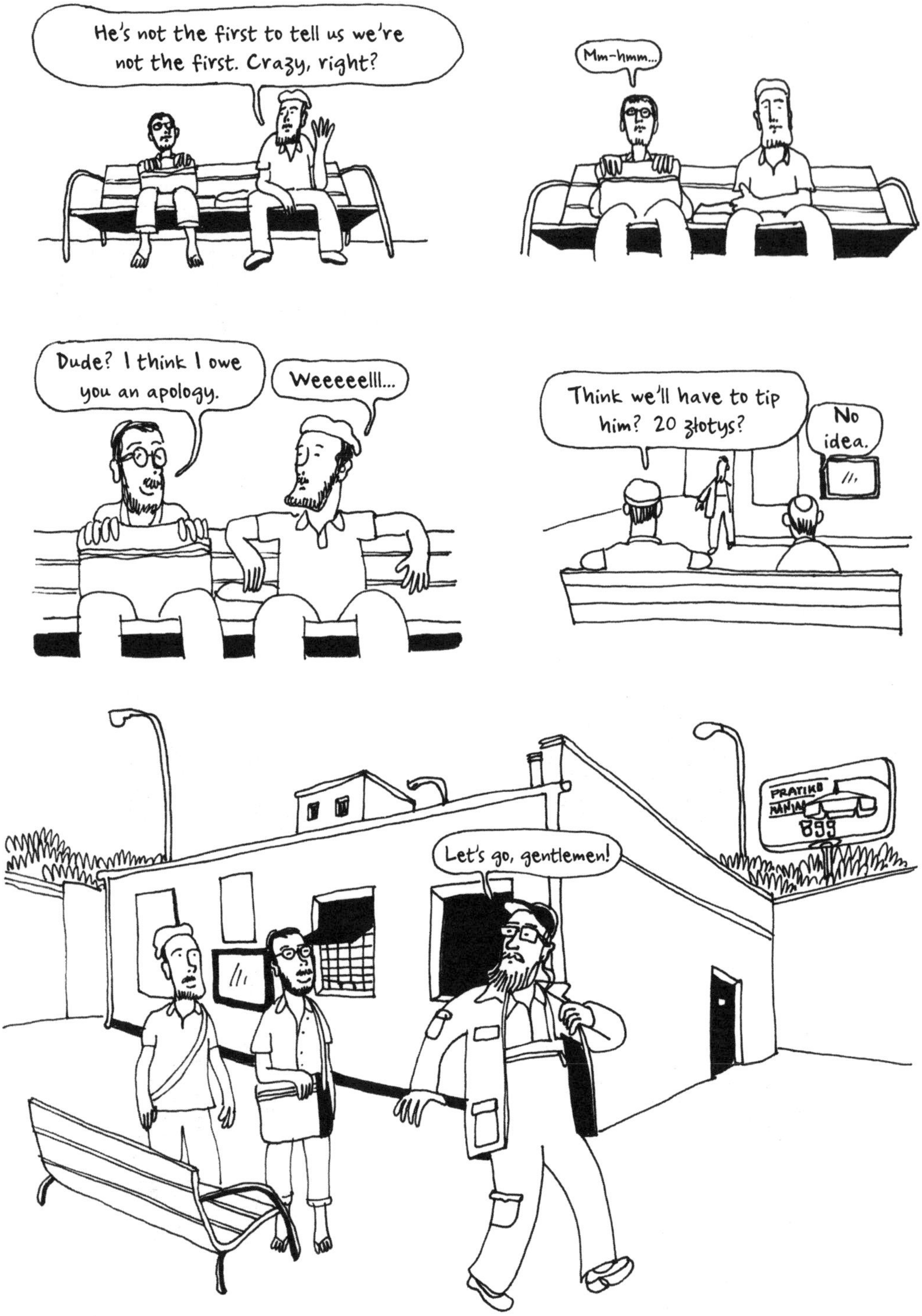

He's not the first to tell us we're not the first. Crazy, right?
Mm-hmm...
Dude? I think I owe you an apology.
Weeeeelll...
Think we'll have to tip him? 20 złotys?
No idea.
Let's go, gentlemen!

With more than 250,000 graves over 30 hectares, this is one of the biggest Jewish cemeteries in Europe.

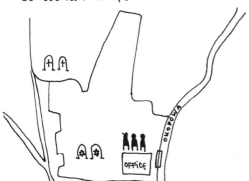

At last, we reach a place that bears witness to how large the Jewish community once was.

Have you been at this job long?

I started in 2002. I'm from Katowice. I moved to Warsaw to join the community.

What did your family do during the war?

They lived down south, under Soviet occupation. My grandfather was sent to Siberia.

Did Poles hide your family?

No! Absolutely not!

Who took care of the cemetery before you?

Ah.

A sad affair...

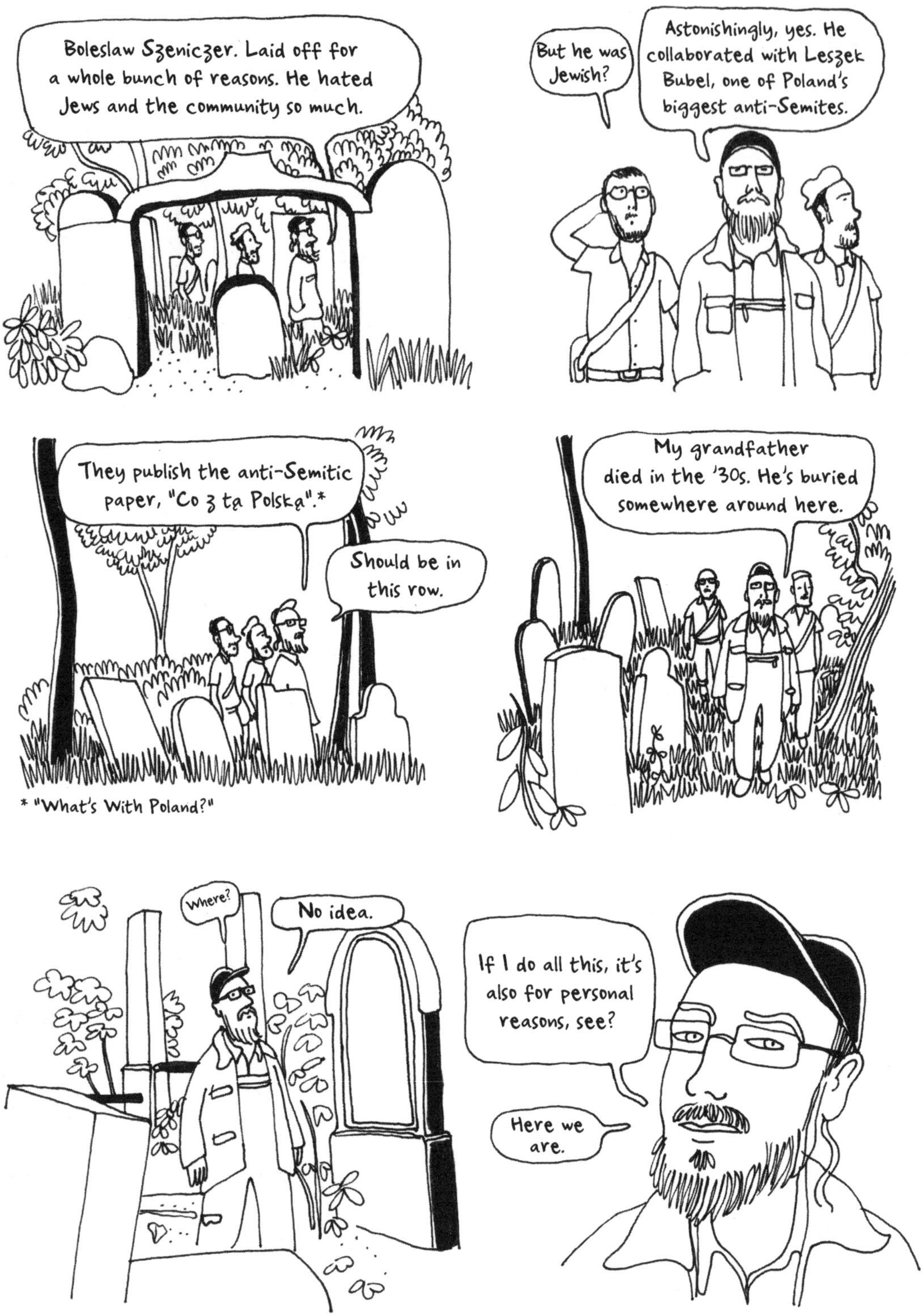
Boleslaw Szeniczer. Laid off for a whole bunch of reasons. He hated Jews and the community so much.
But he was Jewish?
Astonishingly, yes. He collaborated with Leszek Bubel, one of Poland's biggest anti-Semites.
They publish the anti-Semitic paper, "Co z tą Polską".*
Should be in this row.
* "What's With Poland?"
My grandfather died in the '30s. He's buried somewhere around here.
Where?
No idea.
If I do all this, it's also for personal reasons, see?
Here we are.

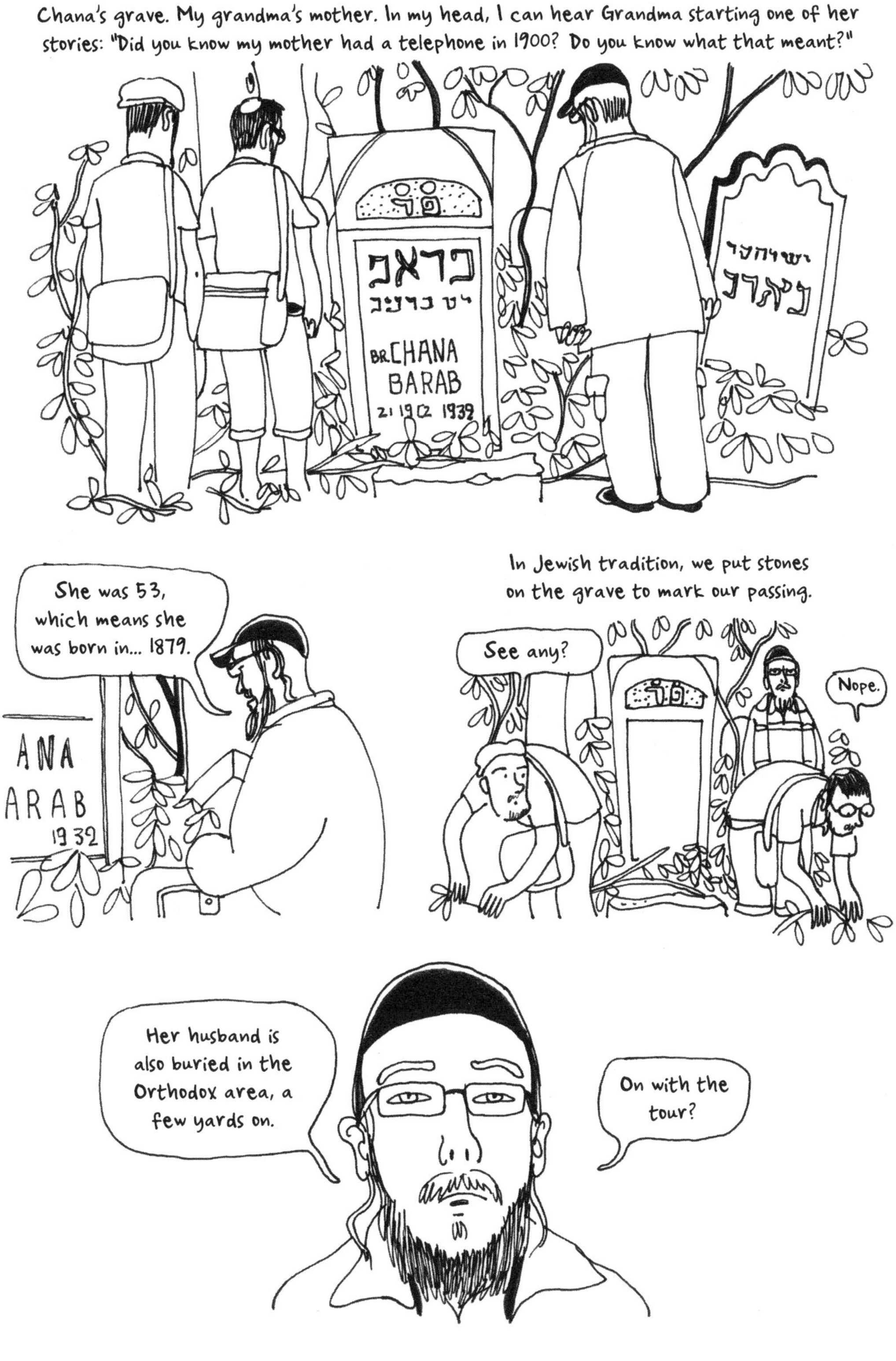
Chana's grave. My grandma's mother. In my head, I can hear Grandma starting one of her stories: "Did you know my mother had a telephone in 1900? Do you know what that meant?"
BR. CHANA
BARAB
She was 53, which means she was born in... 1879.
ANA
ARAB
1932
In Jewish tradition, we put stones on the grave to mark our passing.
See any?
Nope.
Her husband is also buried in the Orthodox area, a few yards on.
On with the tour?

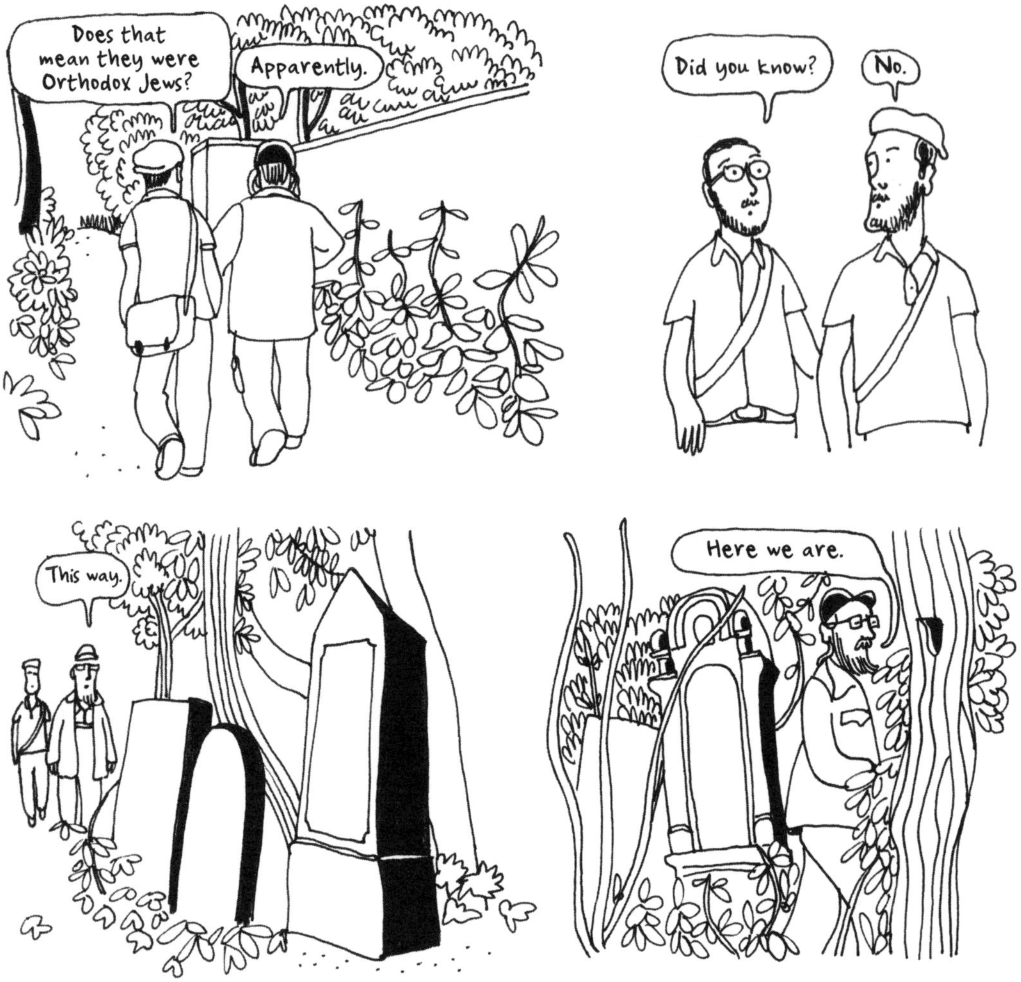
Does that mean they were Orthodox Jews?
Apparently.
Did you know?
No.
This way.
Here we are.

In my head, my grandmother starts another story: "My father built houses. He was a very respected contractor. He only did business with goys!"*

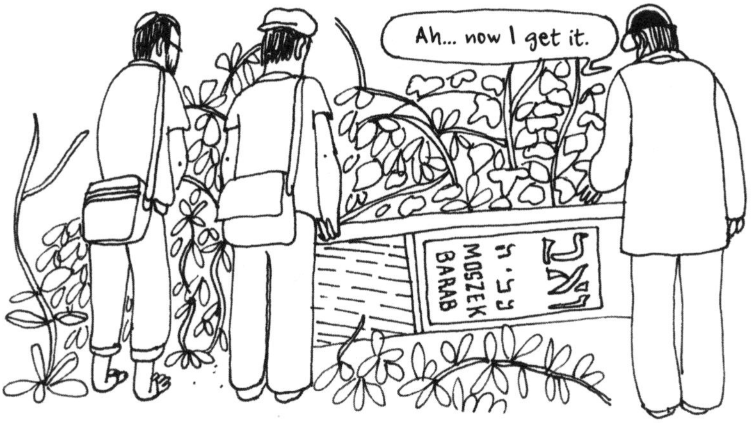
Ah... now I get it.
MOSZEK
BARAB

* Non-Jews.

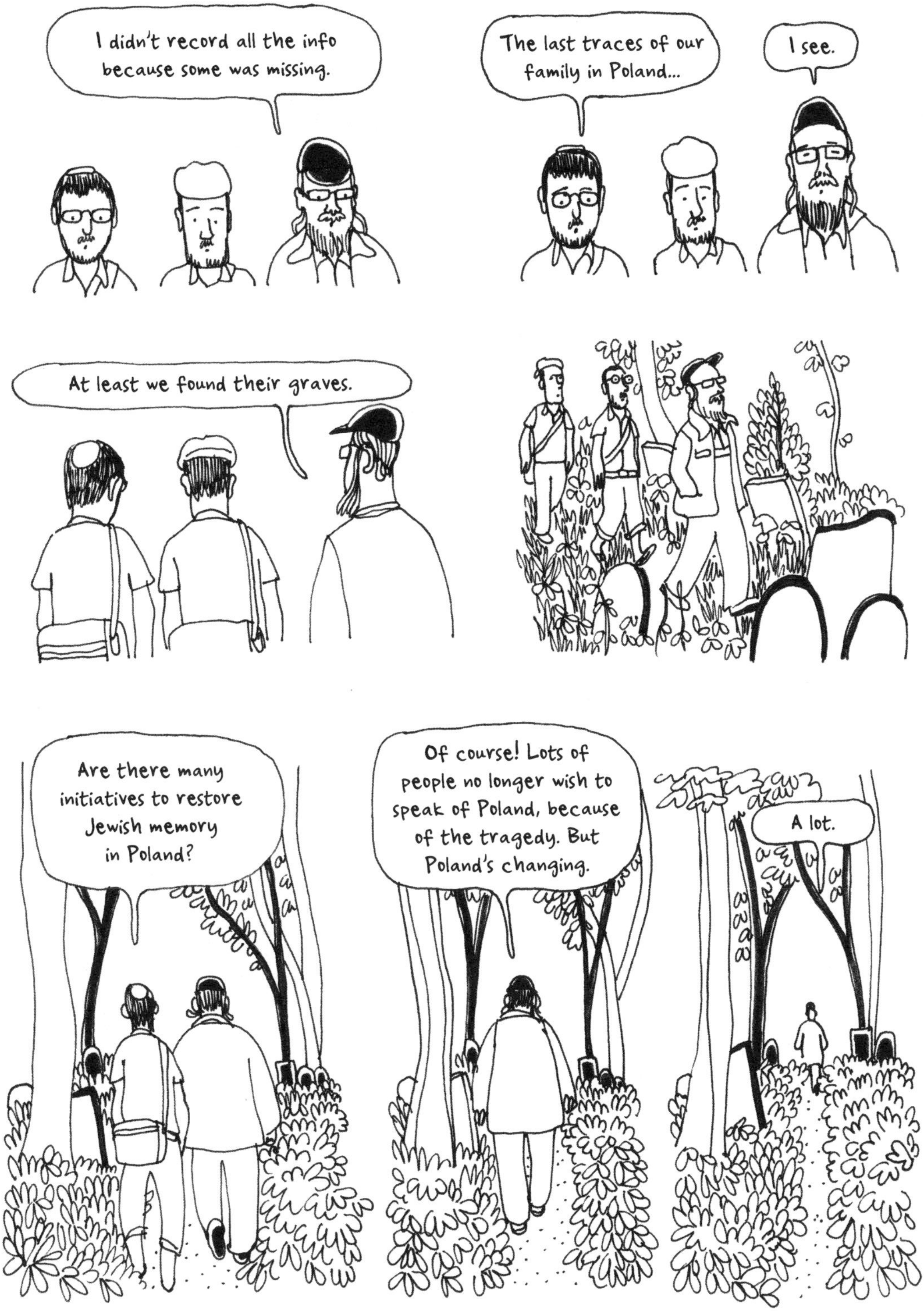
I didn't record all the info because some was missing.
The last traces of our family in Poland...
I see.
At least we found their graves.
Are there many initiatives to restore Jewish memory in Poland?
Of course! Lots of people no longer wish to speak of Poland, because of the tragedy. But Poland's changing.
A lot.

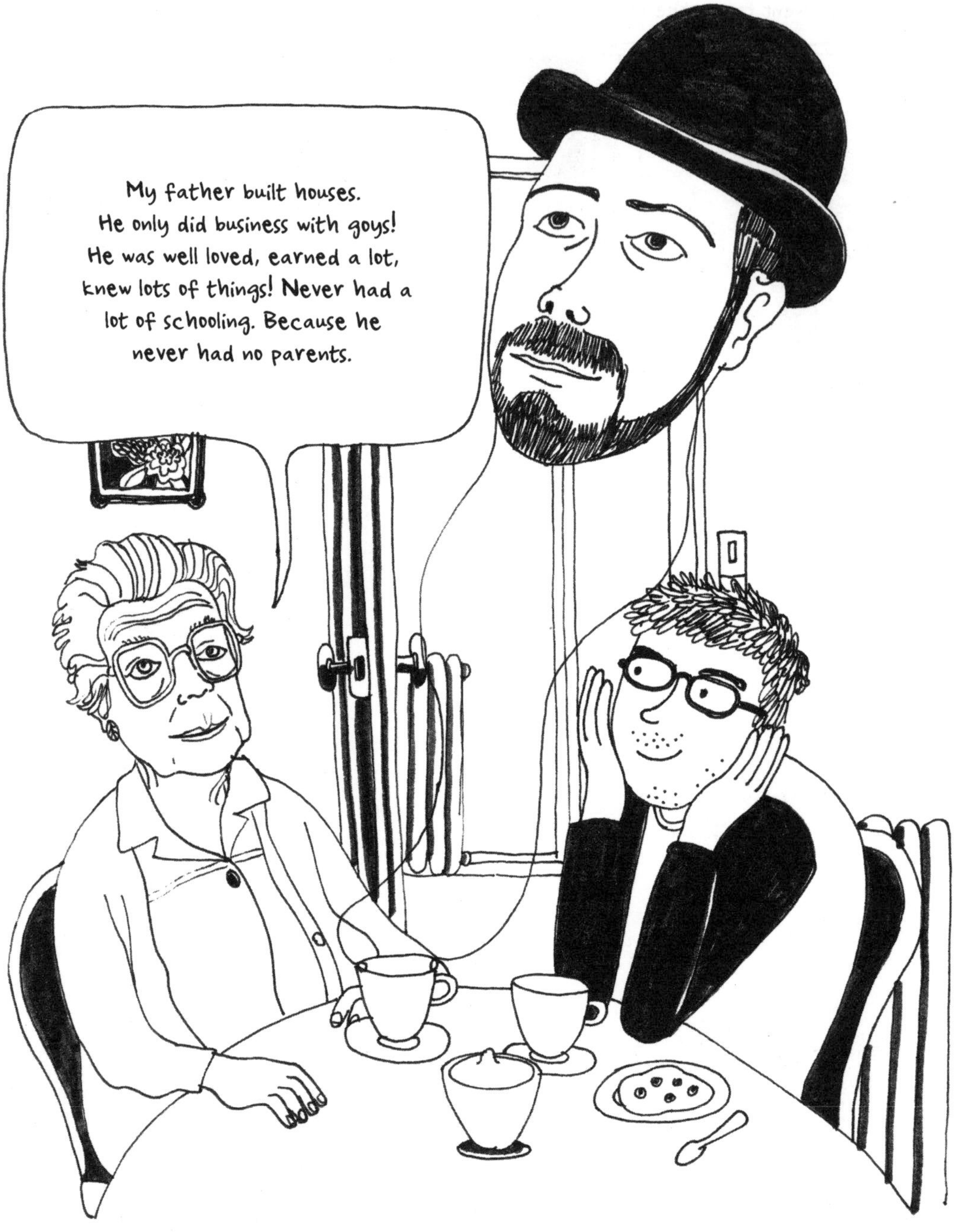
My father built houses. He only did business with goys! He was well loved, earned a lot, knew lots of things! Never had a lot of schooling. Because he never had no parents.

Once upon a time in Warsaw…

He lived with his uncle and grandmother. Not a lot of room! When he came of age, they went to see the rabbi. Because when you needed advice, you asked a rabbi.

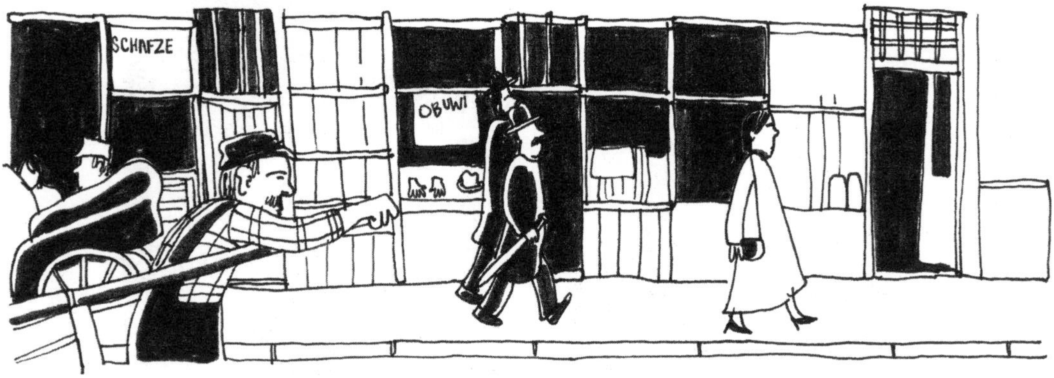
SCHAFZE
OBUWI

There were some interesting people back then.

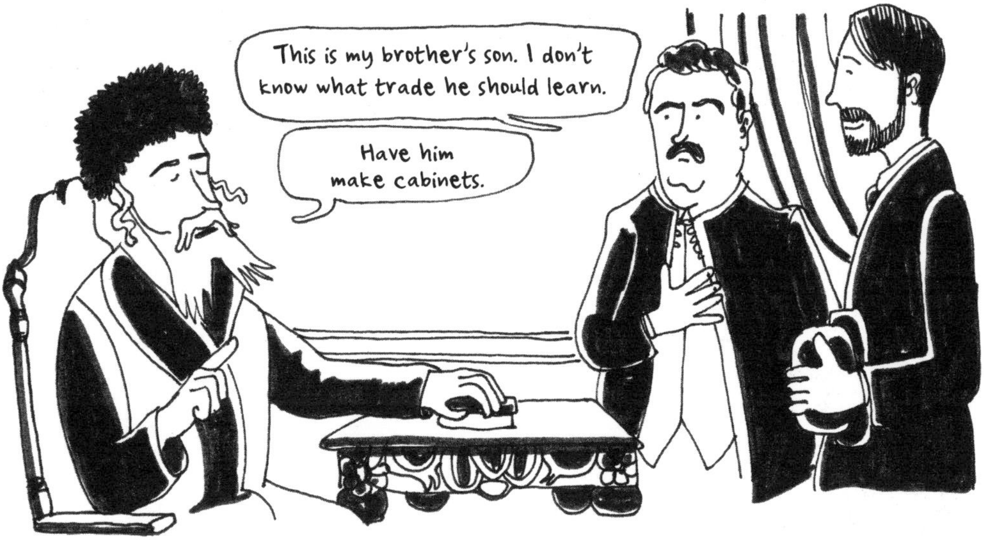
This is my brother's son. I don't know what trade he should learn.
Have him make cabinets.

The rabbi said a cabinetmaker, so he found someone to take him on.

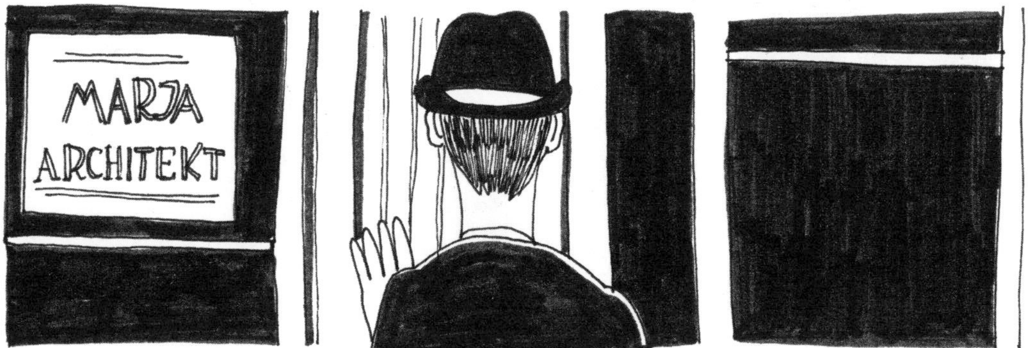
MARJA
ARCHITEKT

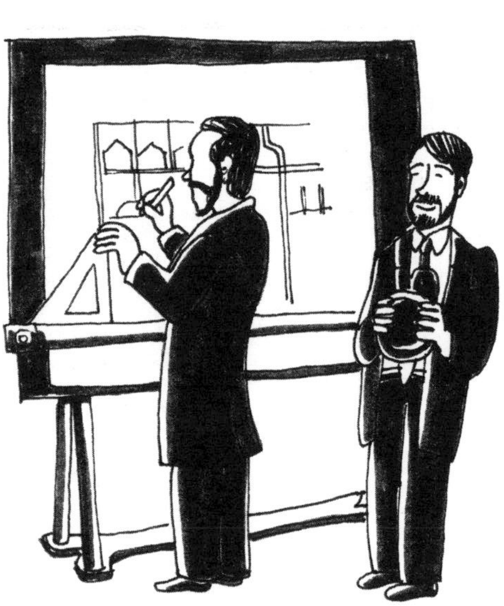
It was an architect
who needed a workman.

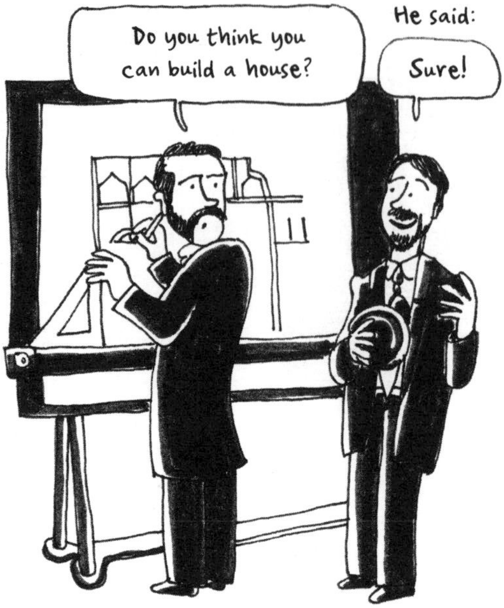
He saw my father was highly competent.
Do you think you can build a house?
He said:
Sure!

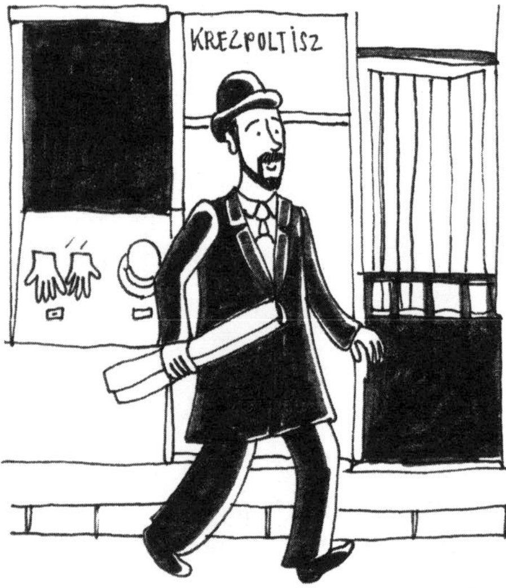
So he started. They gave him some blueprints. He'd never had much schooling, I'm telling you. They gave him the plans and he took them home.
KREZPOLTISZ

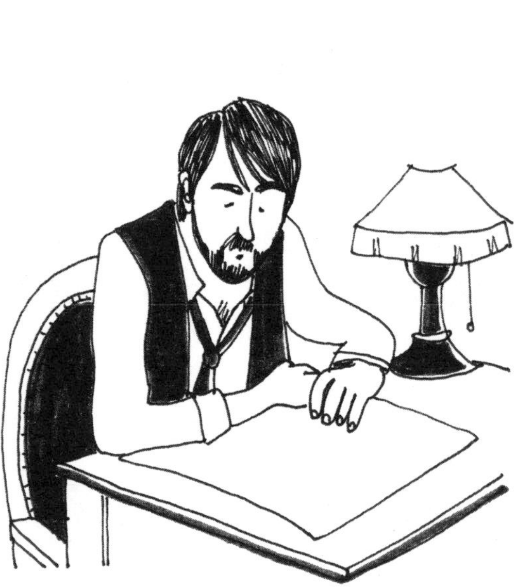
He went over them at home.
Something shocked him.
He didn't like what he saw.

He came up with a good solution.
So he went to the architect and said:

If this goes over here, then that won't work.

The architect, he stared at him and said:

Mr. Barab, I may have an education, but you're a natural! I can draw up plans, but you know how to build them!

So he needed to find people good at woodwork, construction. He had to deal with Polacks, drunks!

ZAHKR I MA

My father was always up on the scaffolding. Once, he had a hundred men working for him.

My father, he knew my mother was always worried about him being up on the scaffolding. So he said:

You know what? I'll give you a telephone!

When he climbed up the scaffolding, he always brought the men cigarettes. Never went up empty-handed.

Fridays or Saturdays were payday. He had a little iron cashbox. Back then they paid with gold pieces. He paid everyone their gold and then bought them a round of vodka and snacks.

PECTOPAH·I RESTAURACJA

ZYWIEC

So you see how well my father did? How could you not love a man like that? With absolute respect!

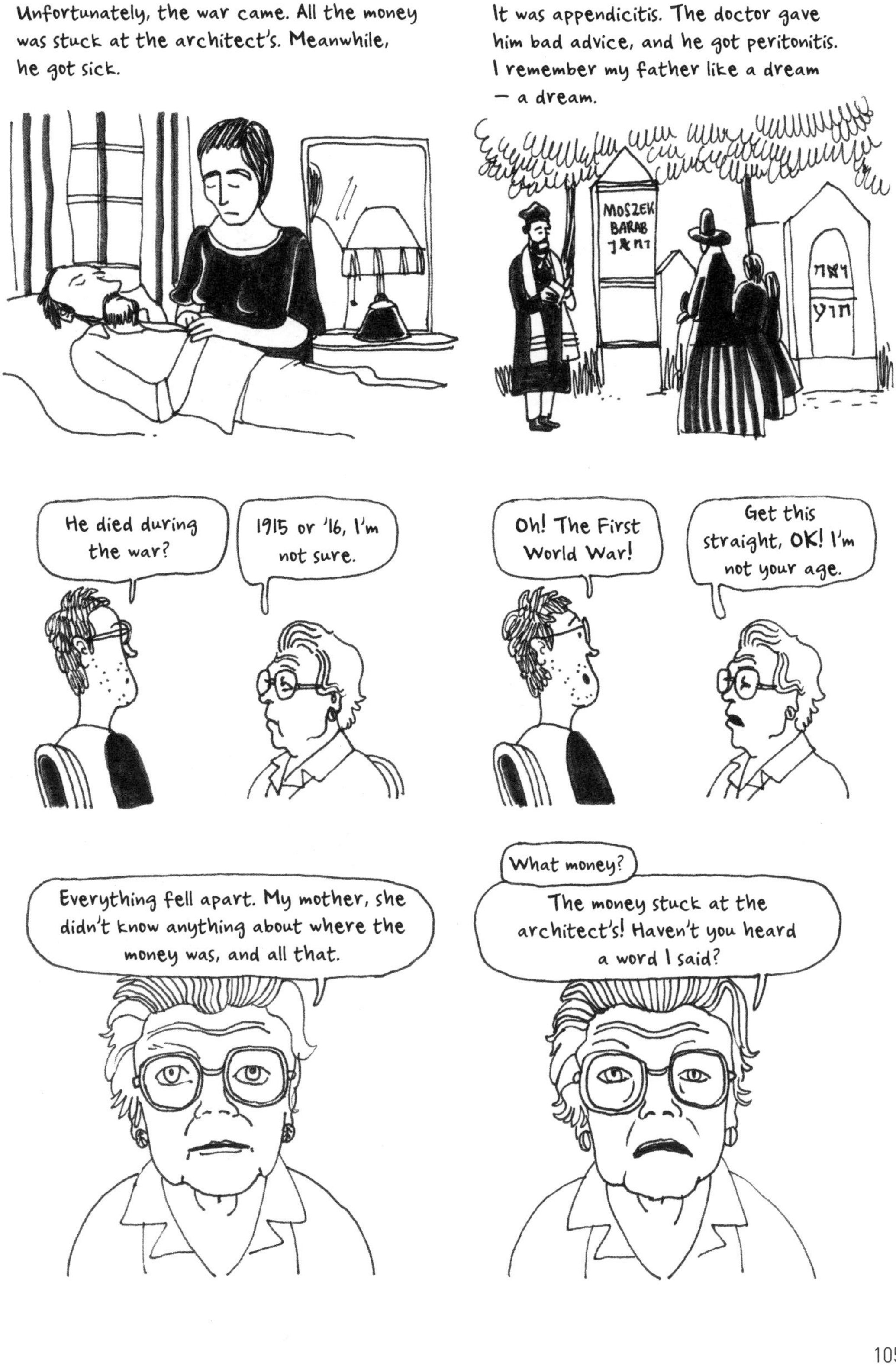
Unfortunately, the war came. All the money was stuck at the architect's. Meanwhile, he got sick.
It was appendicitis. The doctor gave him bad advice, and he got peritonitis. I remember my father like a dream — a dream.
MOSZEK BARAB
He died during the war?
1915 or '16, I'm not sure.
Oh! The First World War!
Get this straight, OK! I'm not your age.
Everything fell apart. My mother, she didn't know anything about where the money was, and all that.
What money?
The money stuck at the architect's! Haven't you heard a word I said?

But since she was was very well-to-do, my mother, she'd bought rich clothes for all her children. And there were a lot of girls — four or five.

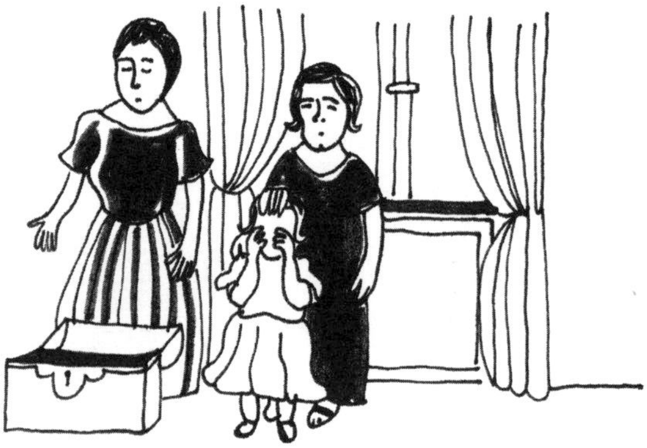

So to my mother they said they could give her whatever she wanted, but only for gold or clothes.

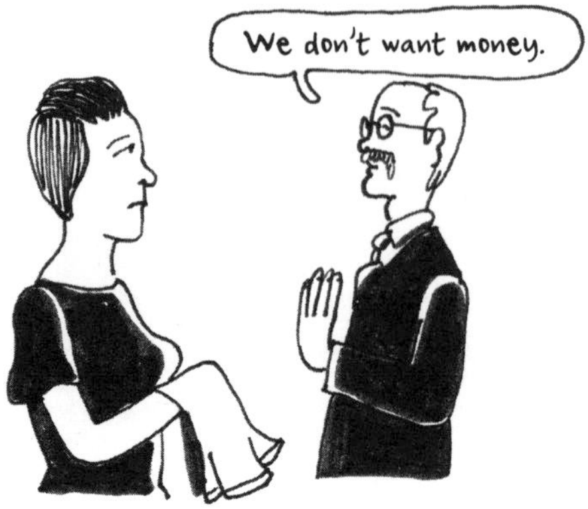
We don't want money.

Back then it was roubles. Back then Russia had occupied Poland. We weren't allowed to learn Polish. Sarah said she went down to the cellar with my American sister to learn Polish.

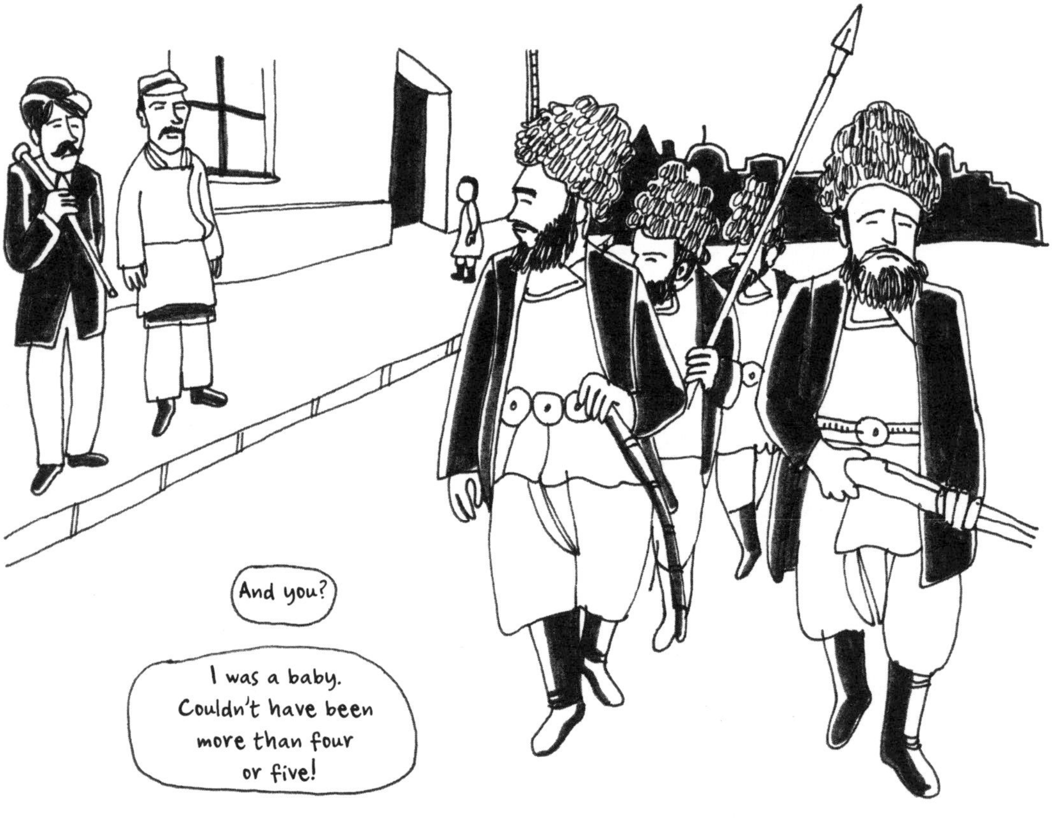
And you?
I was a baby. Couldn't have been more than four or five!

After that, Cossacks came into our house, to see if there were any guns, they said. Real crooks, those Russians! They waved their lances around, threatened us if we didn't do what they said. They stole all our linen. Thieves! Crooks!

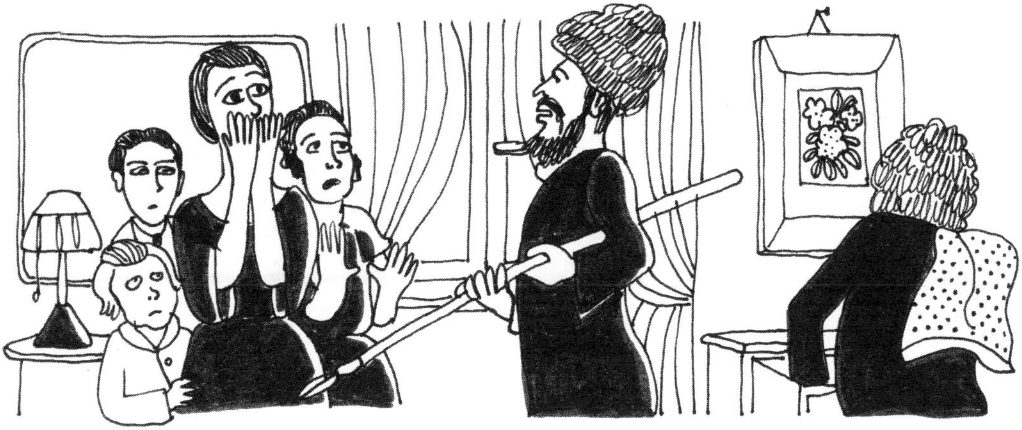

Poverty came later. My mother, she worked. She was a hatmaker. She made samples and sold them.

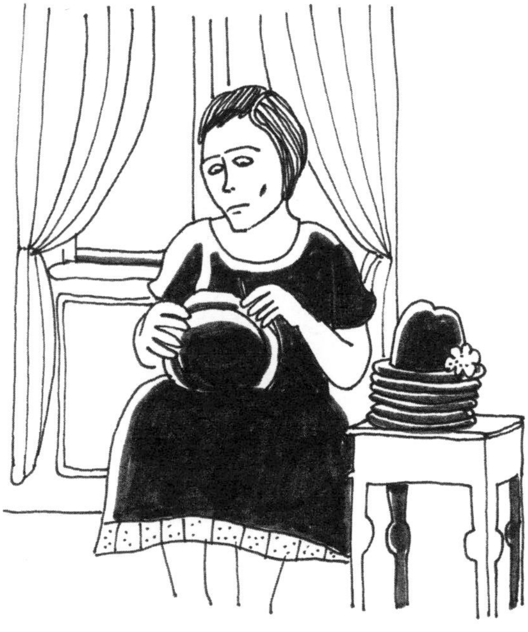

We lived very modestly.

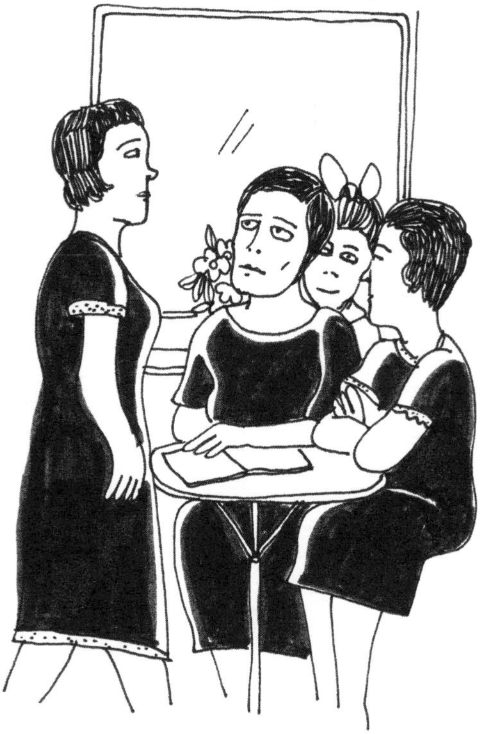

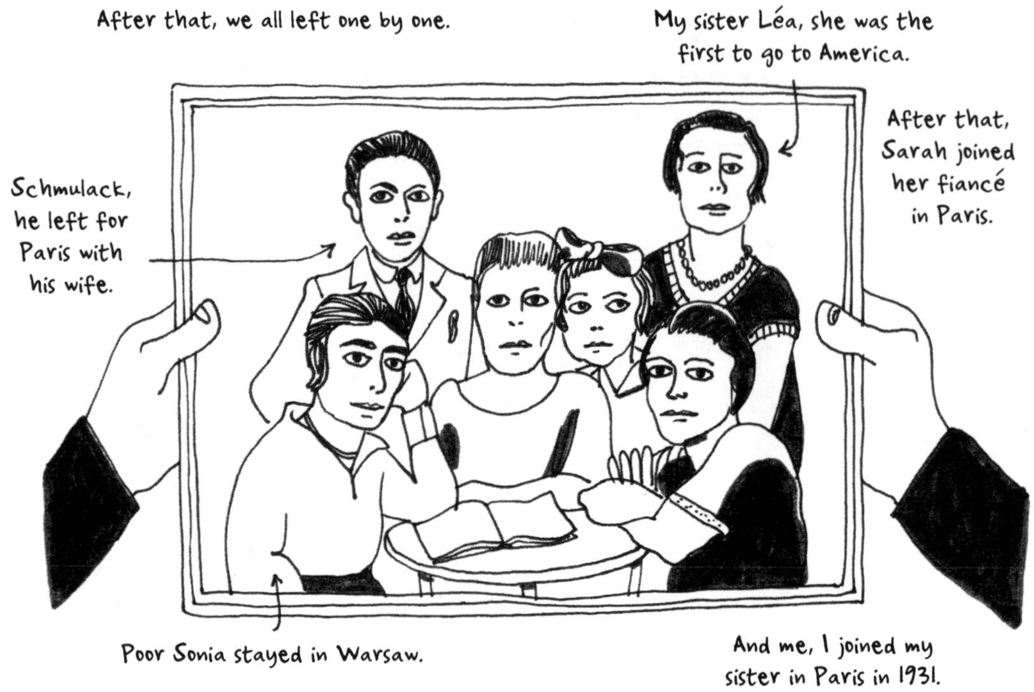
After that, we all left one by one.
My sister Léa, she was the first to go to America.
Schmulack, he left for Paris with his wife.
After that, Sarah joined her fiancé in Paris.
Poor Sonia stayed in Warsaw.
And me, I joined my sister in Paris in 1931.

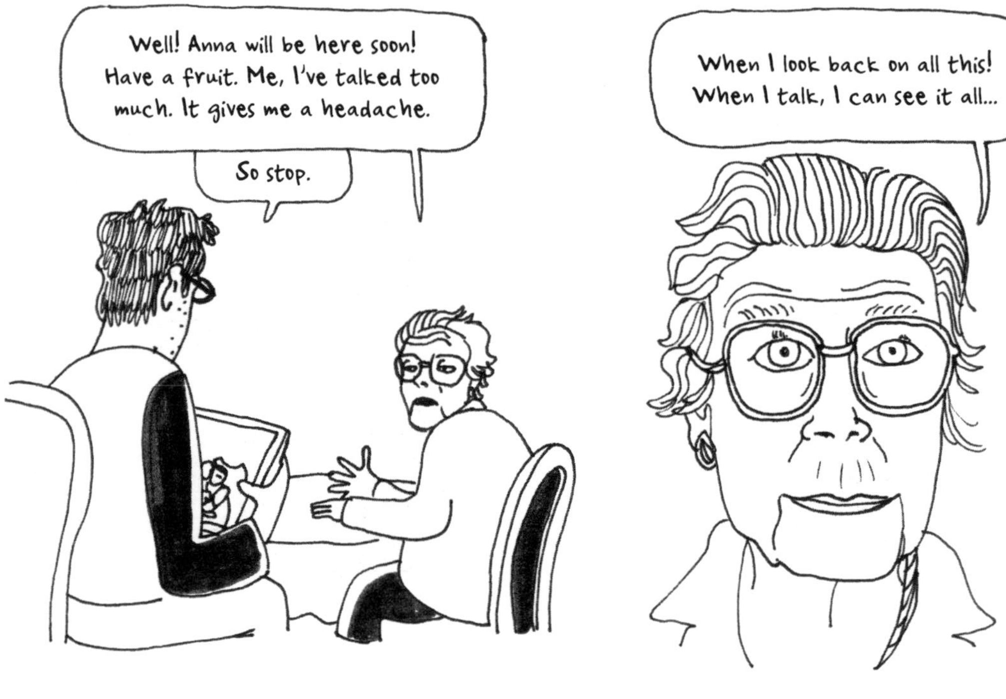
Well! Anna will be here soon! Have a fruit. Me, I've talked too much. It gives me a headache.
So stop.
When I look back on all this! When I talk, I can see it all...

Lost in Translation

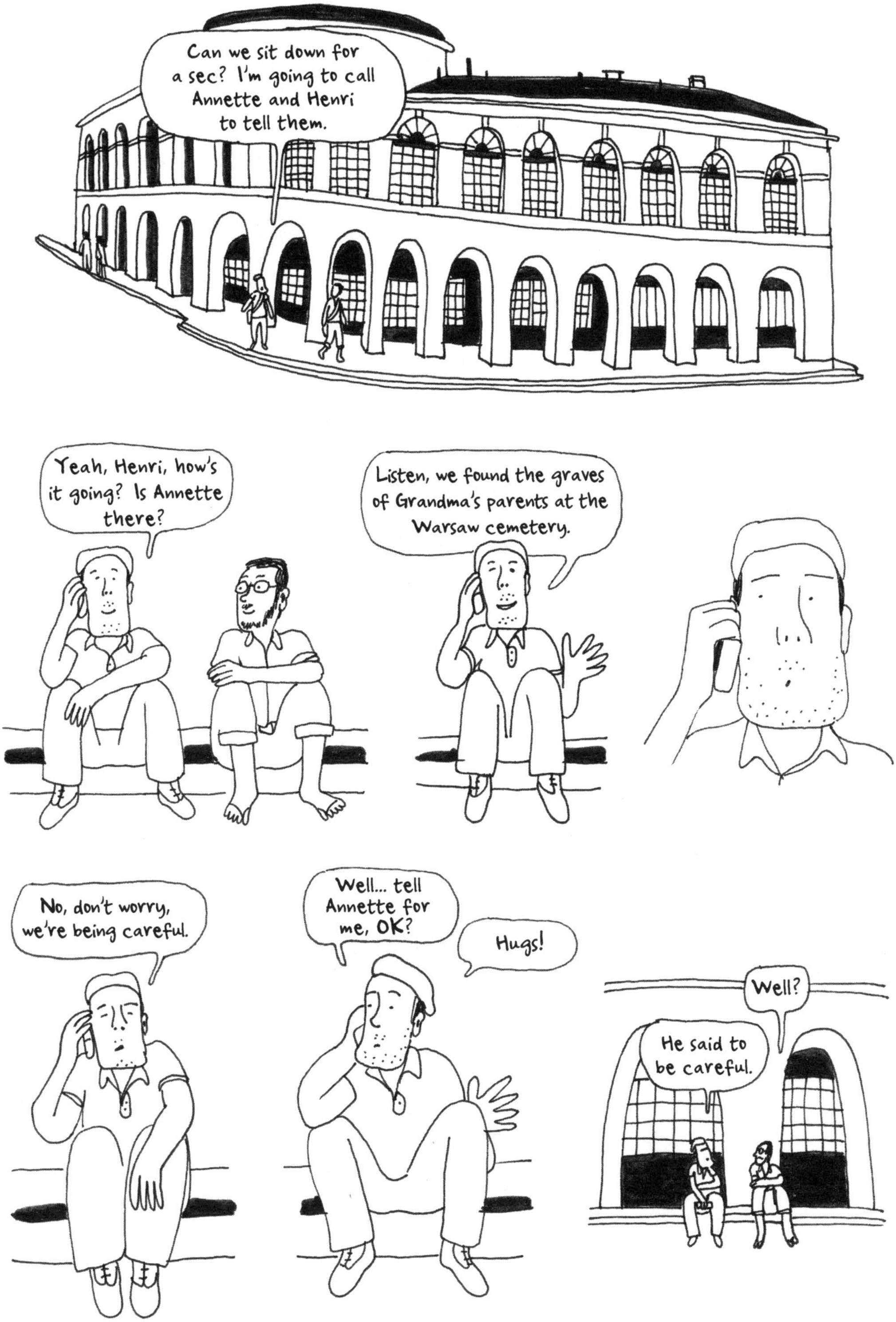

Can we sit down for a sec? I'm going to call Annette and Henri to tell them.
Yeah, Henri, how's it going? Is Annette there?
Listen, we found the graves of Grandma's parents at the Warsaw cemetery.
No, don't worry, we're being careful.
Well... tell Annette for me, OK?
Hugs!
Well?
He said to be careful.

Being Jewish: A User's Guide

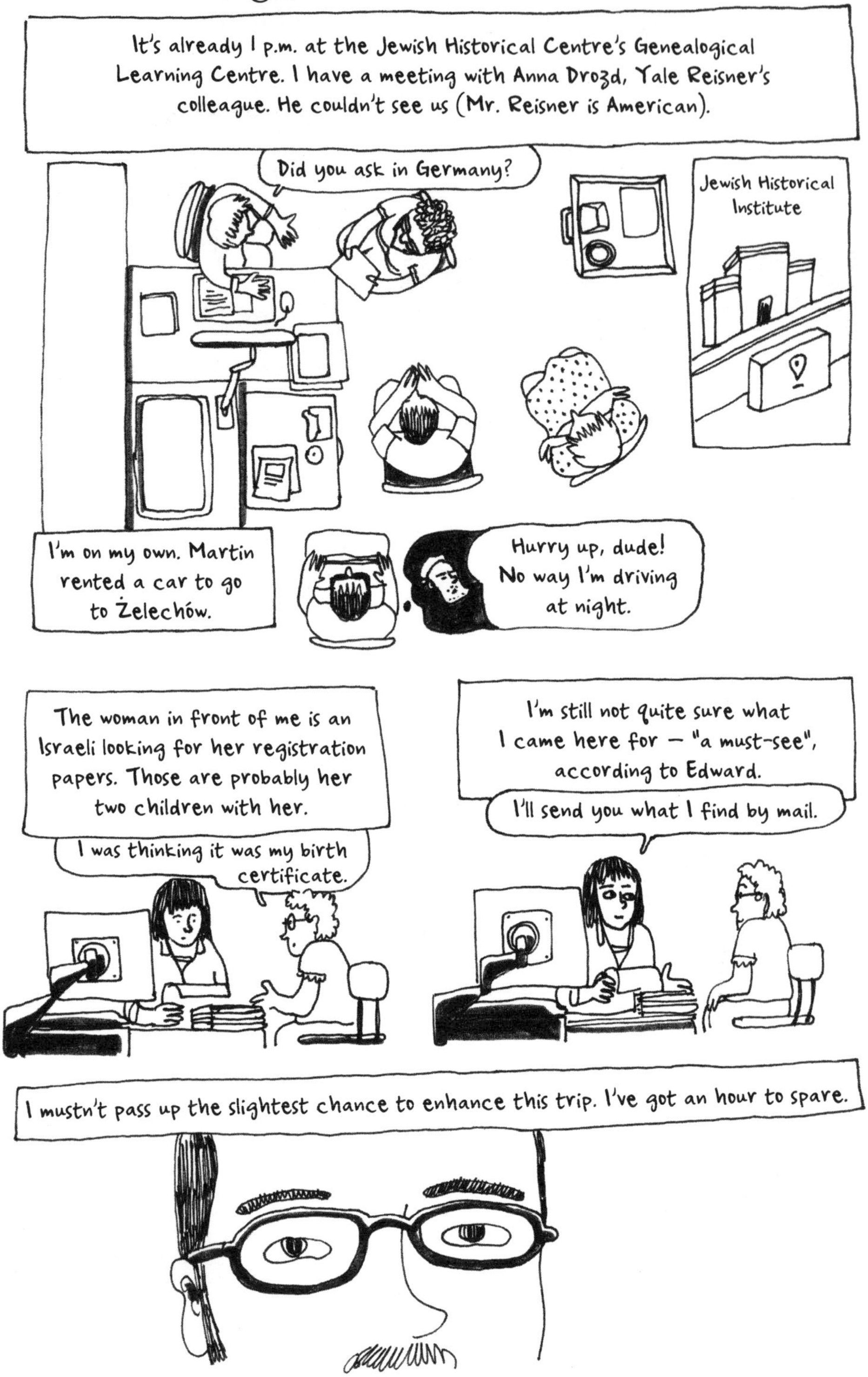
It's already 1 p.m. at the Jewish Historical Centre's Genealogical Learning Centre. I have a meeting with Anna Drozd, Yale Reisner's colleague. He couldn't see us (Mr. Reisner is American).
Did you ask in Germany?
Jewish Historical Institute
I'm on my own. Martin rented a car to go to Żelechów.
Hurry up, dude! No way I'm driving at night.
The woman in front of me is an Israeli looking for her registration papers. Those are probably her two children with her.
I was thinking it was my birth certificate.
I'm still not quite sure what I came here for – "a must-see", according to Edward.
I'll send you what I find by mail.
I mustn't pass up the slightest chance to enhance this trip. I've got an hour to spare.

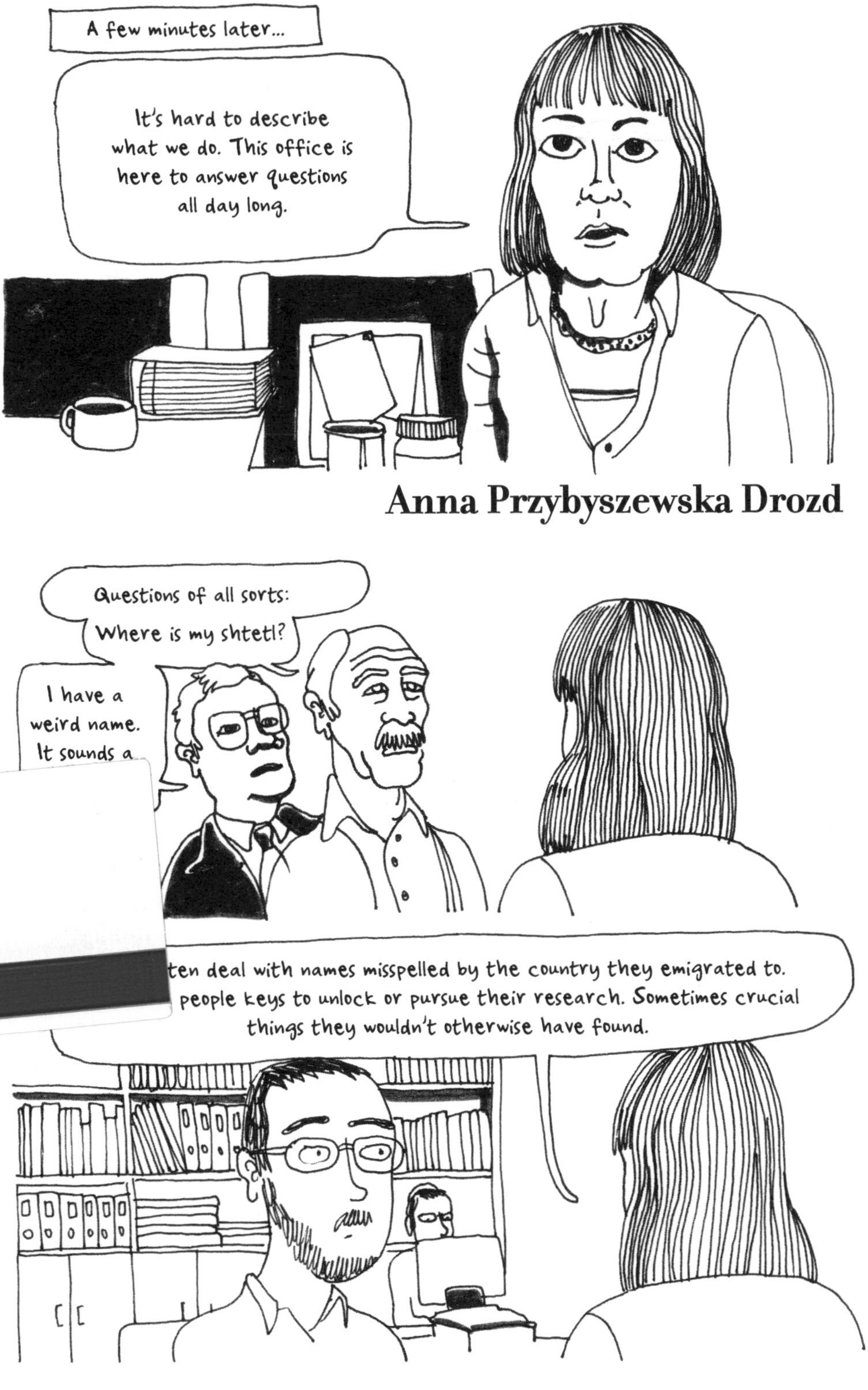
A few minutes later...
It's hard to describe what we do. This office is here to answer questions all day long.
Anna Przybyszewska Drozd
Questions of all sorts: Where is my shtetl?
I have a weird name. It sounds a
ten deal with names misspelled by the country they emigrated to.
people keys to unlock or pursue their research. Sometimes crucial things they wouldn't otherwise have found.

We try to find and collect the civil registers from all over Poland.

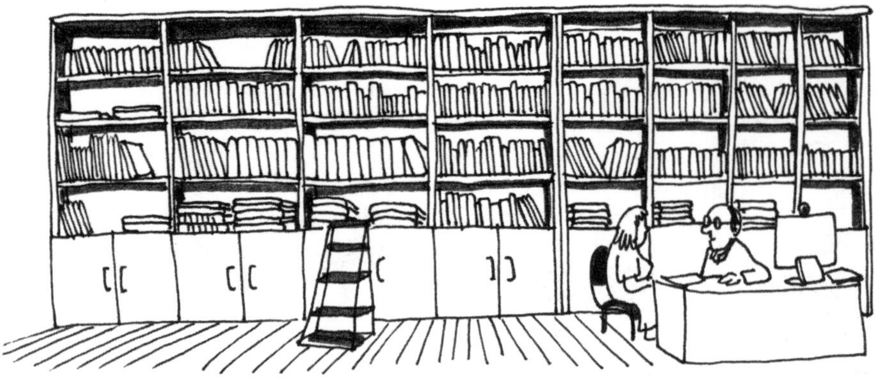

It's harder to find registers for bombed cities like Warsaw.
Sometimes they were only saved thanks to the zeal of town councillors.

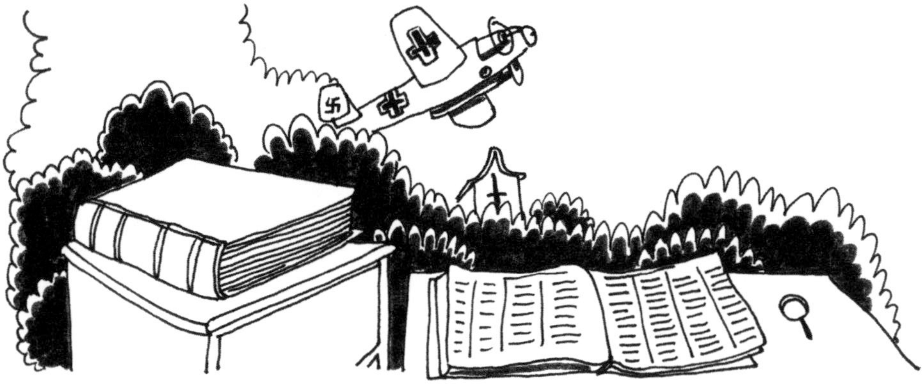

They say the rabbi of a little shtetl fled his village, as it went up in flames,
with the civil registers and a whole bunch of stuff from the synagogue.
He fled across Russia, all the way to the States. But I don't buy it.

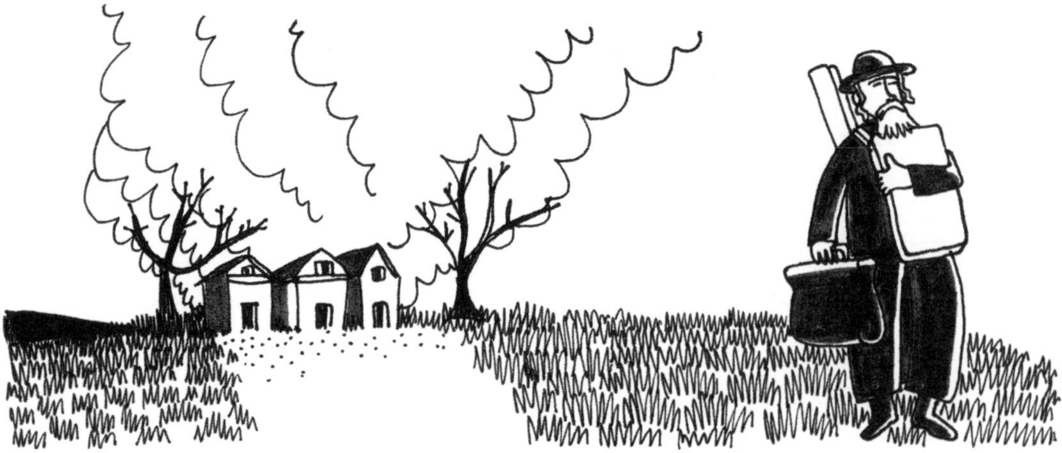

Why would he have gone for the registers at the town hall? Jews were hardly in the habit. I think Christians from the village invented the tale. I know a woman who found his trail in the U.S. He'd gathered, in one room, everything he'd been able to save. But no trace of the registers.

Sometimes people just come across registers. But in such cases, it's very hard to get in touch with them. They usually sell them, and since that's illegal, they leave no number or address.

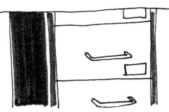

Or else they sell them on eBay, and we can't afford to buy them. Too expensive. Problem is, people buy them. Trying to preserve some bit of memory, they feed the market.

Judaica Poznań, akt vodrzenia 1905

Aktualna Cena	500 zł

zł   Licytuj >

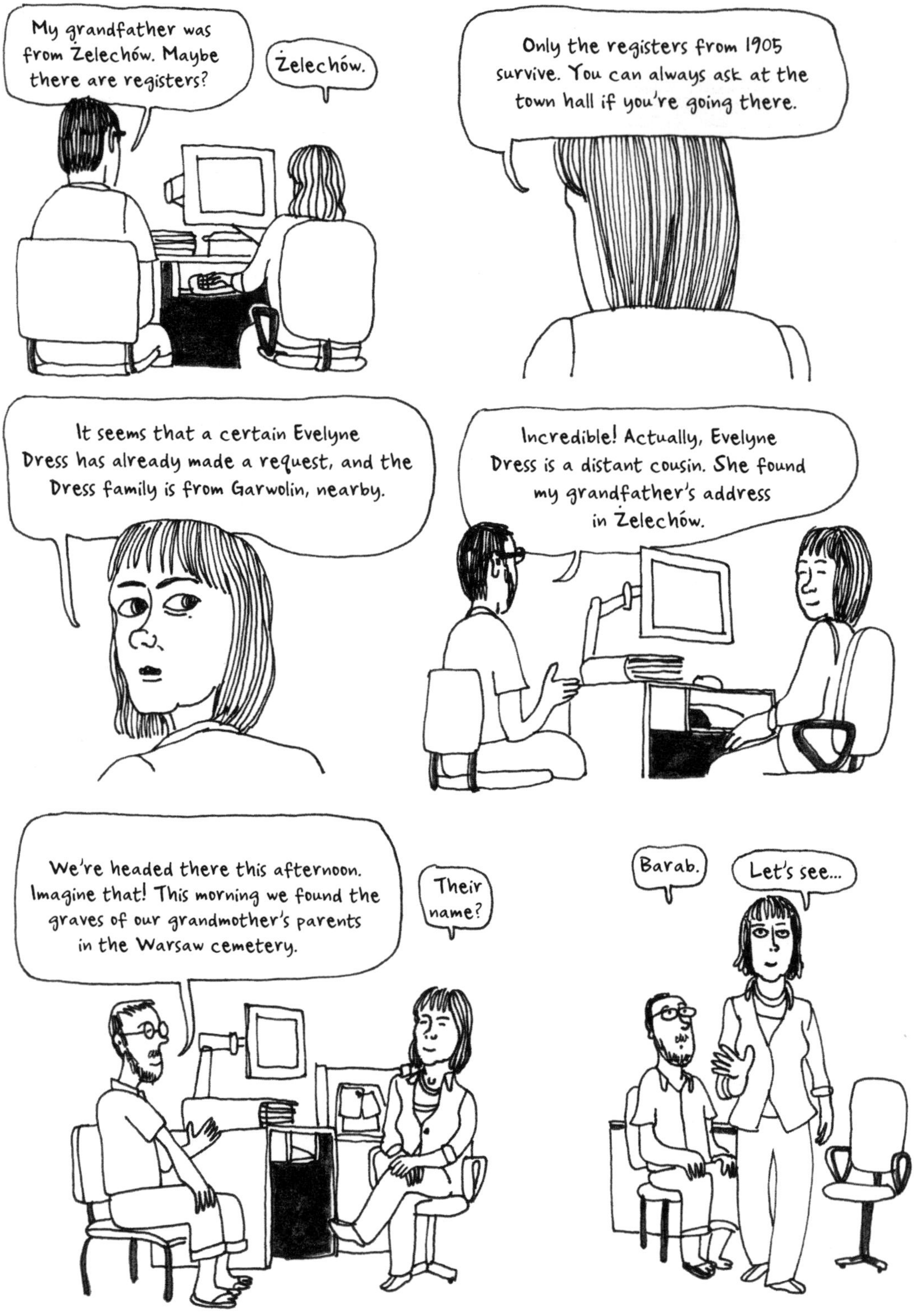
My grandfather was from Żelechów. Maybe there are registers?
Żelechów.
Only the registers from 1905 survive. You can always ask at the town hall if you're going there.
It seems that a certain Evelyne Dress has already made a request, and the Dress family is from Garwolin, nearby.
Incredible! Actually, Evelyne Dress is a distant cousin. She found my grandfather's address in Żelechów.
We're headed there this afternoon. Imagine that! This morning we found the graves of our grandmother's parents in the Warsaw cemetery.
Their name?
Barab.
Let's see...

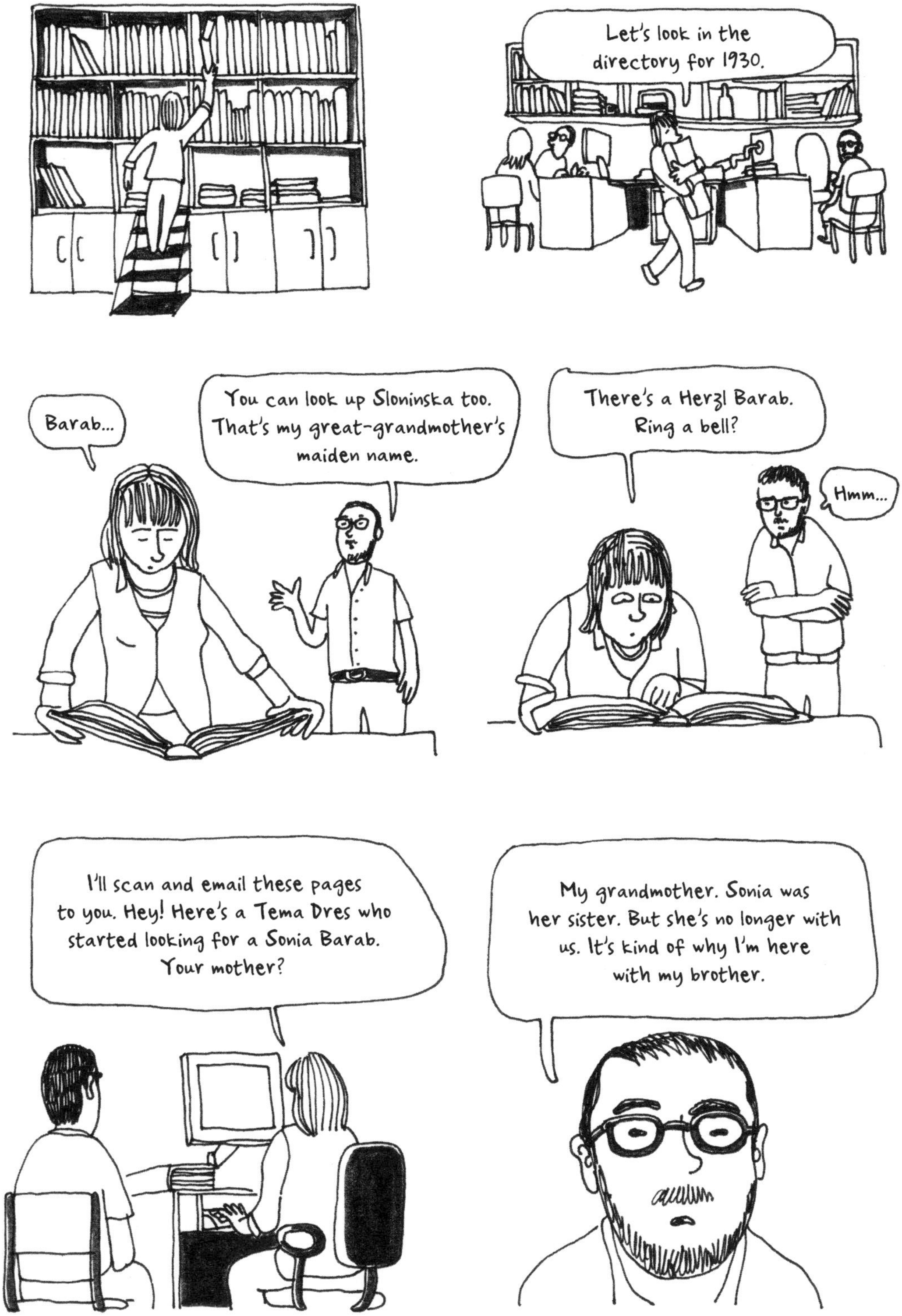
Let's look in the directory for 1930.
Barab...
You can look up Sloninska too. That's my great-grandmother's maiden name.
There's a Herzl Barab. Ring a bell?
Hmm...
I'll scan and email these pages to you. Hey! Here's a Tema Dres who started looking for a Sonia Barab. Your mother?
My grandmother. Sonia was her sister. But she's no longer with us. It's kind of why I'm here with my brother.

When did you start this research?

Yale founded the office 16 years ago. He knew there was going to be high demand from the States. Before that, the communist authorities had made things difficult.

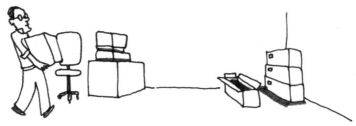

Bit by bit, the number of requests grew. I came in five years later.

There was already too much for two people to do. At first, a lot of letters to file, and later, calls all day long. Now it's email.

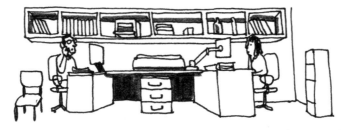

We get from 50 to 100 requests per month. They've changed; at first they all came from abroad, but now more and more Polish people come to see us. Often, they've accidentally discovered evidence of their Jewish roots.

I've heard a bit about that trend.

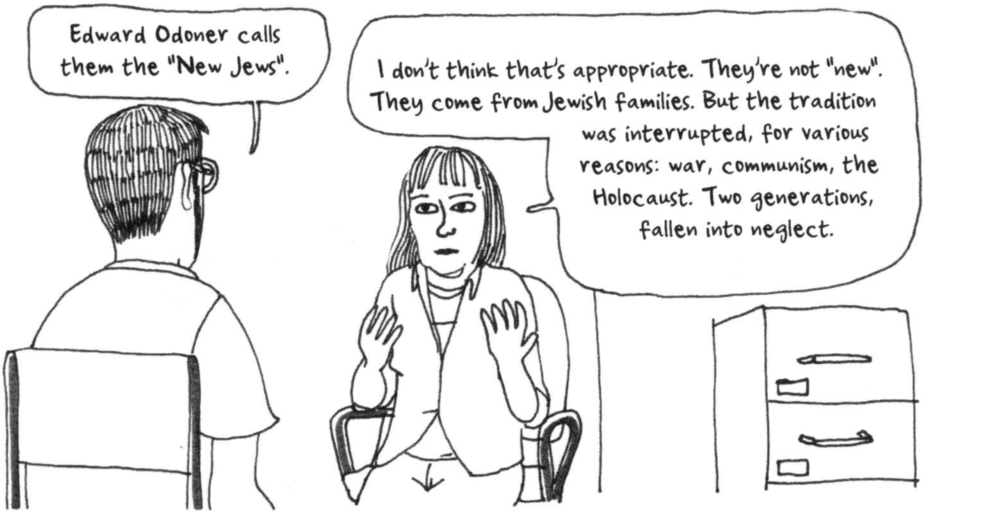
Edward Odoner calls them the "New Jews".
I don't think that's appropriate. They're not "new". They come from Jewish families. But the tradition was interrupted, for various reasons: war, communism, the Holocaust. Two generations, fallen into neglect.

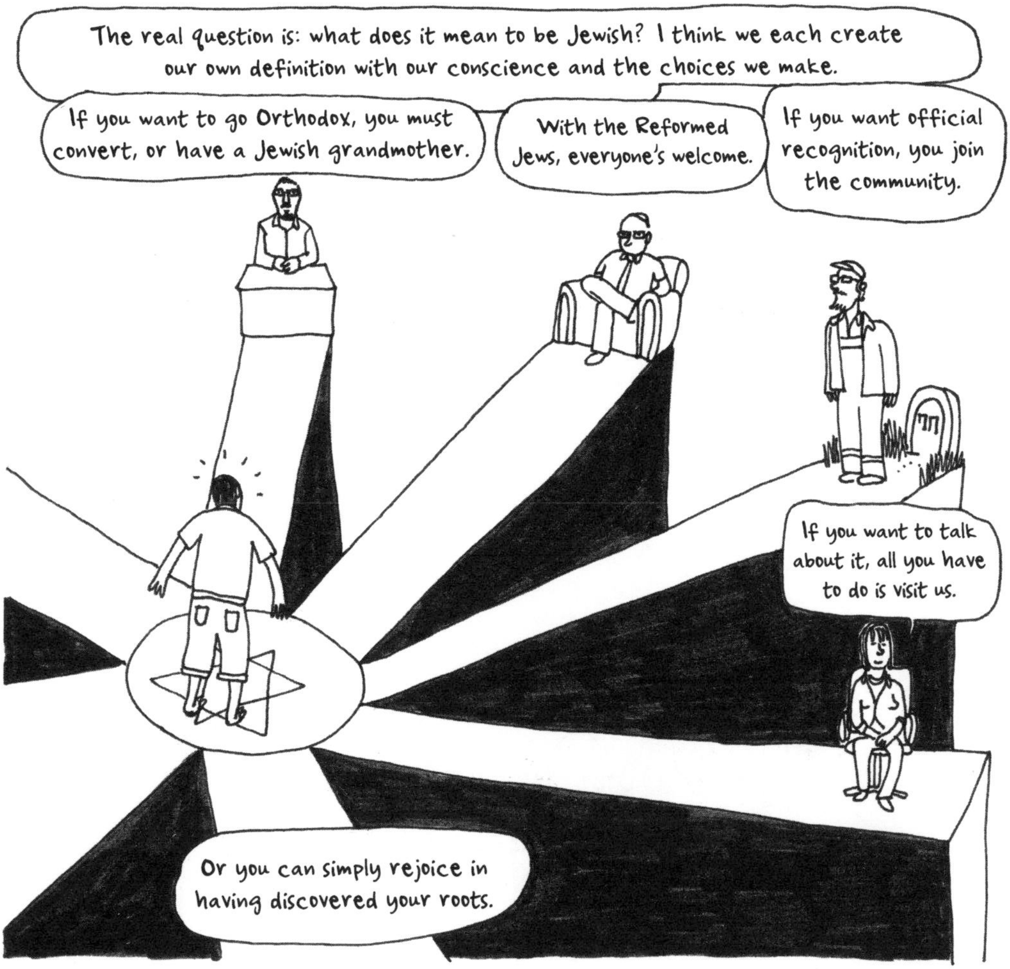
The real question is: what does it mean to be Jewish? I think we each create our own definition with our conscience and the choices we make.
If you want to go Orthodox, you must convert, or have a Jewish grandmother.
With the Reformed Jews, everyone's welcome.
If you want official recognition, you join the community.
If you want to talk about it, all you have to do is visit us.
Or you can simply rejoice in having discovered your roots.

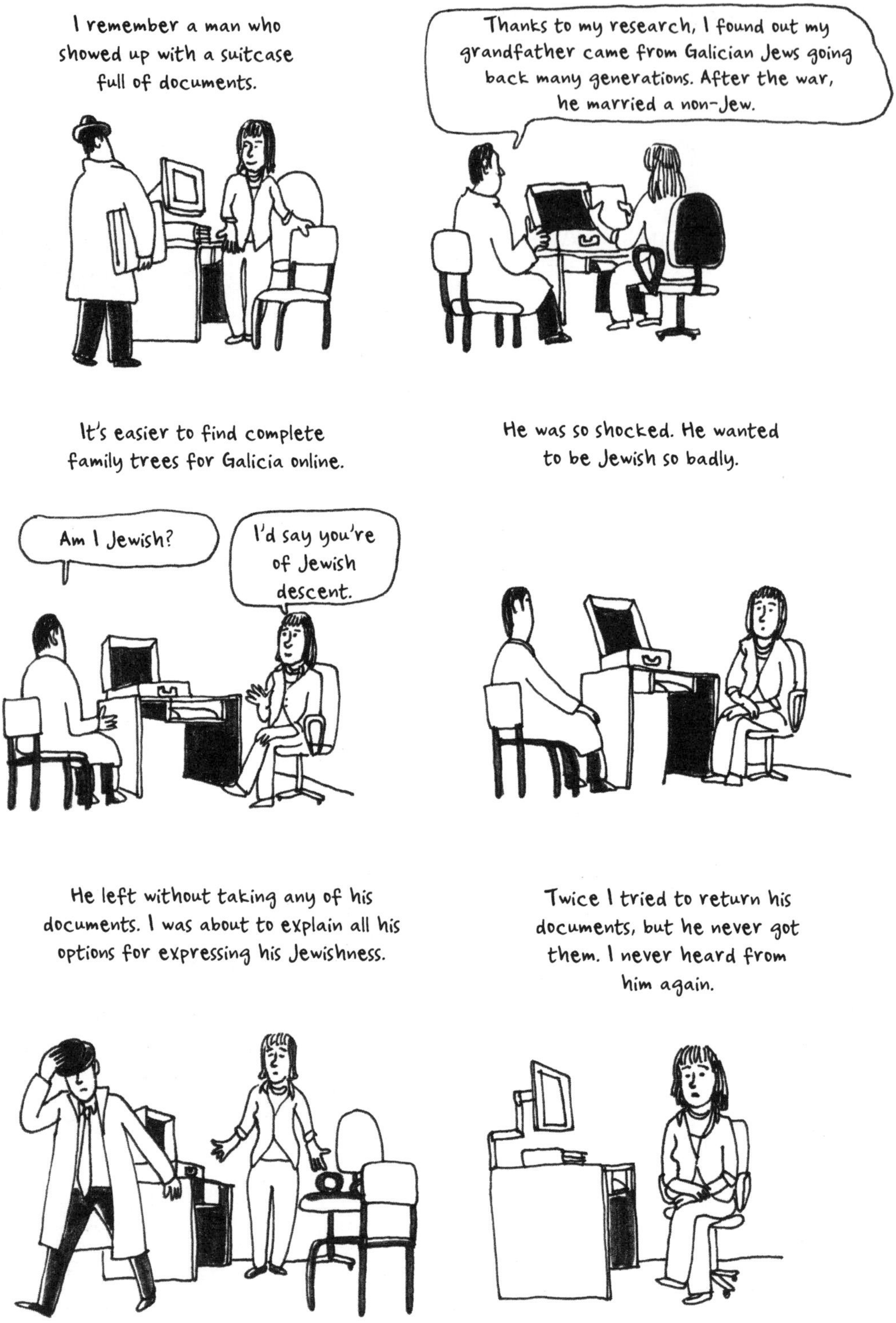
I remember a man who showed up with a suitcase full of documents.
Thanks to my research, I found out my grandfather came from Galician Jews going back many generations. After the war, he married a non-Jew.
It's easier to find complete family trees for Galicia online.
Am I Jewish?
I'd say you're of Jewish descent.
He was so shocked. He wanted to be Jewish so badly.
He left without taking any of his documents. I was about to explain all his options for expressing his Jewishness.
Twice I tried to return his documents, but he never got them. I never heard from him again.

Cold Sweat in Żelechów

3 p.m. and we were on our way at last! Route E21 headed for Żelechów.
We were about to discover the Polish countryside, site of so many fears and fantasies.

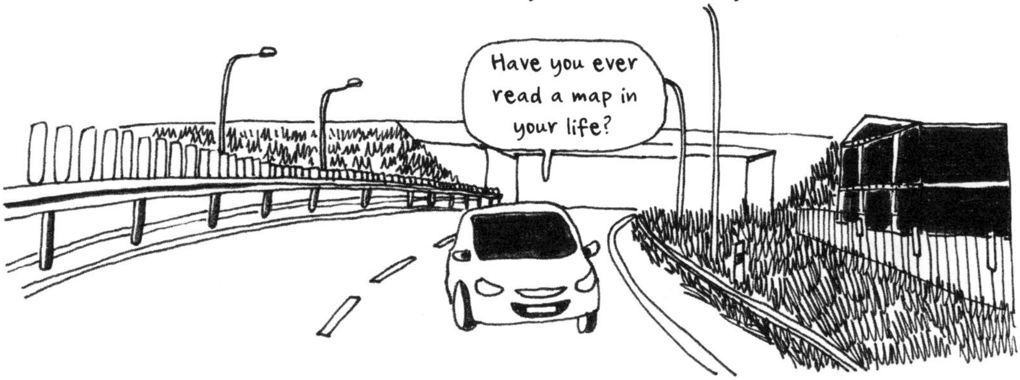
Have you ever read a map in your life?

The dybbuk was reaching unprecedented levels of restlessness in Martin's mouth.

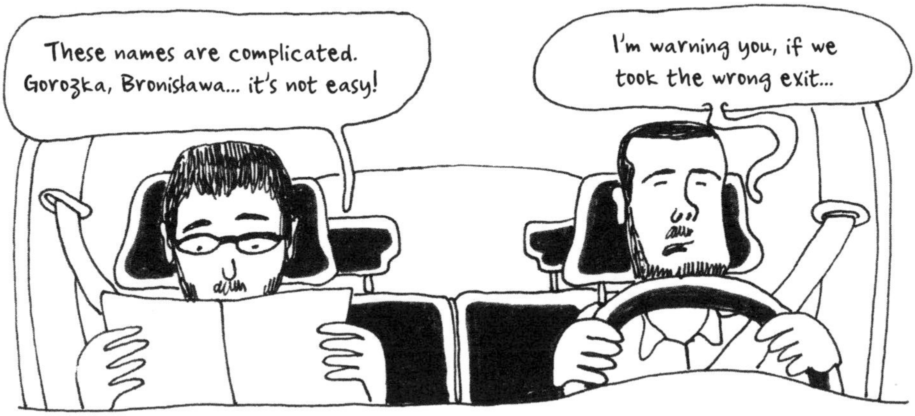
These names are complicated. Gorozka, Bronisława... it's not easy!
I'm warning you, if we took the wrong exit...

It must be said that up till now, no one had been very reassuring.

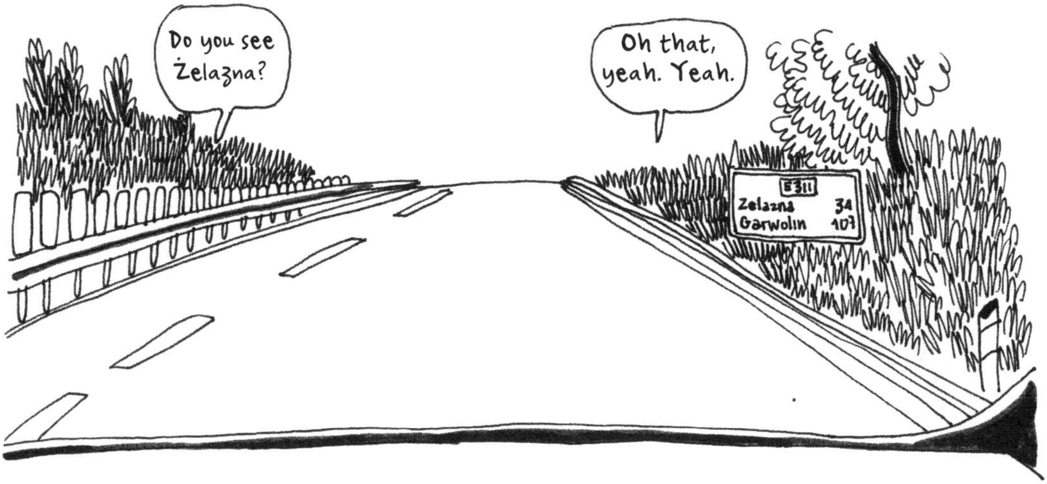
Do you see Żelazna?
Oh that, yeah. Yeah.
Zelazna 34
Garwolin 107

"Anti-Semitism may have vanished from the big cities, but it's still around in the country."

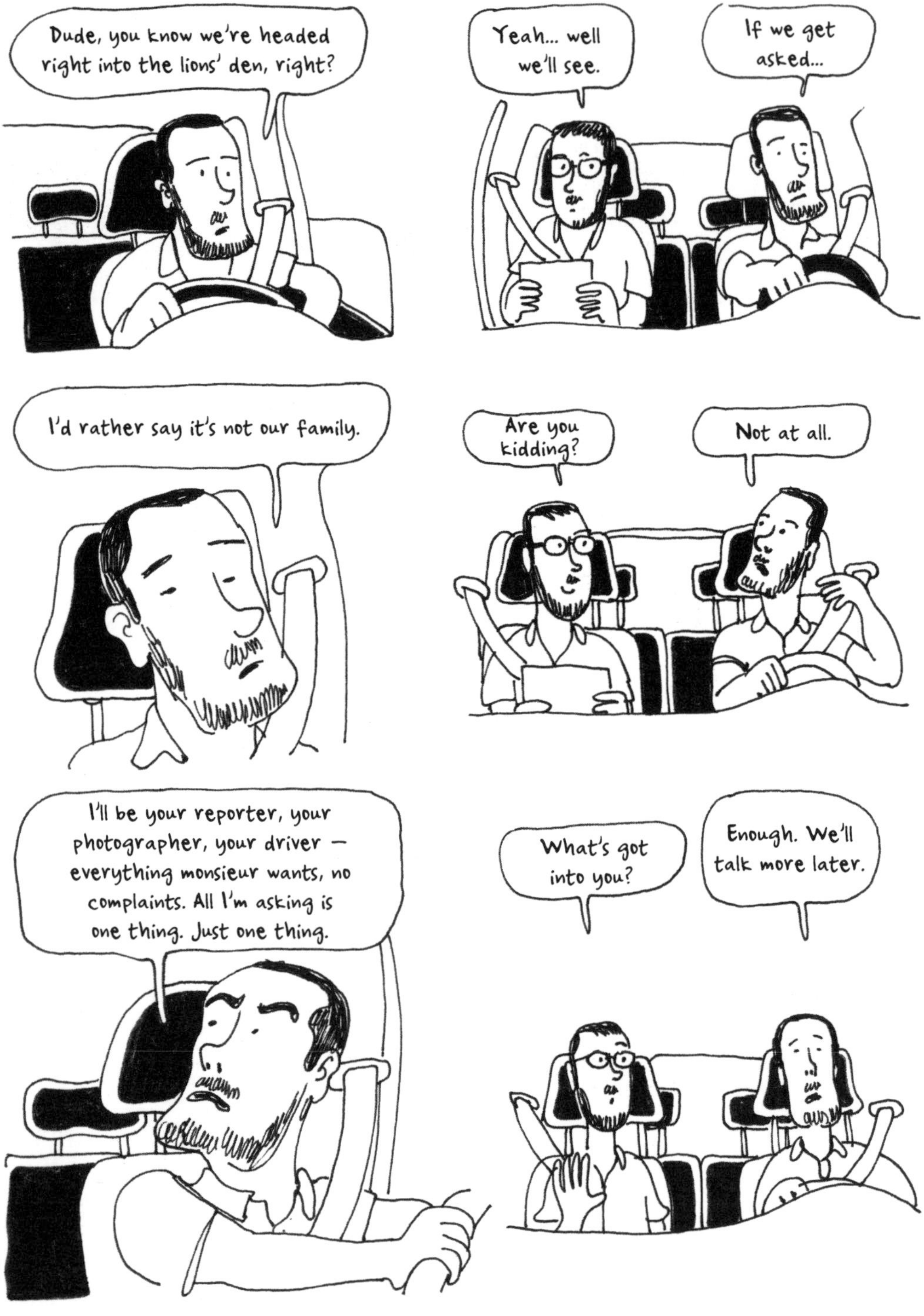

Dude, you know we're headed right into the lions' den, right?
Yeah... well we'll see.
If we get asked...
I'd rather say it's not our family.
Are you kidding?
Not at all.
I'll be your reporter, your photographer, your driver — everything monsieur wants, no complaints. All I'm asking is one thing. Just one thing.
What's got into you?
Enough. We'll talk more later.

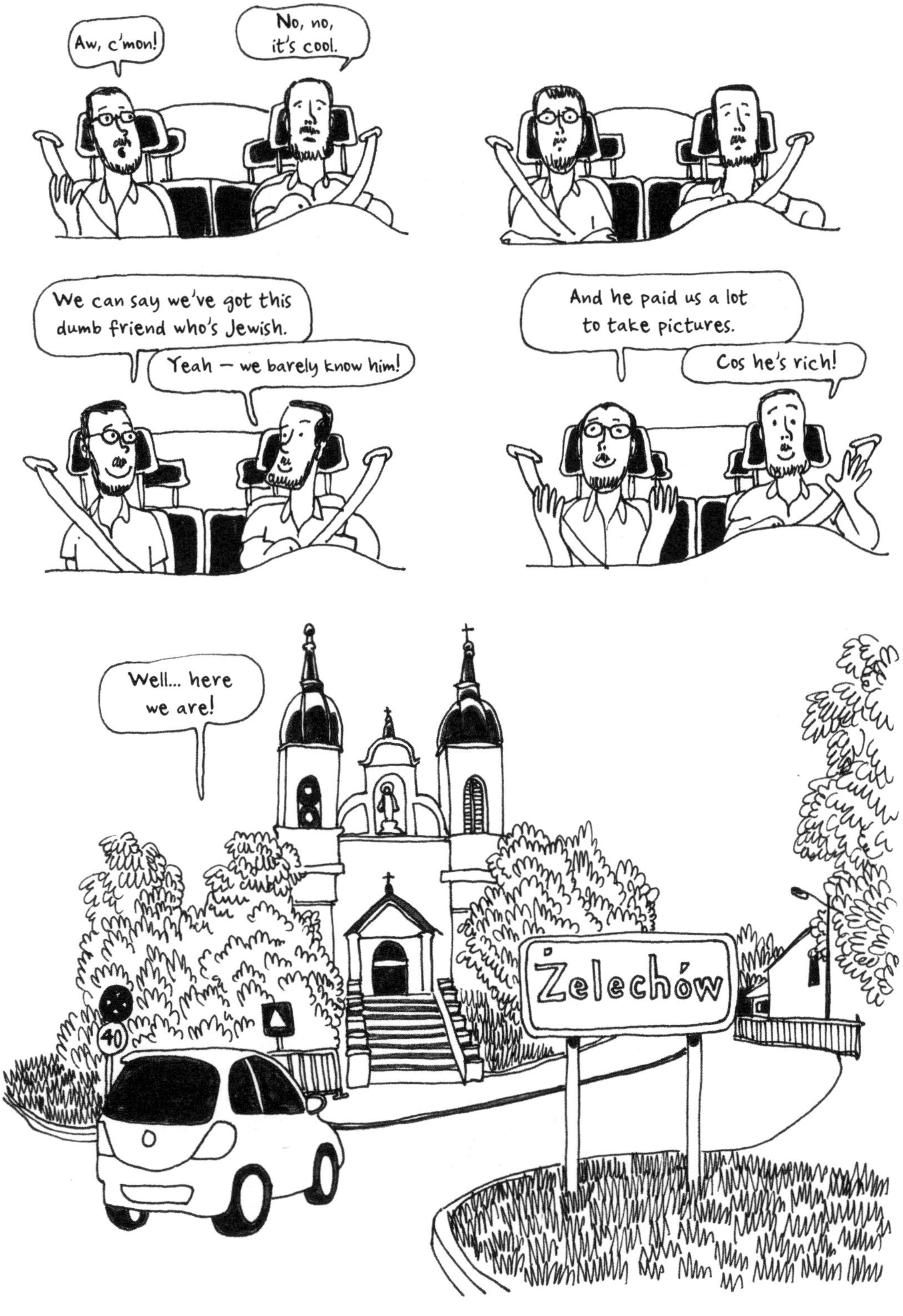
Aw, c'mon!
No, no, it's cool.
We can say we've got this dumb friend who's Jewish.
Yeah – we barely know him!
And he paid us a lot to take pictures.
Cos he's rich!
Well... here we are!
40
Żelechów

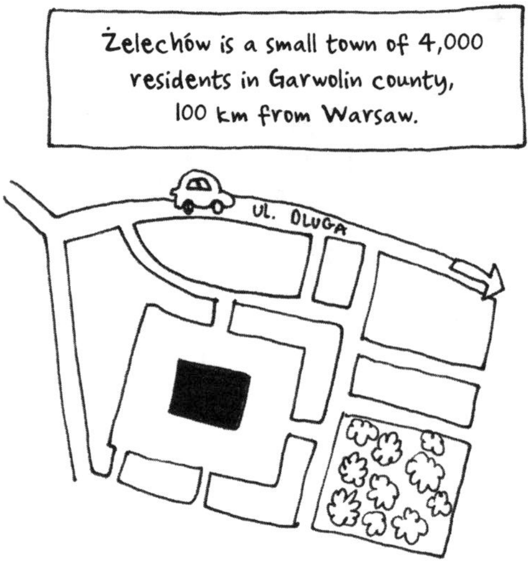
Żelechów is a small town of 4,000 residents in Garwolin county, 100 km from Warsaw.
UL. DLUGA

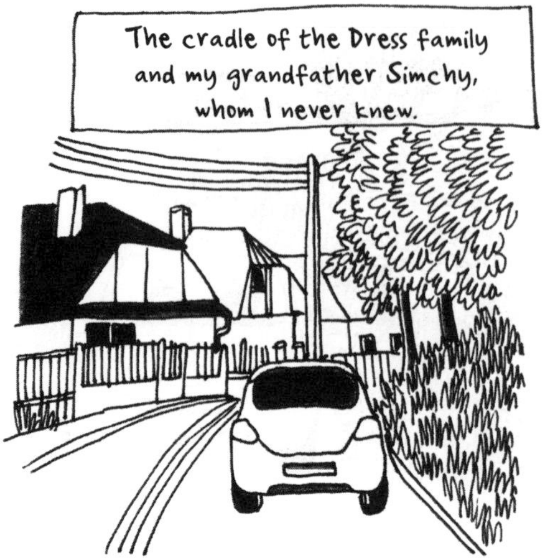
The cradle of the Dress family and my grandfather Simchy, whom I never knew.

Thanks to Evelyne Dress, our distant cousin, I got the exact address of their house.
She was the first to undertake research into our family.

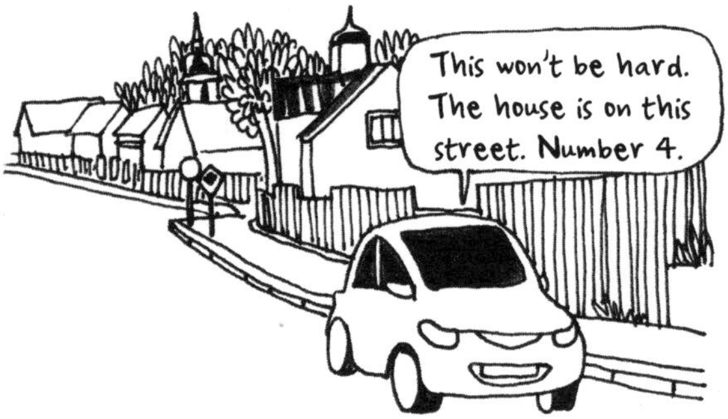
This won't be hard. The house is on this street. Number 4.

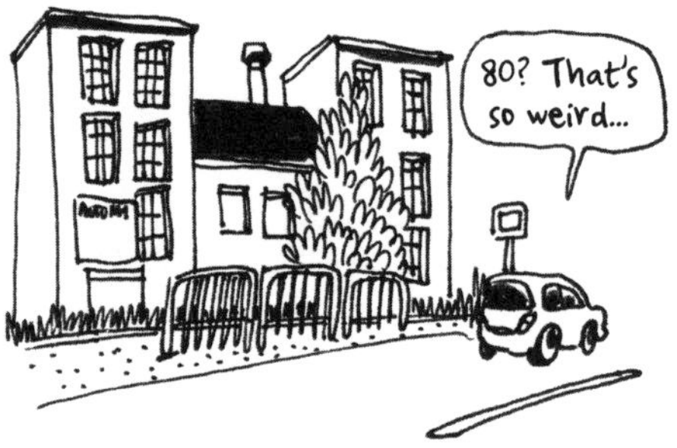
80? That's so weird...

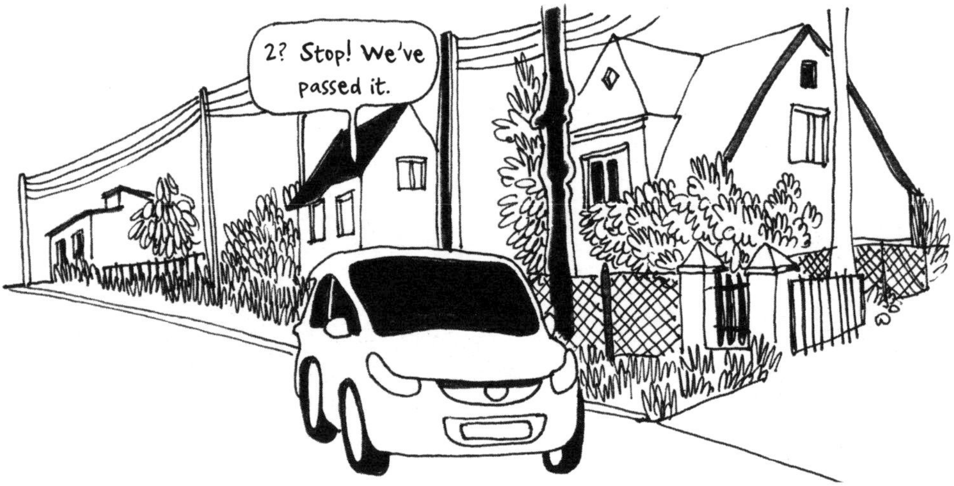
2? Stop! We've passed it.

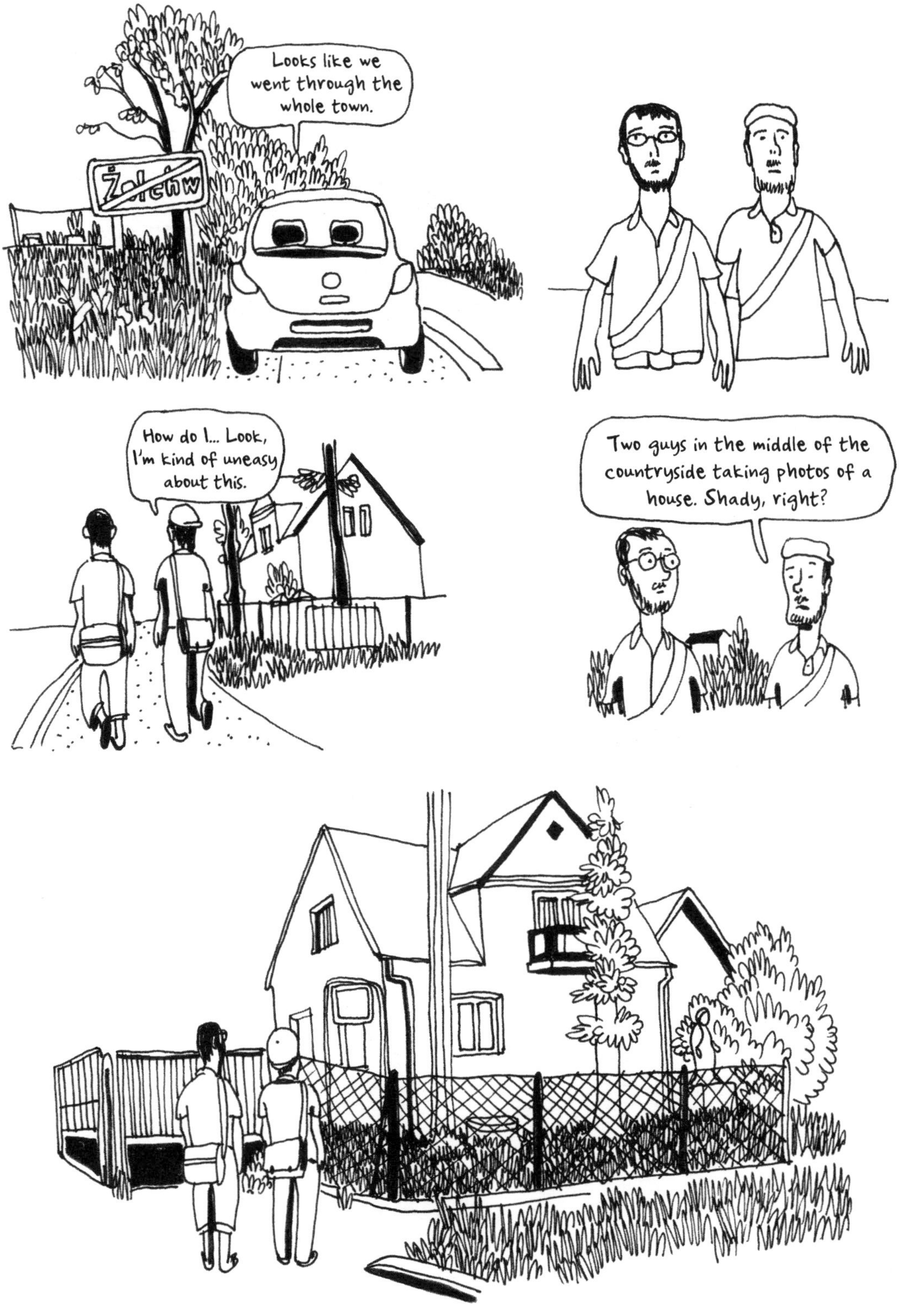
Looks like we went through the whole town.
How do I... Look, I'm kind of uneasy about this.
Two guys in the middle of the countryside taking photos of a house. Shady, right?

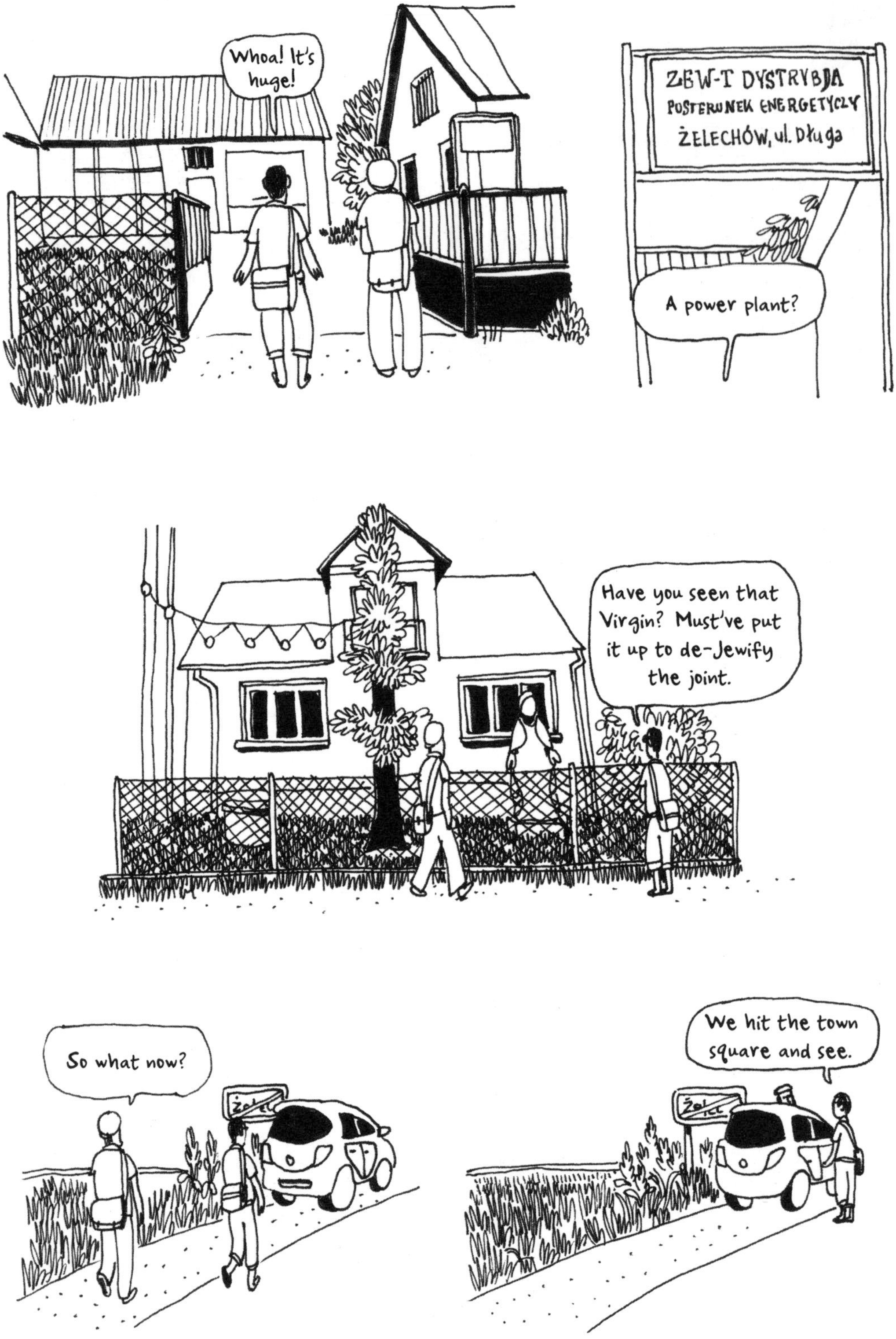

Whoa! It's huge!
ZEW-T DYSTRYBJA
POSTERUNEK ENERGETYCZY
ŻELECHÓW, ul. Długa
A power plant?
Have you seen that Virgin? Must've put it up to de-Jewify the joint.
So what now?
We hit the town square and see.

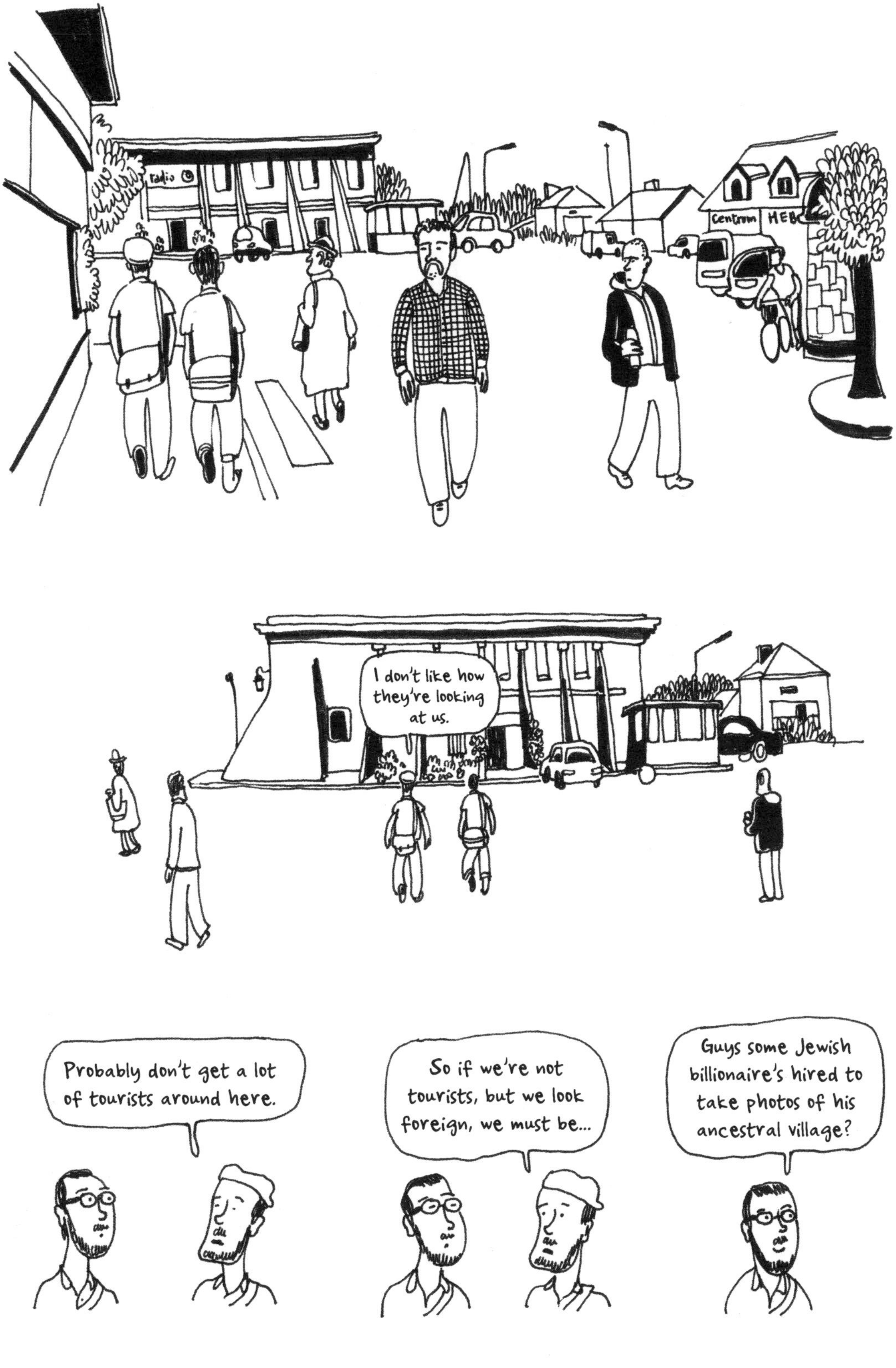
radio
Centrum
I don't like how they're looking at us.
Probably don't get a lot of tourists around here.
So if we're not tourists, but we look foreign, we must be...
Guys some Jewish billionaire's hired to take photos of his ancestral village?

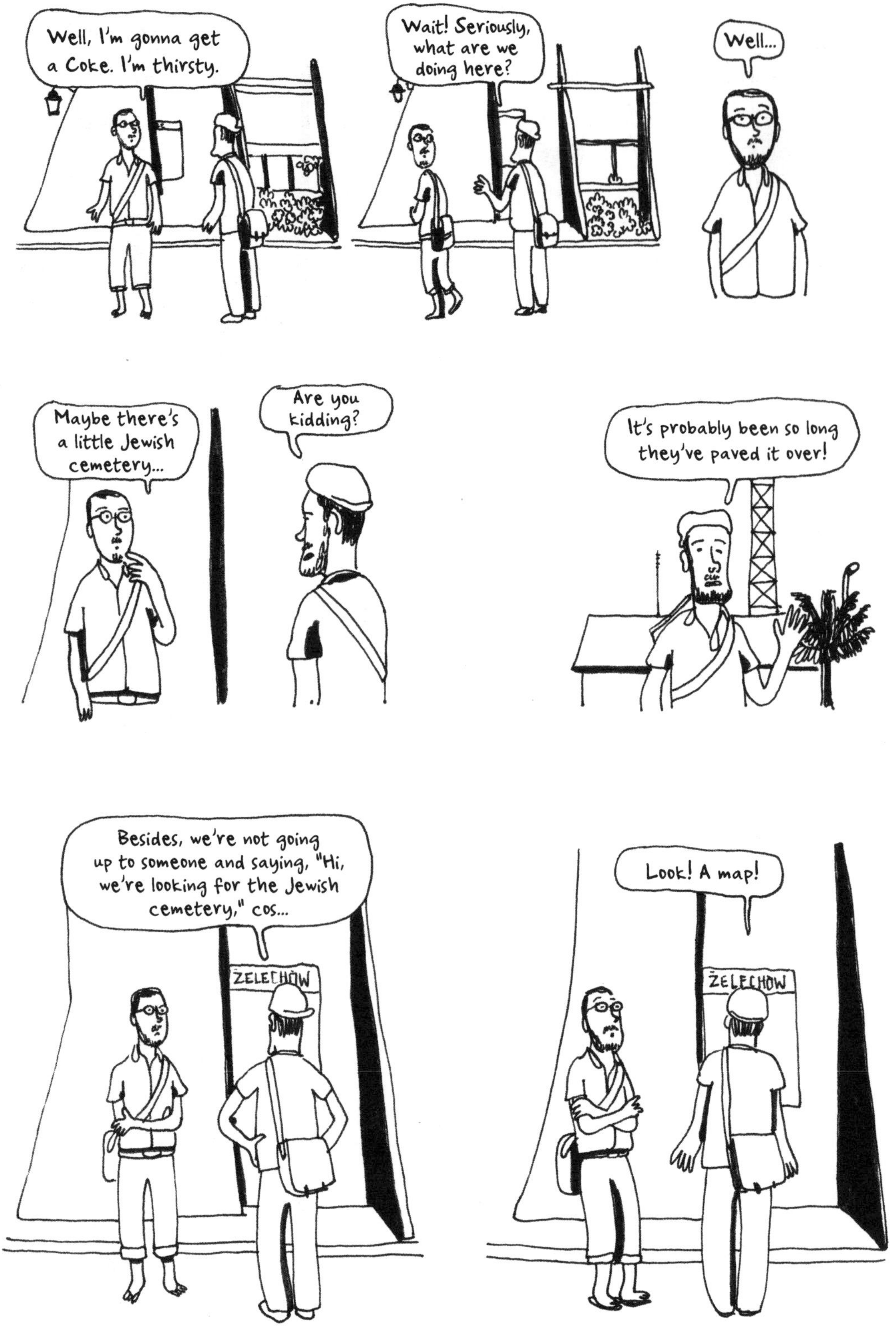
Well, I'm gonna get a Coke. I'm thirsty.
Wait! Seriously, what are we doing here?
Well...
Maybe there's a little Jewish cemetery...
Are you kidding?
It's probably been so long they've paved it over!
Besides, we're not going up to someone and saying, "Hi, we're looking for the Jewish cemetery," cos...
ŻELECHÓW
Look! A map!
ŻELECHÓW

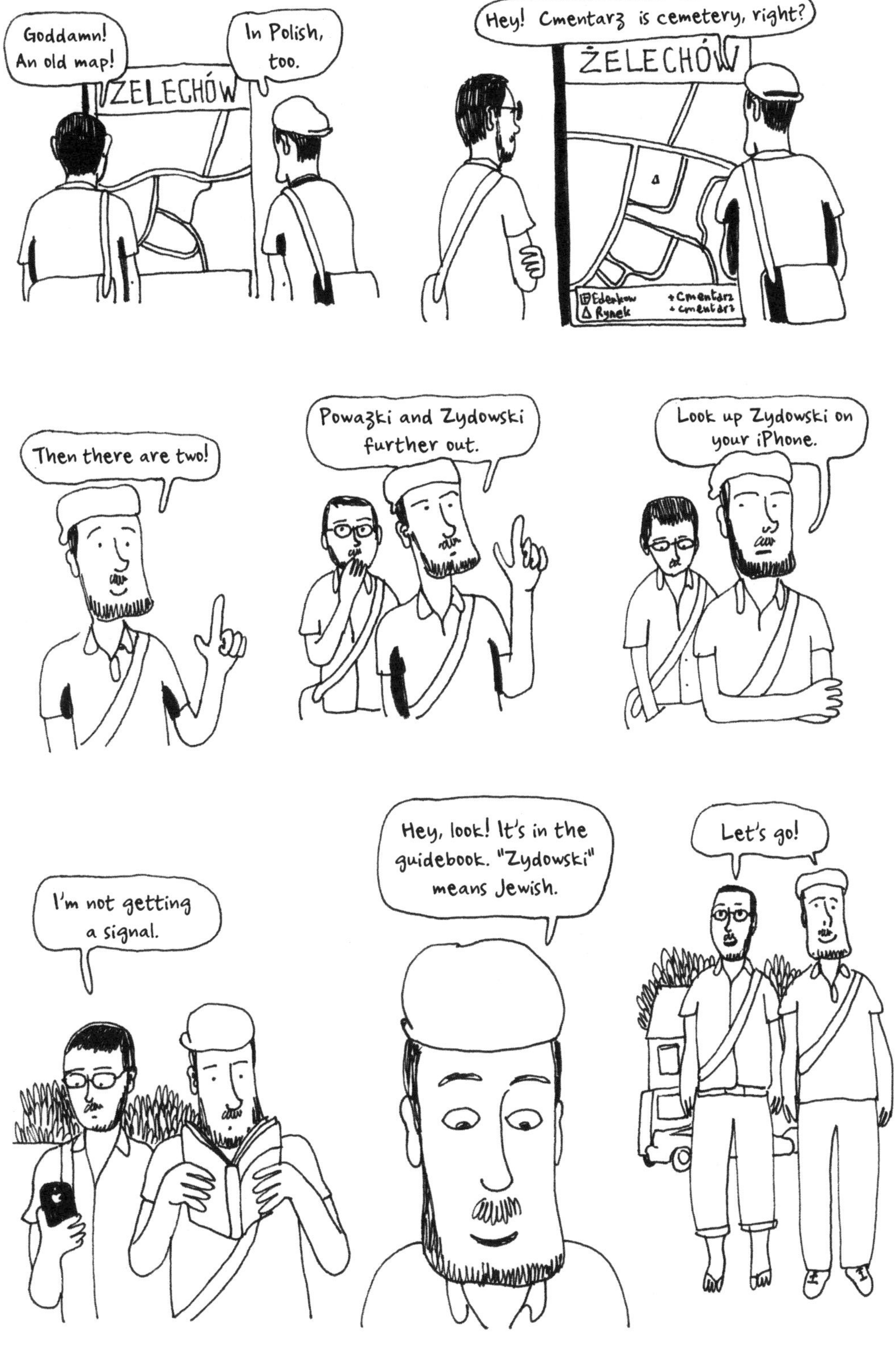
Goddamn! An old map!
ŻELECHÓW
In Polish, too.
Hey! Cmentarz is cemetery, right?
ŻELECHÓW
Ederkow
Rynek
Cmentarz
Cmentarz
Then there are two!
Powazki and Zydowski further out.
Look up Zydowski on your iPhone.
I'm not getting a signal.
Hey, look! It's in the guidebook. "Zydowski" means Jewish.
Let's go!

DLUGA
Market Square
Jewish Cemetery
We must've passed it. Turn around.
No luck, looks like.
Wait! Dude! I saw some weird stones in that field.

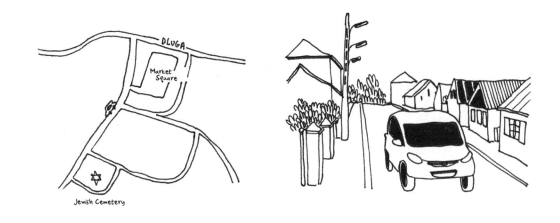

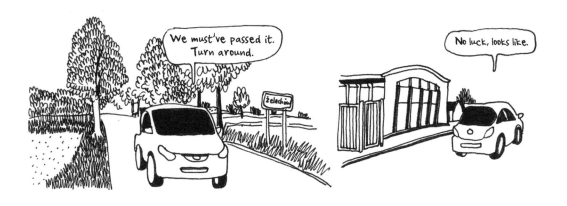

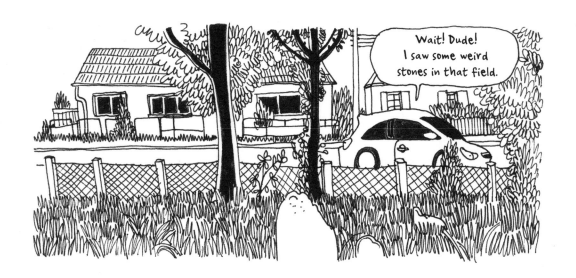

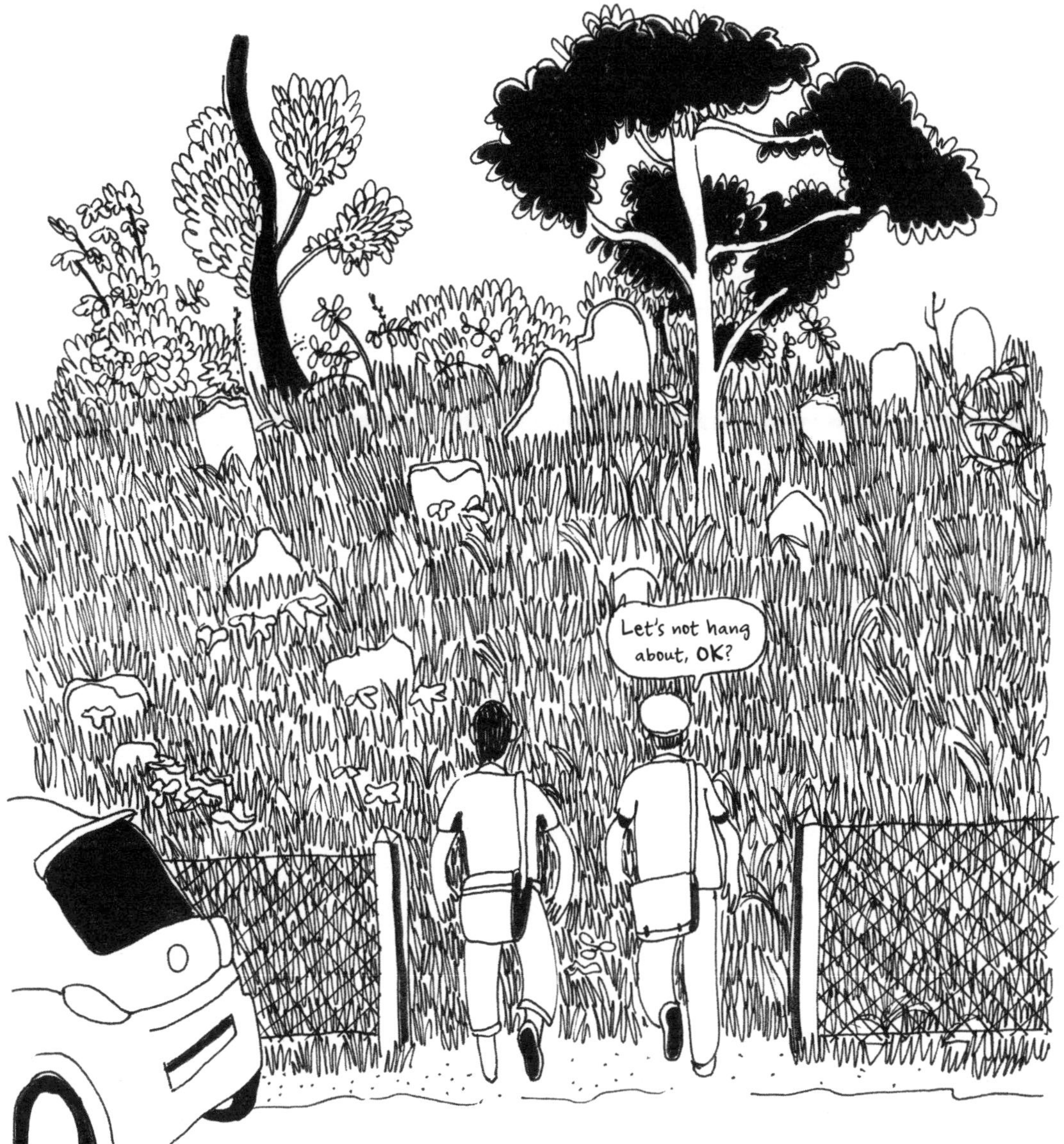
Let's not hang about, OK?

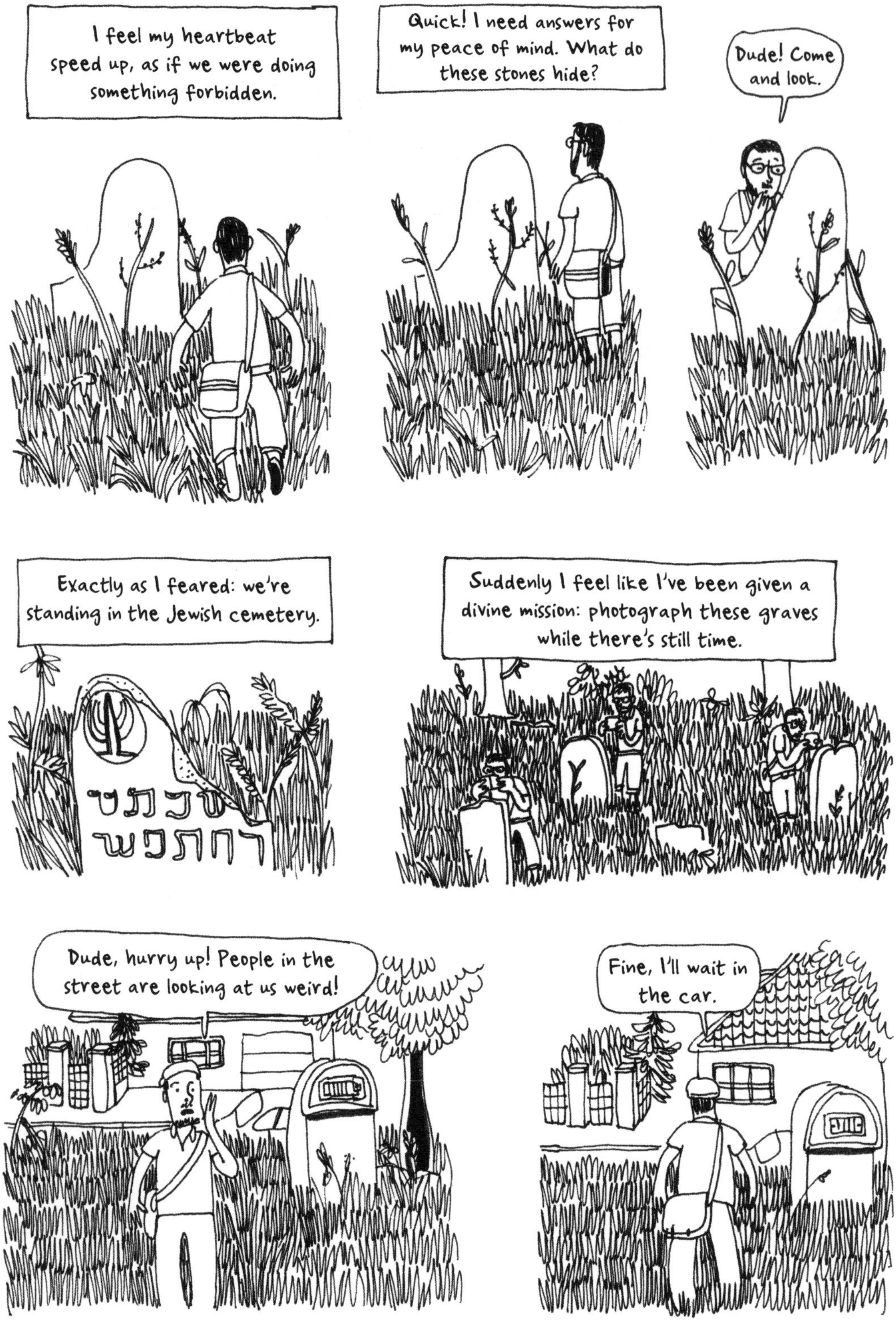
I feel my heartbeat speed up, as if we were doing something forbidden.
Quick! I need answers for my peace of mind. What do these stones hide?
Dude! Come and look.
Exactly as I feared: we're standing in the Jewish cemetery.
Suddenly I feel like I've been given a divine mission: photograph these graves while there's still time.
Dude, hurry up! People in the street are looking at us weird!
Fine, I'll wait in the car.

Here, in this abandoned field, lie the last traces of a community that lived in Żelechów for more than 100 years, traces fading to general indifference. Time has passed so quickly here that these headstones look like the remains of some classical civilization.

The pleasant impressions of tolerance and revival I've had up till now fade abruptly away, making way for absence and indignation.

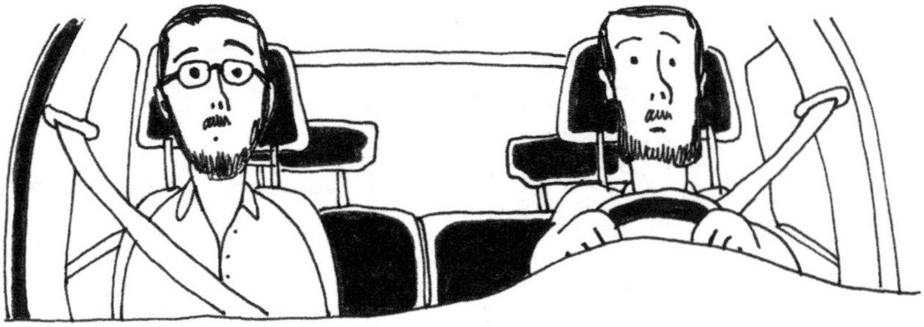

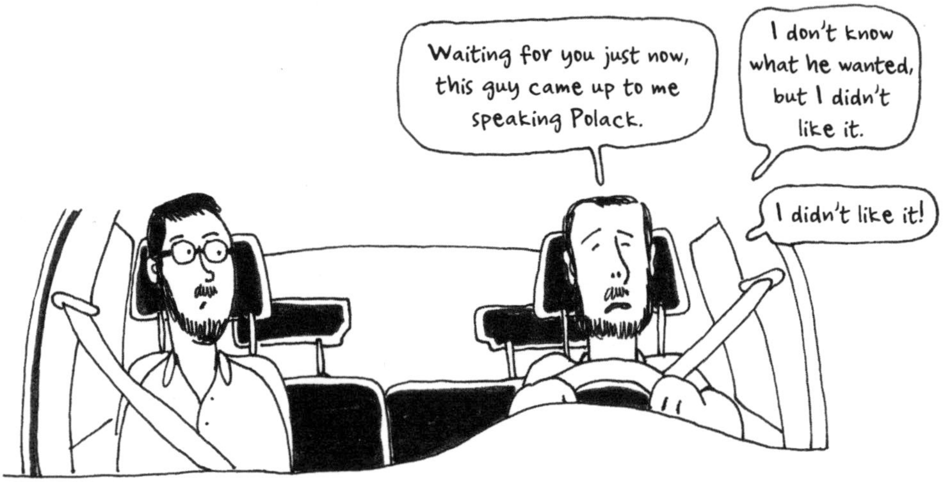
Waiting for you just now, this guy came up to me speaking Polack.
I don't know what he wanted, but I didn't like it.
I didn't like it!

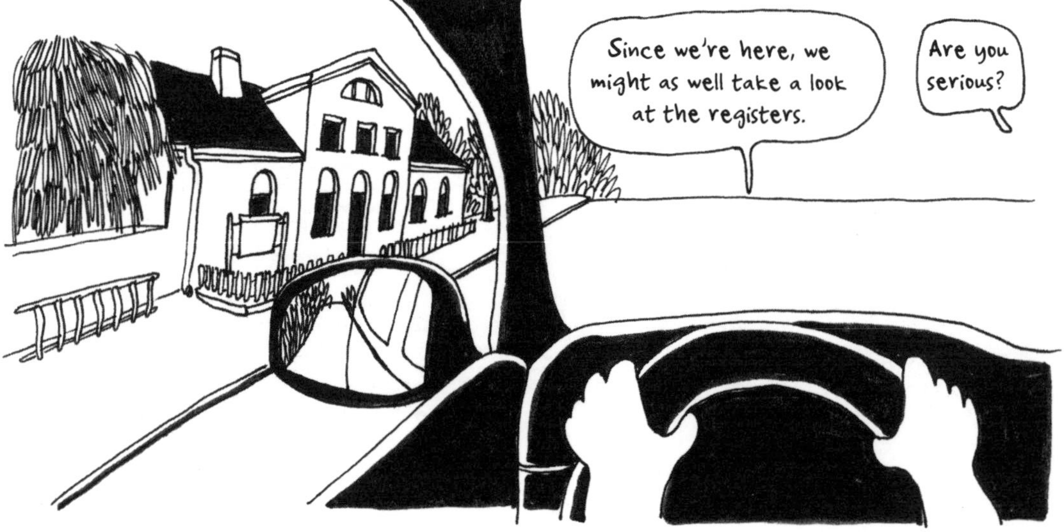
Since we're here, we might as well take a look at the registers.
Are you serious?

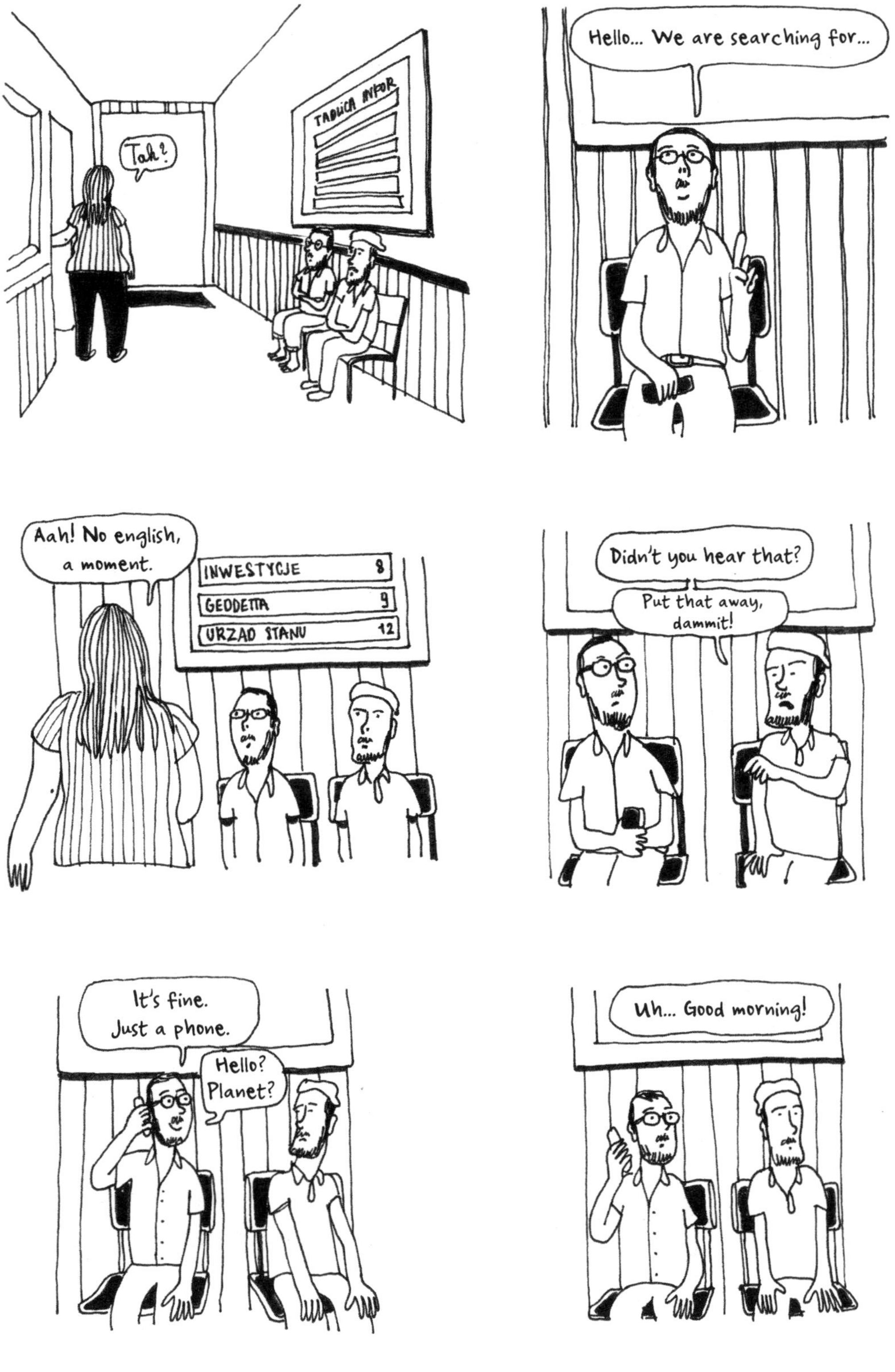
Tak?
TABLICA INFOR
Hello... We are searching for...
Aah! No english,
a moment.
INWESTYCJE 8
GEODETTA 9
URZAD STANU 12
Didn't you hear that?
Put that away,
dammit!
It's fine.
Just a phone.
Hello?
Planet?
Uh... Good morning!

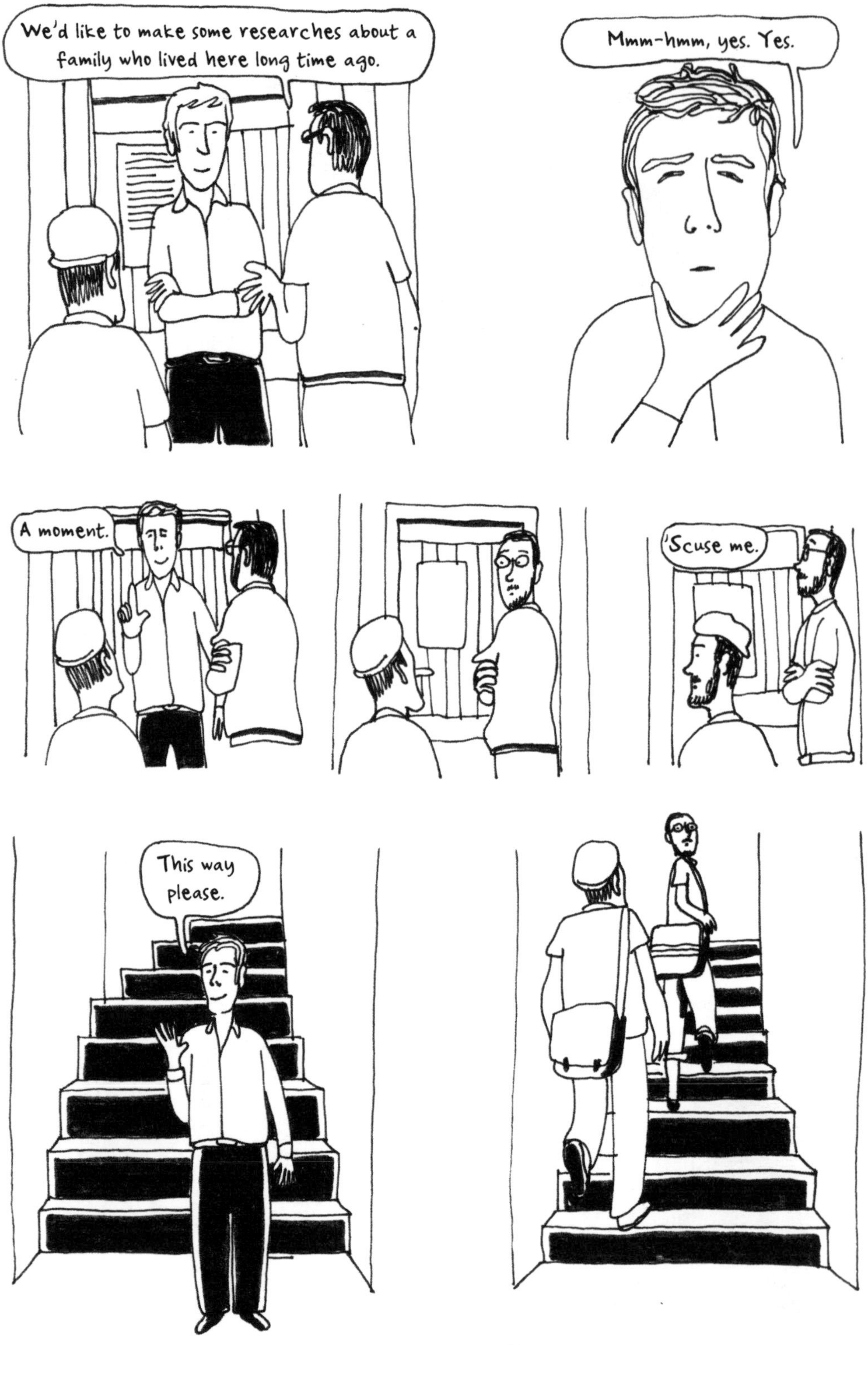
We'd like to make some researches about a family who lived here long time ago.
Mmm-hmm, yes. Yes.
A moment.
'Scuse me.
This way please.

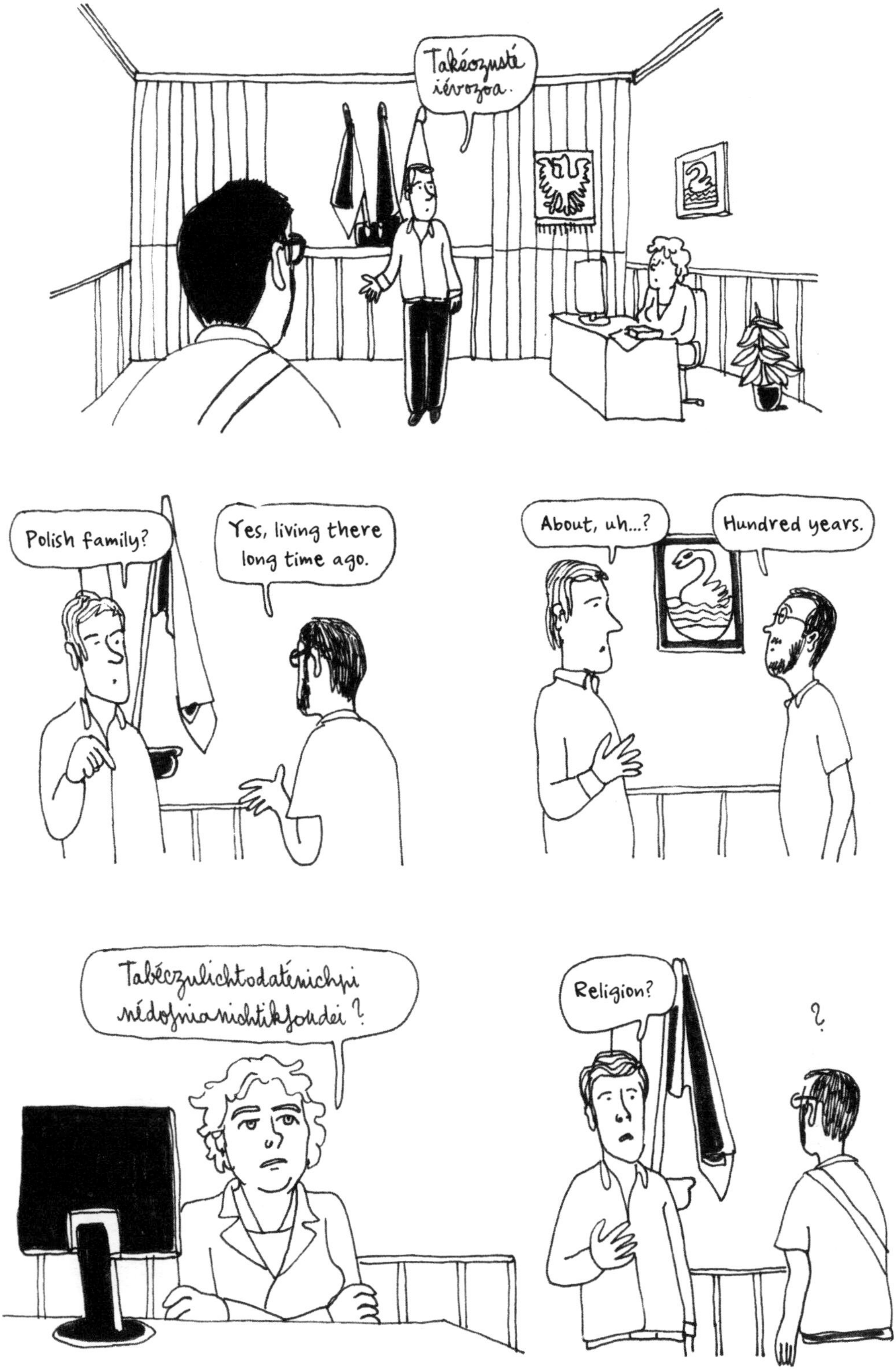
Takéozusté iévozoa.
Polish family?
Yes, living there long time ago.
About, uh...?
Hundred years.
Tabéczulichtodaténichpi nédoźnianichtikjoudei ?
Religion?
?

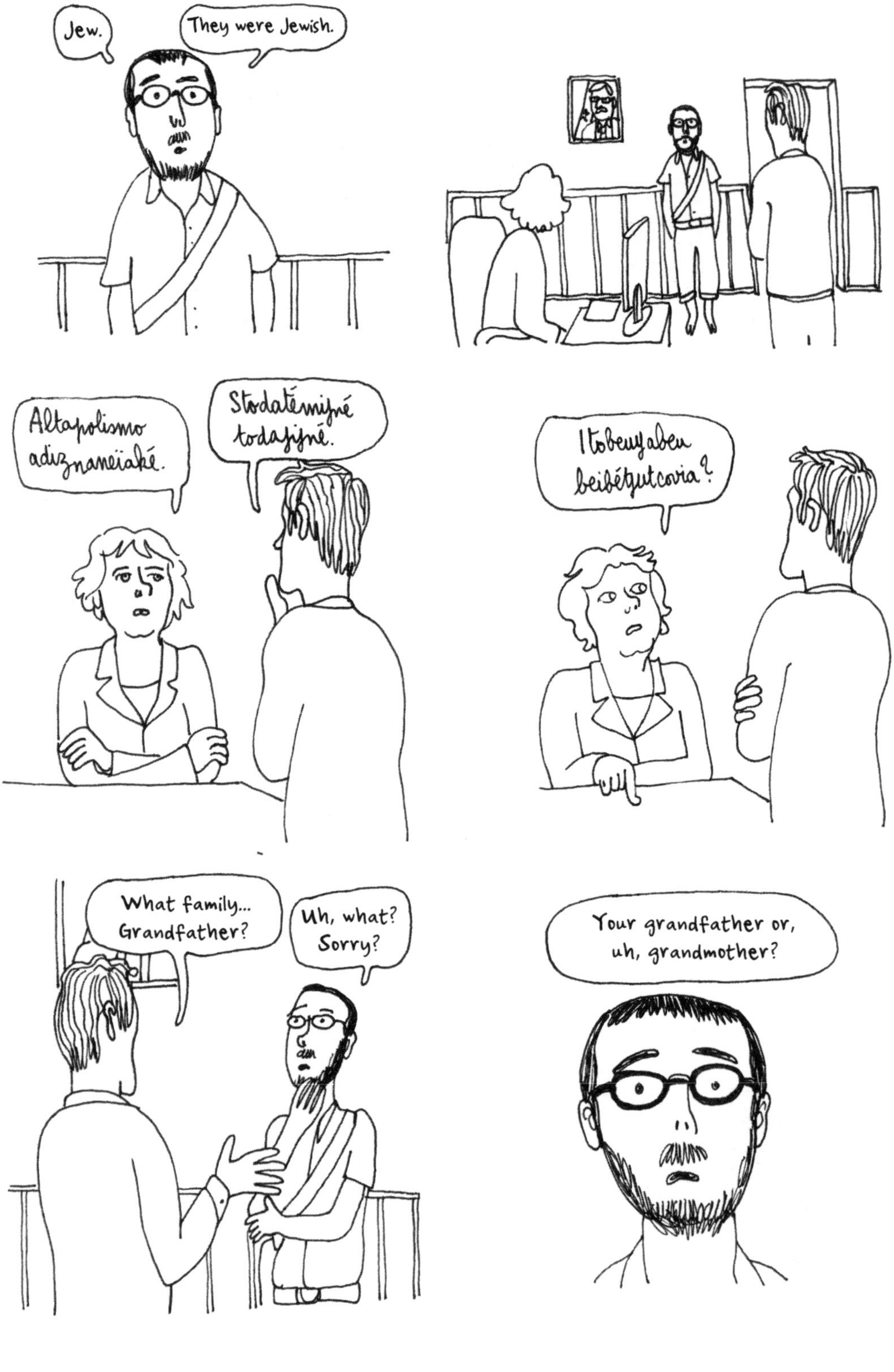
Jew.
They were Jewish.
What family...
Grandfather?
Uh, what?
Sorry?
Your grandfather or,
uh, grandmother?

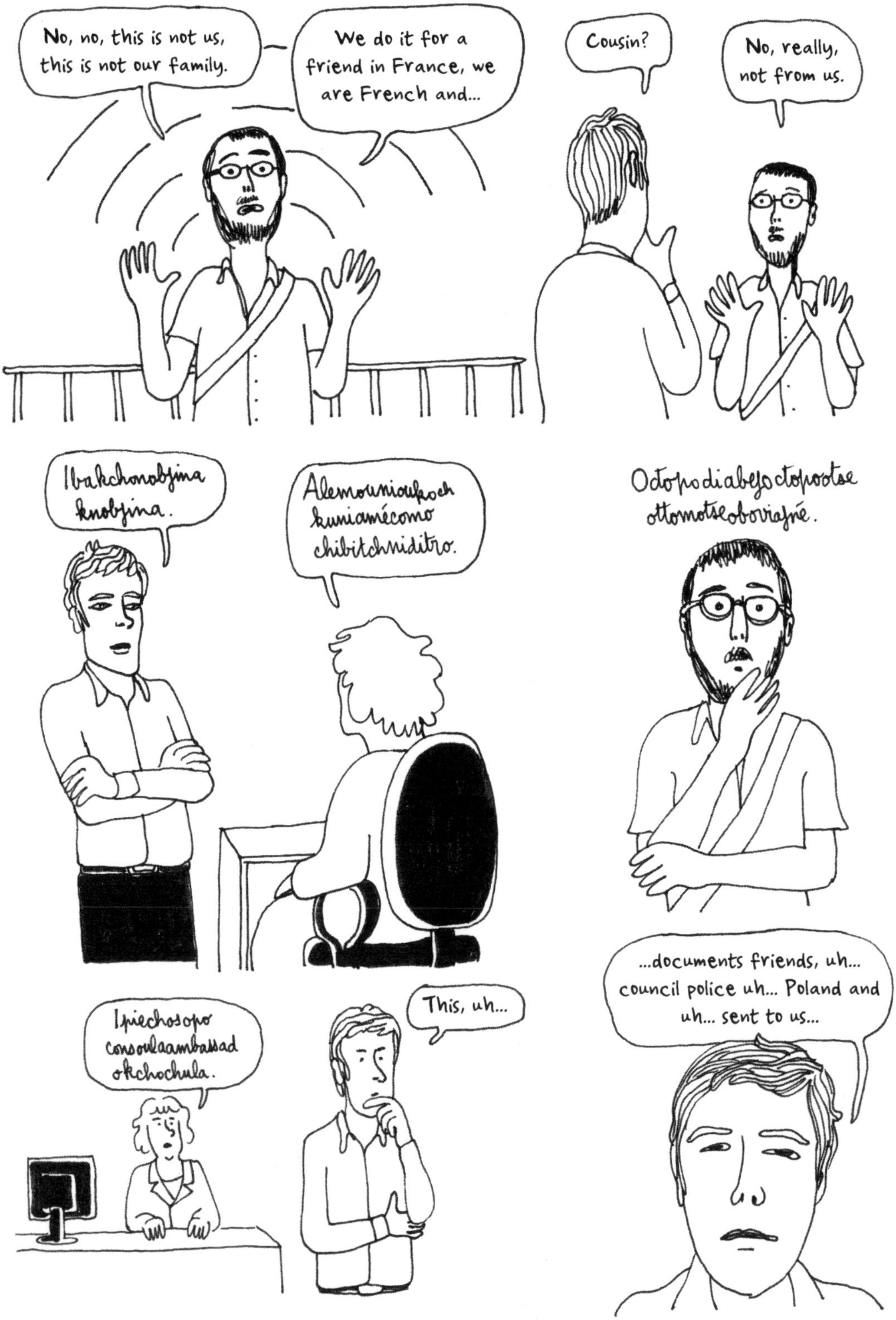
No, no, this is not us, this is not our family.
We do it for a friend in France, we are French and...
Cousin?
No, really, not from us.
Ibakchonobjina knobjina.
Alemouniouhoch kuniamécomo chibitchniditro.
Octopodiabejoctopootse ottomotseobovrajné.
Ipiechosopo consoulaambassad okchochula.
This, uh...
...documents friends, uh... council police uh... Poland and uh... sent to us...

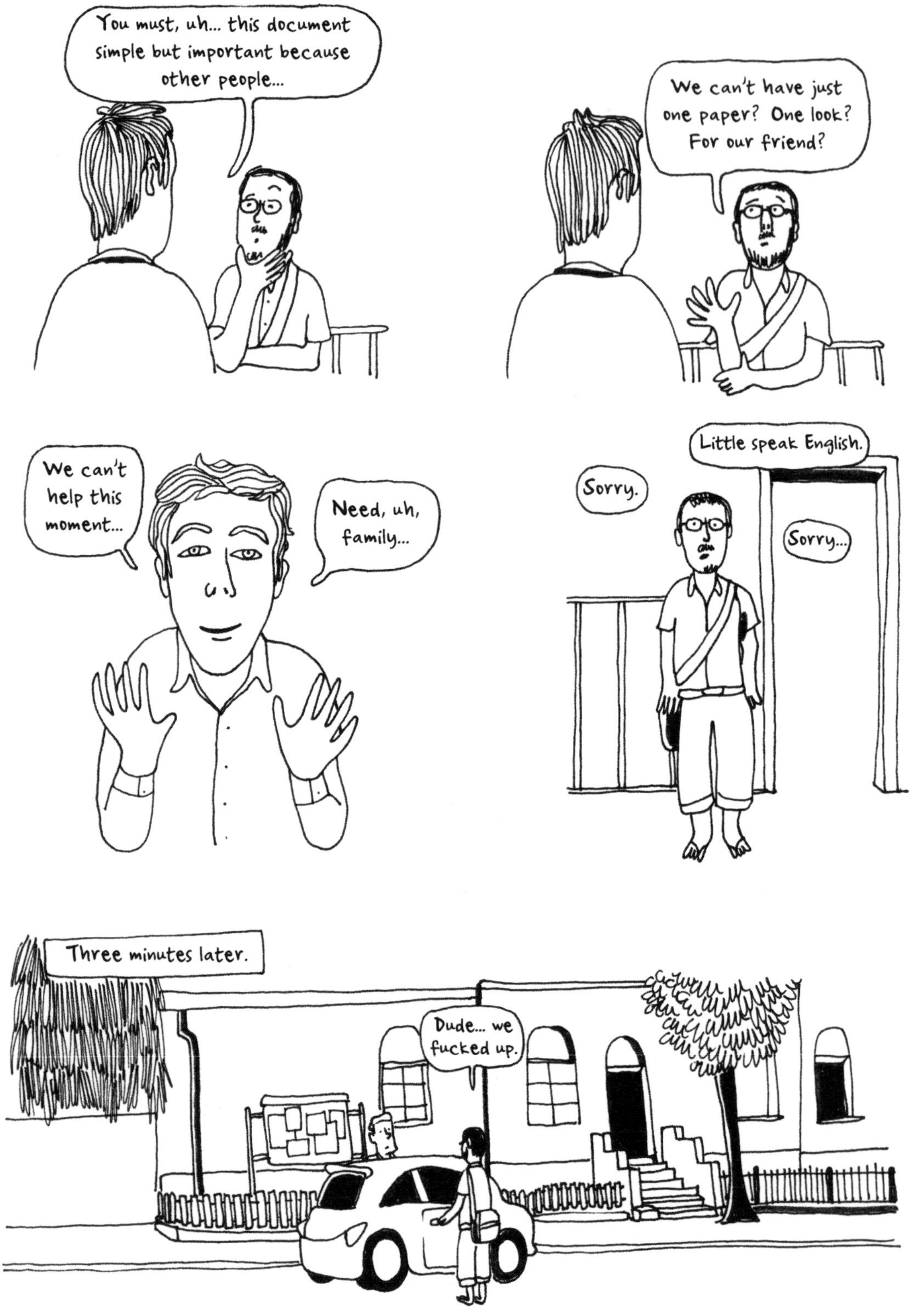
You must, uh... this document simple but important because other people...
We can't have just one paper? One look? For our friend?
We can't help this moment...
Need, uh, family...
Little speak English.
Sorry.
Sorry...
Three minutes later.
Dude... we fucked up.

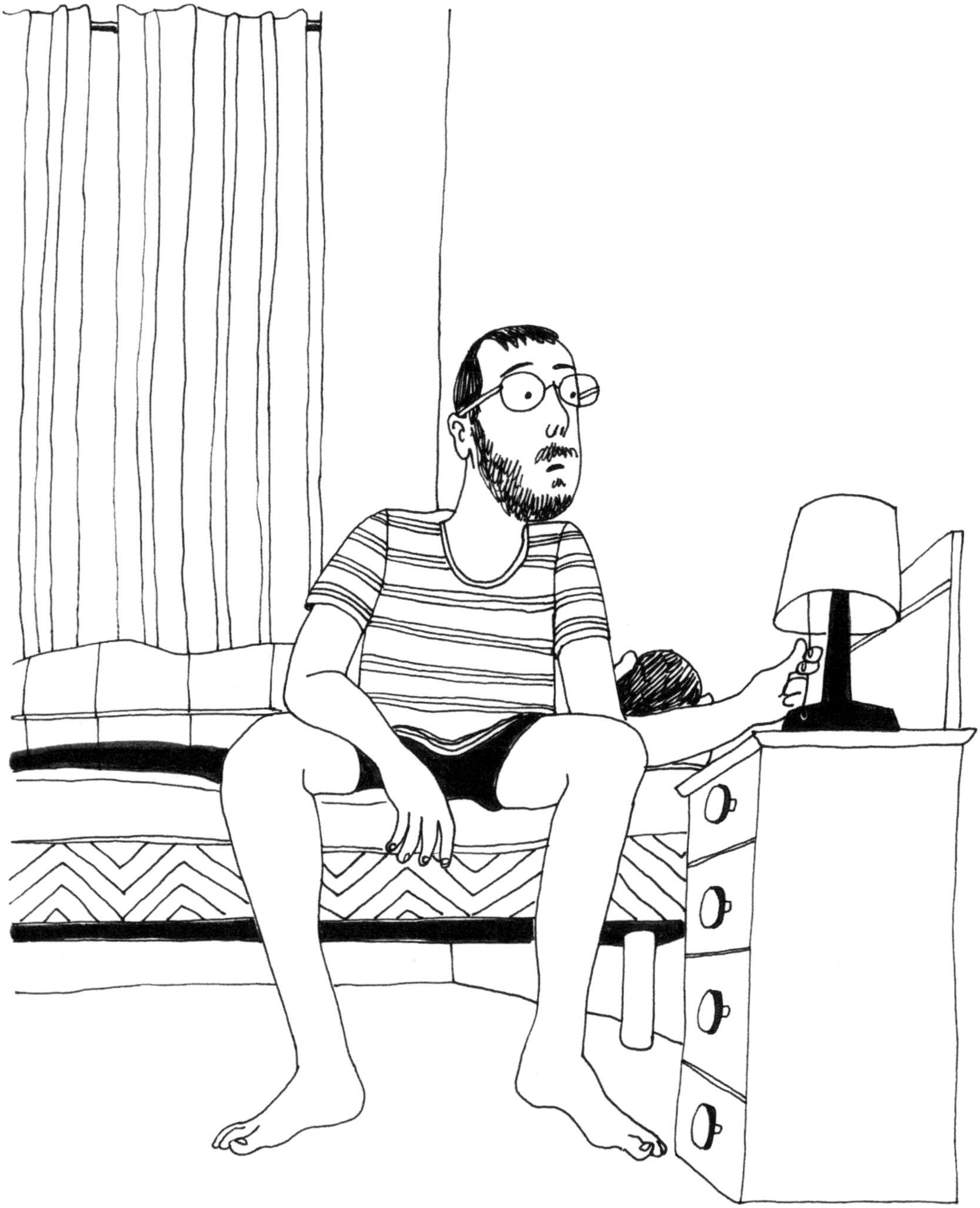

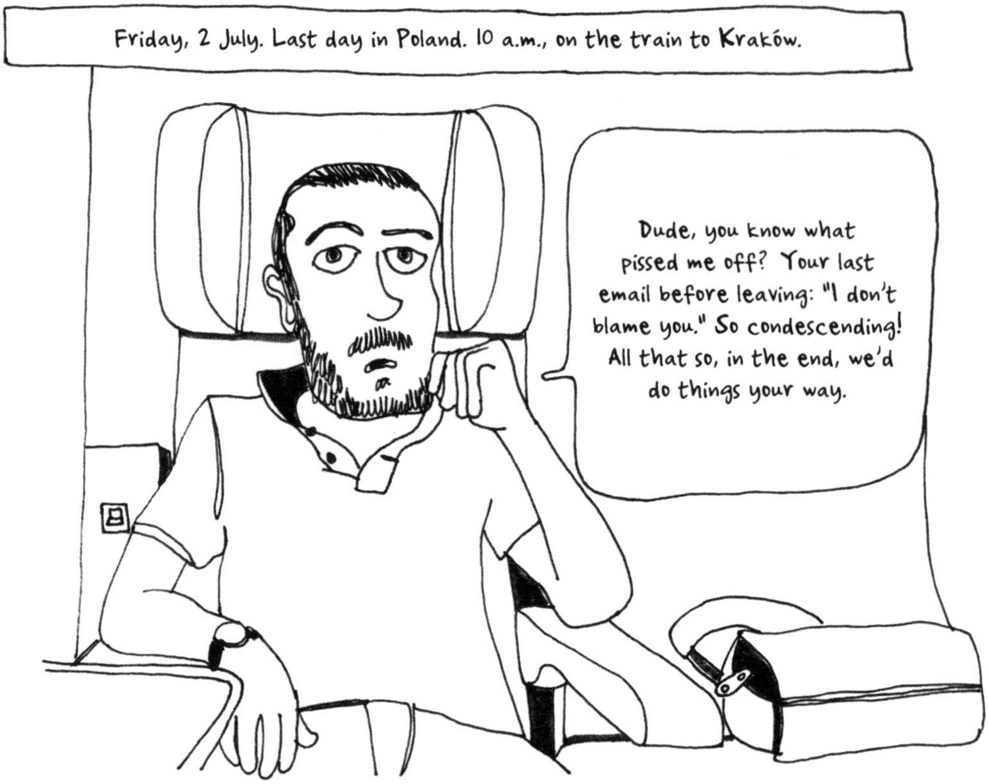
Friday, 2 July. Last day in Poland. 10 a.m., on the train to Kraków.
Dude, you know what pissed me off? Your last email before leaving: "I don't blame you." So condescending! All that so, in the end, we'd do things your way.

Voices Lost in the Landscape

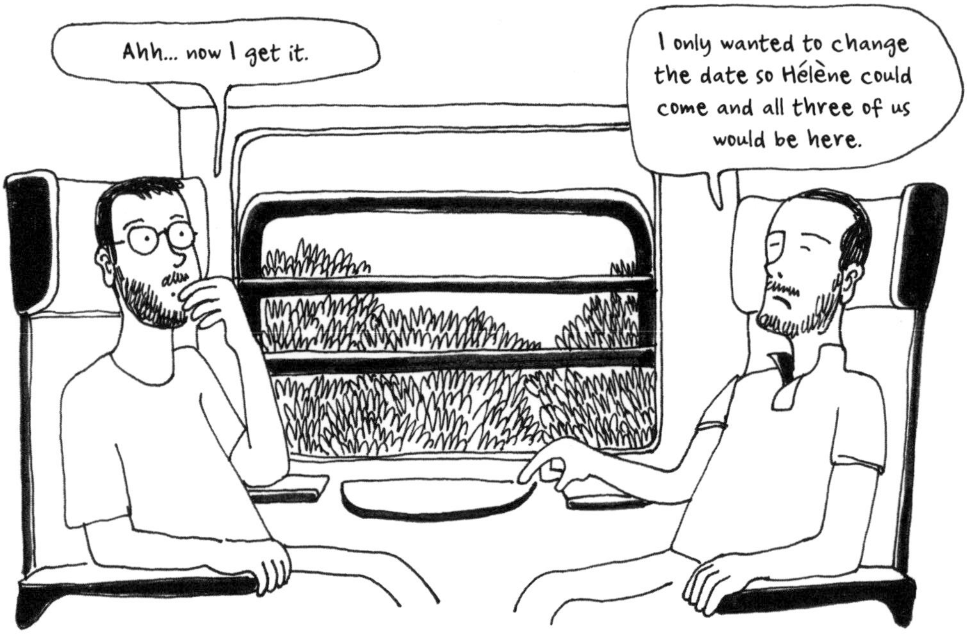
Ahh... now I get it.
I only wanted to change the date so Hélène could come and all three of us would be here.

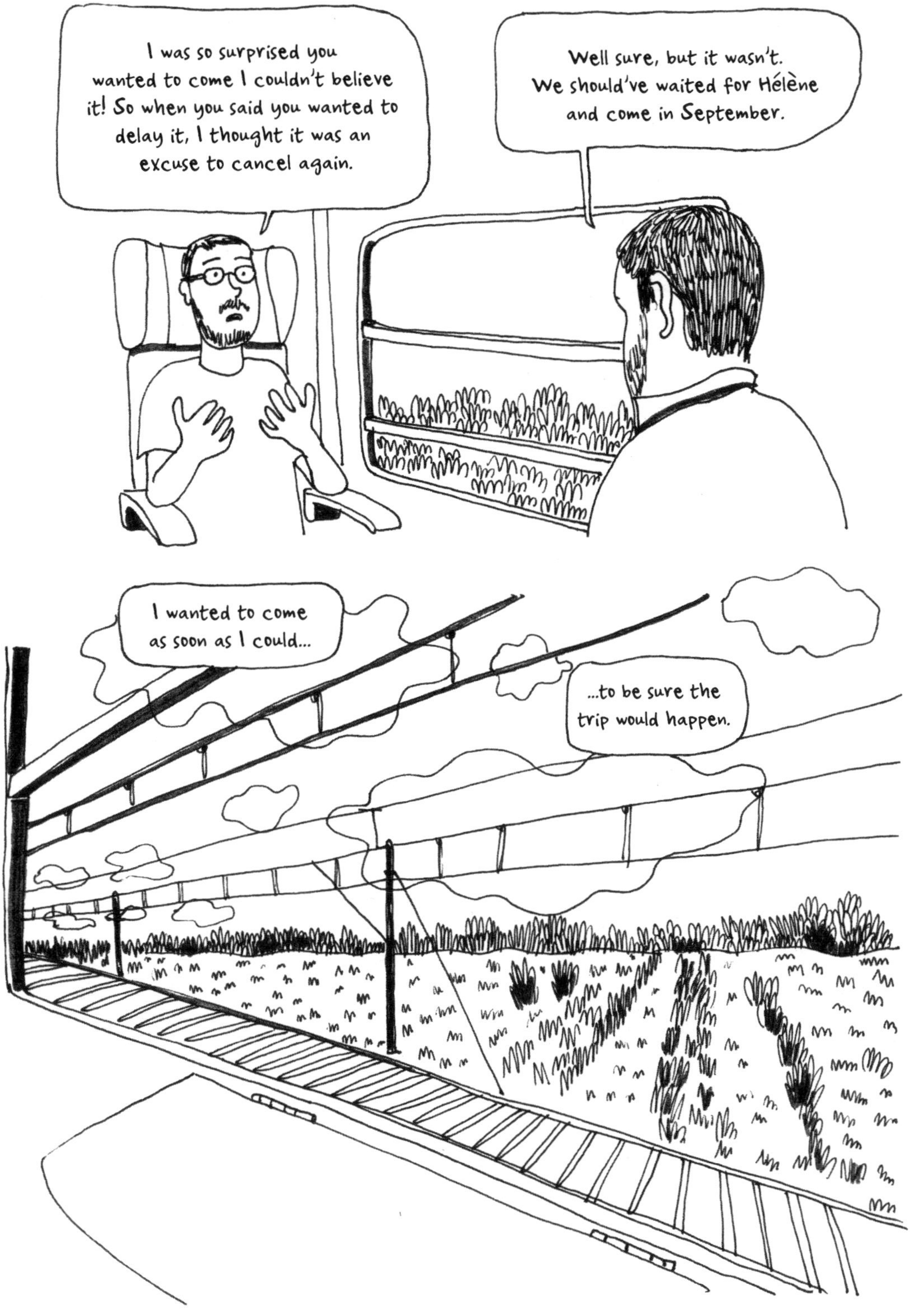
I was so surprised you wanted to come I couldn't believe it! So when you said you wanted to delay it, I thought it was an excuse to cancel again.
Well sure, but it wasn't. We should've waited for Hélène and come in September.
I wanted to come as soon as I could...
...to be sure the trip would happen.

End of the Line

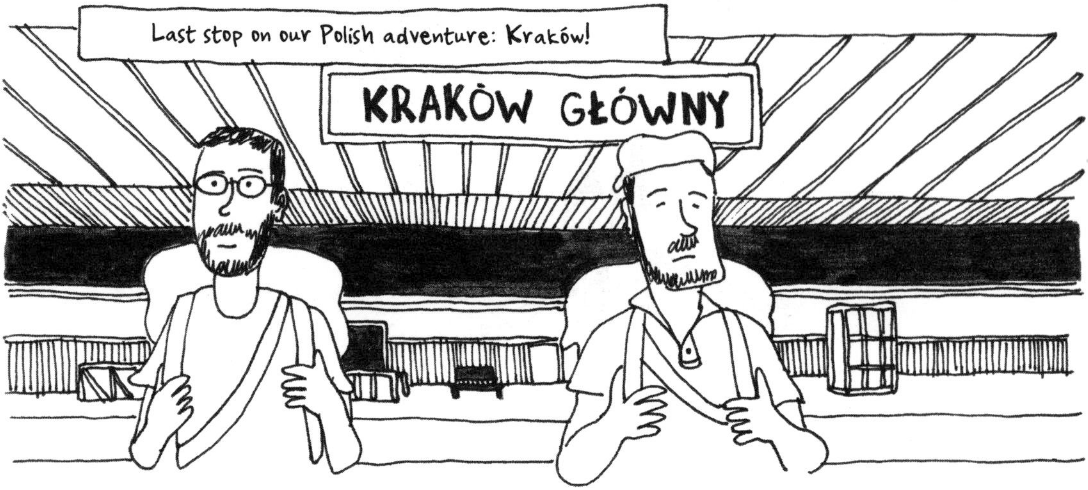
Last stop on our Polish adventure: Kraków!
KRAKÓW GŁÓWNY

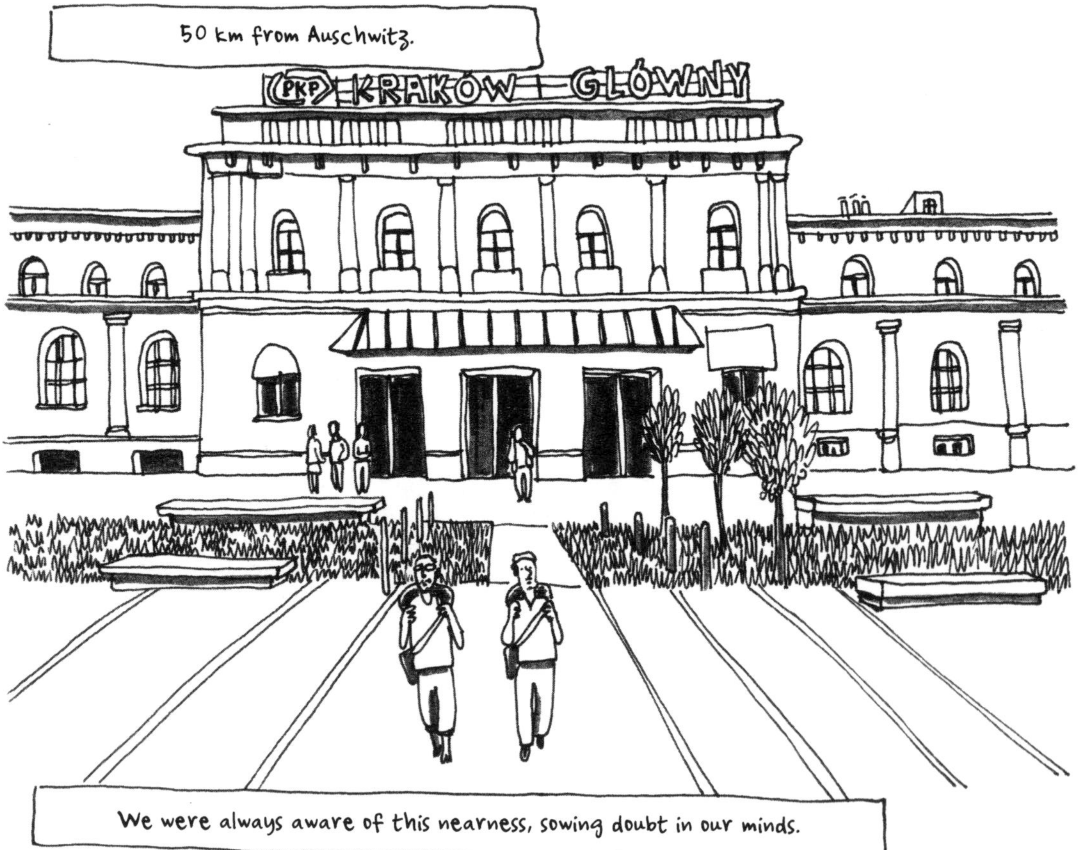
50 km from Auschwitz.
PKP KRAKÓW GŁÓWNY
We were always aware of this nearness, sowing doubt in our minds.

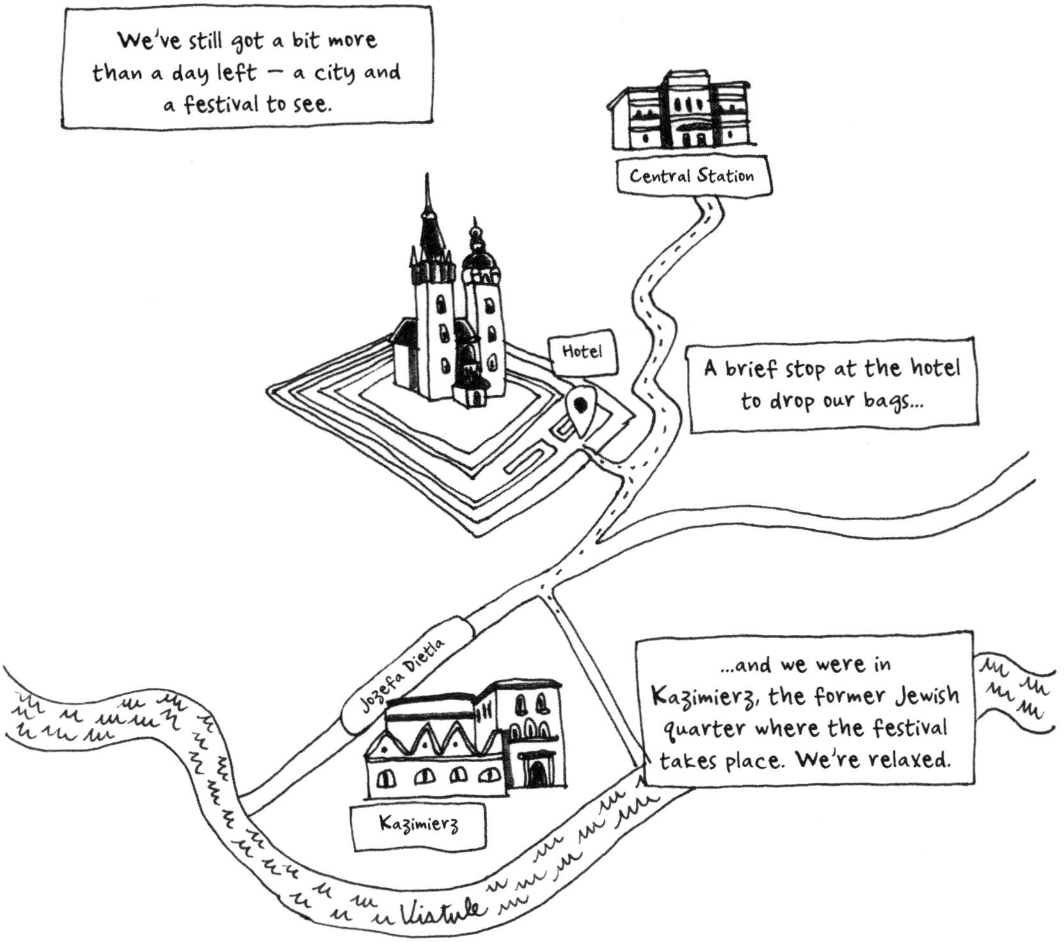
We've still got a bit more than a day left – a city and a festival to see.
Central Station
Hotel
A brief stop at the hotel to drop our bags...
Jozefa Dietla
...and we were in Kazimierz, the former Jewish quarter where the festival takes place. We're relaxed.
Kazimierz
Vistule

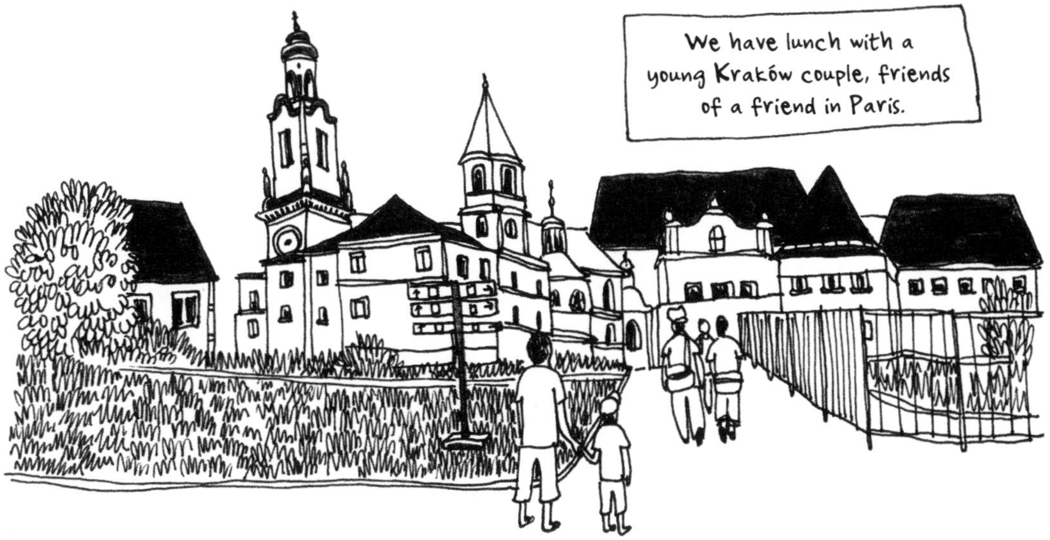
We have lunch with a young Kraków couple, friends of a friend in Paris.

A Bad Omen

We have a date to eat zapiekanki at Nowy Square.

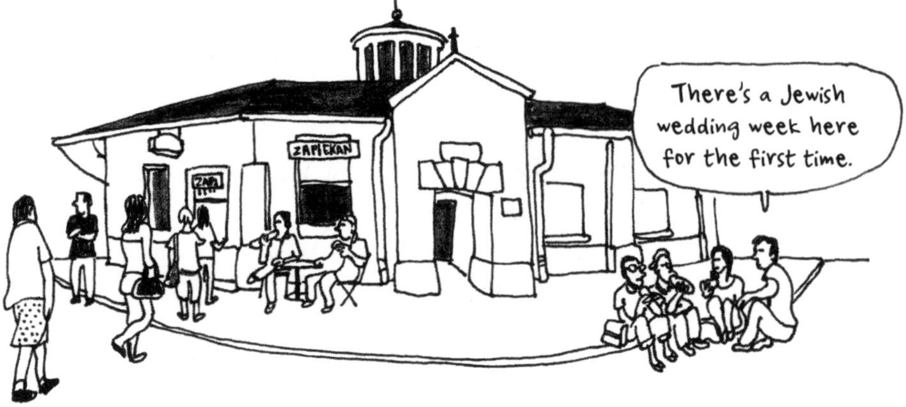
ZAPIEKAN
There's a Jewish wedding week here for the first time.

A zapiekanka isn't high-end gourmet, that's for sure. It's a kind of baguette with toppings (mushrooms, cured meats), and a little glaze of ketchup and chives.

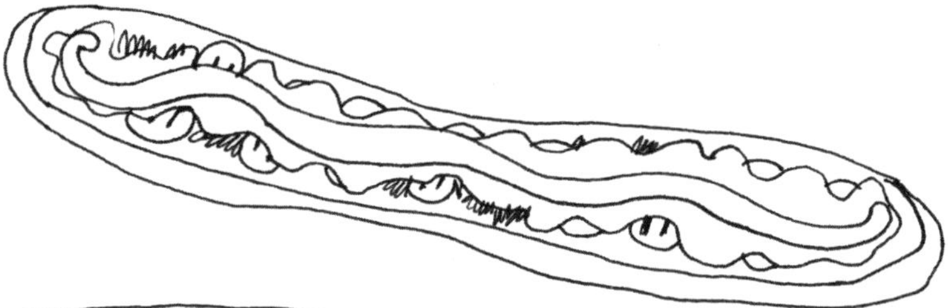

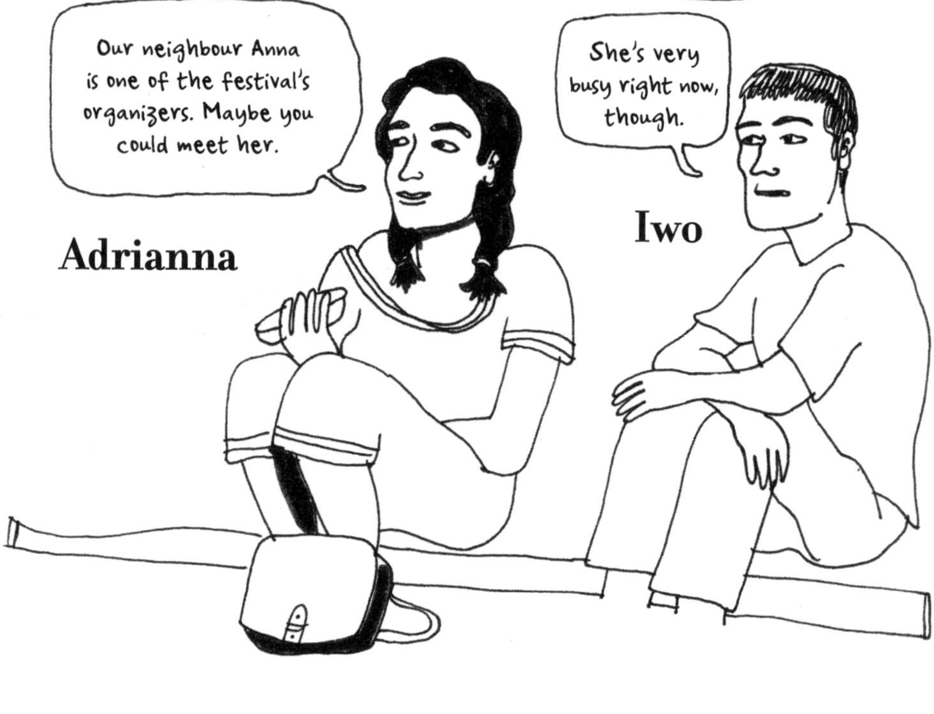
Our neighbour Anna is one of the festival's organizers. Maybe you could meet her.
She's very busy right now, though.
Adrianna
Iwo

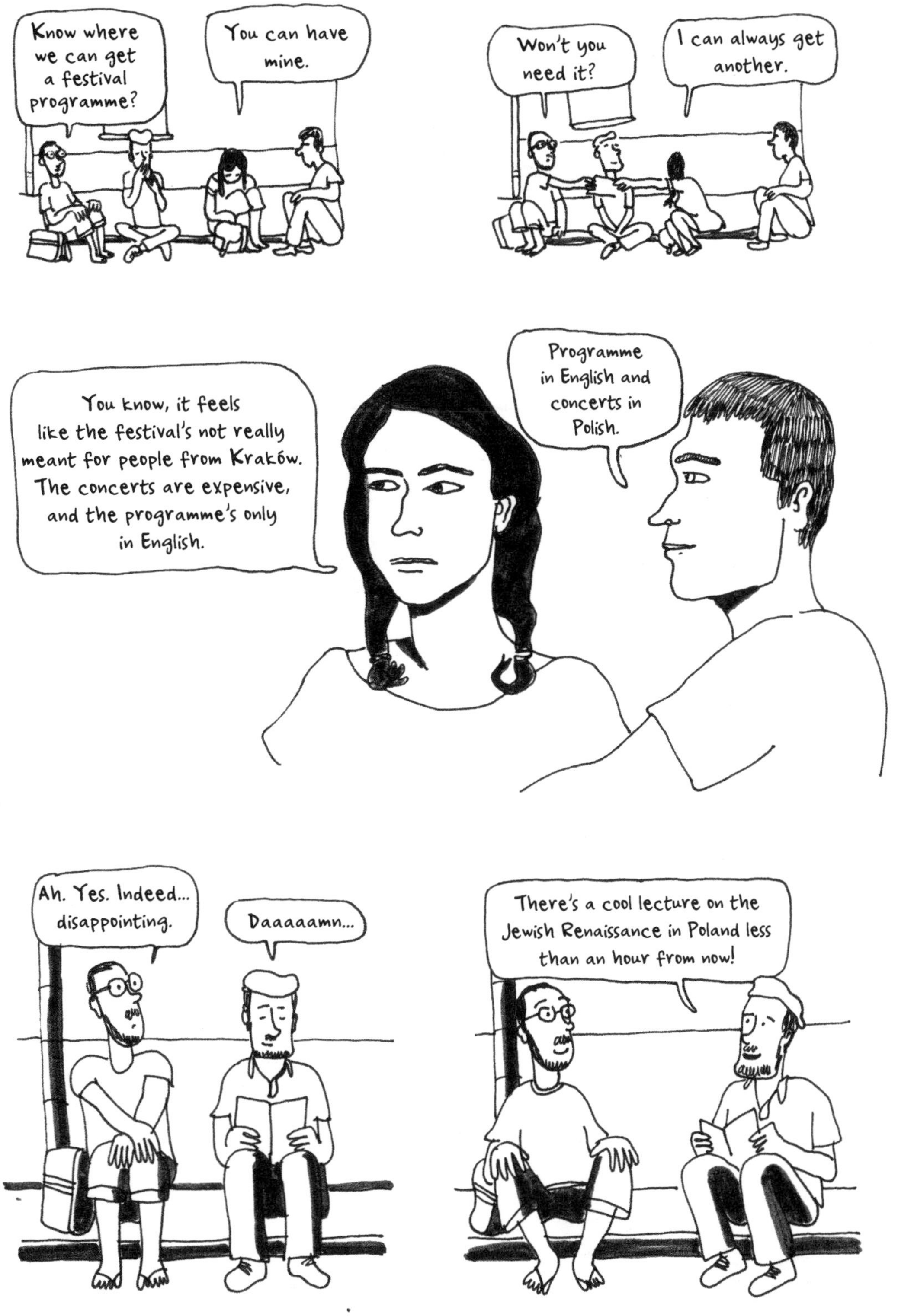
Know where we can get a festival programme?
You can have mine.
Won't you need it?
I can always get another.
You know, it feels like the festival's not really meant for people from Kraków. The concerts are expensive, and the programme's only in English.
Programme in English and concerts in Polish.
Ah. Yes. Indeed... disappointing.
Daaaaamn...
There's a cool lecture on the Jewish Renaissance in Poland less than an hour from now!

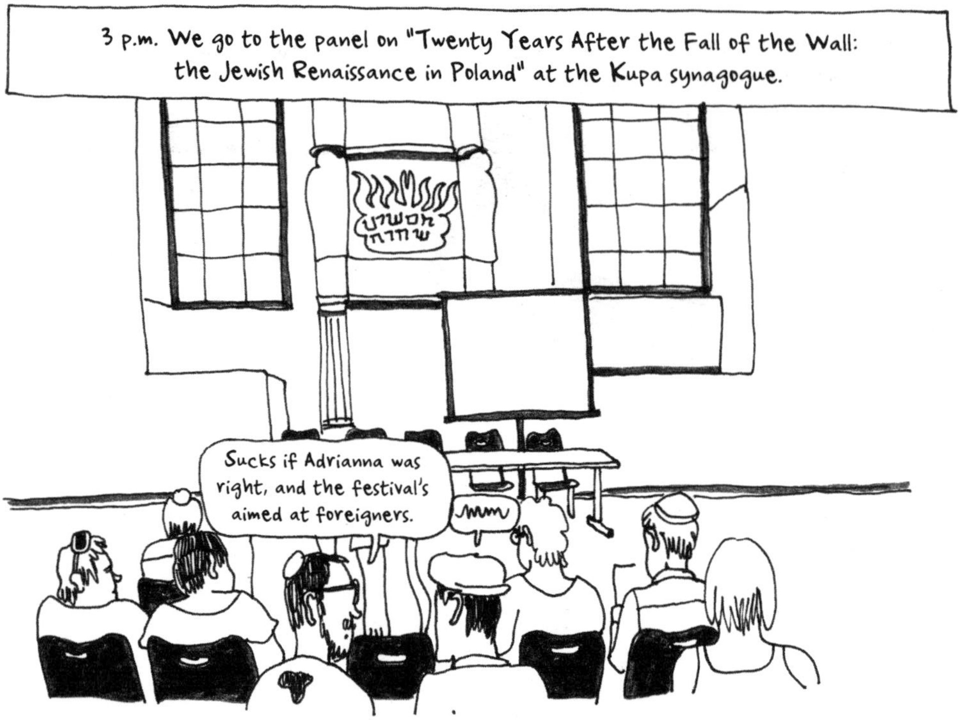
3 p.m. We go to the panel on "Twenty Years After the Fall of the Wall: the Jewish Renaissance in Poland" at the Kupa synagogue.
Sucks if Adrianna was right, and the festival's aimed at foreigners.

People like us

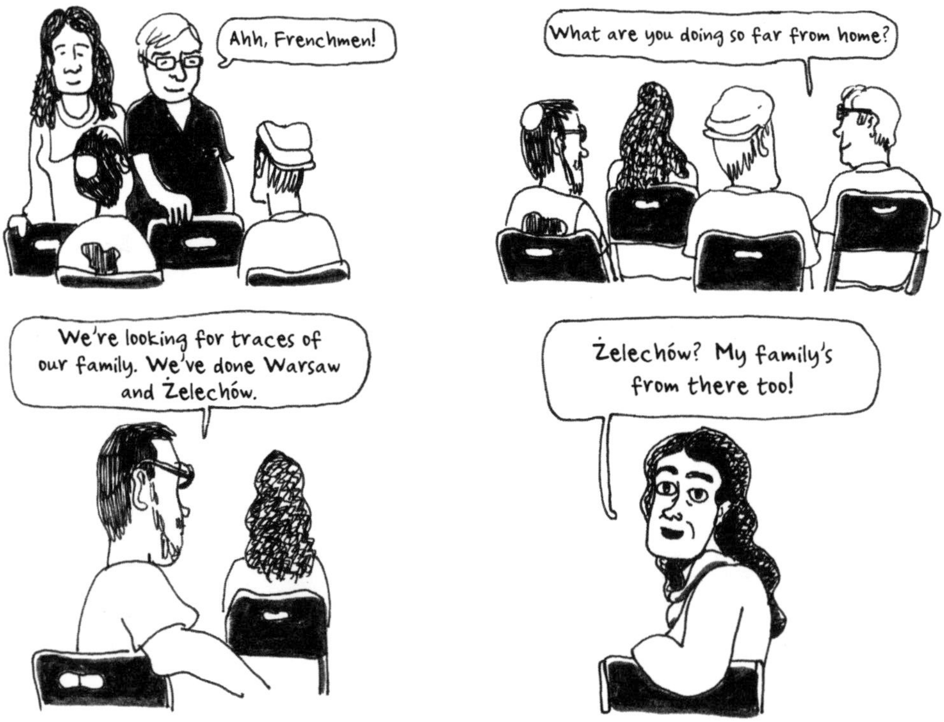
Ahh, Frenchmen!
What are you doing so far from home?
We're looking for traces of our family. We've done Warsaw and Żelechów.
Żelechów? My family's from there too!

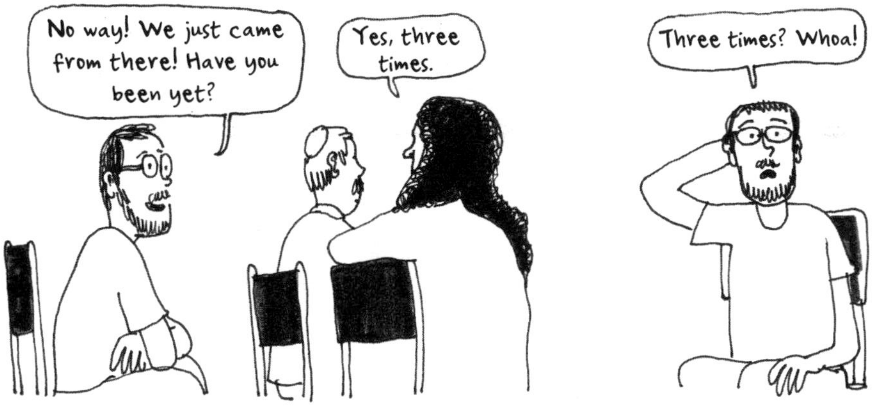
No way! We just came from there! Have you been yet?
Yes, three times.
Three times? Whoa!

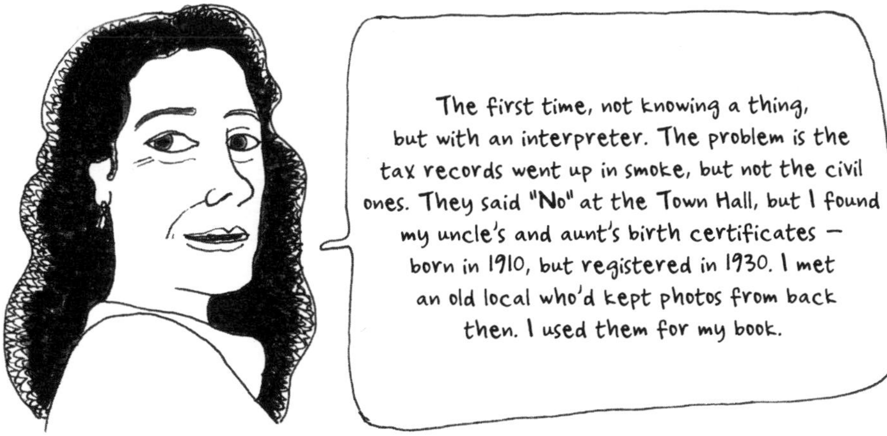
The first time, not knowing a thing, but with an interpreter. The problem is the tax records went up in smoke, but not the civil ones. They said "No" at the Town Hall, but I found my uncle's and aunt's birth certificates — born in 1910, but registered in 1930. I met an old local who'd kept photos from back then. I used them for my book.

Françoise Milewski

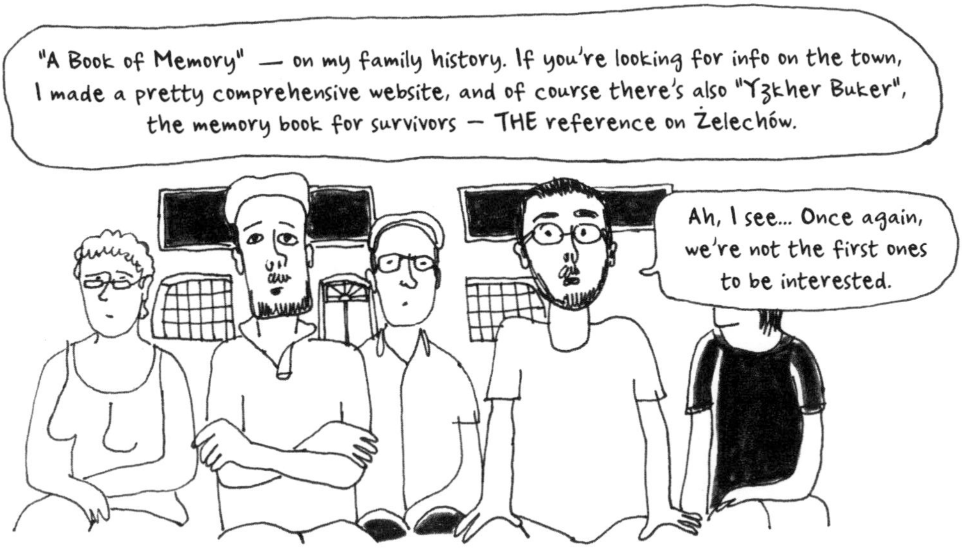
"A Book of Memory" — on my family history. If you're looking for info on the town, I made a pretty comprehensive website, and of course there's also "Yzkher Buker", the memory book for survivors — THE reference on Żelechów.
Ah, I see... Once again, we're not the first ones to be interested.

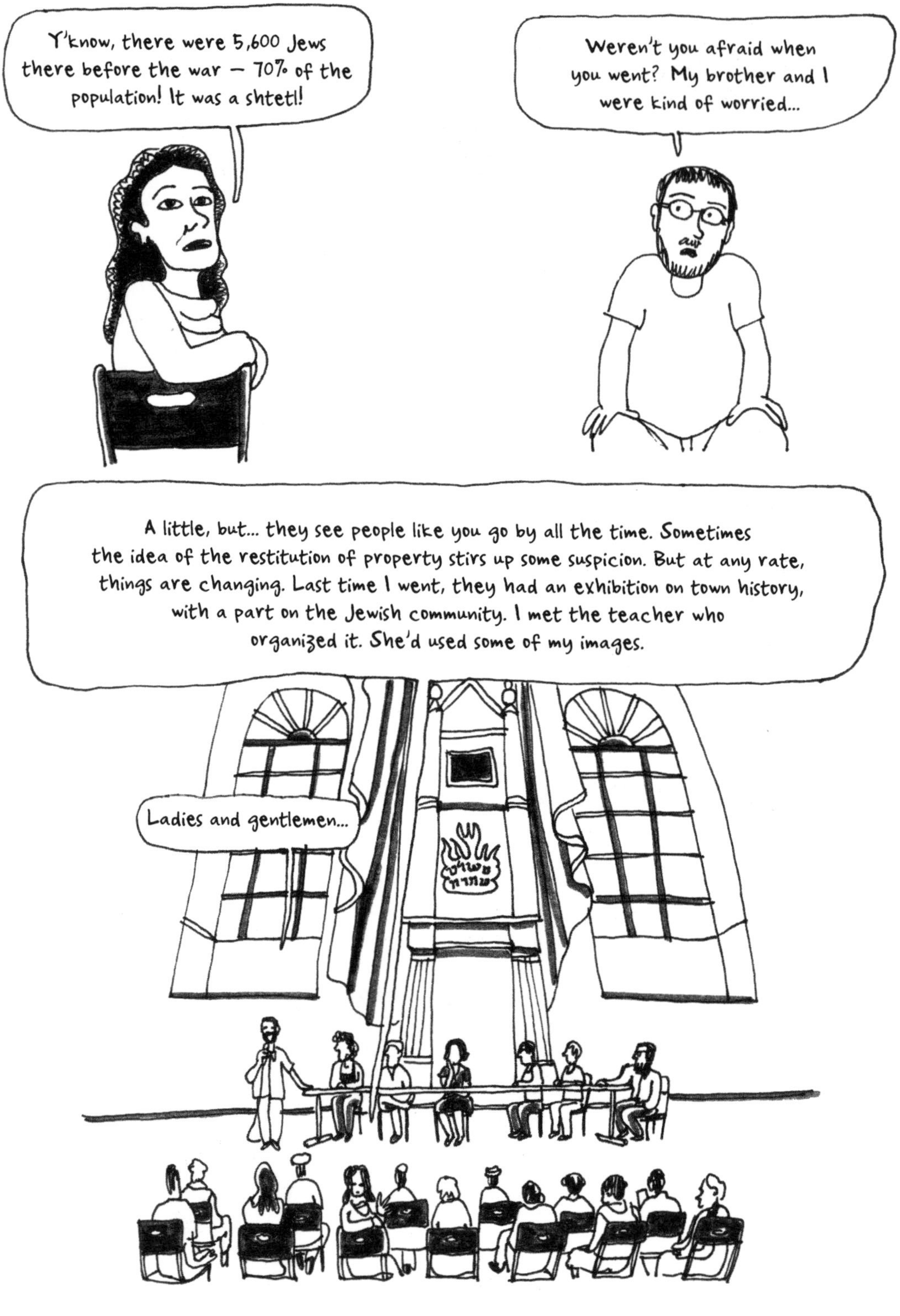
Y'know, there were 5,600 Jews there before the war – 70% of the population! It was a shtetl!
Weren't you afraid when you went? My brother and I were kind of worried...
A little, but... they see people like you go by all the time. Sometimes the idea of the restitution of property stirs up some suspicion. But at any rate, things are changing. Last time I went, they had an exhibition on town history, with a part on the Jewish community. I met the teacher who organized it. She'd used some of my images.
Ladies and gentlemen...

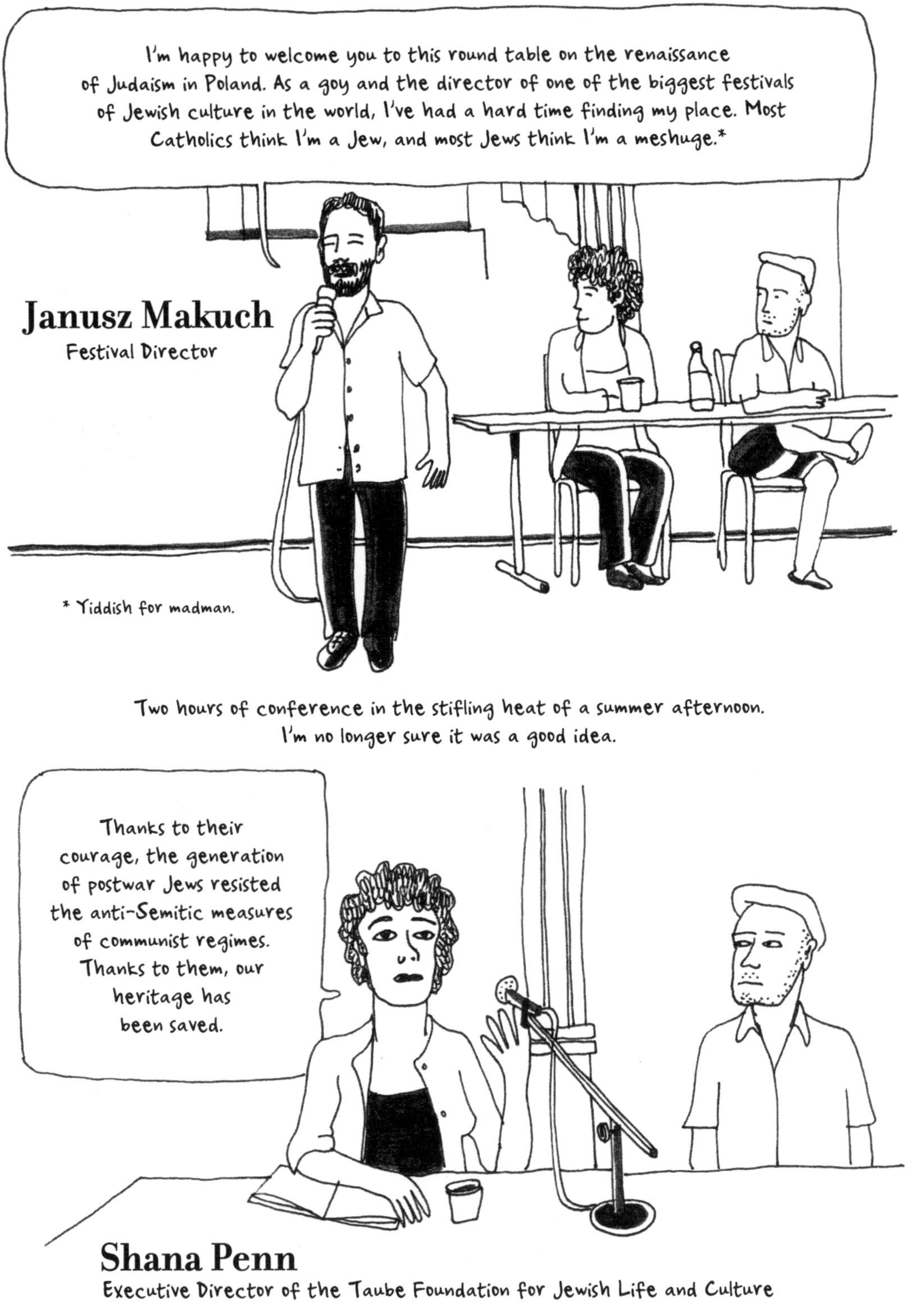
I'm happy to welcome you to this round table on the renaissance of Judaism in Poland. As a goy and the director of one of the biggest festivals of Jewish culture in the world, I've had a hard time finding my place. Most Catholics think I'm a Jew, and most Jews think I'm a meshuge.*
Janusz Makuch
Festival Director
* Yiddish for madman.
Two hours of conference in the stifling heat of a summer afternoon. I'm no longer sure it was a good idea.
Thanks to their courage, the generation of postwar Jews resisted the anti-Semitic measures of communist regimes. Thanks to them, our heritage has been saved.
Shana Penn
Executive Director of the Taube Foundation for Jewish Life and Culture

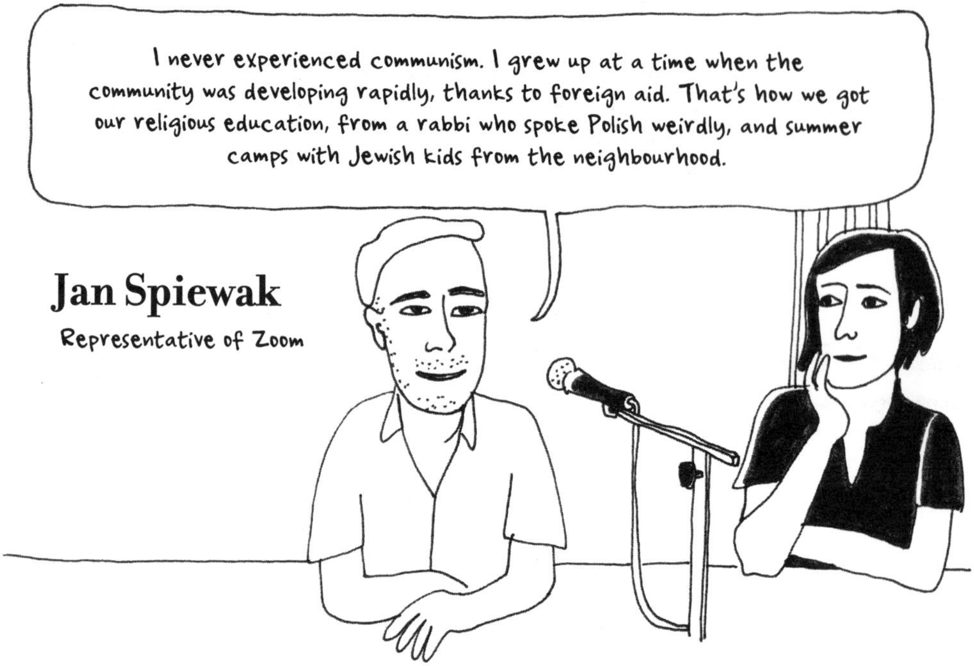
I never experienced communism. I grew up at a time when the community was developing rapidly, thanks to foreign aid. That's how we got our religious education, from a rabbi who spoke Polish weirdly, and summer camps with Jewish kids from the neighbourhood.
Jan Spiewak
Representative of Zoom

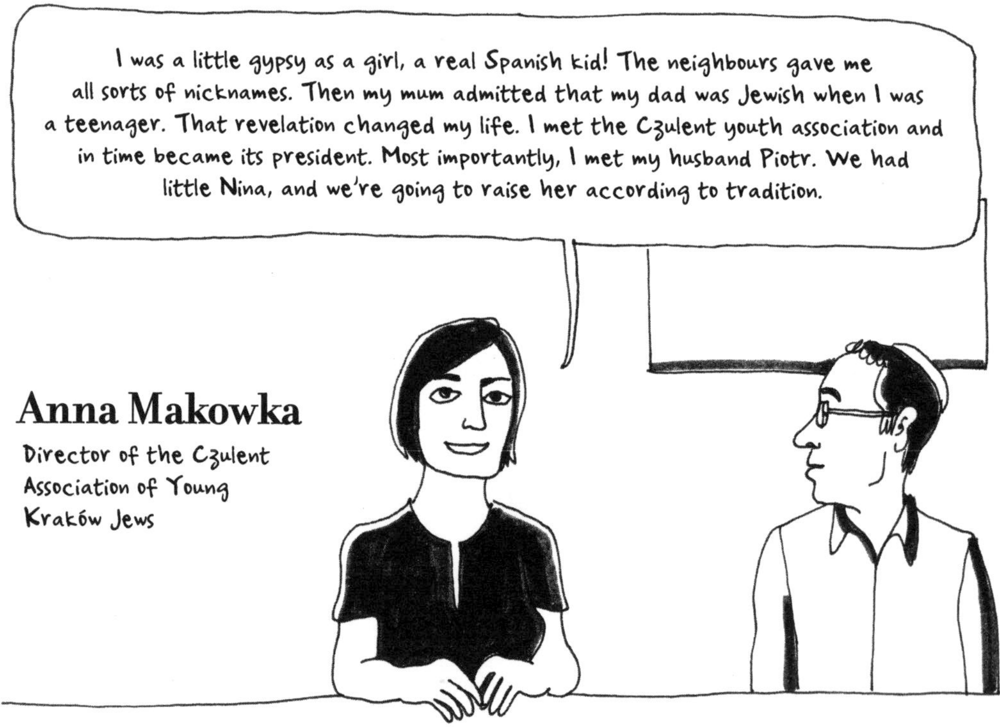
I was a little gypsy as a girl, a real Spanish kid! The neighbours gave me all sorts of nicknames. Then my mum admitted that my dad was Jewish when I was a teenager. That revelation changed my life. I met the Czulent youth association and in time became its president. Most importantly, I met my husband Piotr. We had little Nina, and we're going to raise her according to tradition.
Anna Makowka
Director of the Czulent Association of Young Kraków Jews

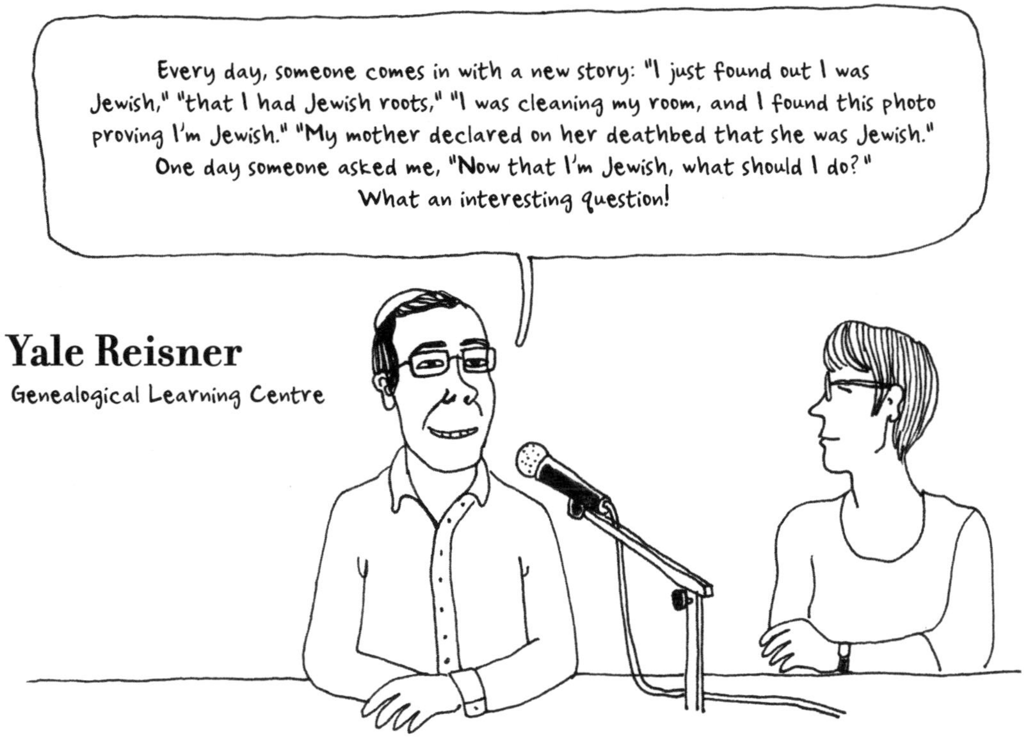
Every day, someone comes in with a new story: "I just found out I was Jewish," "that I had Jewish roots," "I was cleaning my room, and I found this photo proving I'm Jewish." "My mother declared on her deathbed that she was Jewish." One day someone asked me, "Now that I'm Jewish, what should I do?" What an interesting question!
Yale Reisner
Genealogical Learning Centre

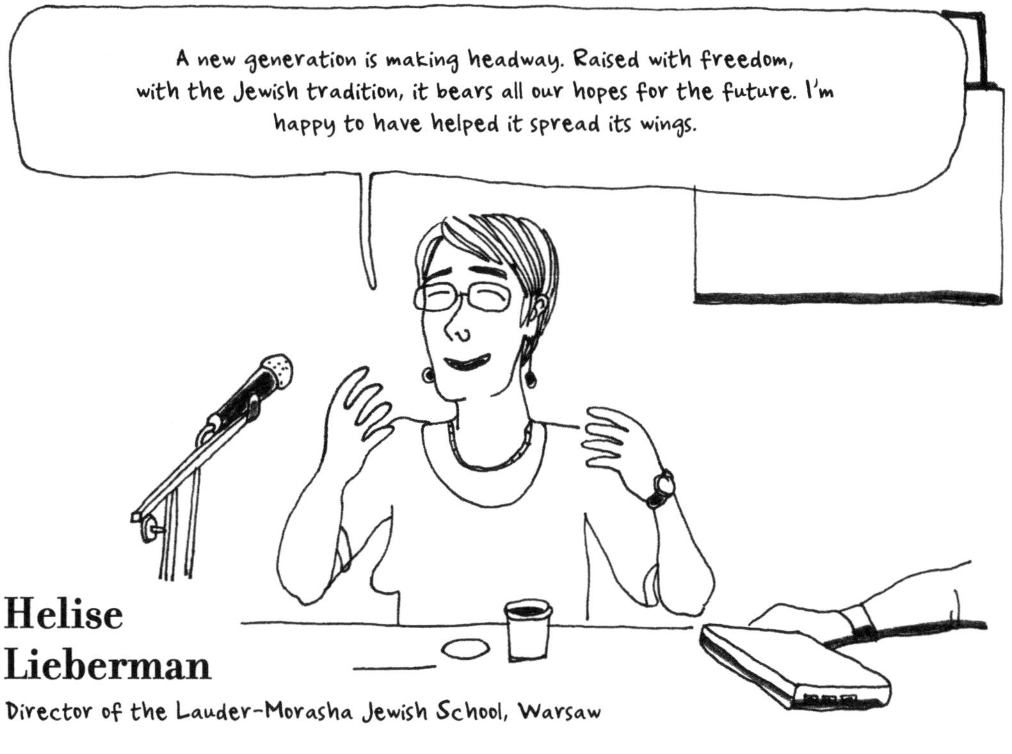
A new generation is making headway. Raised with freedom, with the Jewish tradition, it bears all our hopes for the future. I'm happy to have helped it spread its wings.
Helise Lieberman
Director of the Lauder-Morasha Jewish School, Warsaw

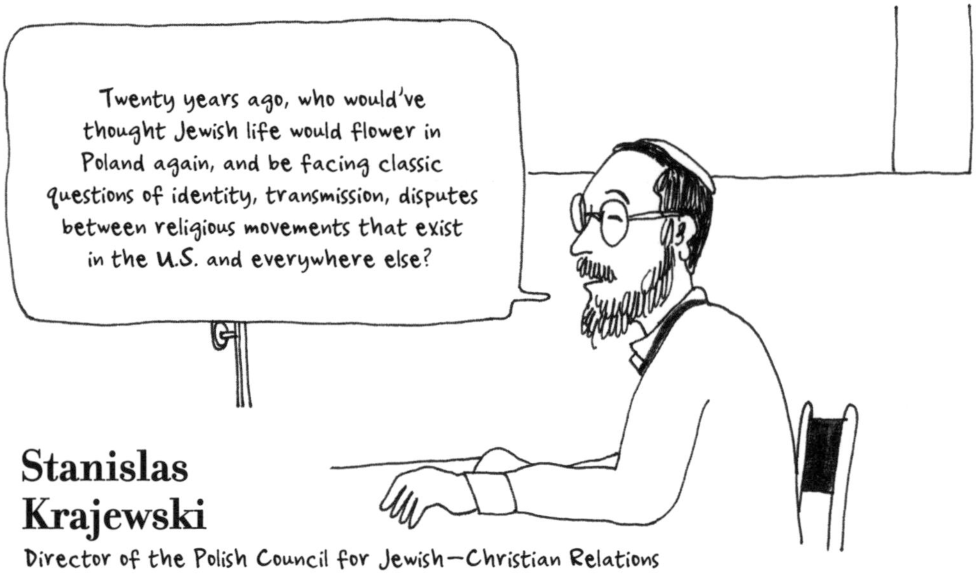
Twenty years ago, who would've thought Jewish life would flower in Poland again, and be facing classic questions of identity, transmission, disputes between religious movements that exist in the U.S. and everywhere else?
Stanislas Krajewski
Director of the Polish Council for Jewish–Christian Relations

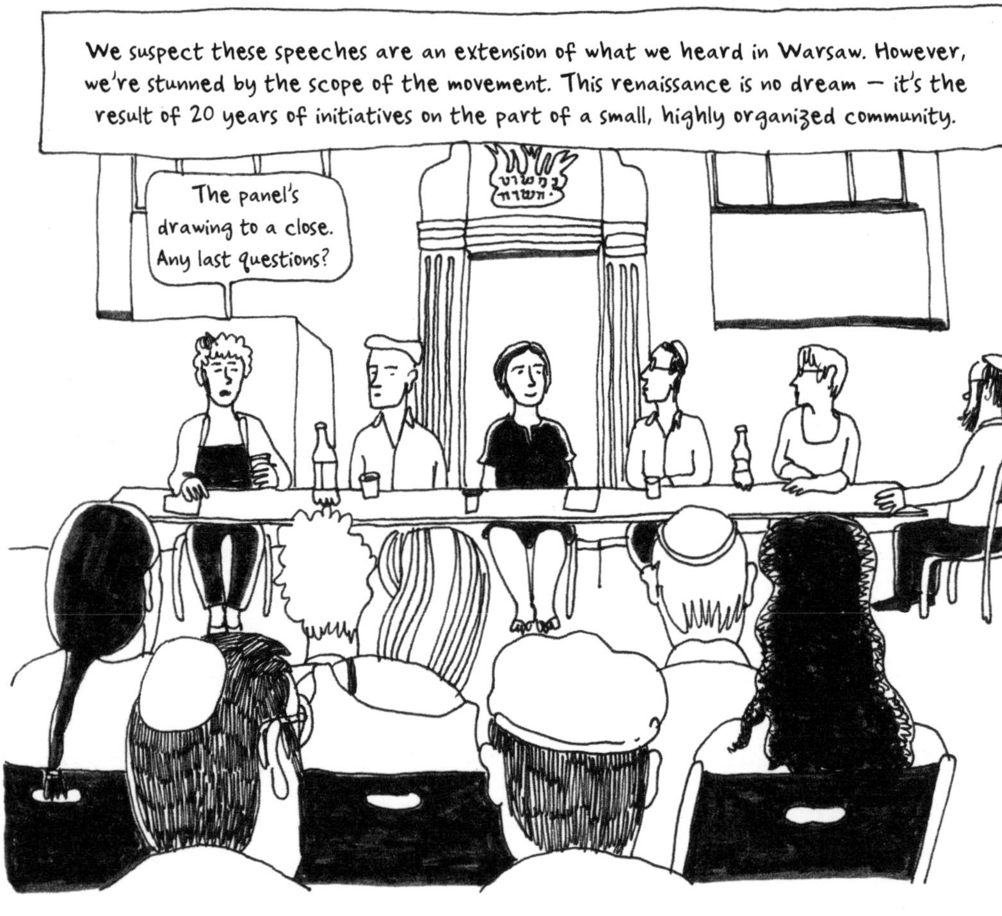
We suspect these speeches are an extension of what we heard in Warsaw. However, we're stunned by the scope of the movement. This renaissance is no dream — it's the result of 20 years of initiatives on the part of a small, highly organized community.
The panel's drawing to a close. Any last questions?

The ones who came back

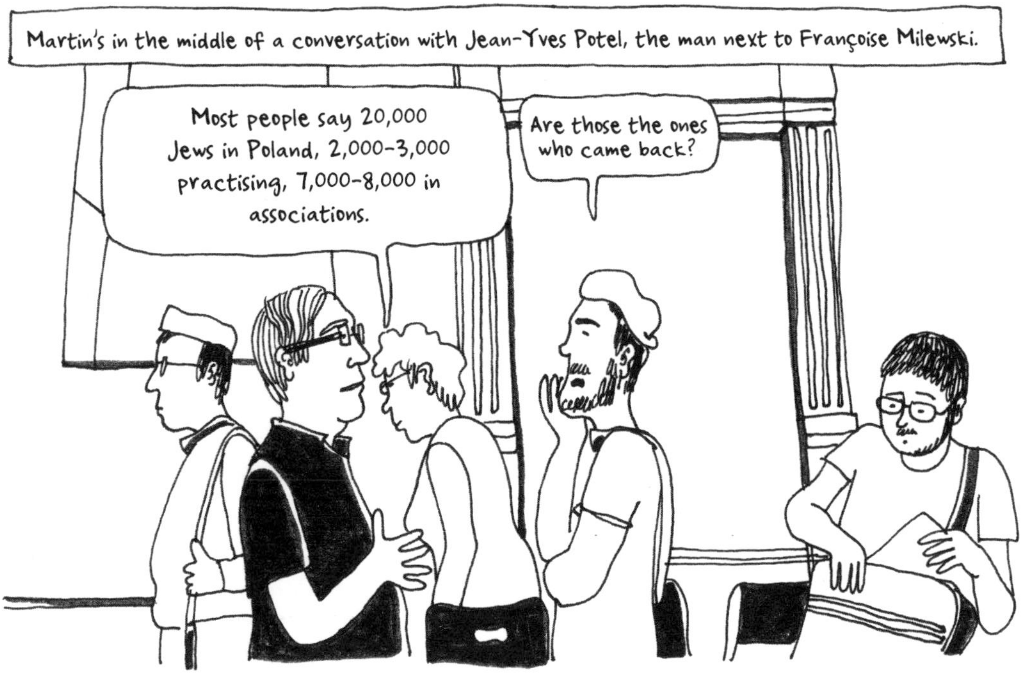
Martin's in the middle of a conversation with Jean-Yves Potel, the man next to Françoise Milewski.
Most people say 20,000 Jews in Poland, 2,000-3,000 practising, 7,000-8,000 in associations.
Are those the ones who came back?

Jean-Yves Potel

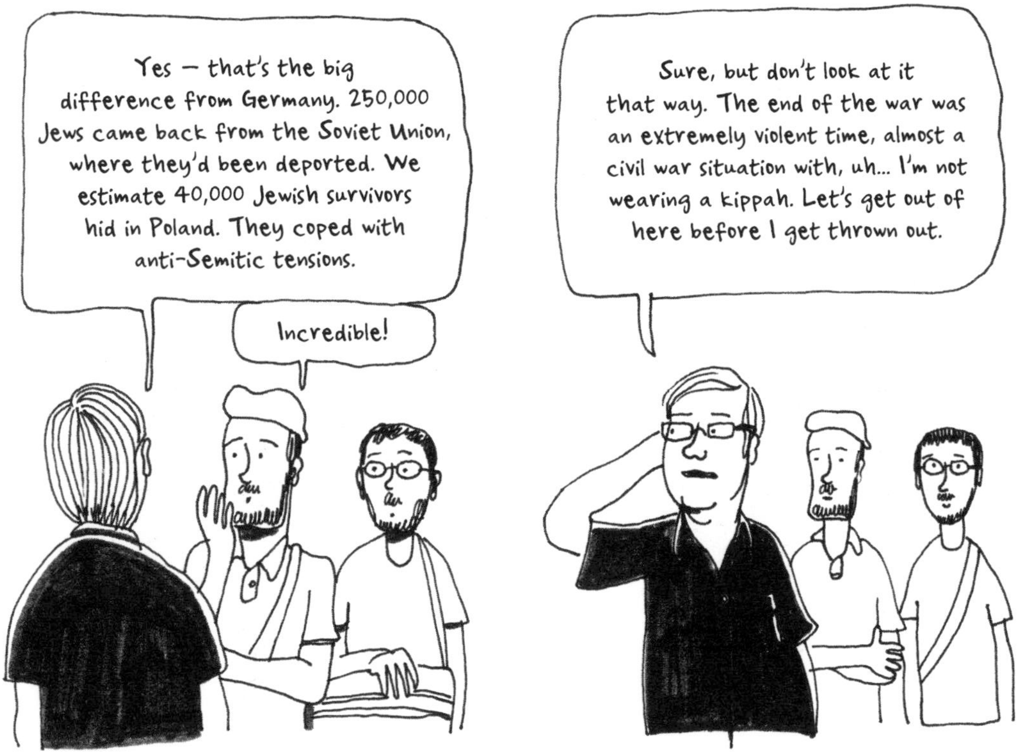
Yes — that's the big difference from Germany. 250,000 Jews came back from the Soviet Union, where they'd been deported. We estimate 40,000 Jewish survivors hid in Poland. They coped with anti-Semitic tensions.
Incredible!
Sure, but don't look at it that way. The end of the war was an extremely violent time, almost a civil war situation with, uh... I'm not wearing a kippah. Let's get out of here before I get thrown out.

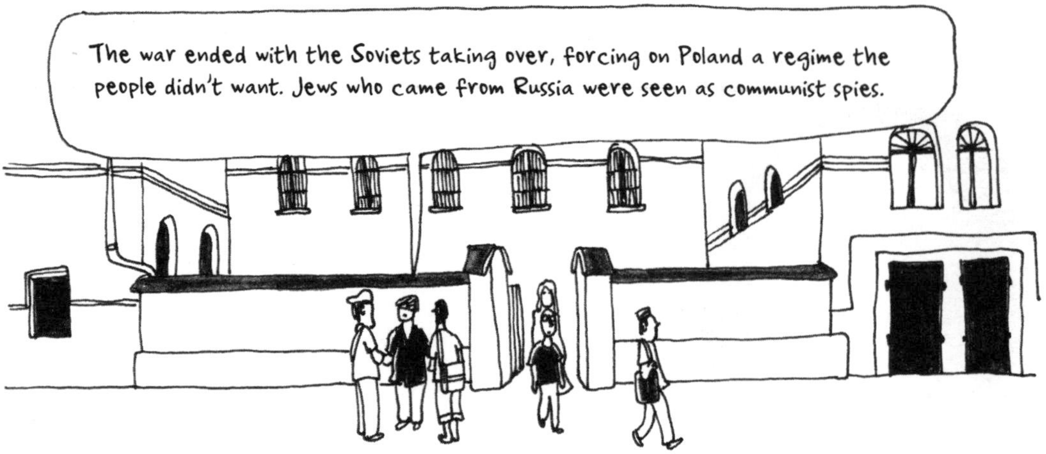
The war ended with the Soviets taking over, forcing on Poland a regime the people didn't want. Jews who came from Russia were seen as communist spies.

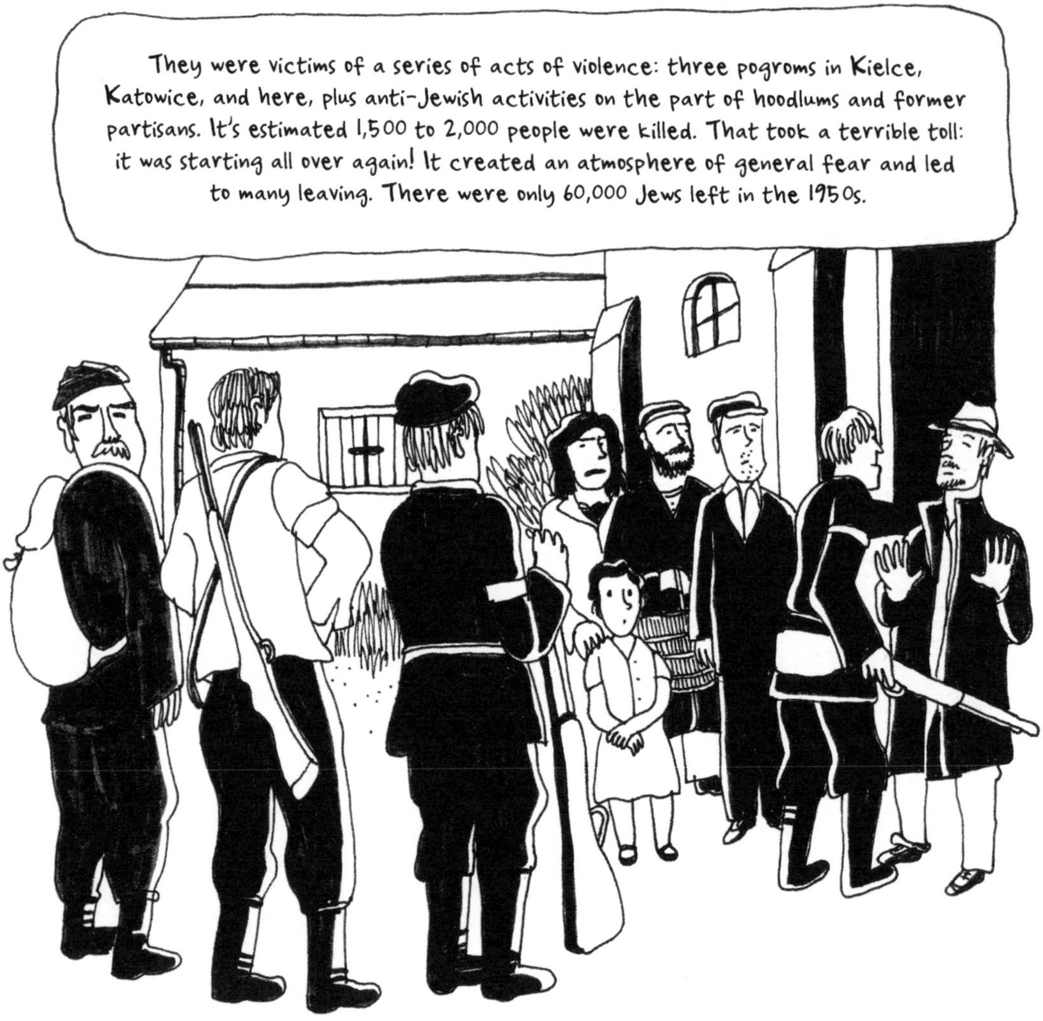
They were victims of a series of acts of violence: three pogroms in Kielce, Katowice, and here, plus anti-Jewish activities on the part of hoodlums and former partisans. It's estimated 1,500 to 2,000 people were killed. That took a terrible toll: it was starting all over again! It created an atmosphere of general fear and led to many leaving. There were only 60,000 Jews left in the 1950s.

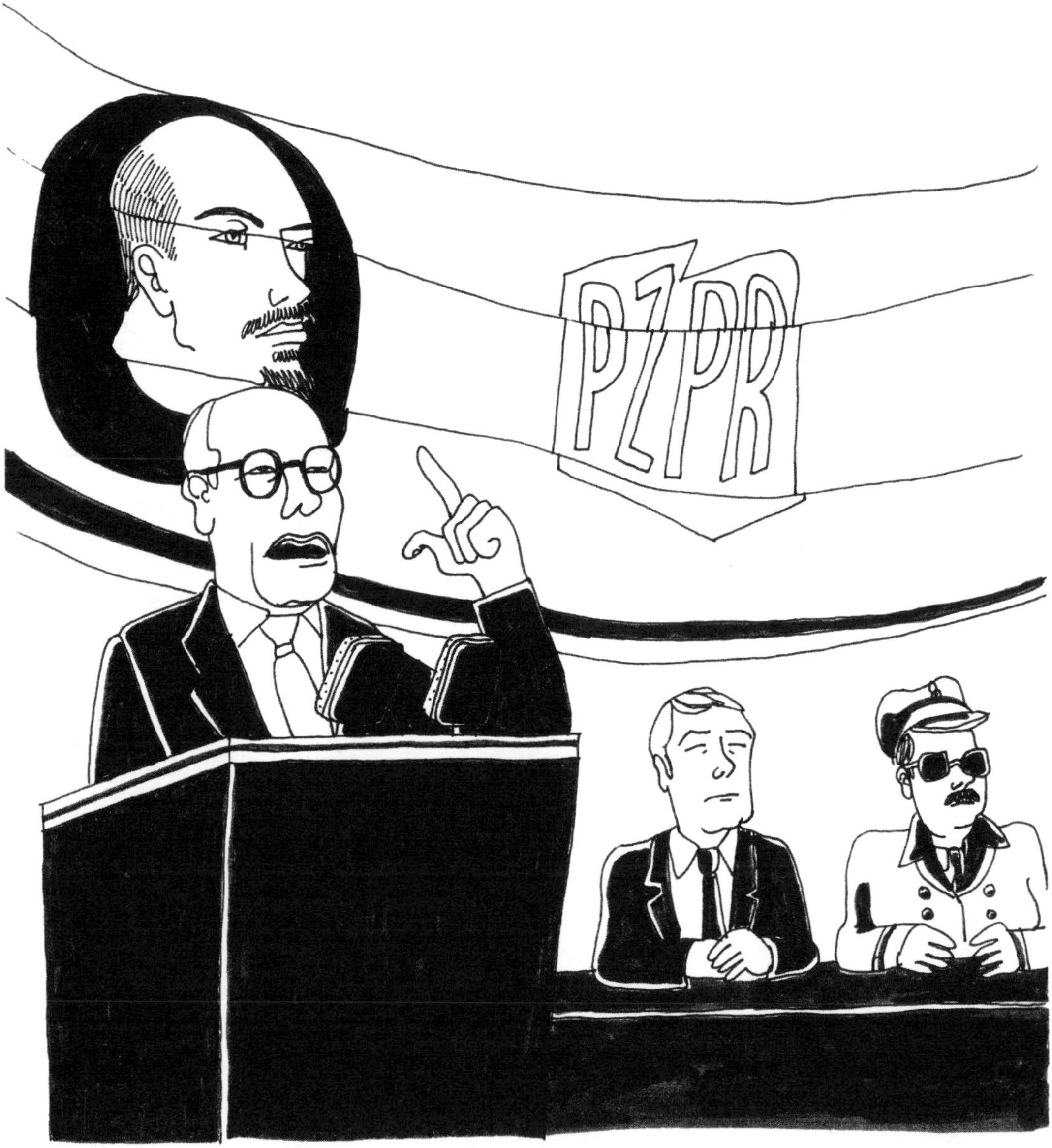
PZPR

Those who remained kept up a Jewish life until '68. There are still schools, associations, newspapers. The strict communist period that began in '49 saw the rise of a patriotic vision of Poland in the name of republican universalism — meaning everyone's a victim, there's no difference between Jews and non-Jews. That was how they erased the Jewish past. Which suited many people, since the Polish attitude towards the massacres hasn't always been blameless.

They made it a political ideology both to conduct anti-Zionist campaigns — "There is a fifth column in our country" — and to advance such ideas as "Those ungrateful Jews: we helped them so much during the war".

This provoked the events of March '68, and the departure of 20,000 people. The darkest time was the early '70s. Only a few Jews, old and assimilated, remained.

Since there'd been no collaborationist state, the regime created a vision of the Polish as innocent victims: "We are blameless."

And that's what's been questioned in intellectual debates over these last 20 years. That's why I called my book "The End of Innocence".

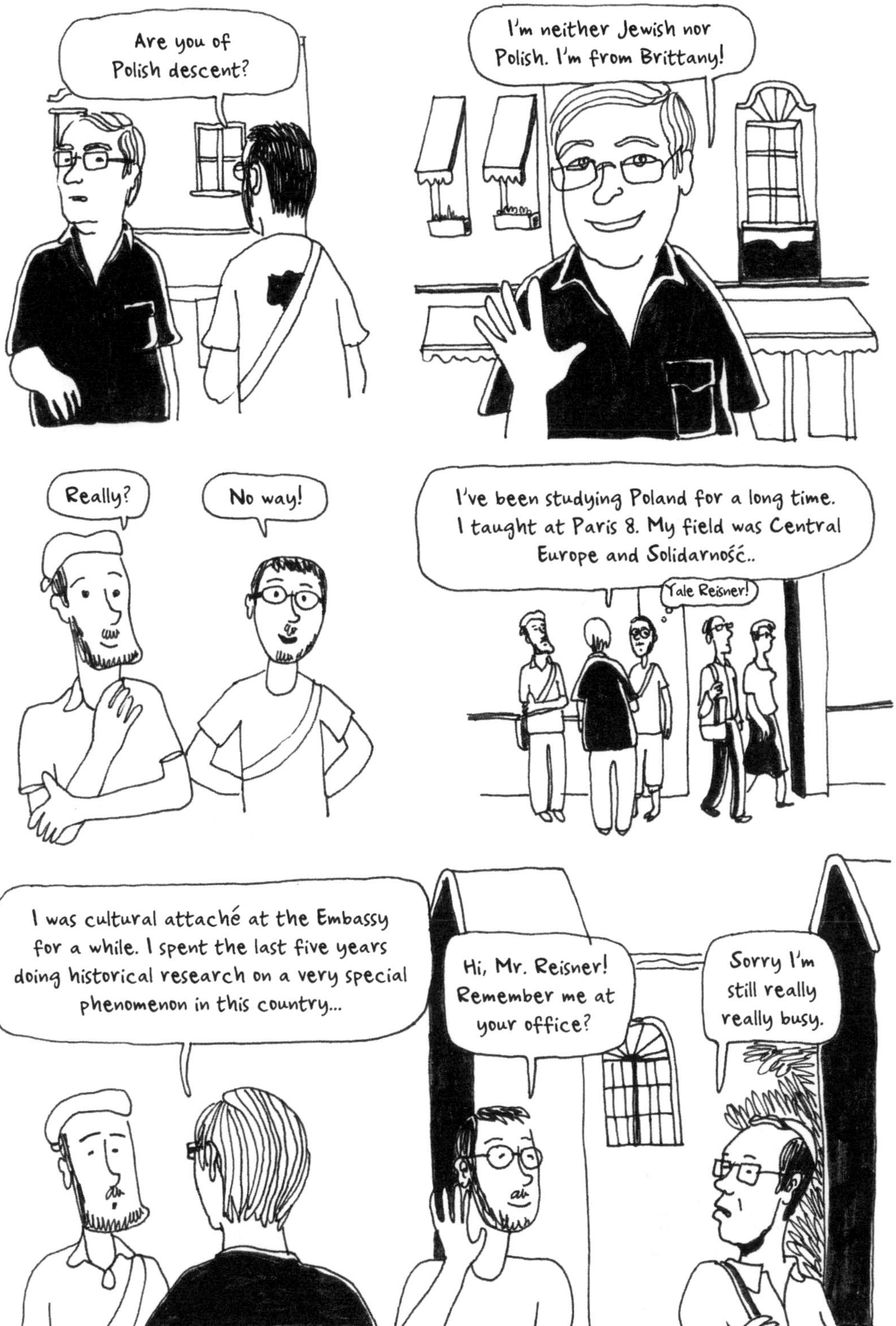
Are you of Polish descent?
I'm neither Jewish nor Polish. I'm from Brittany!
Really?
No way!
I've been studying Poland for a long time. I taught at Paris 8. My field was Central Europe and Solidarność..
Yale Reisner!
I was cultural attaché at the Embassy for a while. I spent the last five years doing historical research on a very special phenomenon in this country...
Hi, Mr. Reisner! Remember me at your office?
Sorry I'm still really really busy.

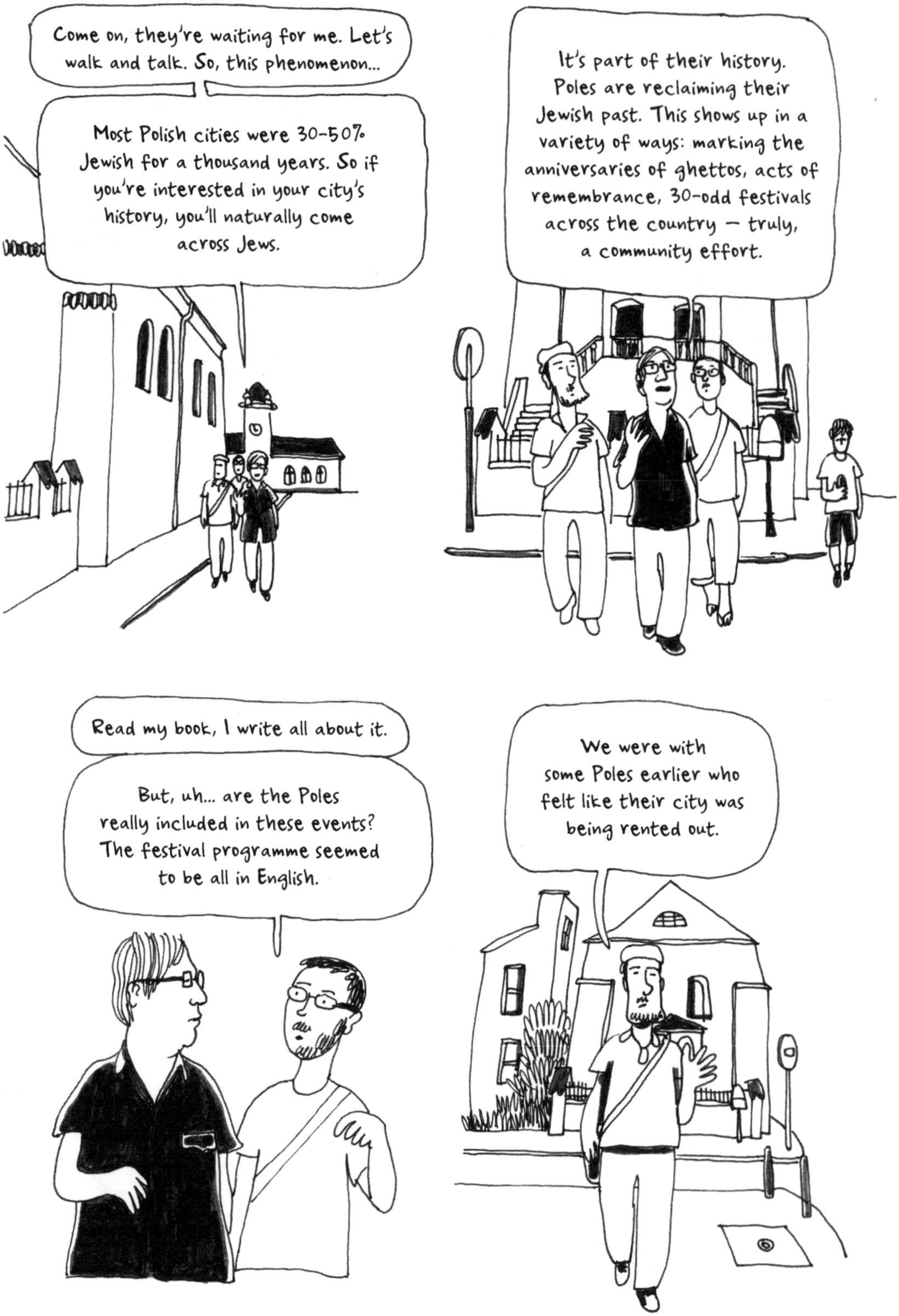
Come on, they're waiting for me. Let's walk and talk. So, this phenomenon...
Most Polish cities were 30-50% Jewish for a thousand years. So if you're interested in your city's history, you'll naturally come across Jews.
It's part of their history. Poles are reclaiming their Jewish past. This shows up in a variety of ways: marking the anniversaries of ghettos, acts of remembrance, 30-odd festivals across the country – truly, a community effort.
Read my book, I write all about it.
But, uh... are the Poles really included in these events? The festival programme seemed to be all in English.
We were with some Poles earlier who felt like their city was being rented out.

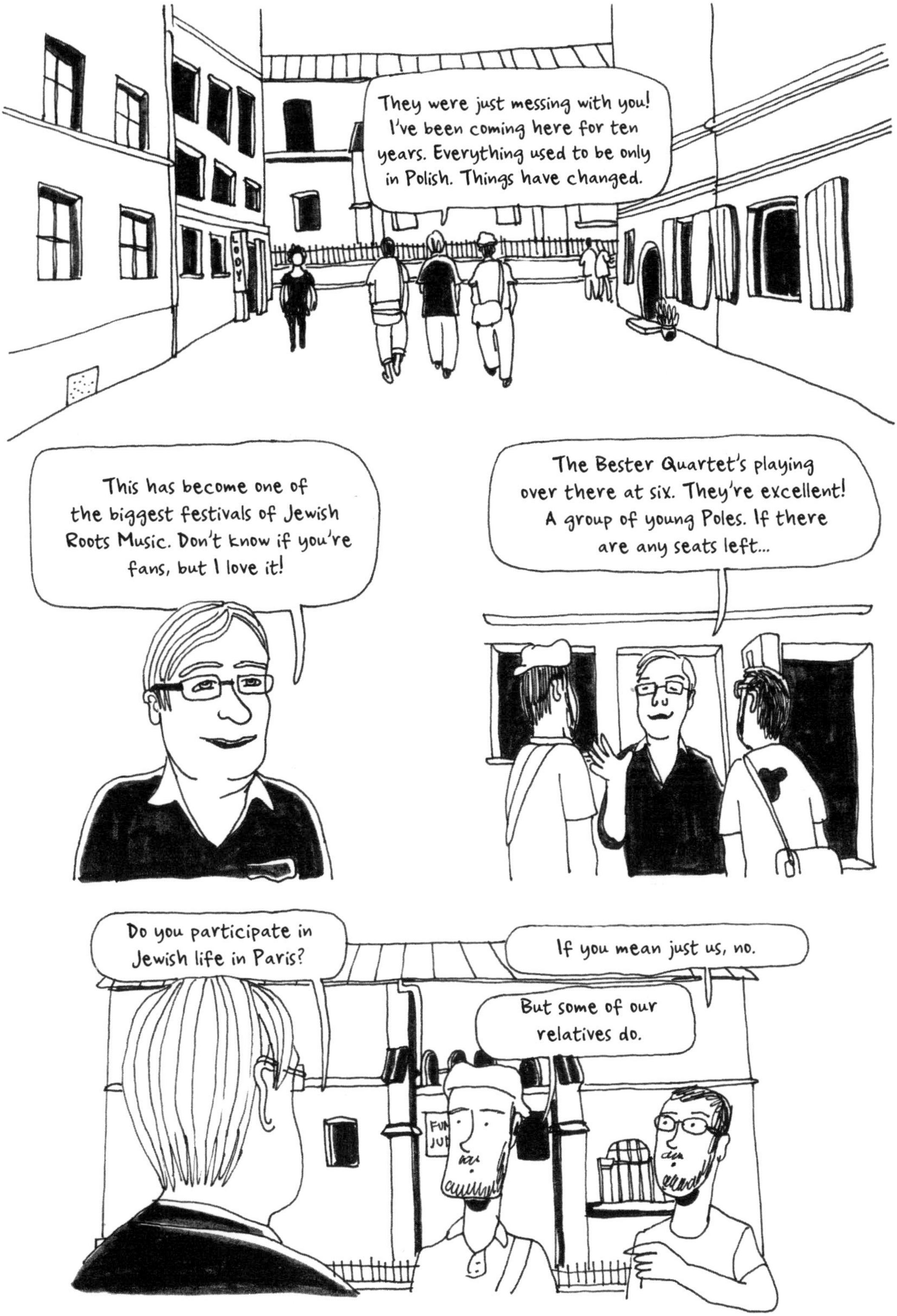
They were just messing with you! I've been coming here for ten years. Everything used to be only in Polish. Things have changed.
LODY
This has become one of the biggest festivals of Jewish Roots Music. Don't know if you're fans, but I love it!
The Bester Quartet's playing over there at six. They're excellent! A group of young Poles. If there are any seats left...
Do you participate in Jewish life in Paris?
If you mean just us, no.
But some of our relatives do.

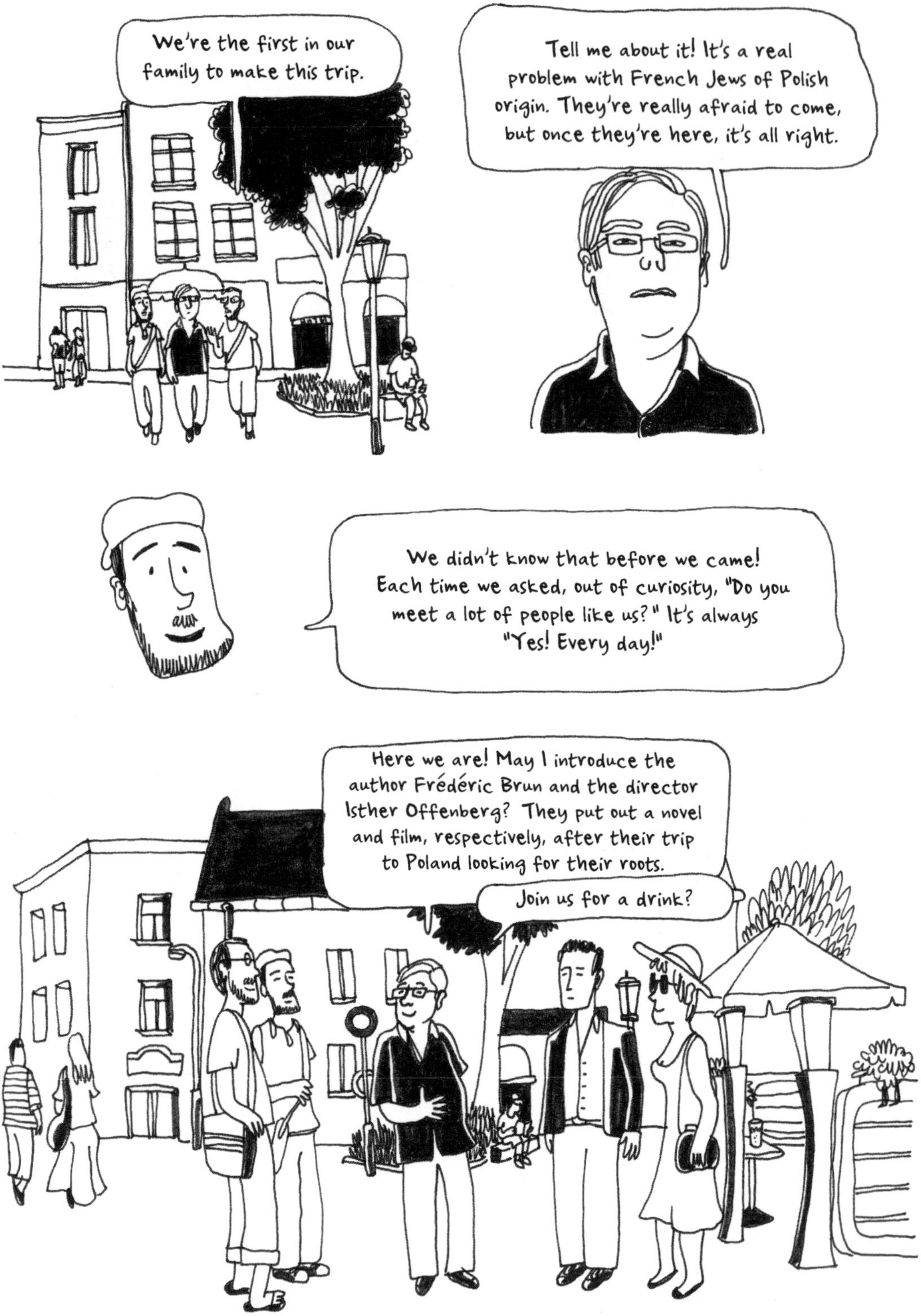
We're the first in our family to make this trip.
Tell me about it! It's a real problem with French Jews of Polish origin. They're really afraid to come, but once they're here, it's all right.
We didn't know that before we came! Each time we asked, out of curiosity, "Do you meet a lot of people like us?" It's always "Yes! Every day!"
Here we are! May I introduce the author Frédéric Brun and the director Isther Offenberg? They put out a novel and film, respectively, after their trip to Poland looking for their roots.
Join us for a drink?

Suspended Animation

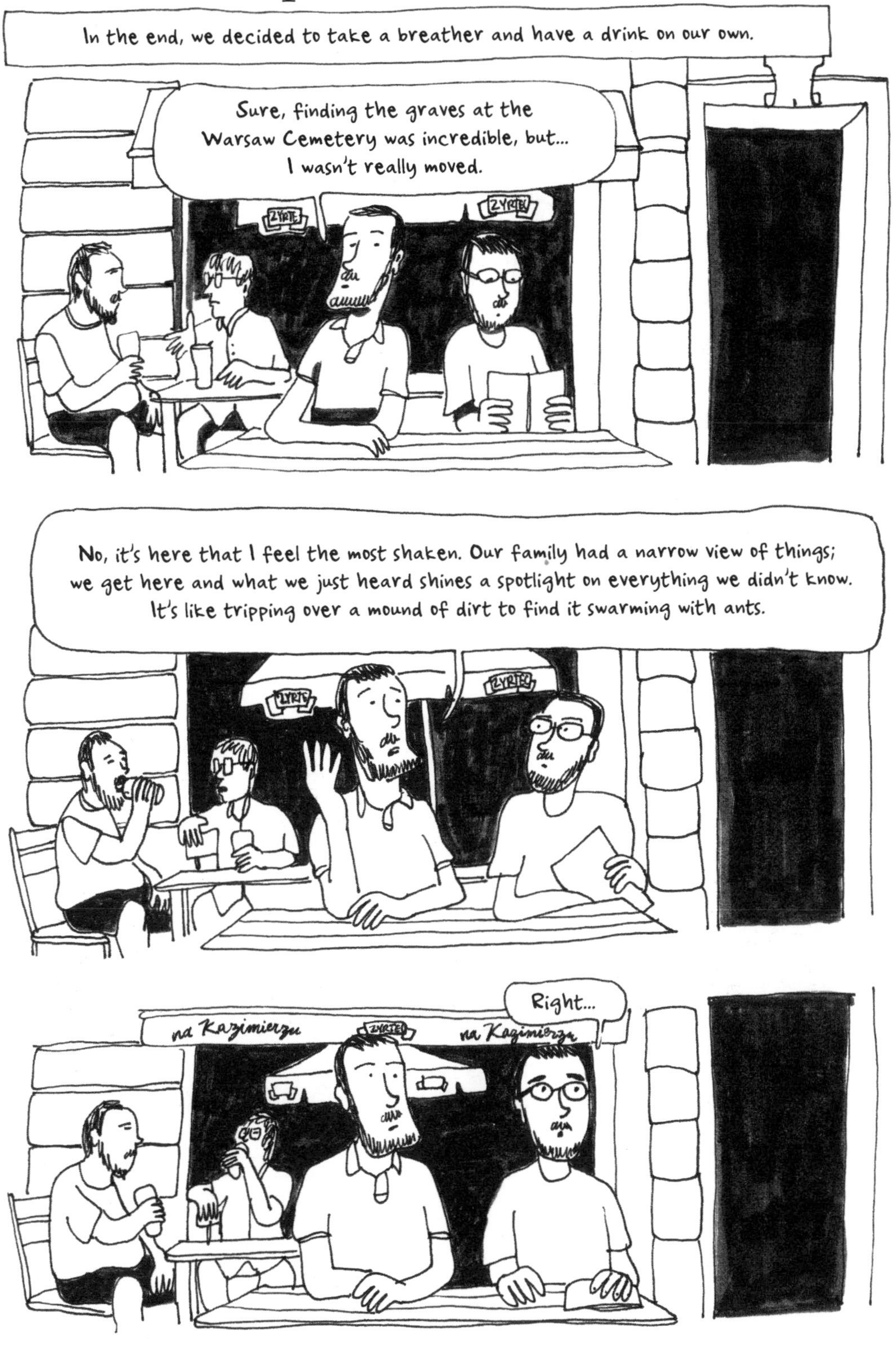
In the end, we decided to take a breather and have a drink on our own.
Sure, finding the graves at the Warsaw Cemetery was incredible, but... I wasn't really moved.
No, it's here that I feel the most shaken. Our family had a narrow view of things; we get here and what we just heard shines a spotlight on everything we didn't know. It's like tripping over a mound of dirt to find it swarming with ants.
na Kazimierzu
Right...

Trampling over Paradise Lost

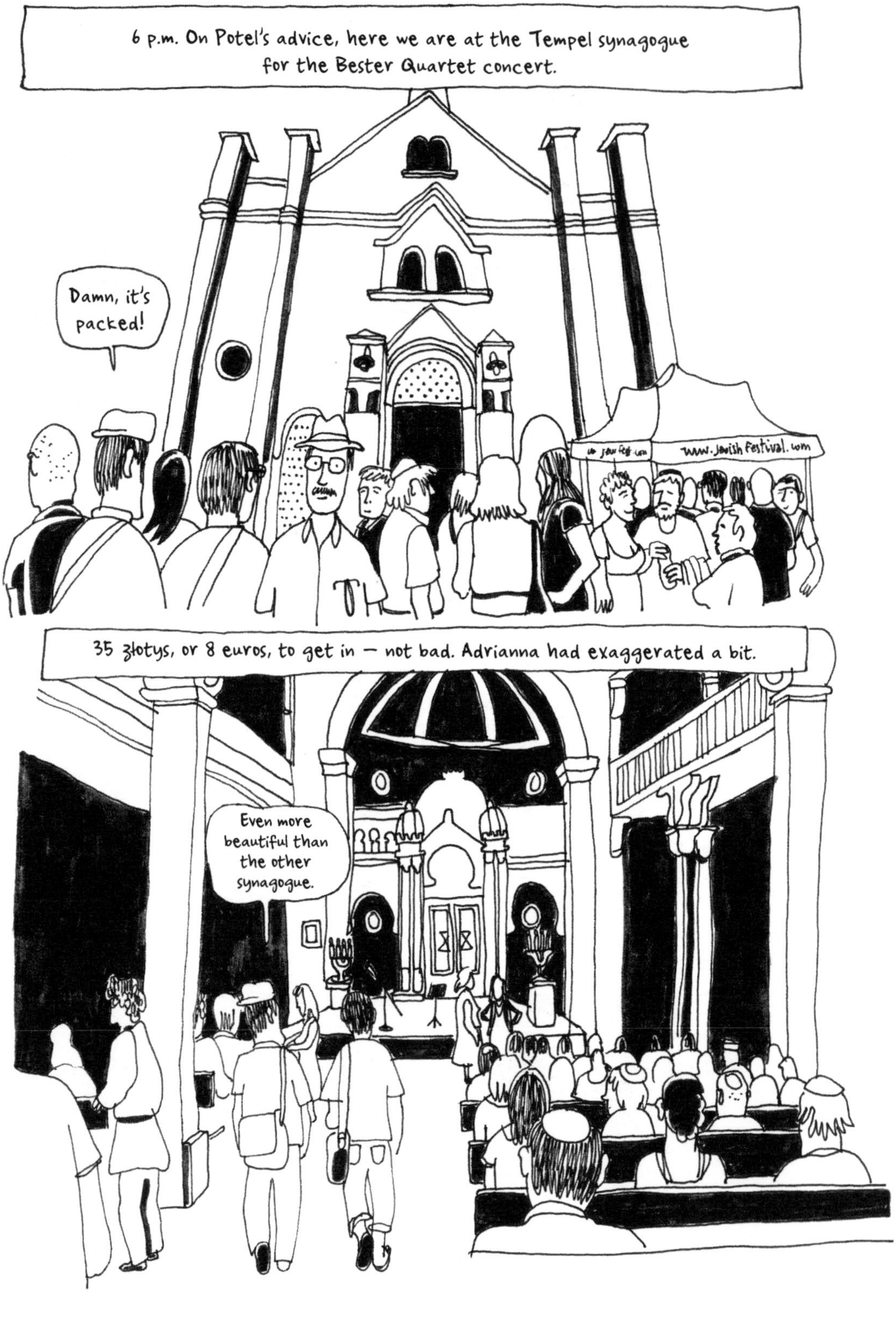
6 p.m. On Potel's advice, here we are at the Tempel synagogue for the Bester Quartet concert.
Damn, it's packed!
35 złotys, or 8 euros, to get in — not bad. Adrianna had exaggerated a bit.
Even more beautiful than the other synagogue.

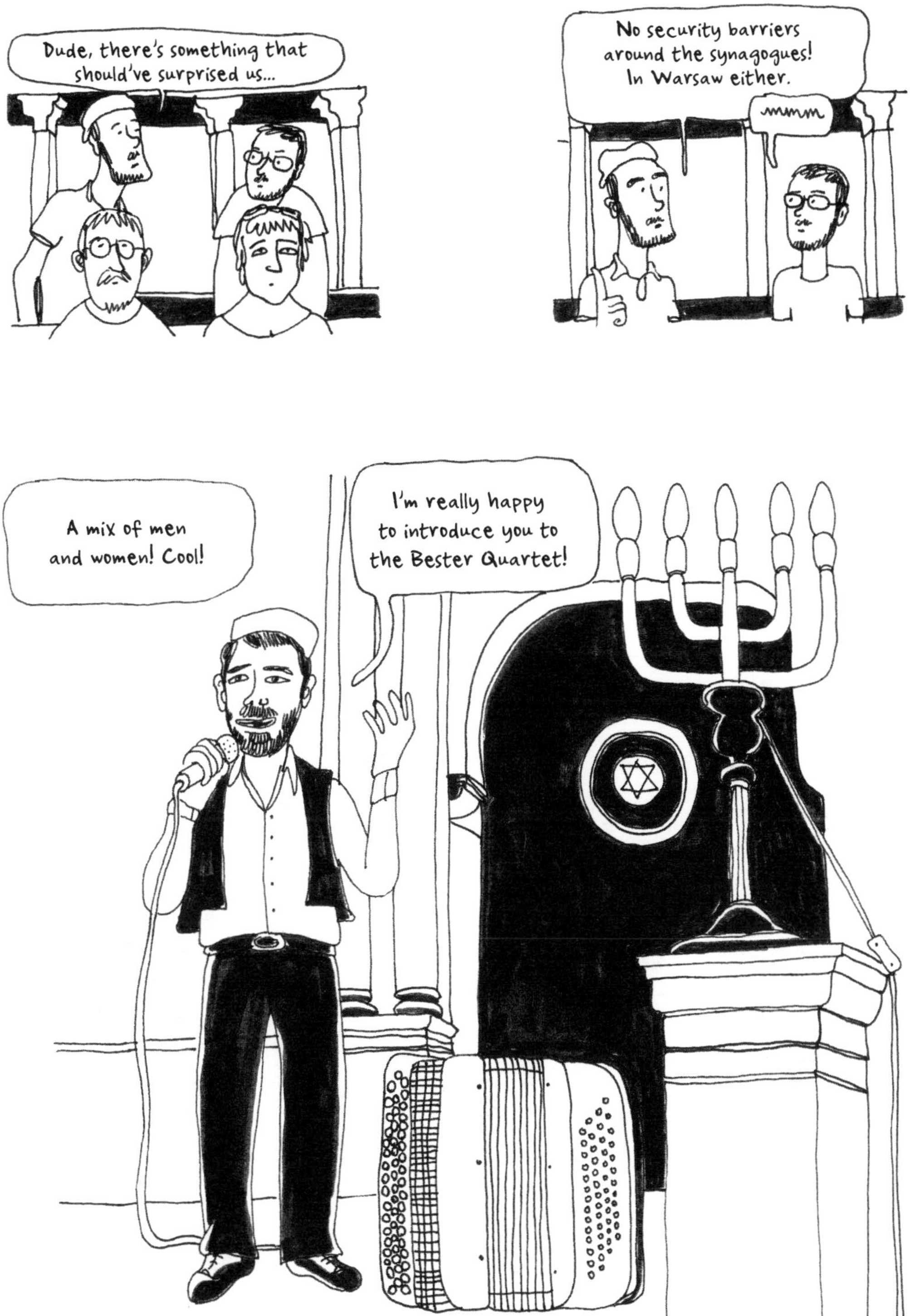
Dude, there's something that should've surprised us...
No security barriers around the synagogues! In Warsaw either.
mmm
A mix of men and women! Cool!
I'm really happy to introduce you to the Bester Quartet!

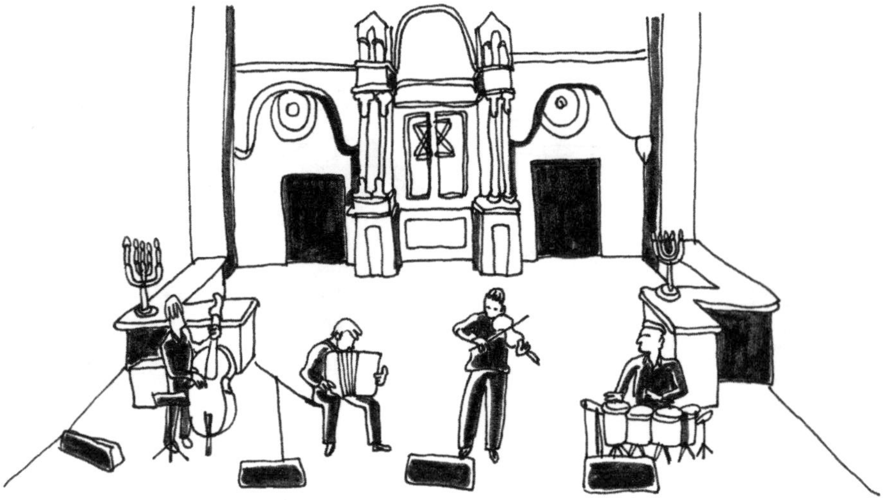

And in the shelter of this sacred place, the first chords of a piercing melody rang out, heading straight for my brain.

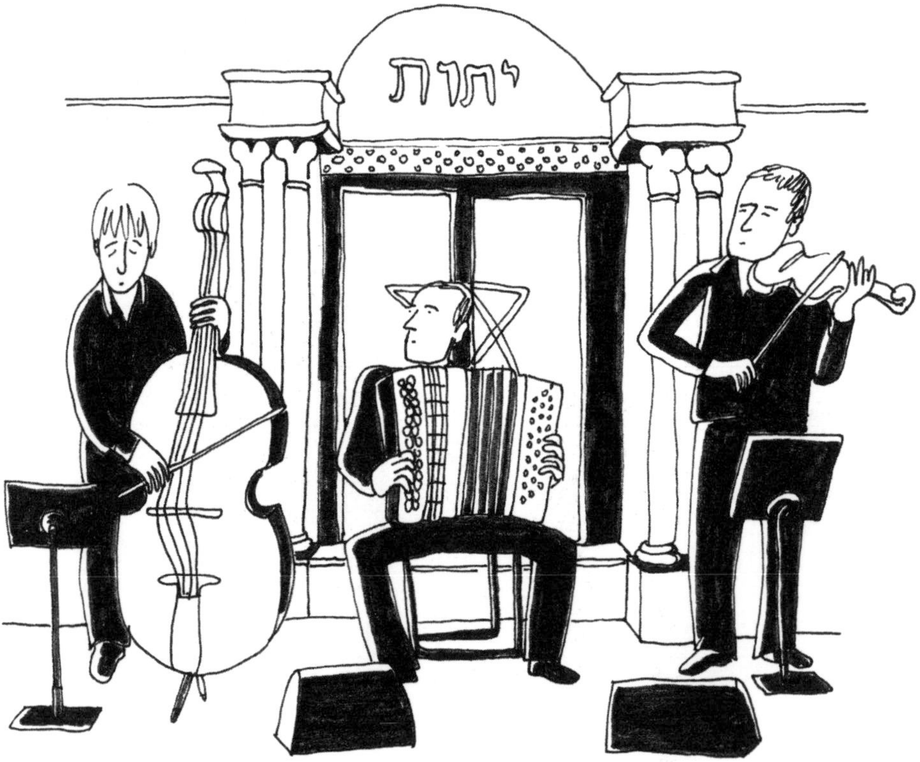

Bester Quartet

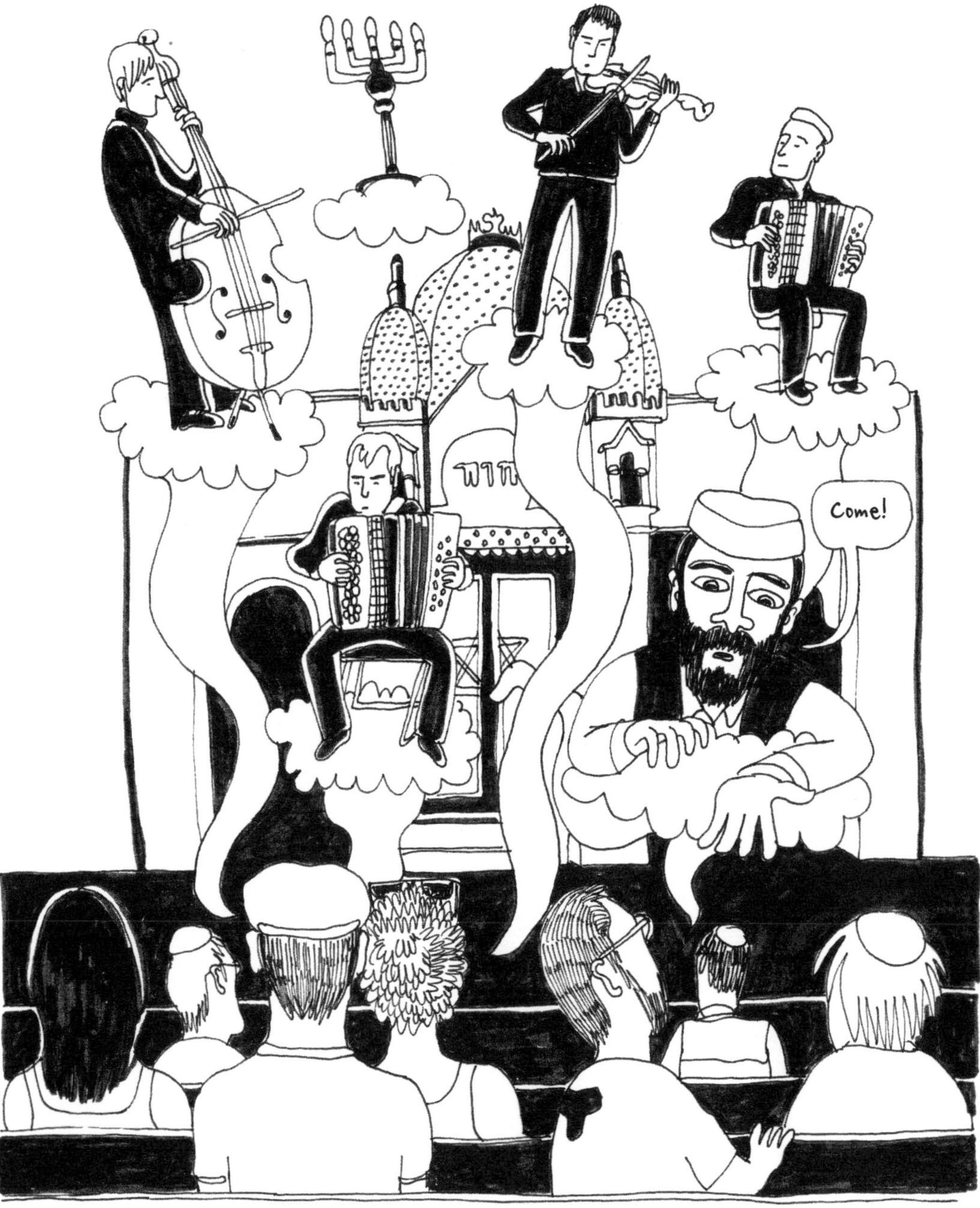
Come!

Spirals of sound passed through the air on either side, slowly filling it. They drew near, then wrapped me up, and carried me away delicately. I tried to fight it, but gave up.

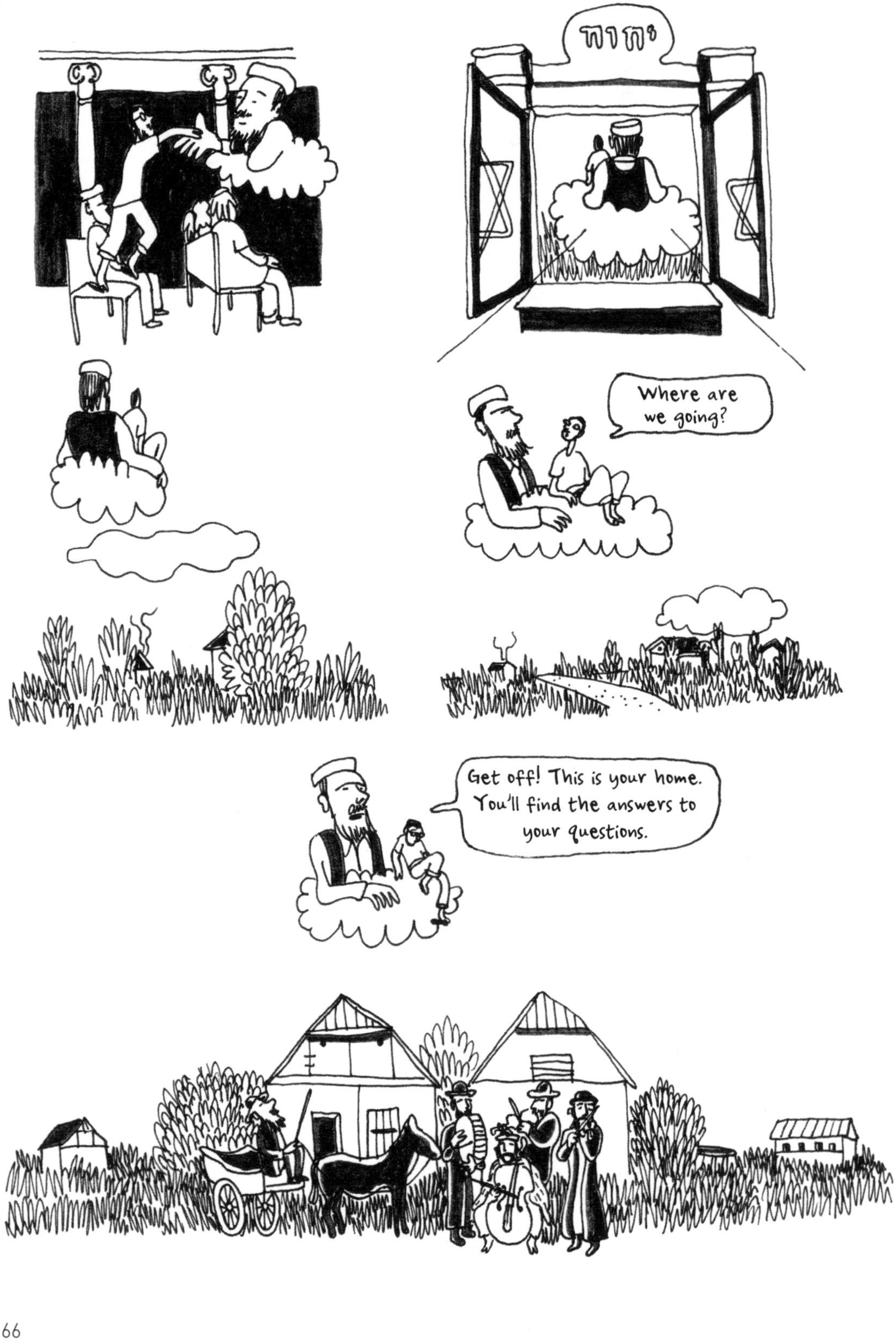
יחוש
Where are we going?
Get off! This is your home. You'll find the answers to your questions.

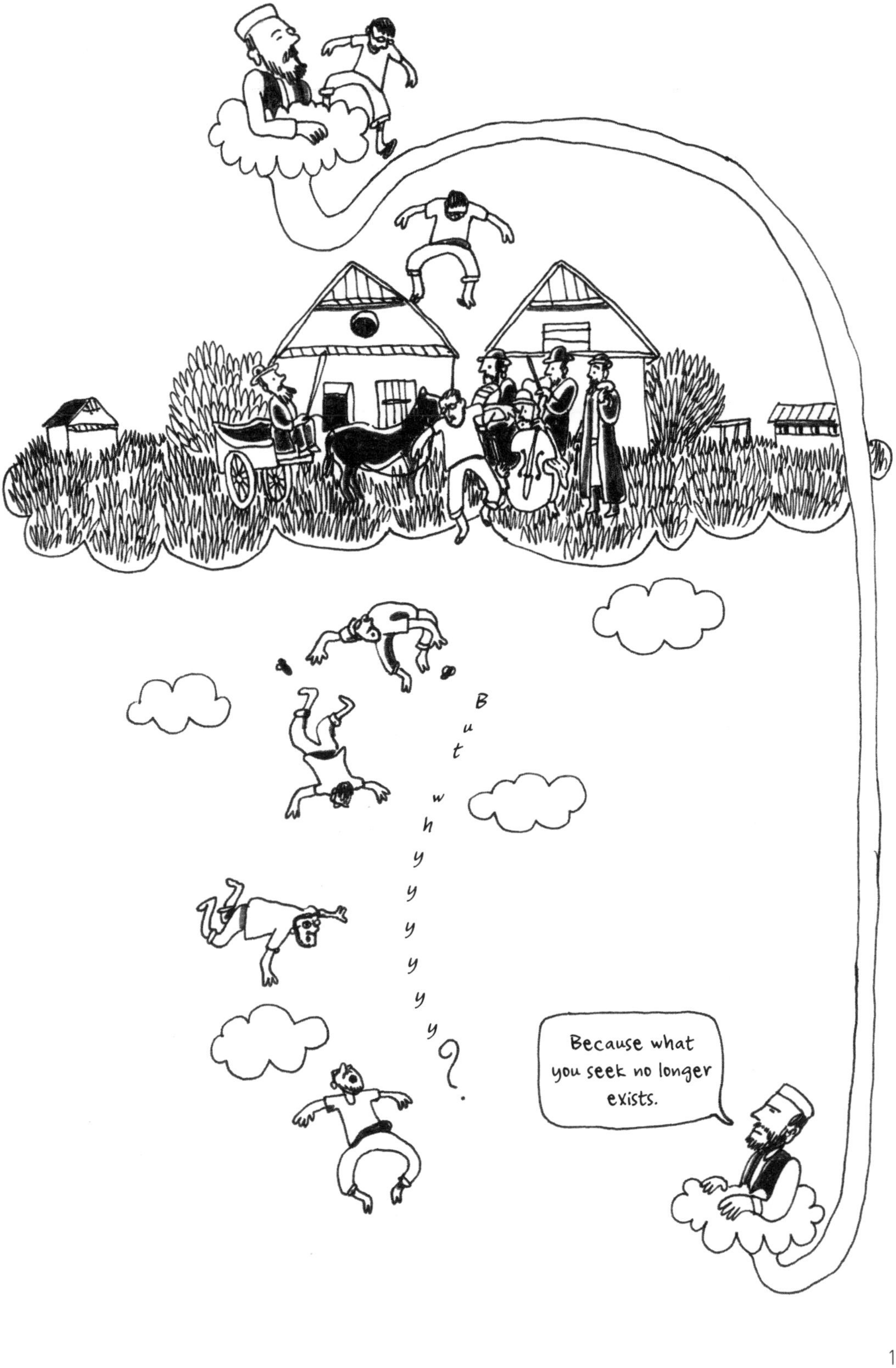

But whyyyyyyy?
Because what you seek no longer exists.

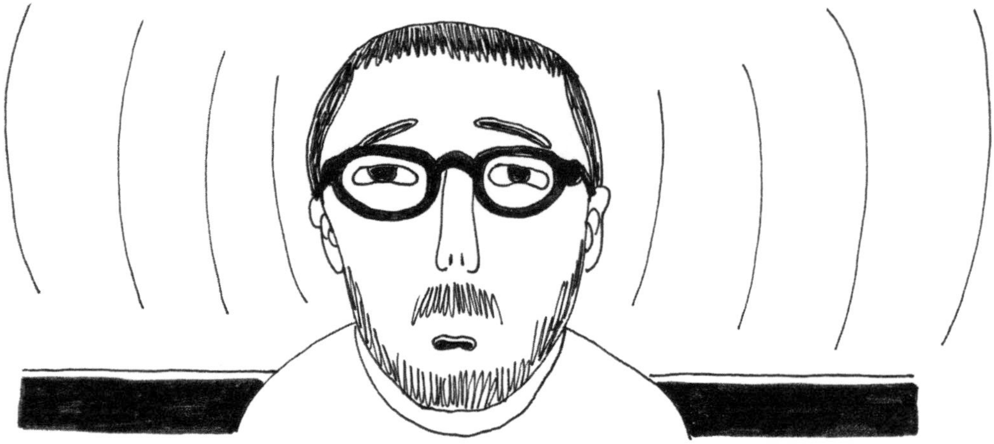

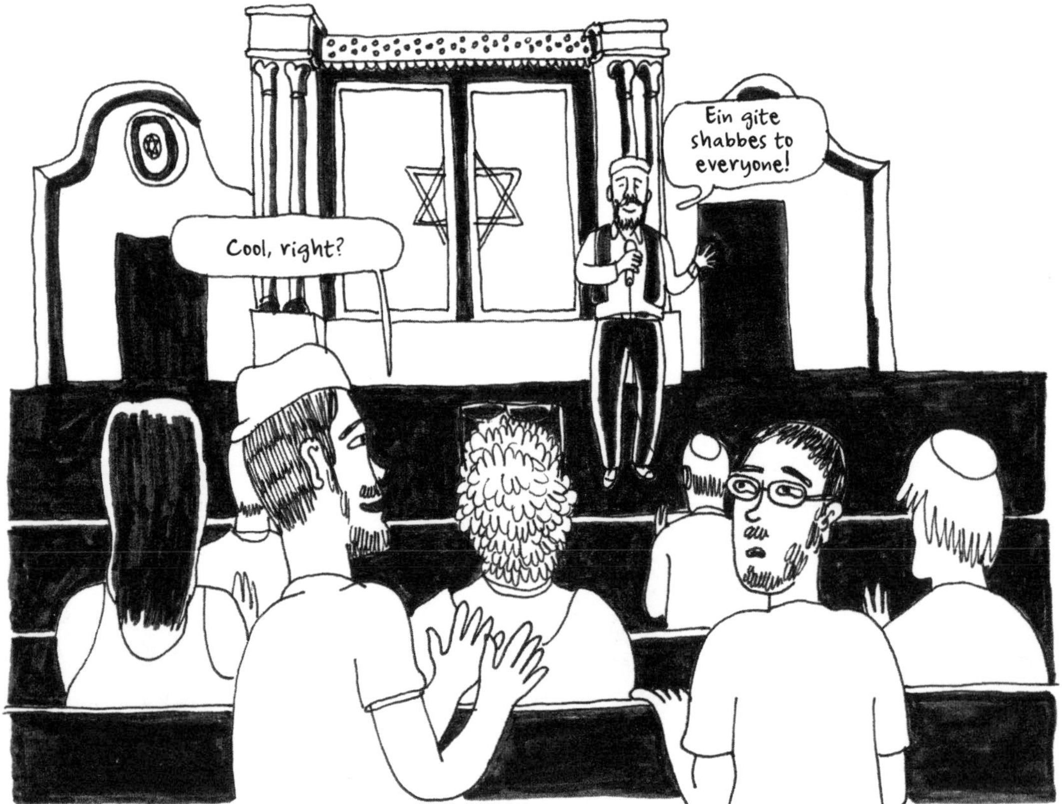
Ein gite shabbes to everyone!
Cool, right?

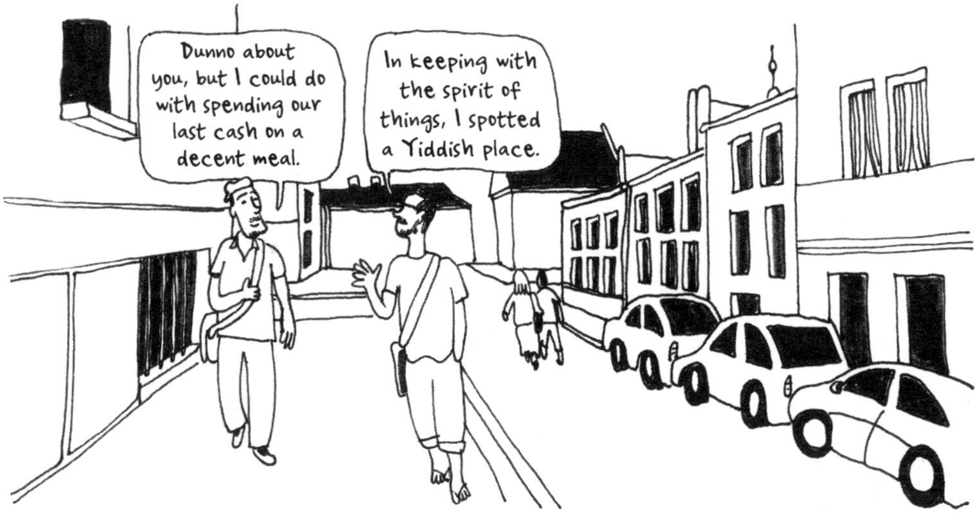
Dunno about you, but I could do with spending our last cash on a decent meal.
In keeping with the spirit of things, I spotted a Yiddish place.

Return to Reality

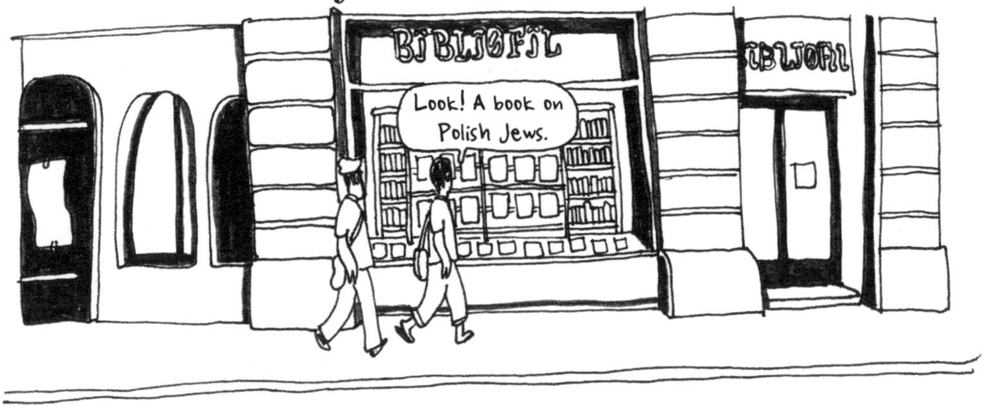
BIBLIOFIL
Look! A book on Polish Jews.

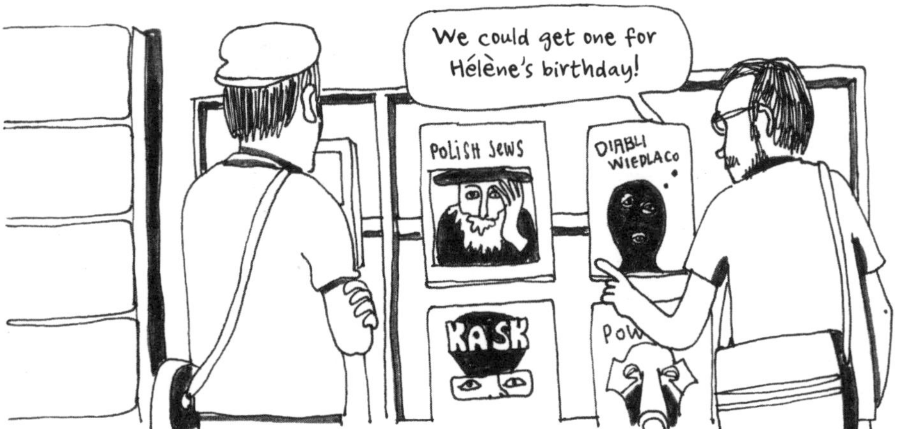
We could get one for Hélène's birthday!
POLISH JEWS
DIABLI WIEDLACO
KASK

A Bit of Fellow-Feeling

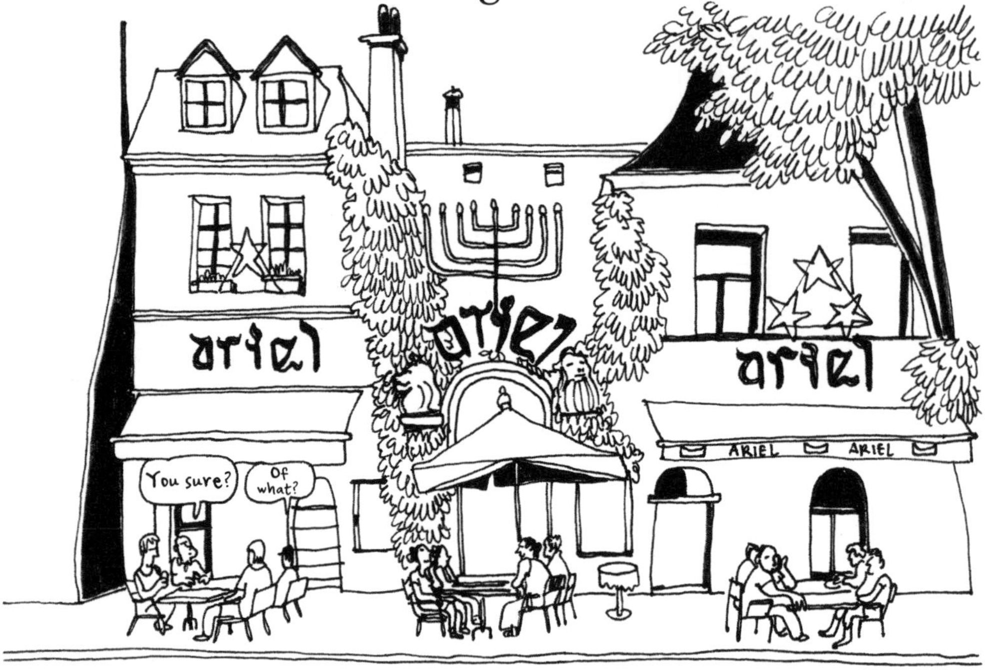

ariel
ariel
ariel
ARIEL
ARIEL
You sure?
Of what?

So what if that world of black and white images no longer existed?
We'd pretend to live as if they did.

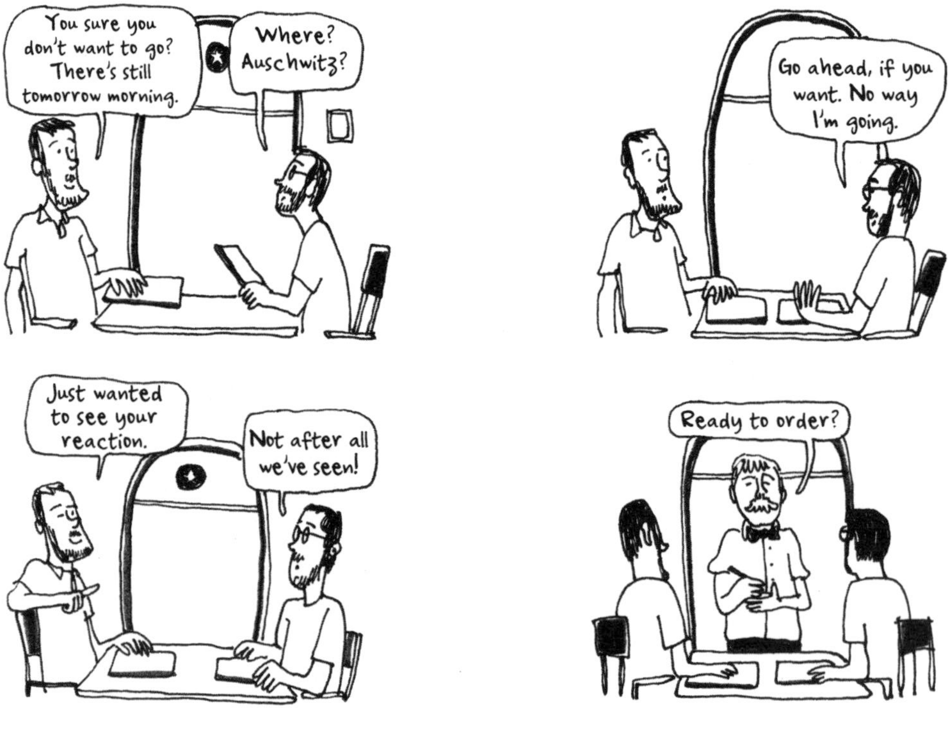

You sure you don't want to go? There's still tomorrow morning.
Where? Auschwitz?
Go ahead, if you want. No way I'm going.
Just wanted to see your reaction.
Not after all we've seen!
Ready to order?

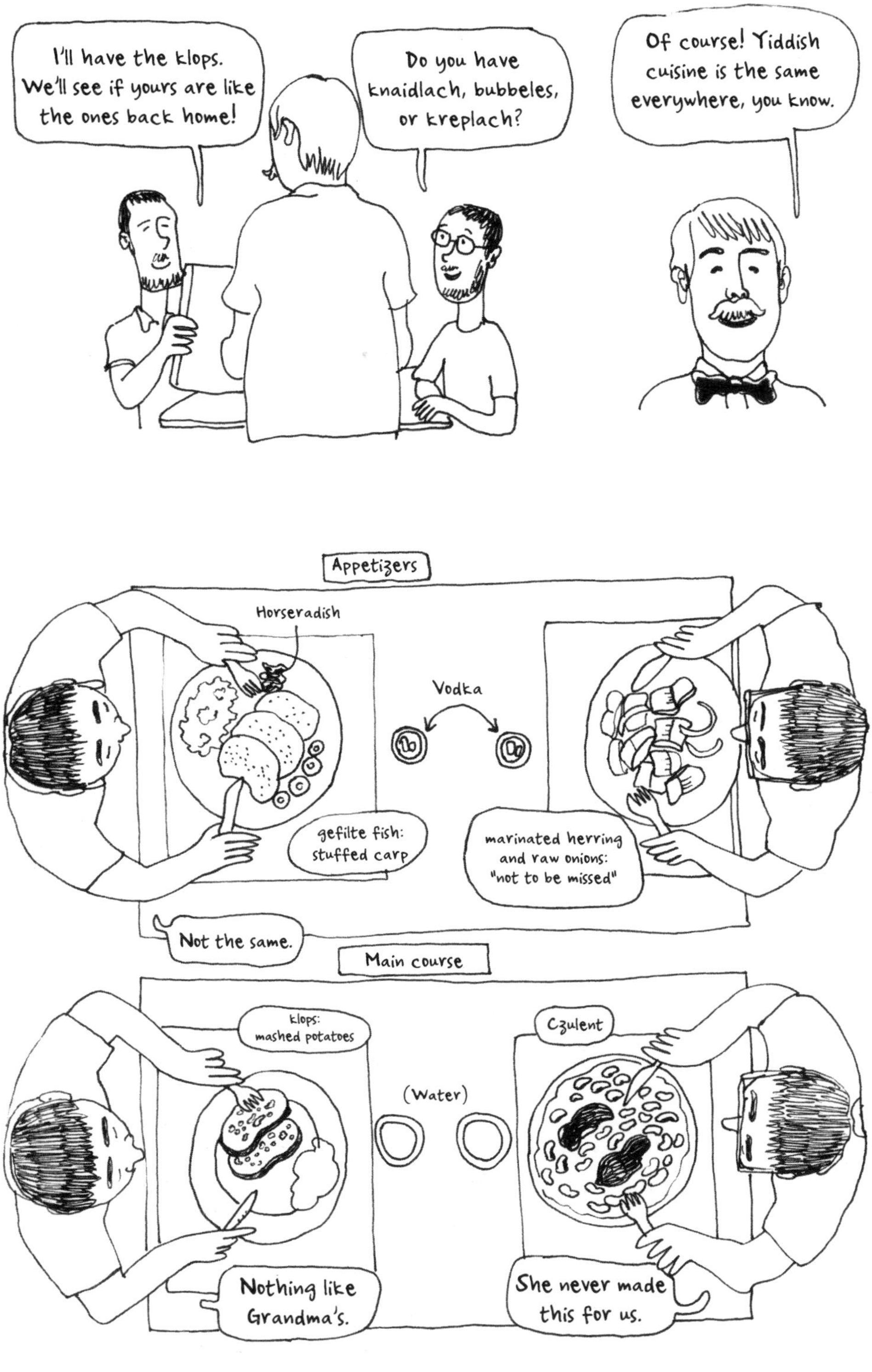
I'll have the klops. We'll see if yours are like the ones back home!
Do you have knaidlach, bubbeles, or kreplach?
Of course! Yiddish cuisine is the same everywhere, you know.
Appetizers
Horseradish
Vodka
gefilte fish: stuffed carp
marinated herring and raw onions: "not to be missed"
Not the same.
Main course
klops: mashed potatoes
(Water)
Czulent
Nothing like Grandma's.
She never made this for us.

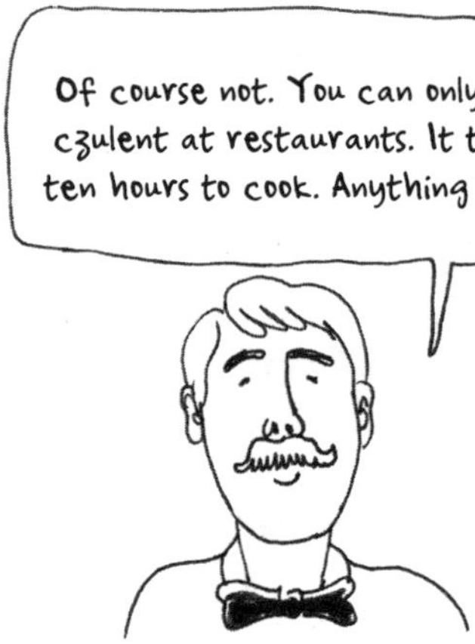
Of course not. You can only get czulent at restaurants. It takes ten hours to cook. Anything else?

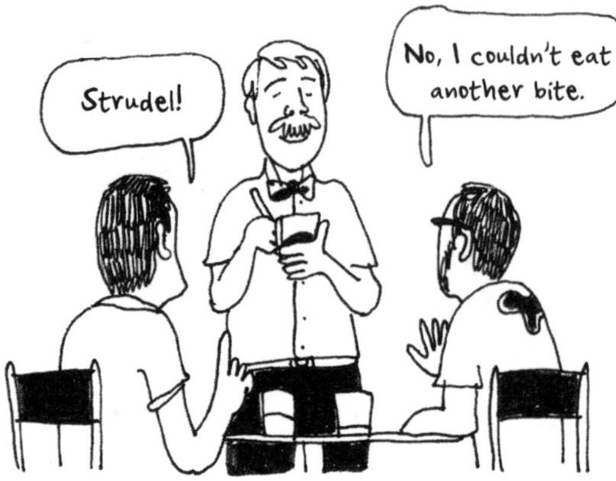
Strudel!
No, I couldn't eat another bite.

And as night fell quietly over the city, we enjoyed the final moments of our Polish adventure.

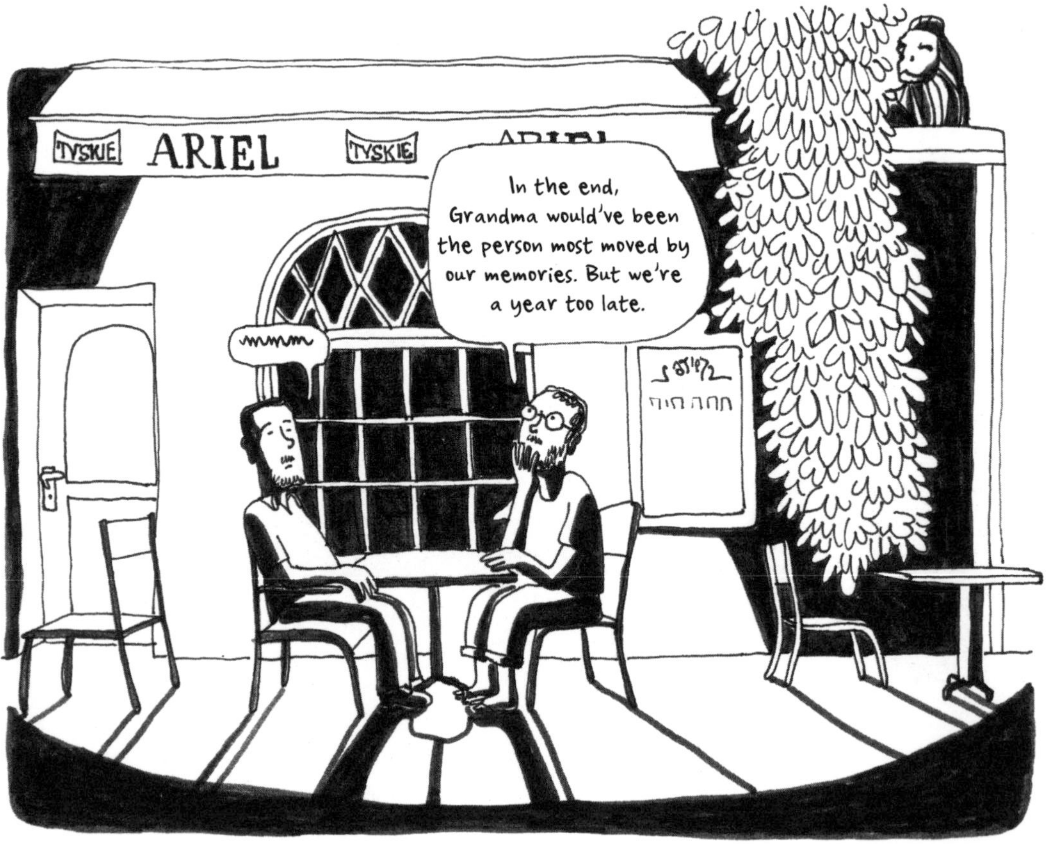
TYSKIE
ARIEL
TYSKIE
In the end, Grandma would've been the person most moved by our memories. But we're a year too late.
mmm

Transit Zones

So, we never went. What did it matter? We would only have perpetuated the nightmare haunting all of us.

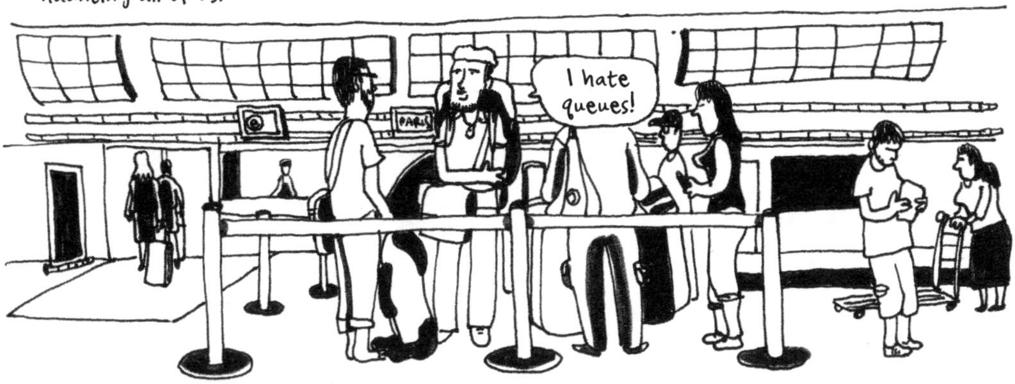
I hate queues!

But today we are no longer the children of those lucky enough to survive the death camps. We are worthy heirs to the Jewish legacy, and its rich, complex history on Polish soil. That broken, hidden part of our identity — we've found it again, at last.

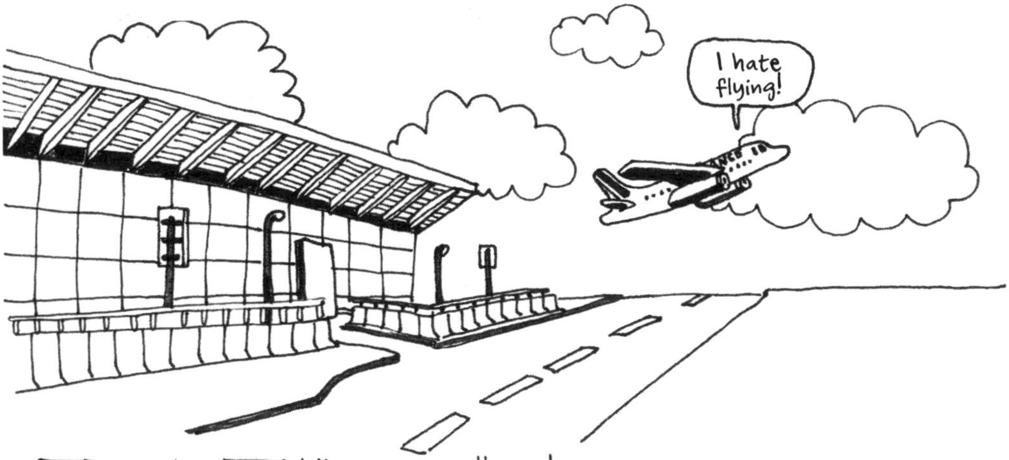
I hate flying!

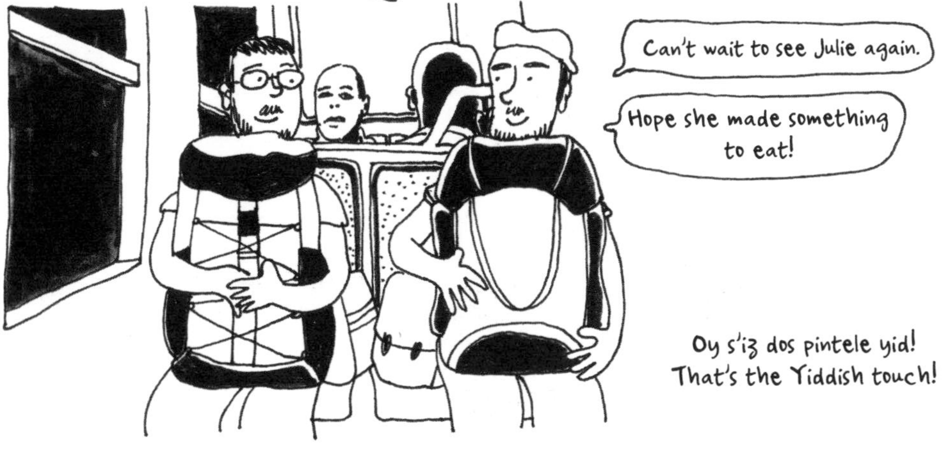
Can't wait to see Julie again.
Hope she made something to eat!
Oy s'iz dos pintele yid!
That's the Yiddish touch!

They'll Never Change

Paris. I've been back for two days, and I feel like my journey won't be over till I meet her.

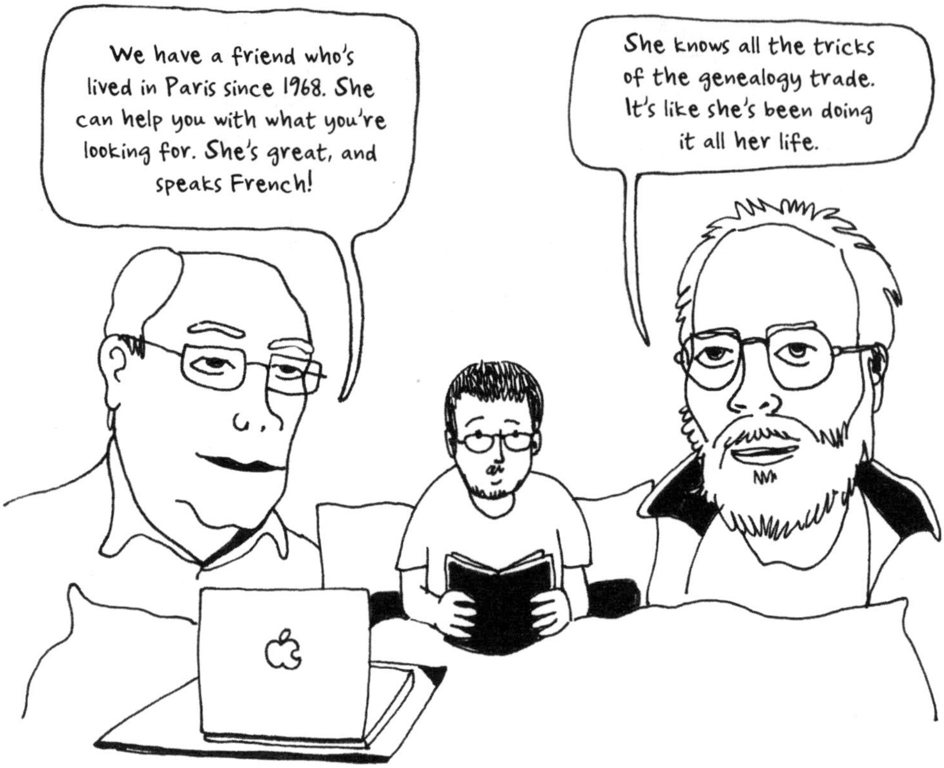
We have a friend who's lived in Paris since 1968. She can help you with what you're looking for. She's great, and speaks French!
She knows all the tricks of the genealogy trade. It's like she's been doing it all her life.

I'm not trying to prolong my meagre search for family history, but I'm curious to dig a bit deeper into the mysterious lives of Jan and Edward.

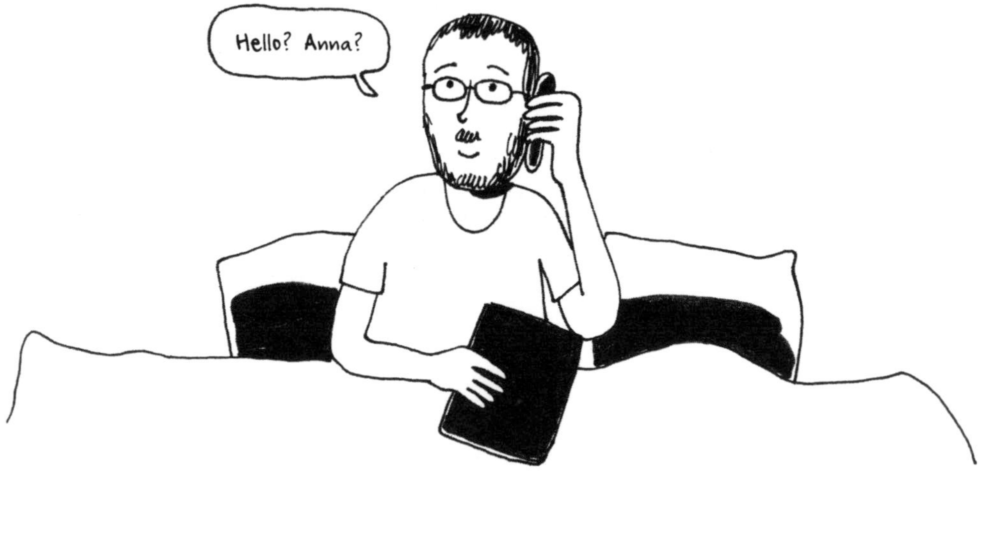
Hello? Anna?

The Porte d'Italie metro stop, that very afternoon. When she heard their names, Anna agreed to meet me that same day.

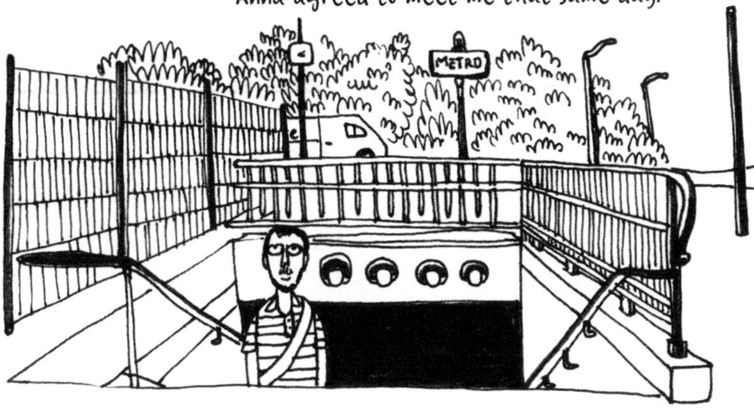
METRO

Once more, I don't know what to expect. I can't rely on my intuition.

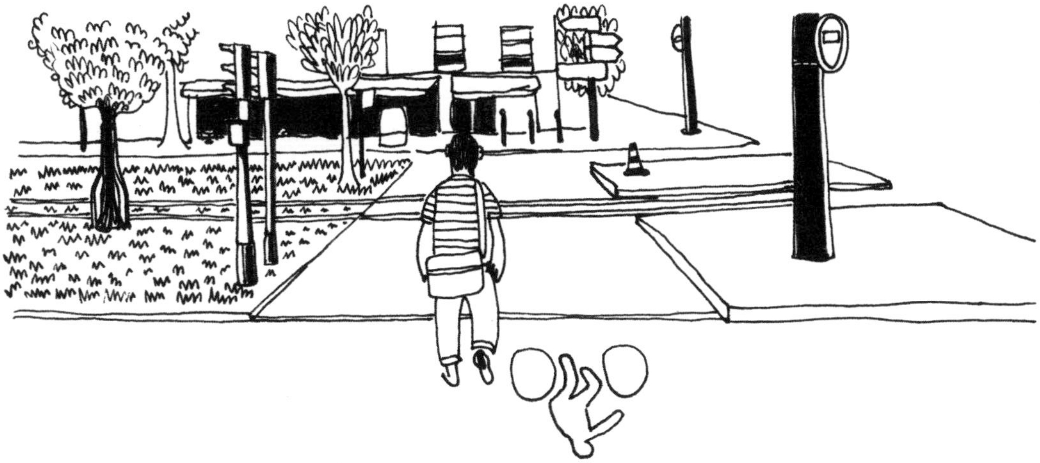

She told me to come to a café on the square.

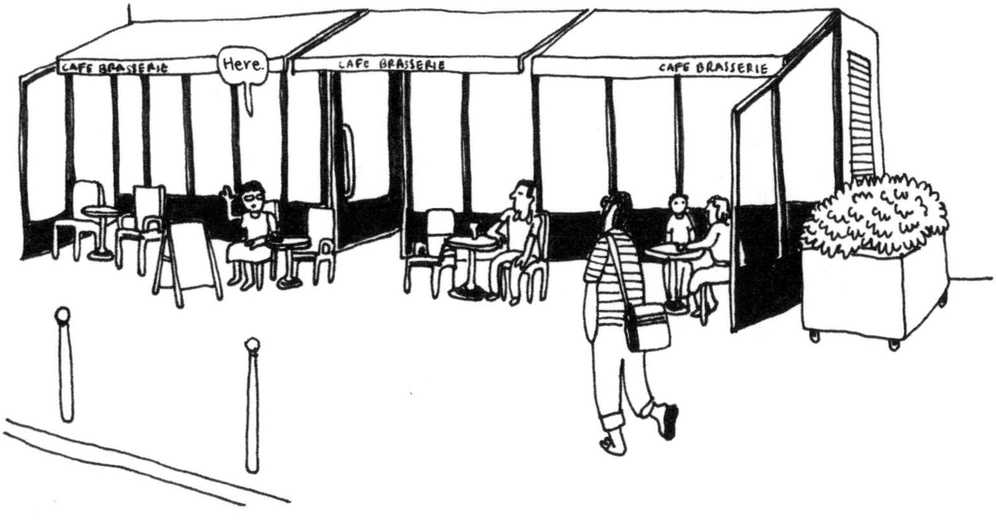
CAFE BRASSERIE
Here.
CAFE BRASSERIE
CAFE BRASSERIE

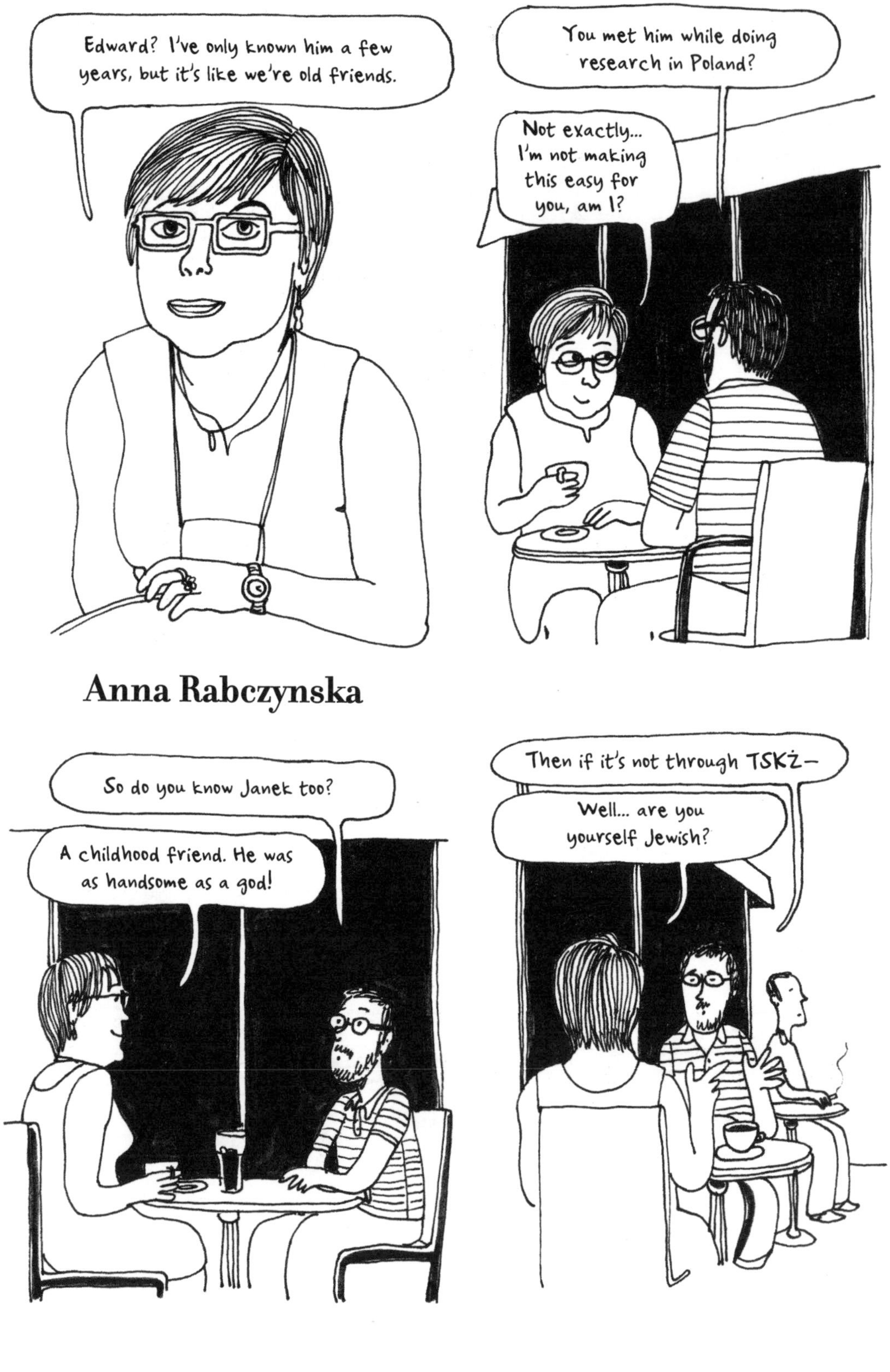
Edward? I've only known him a few years, but it's like we're old friends.
You met him while doing research in Poland?
Not exactly... I'm not making this easy for you, am I?
So do you know Janek too?
A childhood friend. He was as handsome as a god!
Then if it's not through TSKŻ—
Well... are you yourself Jewish?

Anna Rabczynska

I found out when I was 18 — you know, that age when girls start dating. When I was little, my friends were from Uzbekistan, Kazakhstan — I didn't understand why they came from so far away.

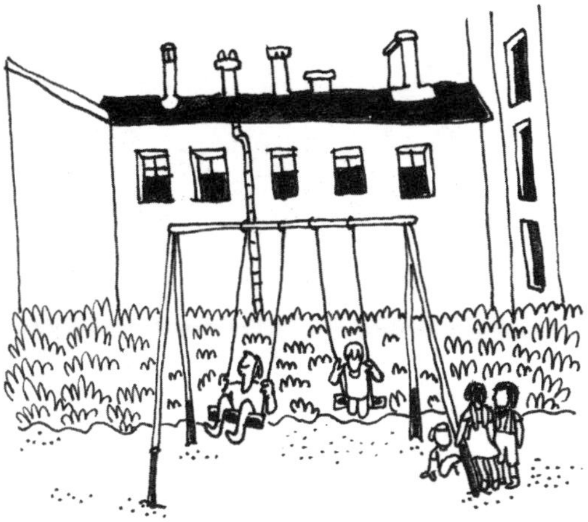

They had completely different personal histories from mine: their families had fled the U.S.S.R. during the war. They kept up traditions and spoke Yiddish at home.

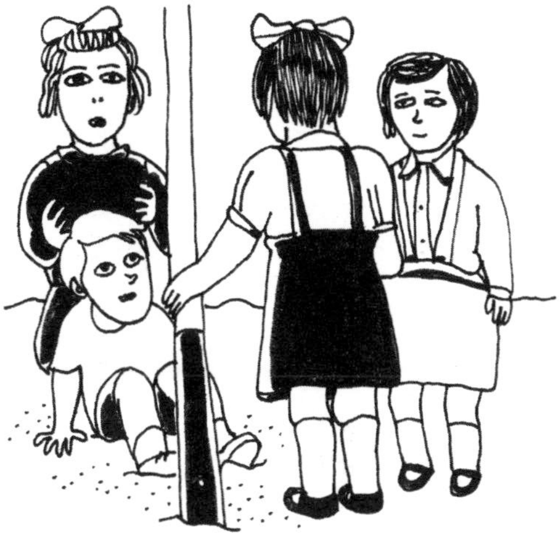

All I had were my parents. They were part of what were called "enlightened Jews" — an entirely assimilated intelligentsia. My father was a diplomat and my mother a biochemist.

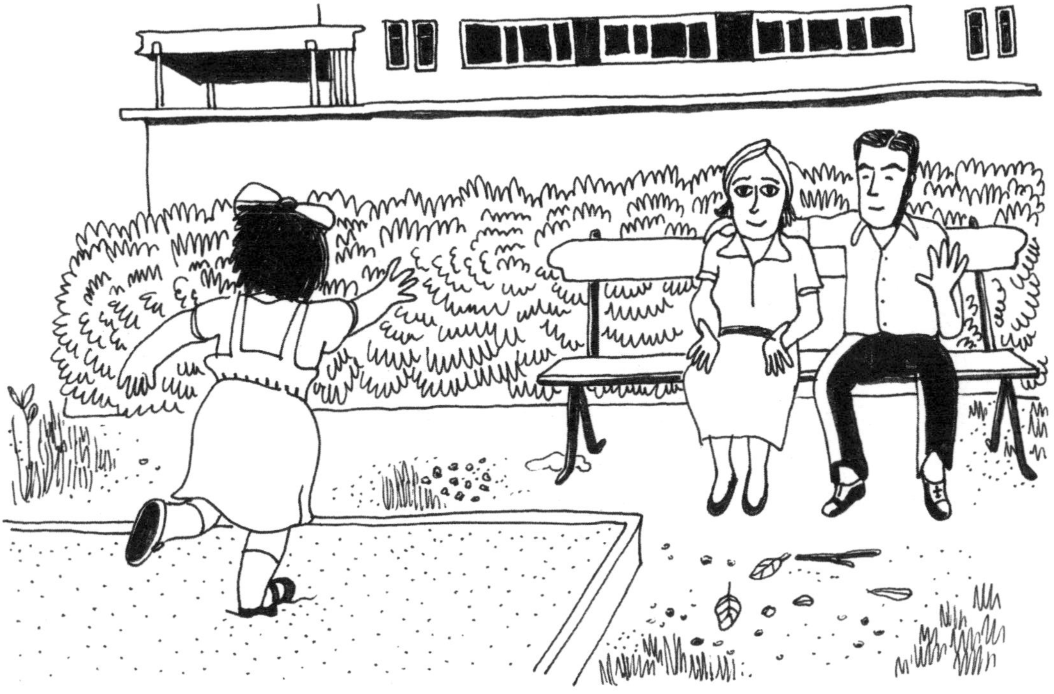

When the war started, my mother, who was studying in Warsaw, found herself in the ghetto. To save her, my father traded two packs of cigarettes for her. No one suspected him.

He was blond and blue-eyed, and had also changed his identity. That was something those who'd fled the U.S.S.R. couldn't understand. They said it was cowardly. They fled to the countryside.

Farmers hid them — whether from the goodness of their hearts, or for money, I don't know. They never told me.

While they were there, they saved the life of a partisan of the Polish Resistance. Since my mother was a doctor, people from the village came to see her. Since then, our families have remained closely tied.

I was 18. I'd maybe heard the word "Jew" twice before in my life. In my head, I thought it meant "atheist". After they told me, my mother never said a word about it again. My father was the one who told me all those stories. Suddenly, everything crumbled, as if with a single blow they'd levelled all the education they'd given me.

I was 20 in 1967, and very political. I knew what was coming, and in March 1968, I was already in Paris.

The first three days after the Six-Day War were euphoric. People in the street were proud of their little Jewish Israelis of Polish descent, who'd beaten up the big bad Egyptian communists.

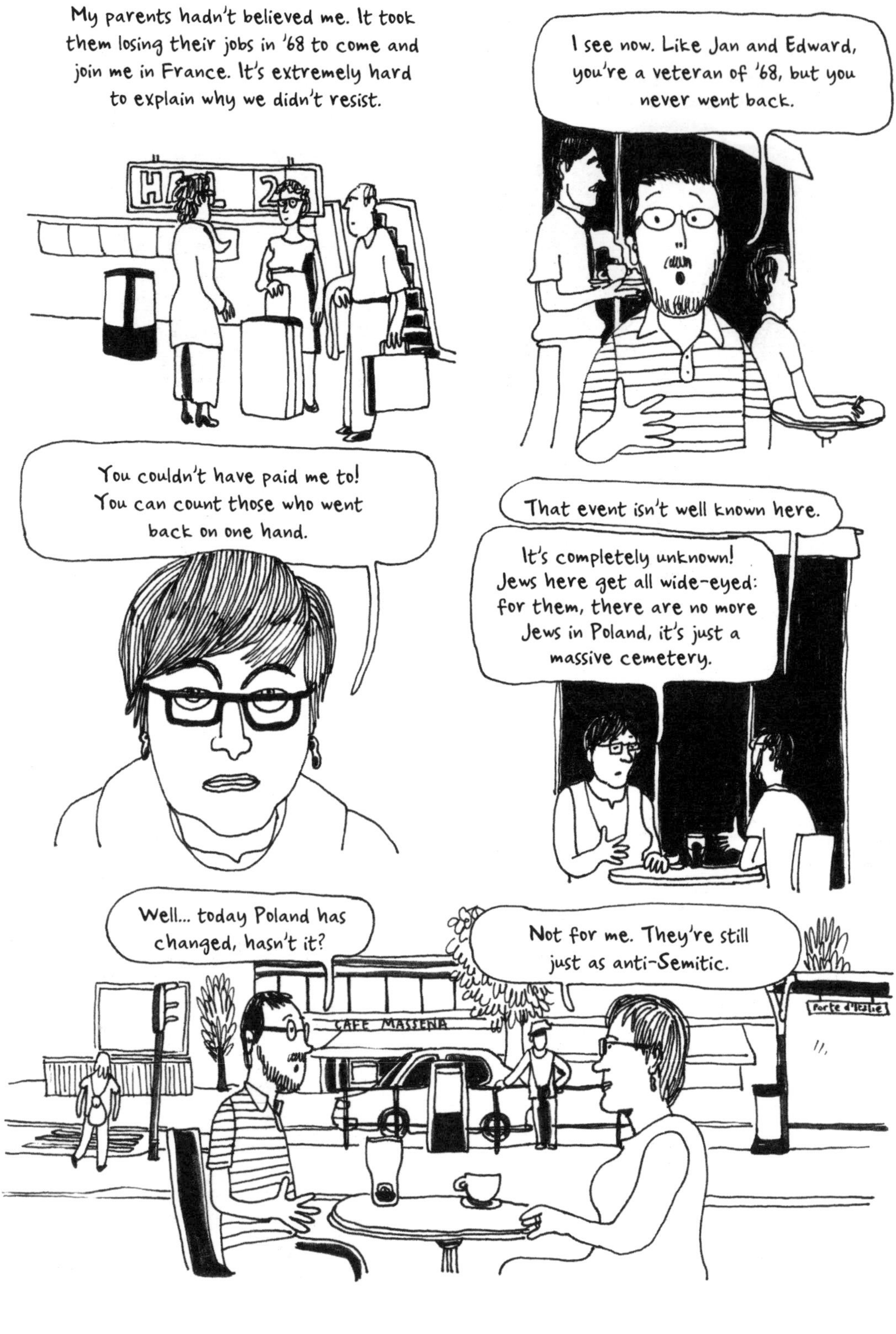
My parents hadn't believed me. It took them losing their jobs in '68 to come and join me in France. It's extremely hard to explain why we didn't resist.
HALL 2
I see now. Like Jan and Edward, you're a veteran of '68, but you never went back.
You couldn't have paid me to! You can count those who went back on one hand.
That event isn't well known here.
It's completely unknown! Jews here get all wide-eyed: for them, there are no more Jews in Poland, it's just a massive cemetery.
Well... today Poland has changed, hasn't it?
Not for me. They're still just as anti-Semitic.
CAFE MASSENA
Porte d'Italie

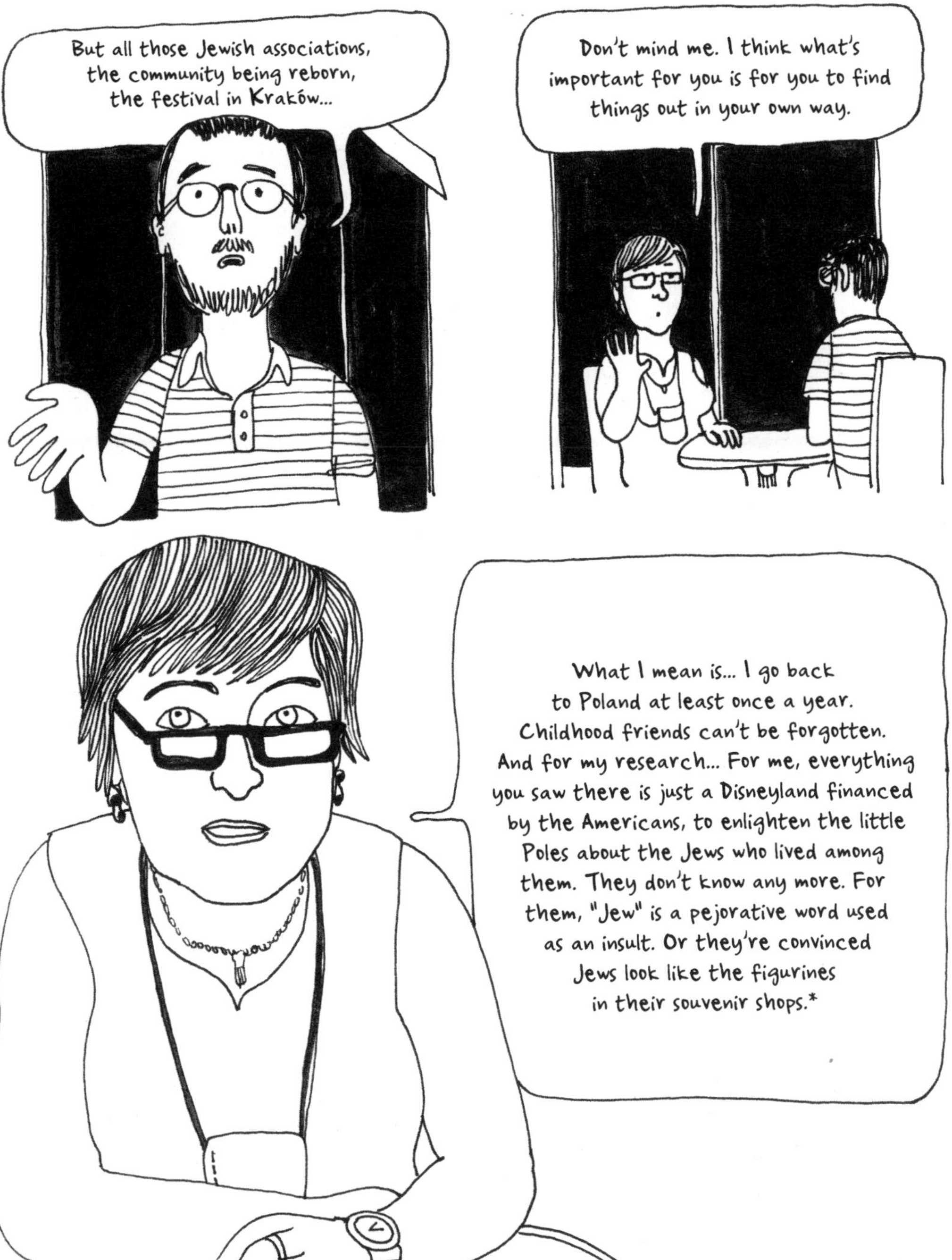
But all those Jewish associations, the community being reborn, the festival in Kraków...
Don't mind me. I think what's important for you is for you to find things out in your own way.
What I mean is... I go back to Poland at least once a year. Childhood friends can't be forgotten. And for my research... For me, everything you saw there is just a Disneyland financed by the Americans, to enlighten the little Poles about the Jews who lived among them. They don't know any more. For them, "Jew" is a pejorative word used as an insult. Or they're convinced Jews look like the figurines in their souvenir shops.*

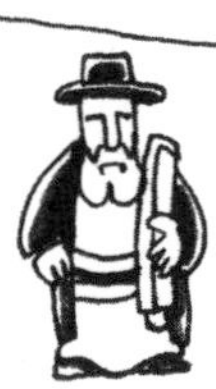

* Anna is referring to the statuettes of bearded, big-nosed, and behatted Jews with a coin in one hand and a Torah scroll or a violin in the other.

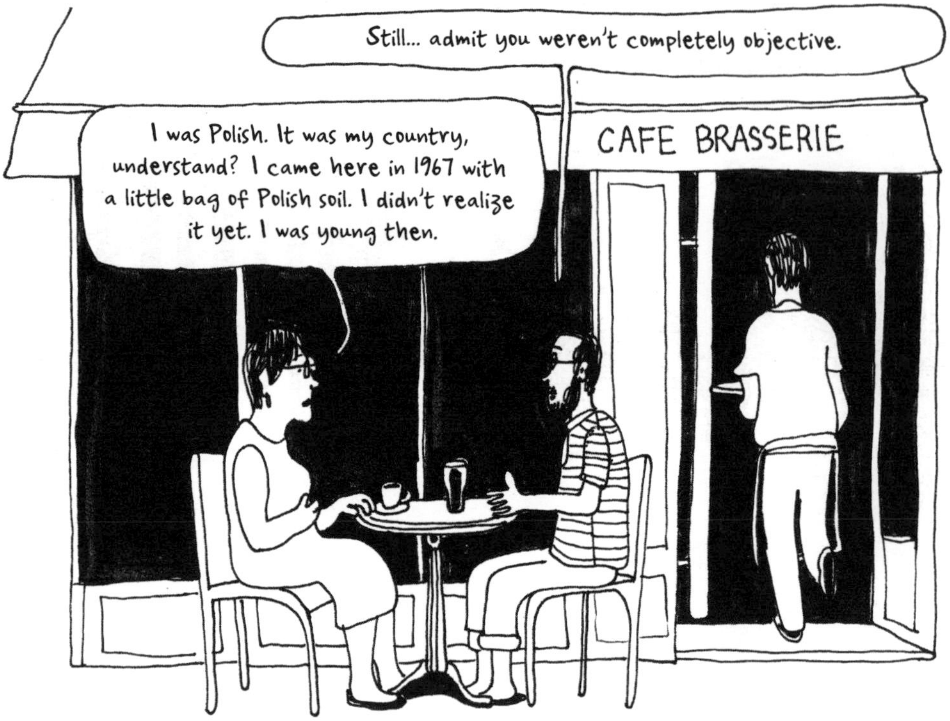
Still... admit you weren't completely objective.
I was Polish. It was my country, understand? I came here in 1967 with a little bag of Polish soil. I didn't realize it yet. I was young then.
CAFE BRASSERIE

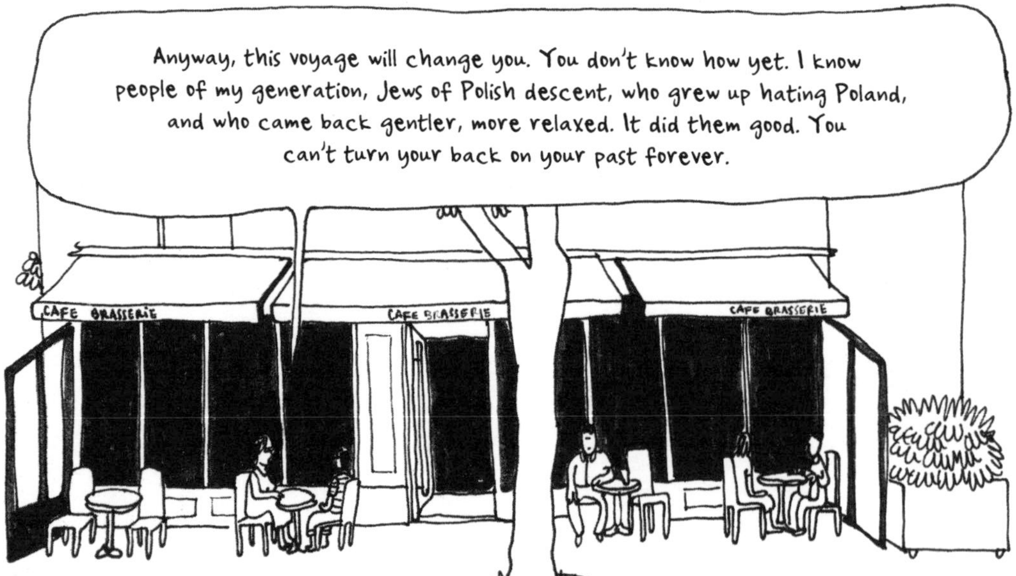
Anyway, this voyage will change you. You don't know how yet. I know people of my generation, Jews of Polish descent, who grew up hating Poland, and who came back gentler, more relaxed. It did them good. You can't turn your back on your past forever.
CAFE BRASSERIE
CAFE BRASSERIE
CAFE BRASSERIE

Putting Things Back in Order

20 April 2011. It's been a little over a year, and I still haven't managed to reach a satisfying conclusion.

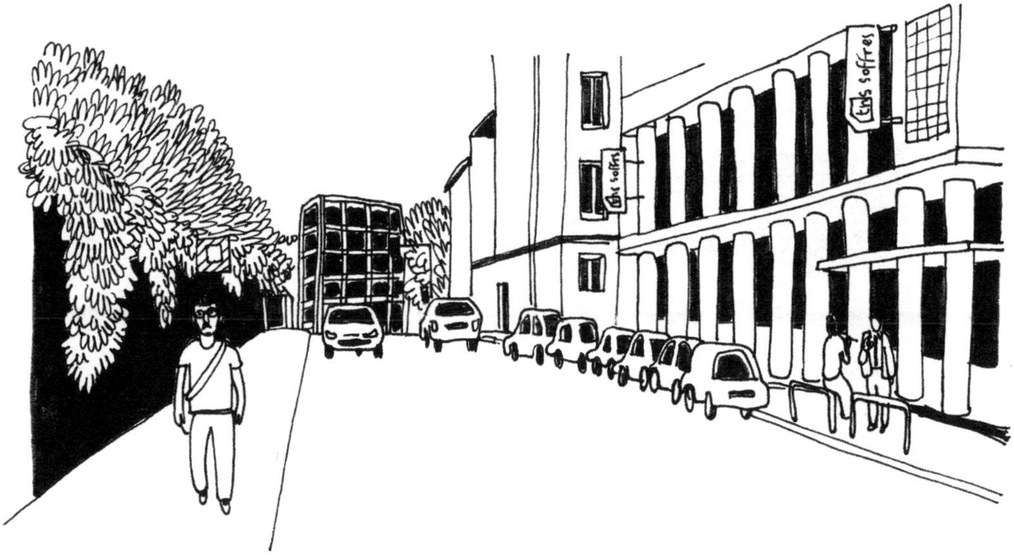

What I got was that when speaking to a Jew of Polish descent, an American Jew living in Poland, a veteran of March '68, a Breton historian, a Pole, or a mere observer, each gave me a more or less optimistic vision of the revival of the Polish Jewry.

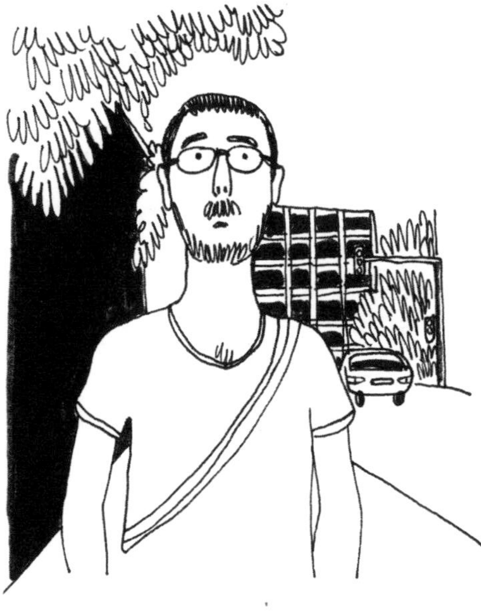

It's a bit before noon, and I'm going to see my grandmother for the first time on my own at the Bagneux cemetery.

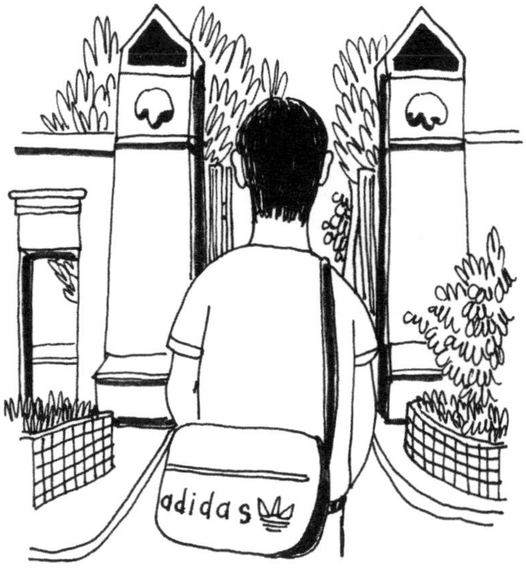
adidas

It's a change from the graveyards in
Warsaw and Żelechów. It's so well kept.

I don't know the path very well, and
I have a very bad sense of direction.

The cemetery's so big that it's very
easy to get lost.

The first Jewish graves! My
grandmother's must be close by.

It's this row, I know it.

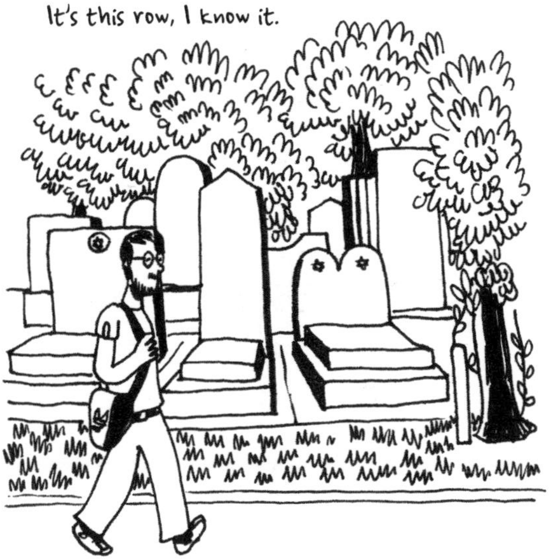

Walking among the graves is a bit like travelling in Poland.

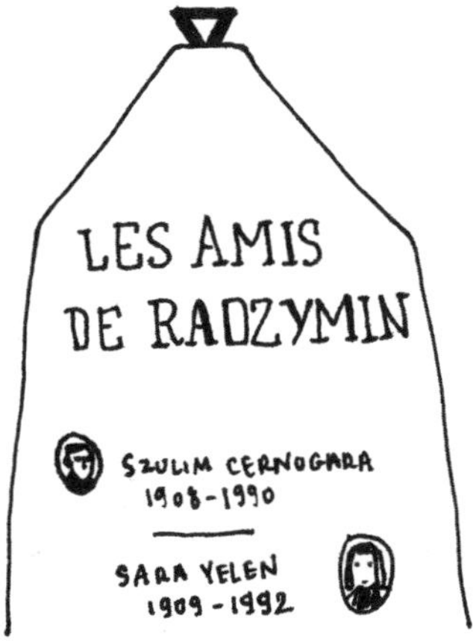
LES AMIS
DE RADZYMIN
SZULIM CERNOGARA
1908-1990
SARA YELEN
1909-1992

Jewish immigrants from Poland are buried here, often by Landsmanshaftn, societies founded by the first immigrants from the same city or shtetl, initially to help each other, gather together, or hold funerals.

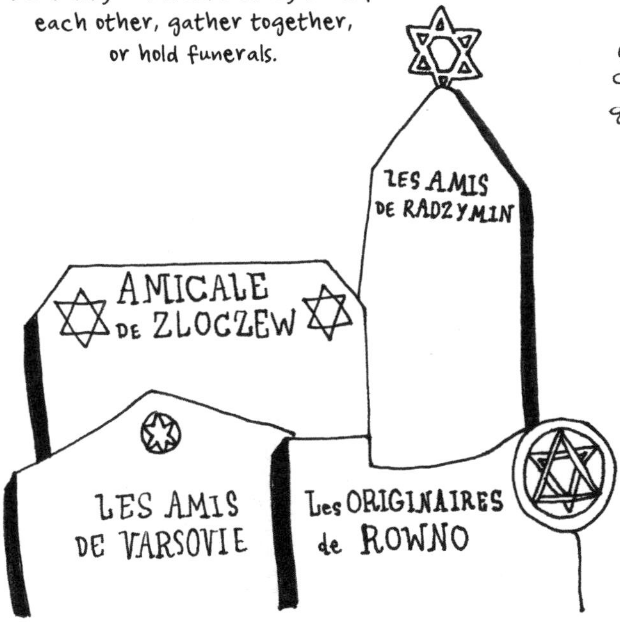
LES AMIS
DE RADZYMIN
AMICALE
DE ZLOCZEW
LES AMIS
DE VARSOVIE
Les ORIGINAIRES
de ROWNO

Żelechów! No longer abstract, that word means the front seat of a Nissan Corsa, an afternoon in the country, and inordinate anxiety. Here is my grandmother's grave.

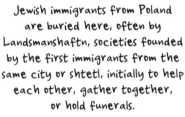

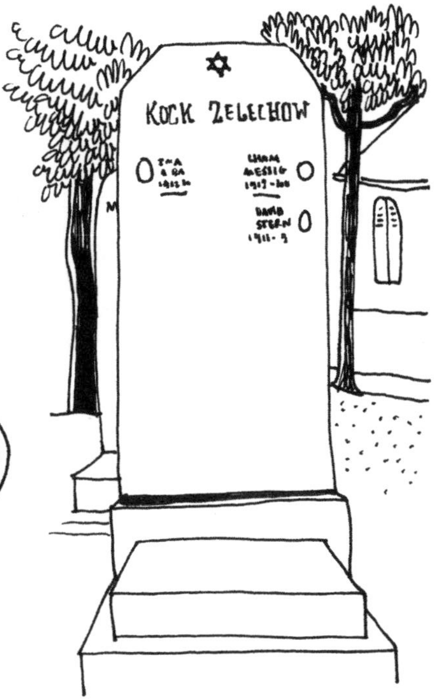
KOCK ZELECHOW

She's buried with strangers from my grandfather's village.

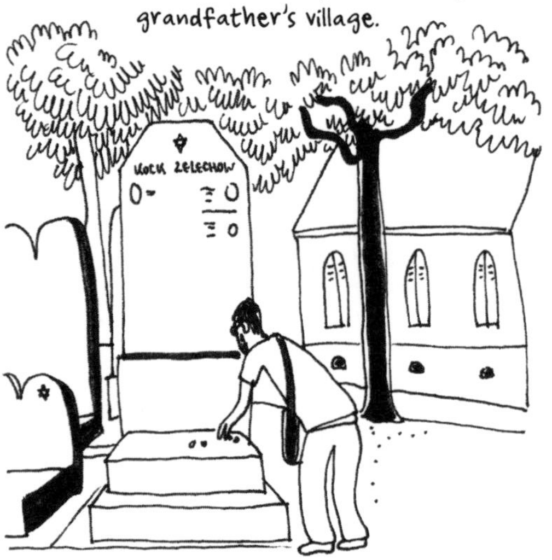

Thanks to the translation talents of the Parisian préfecture, my grandfather Simchy Dres became Simon Dres, and my grandmother Tema Barab, Thérèse Baran. She will never have the same name on her grave as her parents.

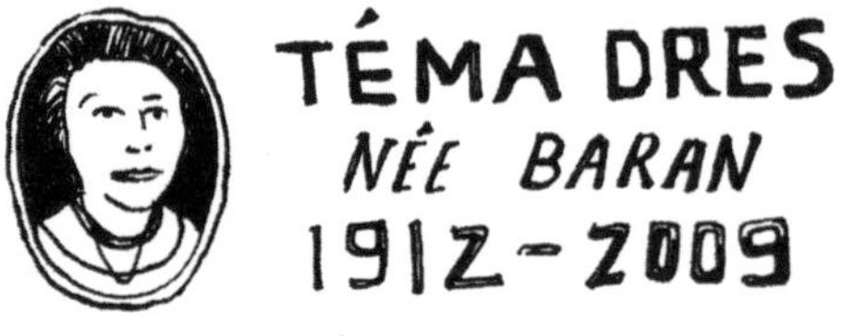
TÉMA DRES
NÉE BARAN
1912-2009

Tragic, how these tiny acts of carelessness can impact a family's destiny forever. Perhaps this story will help put things back in order.

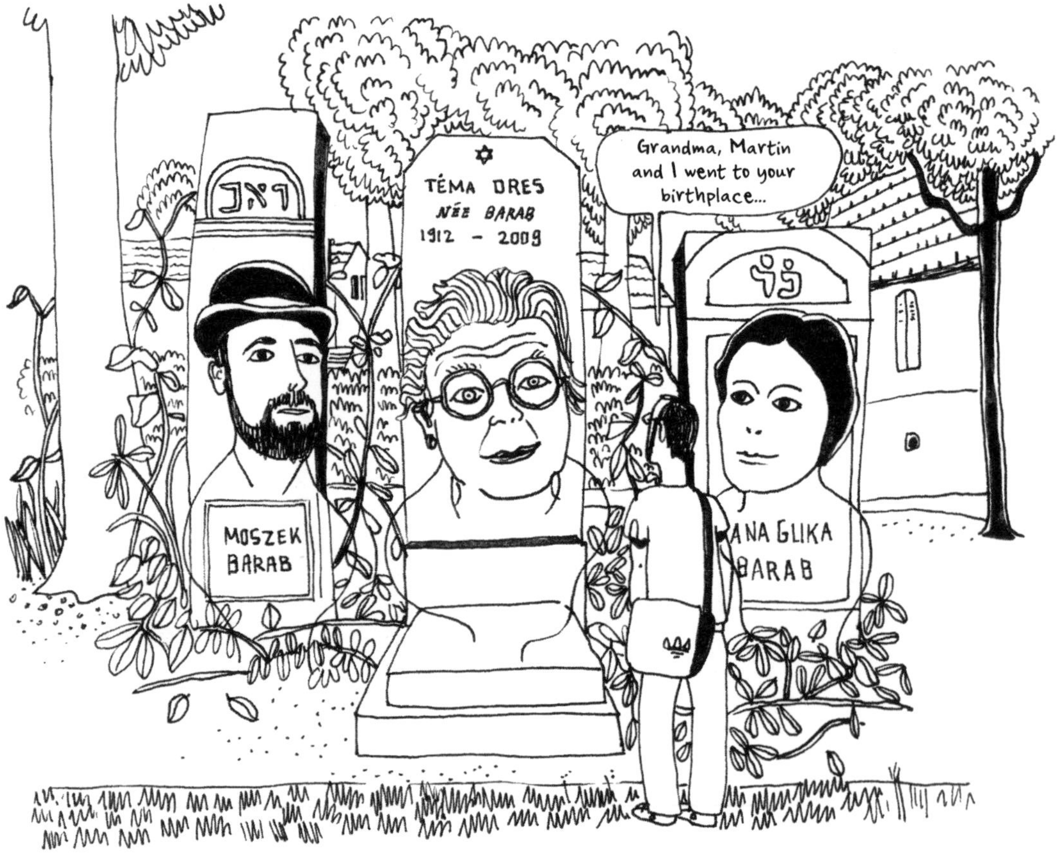
Grandma, Martin and I went to your birthplace...
TÉMA DRES
NÉE BARAB
1912 - 2009
MOSZEK BARAB
ANA GLIKA
BARAB

Author's Note

All the interviews in this book actually happened. The conversations were recorded, and the people and the settings photographed.

When I was putting this together, I set out to transcribe my interviewees' words as faithfully as possible, right down to the errors. The clumsy expressions and inaccurate turns of phrase seemed to add to the uniqueness of each individual. Preserving these allowed me to depict our experience with utmost honesty.

These witnesses were not always speaking in their mother tongue.

I have carried this technique through into the dialogue of this book, even if I don't always mention it. During our first meeting, Jan Spiewak spoke to me in English so his friend Danka could contribute. Then, while walking through Jewish Warsaw with Jan and Martin, we spoke French. At TSKŻ, everyone we met was Polish, and our conversations were in English. Our interviews with Rabbi Zarcynsky, Isroel Szpilman at the Warsaw cemetery, and Anna Drozd at the Genealogical Learning Centre were also conducted in English. Rabbi Burt Schuman, who was American, wished to speak with us in French. Some wordings may seem surprising.

My apologies to the Polish for massacring their language in my tale.

Her Name Was Tema

Her name was Tema; she was our grandmother. Our journey to Poland all started with her. This journey reunited me with my brother Jérémie. Here we were, sharing a bed and a room again, long after our last family vacation. In Poland. In Warsaw.

She passed away in September 2009. I was in Israel then. Although she had spoken to me of this country for so long, she decided to move on before I could tell her about my time there. That was the first year I didn't send her a postcard since learning to write.

Our grandmother was a link across several generations. A link between the war and today: for although tradition called for silence, she could never stop talking to us. She knew how to re-create the fear she experienced in occupied Paris. A Paris where she survived by hiding in a closet even as her ears, accustomed to Yiddish from her childhood, were flooded with the orders of Nazi soldiers.

She linked us all – grandchildren, aunts, and uncles. What with everything that had happened to her, we thought she'd be with us forever. The floor of her apartment in the 11th Arrondissement, which her feet had trod for almost fifty years, had the impudence to succeed where the Nazis had failed.

Our grandmother recounted her Warsaw childhood so well that after more than a hundred years, we seem to remember it ourselves. During this journey towards the unknown, three moments in particular stood out.

The first trail we followed led us to the graves of our great-grandparents in Warsaw. It was an intense moment when the surprise of having reached our goal won out over the anticipated emotion. A few hours away from our Parisian lives, in the subdued light of the Jewish cemetery, we took the measure of the moment. This encounter anchored our journey in a concrete and objective reality that lent our quest, however unnecessarily, the luxury of pertinence.

Exhilarated by this early triumph – due entirely, I admit, to Jérémie's stubbornness – we set out for Żelechów, a tiny town south of Warsaw, the birthplace of our grandfather Simon. Nothing in the village recalled our family's forgotten presence. Nothing but a bronze plaque at the market square. The inscription was no commemorative message, but an old, very rough map with Polish captions. I don't know what association of ideas led us to pick out one word among all the others: Zydowski. Zydowski, which means "Jewish", was carved beside Cmentarz, or "cemetery". Once more, we found the hidden but quite tangible presence of our roots.

We reached Kraków during the festival of Jewish culture. There we met people of every outlook and, against all expectation, we realized that our quest, which seemed quite extraordinary to us, was quite commonplace for others. Other uprooted people following the traces of a past they never knew, but which nevertheless formed and fashioned them. Quietly, without making a fuss, the children of Poland were returning to their past, bumping up against it, rediscovering bits of often overshadowed personal history. Jérémie and I made our return in our grandmother's footsteps. We had gone our pretty much separate ways since adolescence. In a way our grandmother, from her distant, eternal abode, guided our steps to reunite far away in time and space, in Poland, the land of her birth. Her name was Tema; she was our grandmother.

Martin Dres

In the Warsaw cemetery...

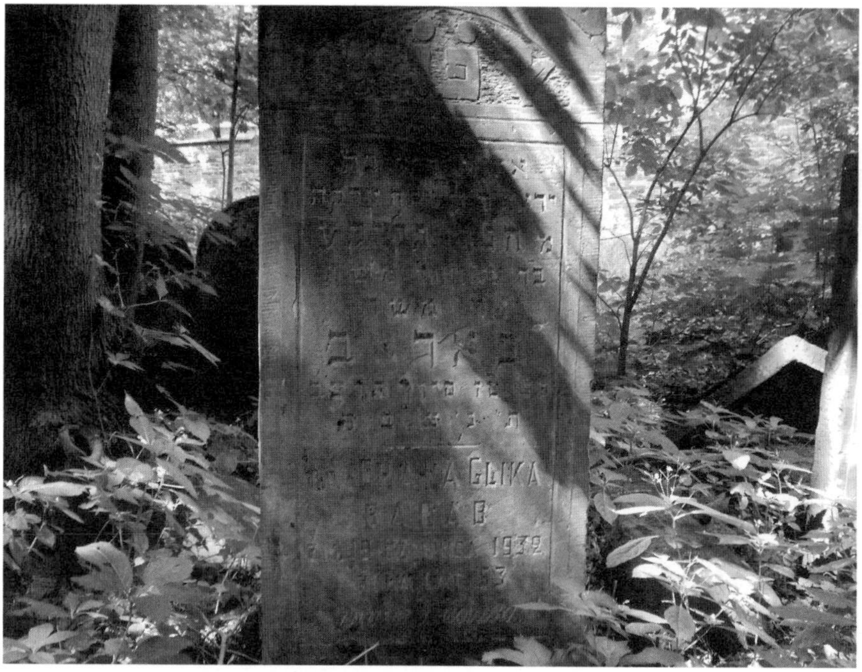

The grave of Chana Glicka Barab, my grandmother's mother.

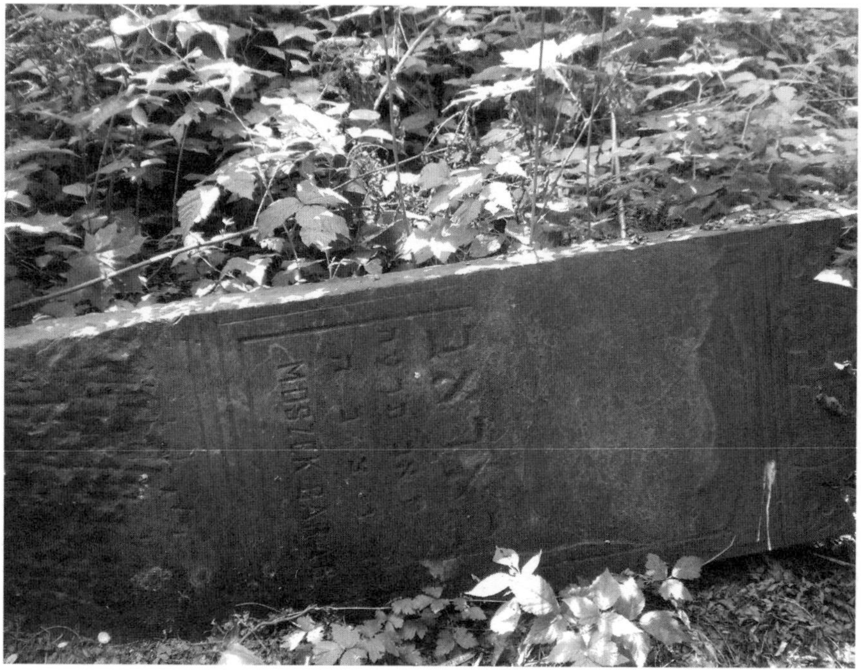

The grave of Moszek Barab, my grandmother's father.

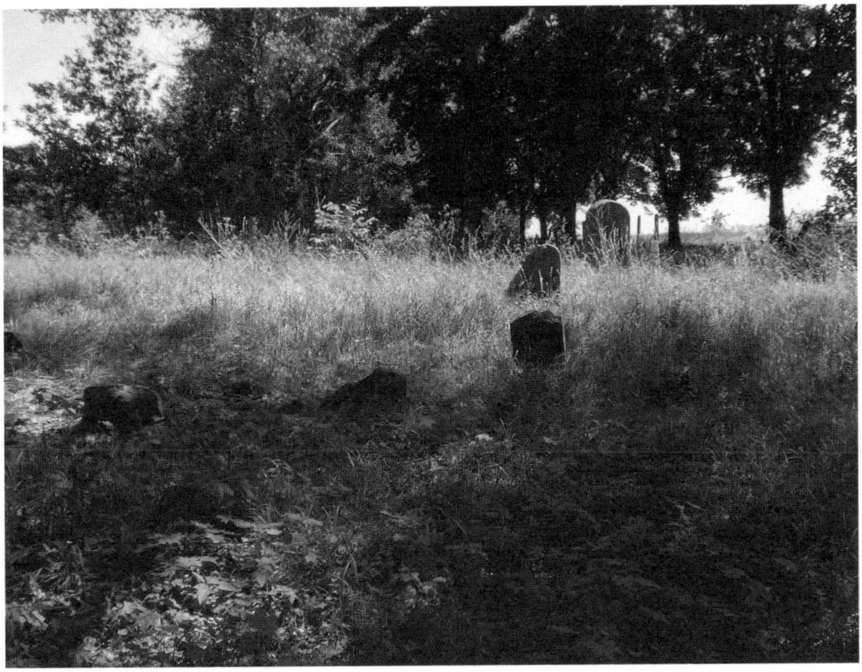

The wild charm of the Polish countryside? No, the Jewish graveyard in Żelechów.

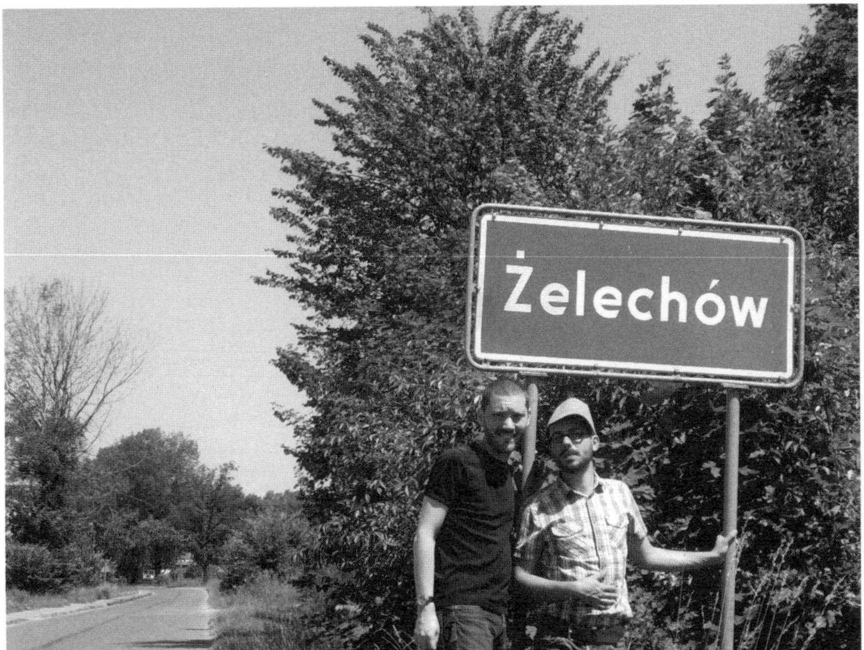
Żelechów

Veni, vidi, vici.

A host of family photos held pride of place on my grandmother's dressing-table. Some, in old silver frames, evoked a foreign world, the world of the past.

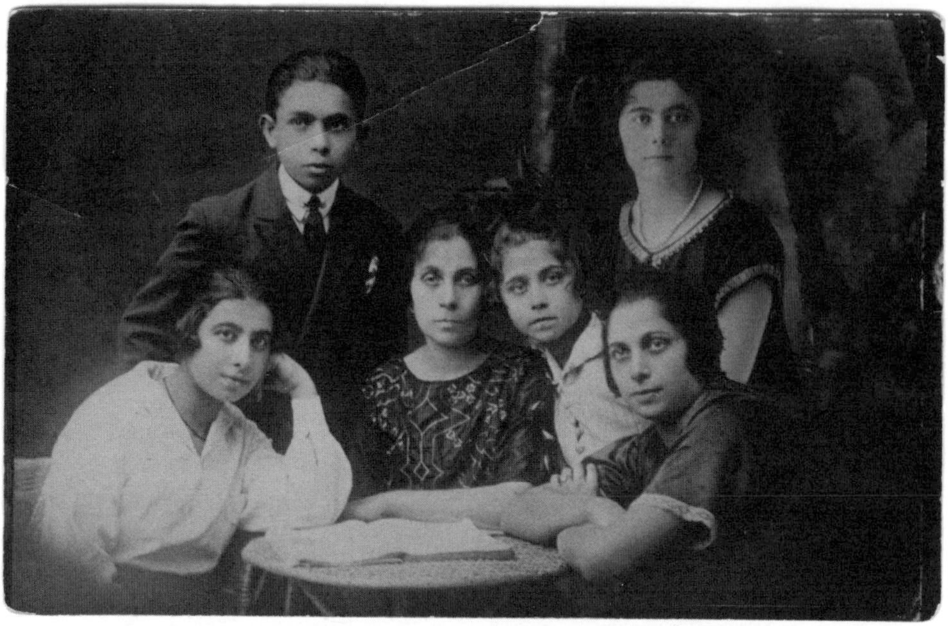

The Barab family in Warsaw: my grandmother (the youngest), her mother Chana (centre), and, clockwise from left, her brother and sisters Sonia, Schmulack, Sore, and Léa.

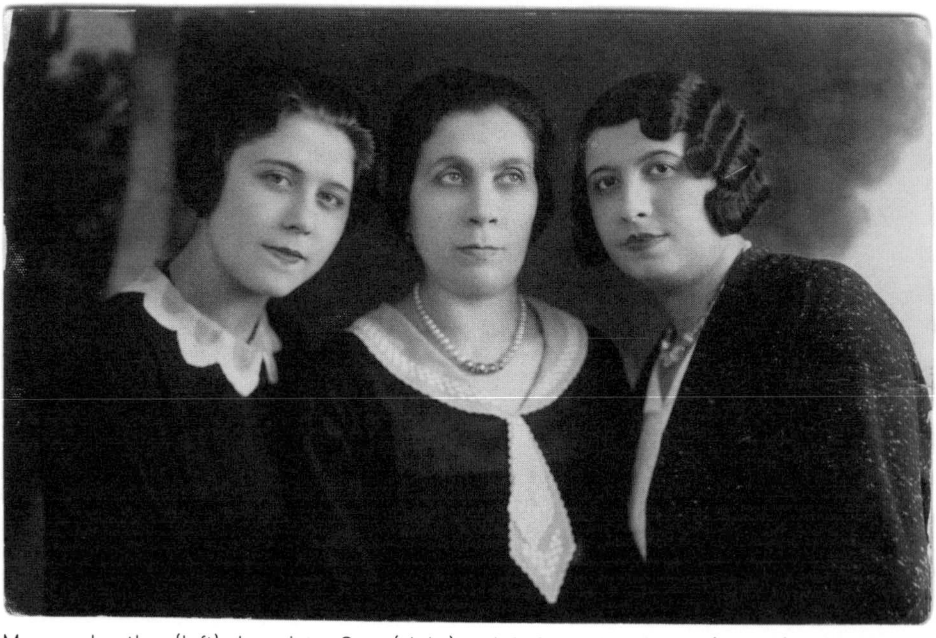

My grandmother (left) , her sister Sore (right) and their mother Chana (centre), shortly before leaving for Paris.

Moszek Barab, a building contractor in Warsaw,
and my grandmother's father.

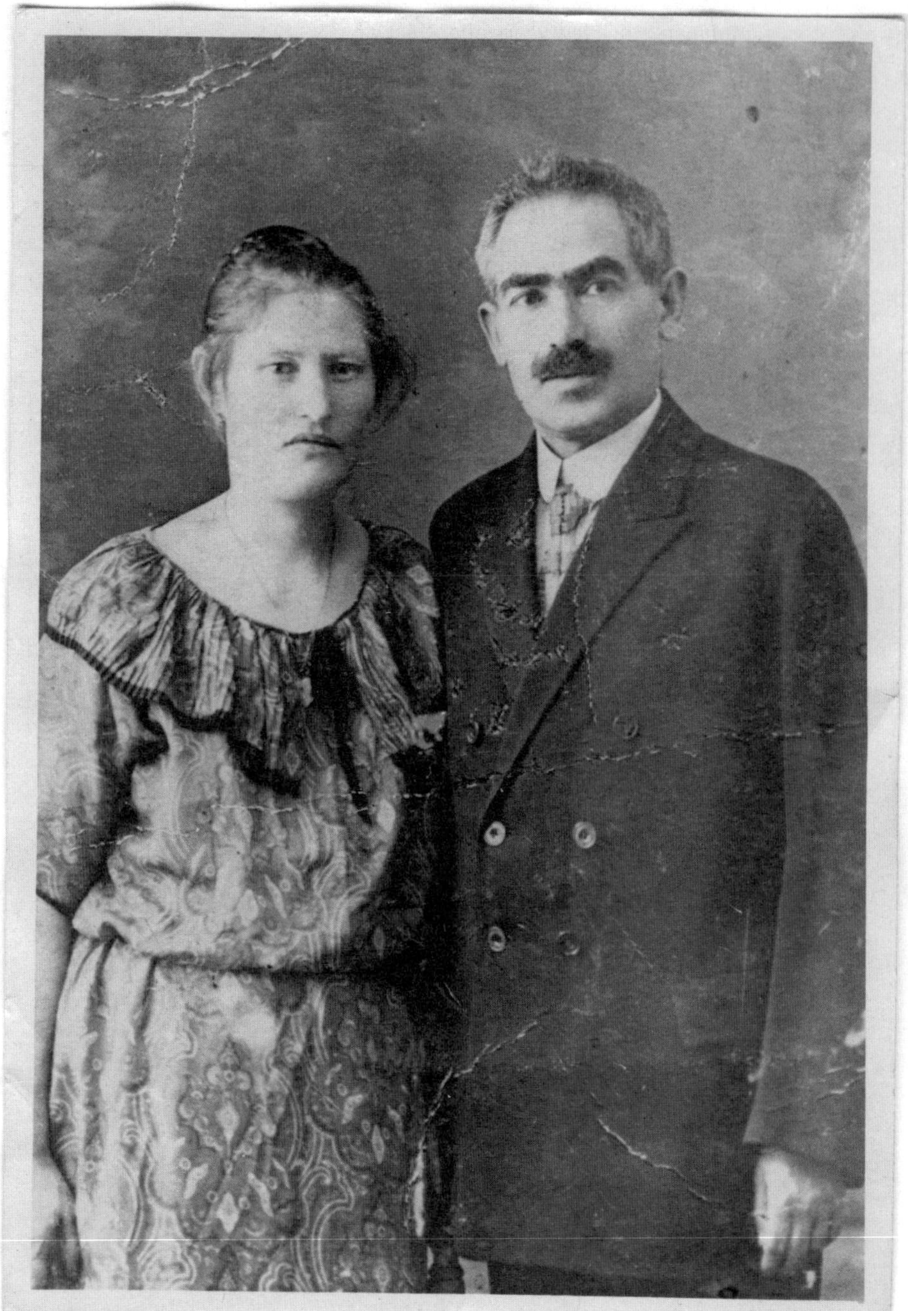

Gela and Yankiel Dress, my grandfather Simchy's parents, originally from Żelechów, having just reached Paris in 1921. Yankiel would die during deportation, and Gela disappeared a few decades later.

My grandparents, a few years after the war...

...in front of their clothing boutique on the Boulevard Voltaire in Paris...

...and in Villeparisis, where they'd bought a country house. During the war, my grandfather and his family had taken refuge in a nearby pension. A glimpse of my Aunt Annette running towards them.

My grandfather liked to go and relax in Villeparisis on Sundays, or during the month of August. Sometimes he played cards with the family, and with his friends from the Żelechów Landsmanshaft.

One of my favourite photos of my grandmother since, when I picture her telling me her incredible stories, this is the face I see, slightly amused and always perfectly groomed.

Acknowledgements

...those who took part in this project:

my brother and partner, Martin, who agreed to travel with me, and then to get depicted unflatteringly, and finally to write a moving testimony; all the people we met in this book, for their availability and support, especially Jan Spiewak, Edward Odoner, Jan Lapter, and Anna Rabczynska; Jean-Yves, for following the project right from the start, and for his wonderful preface; the team at Cambourakis – Frédéric, Chiara, and Sylvain; my aunt, Evelyne Dress, for her information on Żelechów; Camille, for her class on perspective; Tomoë, for her advice on the cover; Fred, for the book's website;

the Foundation of France, for its support in realizing the project;

those on whom my grandmother counted a great deal, especially Annette, Henri, Sandra, Olivier, their children, Anna;

my sister Hélène, who couldn't come with us on the trip;

my dear Gladys, for her support and advice;

my mother, Philippe, my brothers and sister, Raphaël and Zoé;

my father, for his help, the family in Singapore – Pandit, Prita, and Yanti;

my maternal grandparents Hadassa and Maurice Guini;

all my friends who helped, supported, and encouraged me.

About the Author

 Born in 1982, Jérémie Dres lives and works in Paris. He graduated from the École des Arts Décoratifs in Strasbourg. Since 2007, he has worked in multimedia, graphic design, and illustration. Along with his comics projects, Dres works in digital art, installations, and performance pieces.